WINE AND CULTURE

VINEYARD TO GLASS

Edited by
Rachel E. Black and Robert C. Ulin

BLOOMSBURY
LONDON · NEW DELHI · NEW YORK · SYDNEY

Bloomsbury Academic

An imprint of Bloomsbury Publishing Plc

50 Bedford Square
London
WC1B 3DP
UK

175 Fifth Avenue
New York
NY 10010
USA

www.bloomsbury.com

First published 2013

© Rachel Black and Robert Ulin, 2013

All rights reserved. No part of this publication may be reproduced or transmitted in
any form or by any means, electronic or mechanical, including photocopying,
recording, or any information storage or retrieval system, without prior permission
in writing from the publishers.

Rachel Black and Robert Ulin have identified their rights under the Copyright,
Designs and Patents Act, 1988, to be identified as editors of this work.

No responsibility for loss caused to any individual or organization acting on or
refraining from action as a result of the material in this publication can be
accepted by Bloomsbury Academic or the author.

British Library Cataloguing-in-Publication Data
A catalogue record for this book is available from the British Library.

ISBN: HB: 978-0-8578-5400-1
PB: 978-0-8578-5401-8
ePub: 978-0-8578-5420-9
ePDF: 978-1-4725-2075-3

Library of Congress Cataloging-in-Publication Data
A catalog record for this book is available from the Library of Congress.

Typeset by Apex CoVantage, LLC, Madison, WI, USA.
Printed and bound in India

WINE AND CULTURE

CONTENTS

ACKNOWLEDGMENTS

We would like to thank all of the contributors who participated in this volume. A special thank you is due to Emily Contois and Chris Maggiolo, graduate students in the Boston University Gastronomy, for their help with preparing the manuscript and compiling the index. We are thankful for the support of our respective spouses Suzanne Bamonto and Doug Cook.

LIST OF ILLUSTRATIONS

Introduction

RACHEL E. BLACK AND ROBERT C. ULIN

Wine has long been and continues to be an important commodity that generates significant interest because of its commercial, symbolic, cultural, and aesthetic value. On the academic side, historians, geographers, and economists continue to write prolifically about wine worldwide, documenting the involvement of elites and now multinational corporations in the development of winegrowing estates and global markets. There is, additionally, much enthusiasm for popular publications by wine writers and critics such as Robert Parker and magazines such as the *Wine Spectator*, all of which taken together are highly regarded for their authoritative evaluations and rankings of wine. Perhaps the most significant measure of interest is the consumption of wine that continues to rise robustly with globalization, clever advertising, and the proliferation of new winegrowing areas, such as China, to both cultivate and meet consumer demands.

Curiously, by comparison, anthropological research on wine as an exclusive topic of inquiry is scant over the past twenty years. This collection of essays from around the world therefore breaks new ground in that the authors not only address the importance of wine as a commodity, but also most importantly link their research on wine to a number of critical issues at the forefront of the social sciences and humanities. Contained in this volume are essays that address globalization, local agency, representation, social class, the invention of tradition, socialist and postsocialist cultures of wine, gender, and the uses of history and culture to support the quality and authenticity of wine. However, before we pursue more closely what the scope of the book entails, it makes sense to explore why there has not been a significant legacy of wine research on the part of anthropologists given the rather remarkable topical and geographical breadth of their research over the past century.

PAST MODELS AND CURRENT DIRECTIONS

Those familiar with the history of anthropology know well that there is an intimate relationship between European colonialism and the development of academic anthropology in North America and Europe. Apart from America's own indigenous population, anthropologists took advantage of opportunities for field research among African, Asian, and Pacific peoples who came under colonial rule. This is not to say that anthropologists simply aided and abetted the colonial effort; numerous anthropologists criticized the exploitation and cruelty often associated with colonialism and, moreover, like Paul Radin, Margaret Mead, and Marcel Griaule, wrote ethnographic accounts of indigenous peoples that celebrated their diversity and humanity. However, as the contributors to the important Talal Asad (ed. 1973) volume have argued, the tradition of fieldwork among small-scale indigenous populations was cultivated in the midst of the colonial process and therefore unwittingly became part of the legacy of the discipline reproduced until relatively recently.

It is surely not our intent to elaborate anthropology's relation to colonialism, as this well-traveled territory would take us far from the topic at hand. Nonetheless, there are good reasons why anthropologists have not written much about wine, or, for, that matter, food, related to how the discipline developed historically, especially its focus on fieldwork in small-scale indigenous societies. It would be wrong, though, to conclude that anthropologists paid no attention to food or drink altogether. One is reminded of Franz Boas's (1964) classic ethnography on the Netsilik Eskimo that documents life in the social round inclusive of Eskimo foods and recipes. Moreover, ritual has long been a focus of anthropological writings, given the influence of Emile Durkheim, Marcel Mauss, and later Victor Turner, and thus food and drink such as palm wine in West Africa or manioc beer in the Amazon that are consumed with ritual are often highlighted in these accounts. It is thus clear that anthropologists have long noted what indigenous peoples consume in both the "raw and cooked" versions.

Acknowledging the attention devoted to food and drink in classical ethnography is not to suggest that the contributions of ethnographers today lack novelty. To the contrary, the classical iterations of fieldwork born in the colonial milieu precluded the sort of critical and intensive exploration of food and drink that marks the contemporary research agenda of social and cultural anthropologists. With few exceptions, most classical fieldwork was carried out among indigenous peoples in locales constructed as circumscribed. That is, the specific locale of ethnographic research until relatively recently was the village, band, or tribe as a singular unit of analysis associated with a specific territory. Culture was thus regarded as coterminous with a geographically limited or bounded group of people. Apart from an emphasis on ranked lineages, the people themselves, as well as the culture associated with them, were often regarded as homogeneous, suggesting an organic composition that was isomorphic with nature.

This representation of circumscribed peoples and their cultures may appear as a caricature in light of the significant theoretical differences among classical anthropologists that incorporated functionalism, structuralism, structural functionalism, and historical particularism. The point, however, is not that these theoretical traditions lack difference, as surely they did, but rather that, methodologically, anthropology had constructed through its own historical formation a tradition of research focused on societies as cultural isolates. This was as much true of Boasian historical particularism as it was of French and British structural and functional anthropology invested theoretically in history's negation.

The idea that fieldwork in terms of participant observation took place in geographically and culturally circumscribed societies is only part of the problem associated with the legacy of colonial anthropology. Anthropology itself was nearly unique in carving out a research agenda that was exclusive, or nearly so, to indigenous societies. The identity of anthropologists and anthropology was profoundly associated with conducting empirical research by living among an indigenous society for a sustained period of time. In part, this initiative owes its origins to the Enlightenment and the fascination of writers such as Jean-Jacques Rousseau with civilization's ultimate corruption of human nature and the unrealized social potentials of "natural man." This meant anthropology both as a discipline and as a perspective was tied historically to the lives of indigenous peoples. Although some anthropologists in Europe conducted their research in the European countryside, Alpine regions, and in Southern Europe where initially rural people were likewise viewed as the analogs of natural humanity (Comaroff and Comaroff 1992), for the most part it was the colonies and colonized peoples to whom these anthropologists turned the majority of their attention.

Surely one can argue today that anthropology has long surpassed its colonial legacy and research tradition exclusive to circumscribed indigenous

cultures. There is some truth to this belief except for the fact that some historical connections are reproduced in the subtlest of ways. This is surely Johannes
Fabian's point in what he has characterized as the "denial of coevalness"
(1983). According to Fabian, anthropology makes use of unrecognized rhetorical strategies whereby indigenous peoples are regarded as noncontemporane-
ous. Such rhetorical strategies are implied in commonly used dichotomies such
as modern and traditional or urban and rural. Fabian maintains that these
dichotomies are not benign rhetorical strategies in that they place indigenous
peoples in a subordinate position to the anthropologist, the very consequence
most contemporary anthropologists have sought to avoid in rejecting evolutionary models of human culture.

The appeal to colonial anthropology, bounded cultures, and the denial of
coevalness remain germane to the concerns of a volume concretely grounded in
the ethnography of wine. For example, Fabian's point about coevalness applies
to a socially differentiated winegrowing community in that the modernity of
current wine technology is often invoked by elites and oenologists to dismiss
the veneration of tradition, invented or otherwise, on the part of small-scale
growers who live at what appears to be the margins of winegrowing history
and discourse.

Our objective here is to suggest why anthropologists until recently paid
such little attention to wine, and food more generally, toward the end of better
appreciating the uniqueness and importance of research on the anthropology
of wine. While the anthropology of wine is today as broad as the many world
regions where grapes are cultivated and vinified, as a specific arena of research
it depended largely on the maturation of the anthropology of Europe. This was
not only the case because of the history and dominion of European winegrowing regions, albeit very important, but also that the development of a Euro-
peanist anthropology, and a North American anthropology as well, foretold
an important shift in anthropological theorizing and the identity of its object
domain. Doing ethnography "at home" or in a culture closely related to one's
own was problematic for the developing discipline of anthropology, a social
science initially geared toward constructing Otherness. Until the second half of
the twentieth century, most anthropologists felt that doing fieldwork in Western cultures lacked objectivity and therefore validity. There was also a certain
discomfort to doing anthropology at home as the critical gaze turned inward.
Although the list of anthropologists who have conducted research in Europe is
significant, inclusive of Eric Wolf, Ernestine Friedl, and Jane Schneider to name
just a few, the acceptance of the anthropology of Europe was arguably slow
for a discipline whose identity remained heavily invested in research among

indigenous societies. This is not to say that anthropologists working among indigenous populations and peasants have paid no attention to food and drink beyond its local articulations—research on plantation agriculture and global commodities such as coffee and sugar stand as important and not exceptional examples that have contributed significantly to the interest in the anthropology of food. However, interest in wine as a topic of research in its own right has matured as a theme in conjunction with the growing acceptance and recognition of the anthropology of Europe and North America that has opened the door for a whole group of younger anthropologists interested in drink.

Anthropological research today has changed considerably, moreover, from its classical emphasis on the totality of life in the social round in that ethnographers working in both indigenous communities and those of much larger scale are likely to focus on a smaller set of issues and problems as they link local lives to regional, national, and transnational economic, political, and social processes. Furthermore, along with the movement of peoples, labor markets, and commodities that go along with transnationalism and globalization, quality fieldwork has become by necessity multi-sited. Most contemporary anthropologists have a sense of culture that is translocal and porous rather than circumscribed, and are prepared, therefore, to pursue their research agenda in a number of geographical locations. Again, this is not entirely new as anthropologists such as Oscar Lewis followed his Puerto Rican informants from the island to the continental United States. However, rather than being exceptional, this has become the standard. When studying drink and food, not to mention the associated reproduction of labor, culture, and social relations, the capacity to conduct research through the cycles of production and consumption necessitates multi-sited research inclusive of the archives and historical narratives.

We can see, therefore, that an anthropology fashioned in the midst of colonialism and dedicated to studying life in the circumscribed social round is ill prepared to study the complexities of contemporary life defined by rapid transfer of technologies, the mobility of people and culture, and the multiplicities of forms that globalization takes in linking diverse populations throughout the world. The focus on food and drink by classical anthropologists, while noteworthy, was simply not prepared to address their contemporary articulations. While it may be true that much has changed historically, it is also the case that anthropologists are theorizing the contemporary world and their own discipline quite differently.

There are a number of reasons why anthropologists and other academics have not seen the anthropology of food and alcohol as serious areas of study. First, most scholars associated food, wine, and alcohol first and foremost with pleasure and therefore deemed them unworthy of serious investigation or theorizing. In the case of alcohol, particularly in North America, academics have taken up a disease prevention stance; this has largely precluded the study of the social and cultural value of alcohol (Black 2010). Second, wine is categorized simply as alcohol and becomes another dangerous intoxicant; once again, this overshadows the ritual, symbolic, and social importance of wine in many cultures. For instance, there would be no Catholic mass without wine. Last, we should rethink the categorization of wine as simply alcohol: for many cultures now and in the past wine is food. From a practical perspective, wine is an important source of calories. In many European countries, along with water, wine is ever-present on the dining table and is rarely consumed outside of meals. This may be changing, but it is important that scholars note these changes and try to understand the social, cultural, and economic shifts signaled by the French and Italian polices' cracking down on drinking and driving, for instance. Although associated with the pleasures of the table, wine offers an important site for anthropological investigation into larger social issues.

This brings us back to the anthropology of wine and what is potentially fresh and unique in today's scholarship focused on wine. Scholars from multiple disciplines would agree that wine as a commodity is symbolically charged because of its long-standing associations with religion, ritual, debauchery, sexuality, and sociability more generally. In this regard, wine is a window on actual and symbolic processes that point beyond the commodity itself. In fact, this is somewhat the problem with popular accounts of wine in that apart from social class, refinement, or perhaps the contrary but nonetheless important with bulk wines, wine tends to be discussed and written about as an object in itself. There is no shortage of articles, news reports, and books that discuss the colors, aromas, tannins, acidity and so on associated with particular wines. It is not that the biochemistry and technical skills reflected in wines is unimportant; for example, they are essential in understanding consumer preferences and professional ratings even if they are based on unacknowledged social and cultural assumptions. As anthropologists who research wine, we are well aware of the blending of technology, science, and tradition, or their oppositions, in making what are widely regarded as venerable wines. Even the issue of *terroir* and the linking of taste to place are given a paramount position in how we evaluate and appreciate wine. However, and here is where this volume makes a special contribution, the reputed qualities of the wine itself are only a departure point for a much broader and critical commentary on wine.

The readers of this volume will not only be exposed to richly textured ethnographic accounts of wines from a number of world areas, but they will also have a critical exposure to the peoples and diverse traditions, contested and otherwise, too often ignored or eclipsed by narratives specifically devoted to the commodity itself. This is an especially important point because wine is often discussed, like most commodities under late capitalism, as if it were re-mote or divorced from the social relationships of its production, circulation, and consumption, thus ostensively and wrongly giving the impression that it has a life of its own. Because of the symbolic capital invested in their represen-tation, elite wines in particular seem especially prone to the reified discourses of connoisseurs and aficionados that reproduce social class while expunging concrete images of social labor. In analogous terms, this is exactly what is at risk with the now common notion of *terroir*. *Terroir* is meant to draw our imagination to the natural conditions of climate and soil as a signifier of dis-tinction and in so doing reinforces the sense that the standards of excellence as well as the commodity itself is nothing more than natural—a point of view written into the French Appellation d'Origine Contrôlée (AOC) legislation of the early twentieth century. Such rhetorical moves take us away from the unro-mantic images of concrete human subjects as they toil in the vineyards, experi-ence harsh living conditions, and even face gender and class exploitation that are quite contrary to how we wish to imagine wine.

This volume is, therefore, most fundamentally about wine as a sociocultural and historical commodity and thus it brings anthropology's unique emphasis on culture, social relations, representation, and power to a critical understand-ing of wine. Themes such as the dismissal of tradition and its opposition to science will be explored and deconstructed as will the importance of wine to local and national identities negotiated from differently positioned subjects. As noted, wine is utilized in this book to raise important questions about global-ization, markets, cultural constructions of history, and identity without losing the pleasures associated with reading about wine. None of this would have been possible in a classical version of ethnographic research tied to the identity of locally circumscribed indigenous populations nor in conventional volumes of wine that fail to pay significant attention to the social relations through which wine is produced, circulated, and symbolically represented.

STRUCTURE OF THE VOLUME

We have chosen to structure this volume around four broad themes that bring together a variety of perspectives on the anthropological study of wine. Each section opens with a short introduction that highlights some of the common analytical threads and theoretical approaches.

The first section is entitled "Rethinking *Terroir.*" With the renewed debate on this topic in the wine, food, and anthropological worlds, it made sense to showcase the ways in which anthropologists are reconsidering, advancing, and challenging this debate. Based on ethnographic findings, anthropologists are looking beyond a geological and climactic definition of *terroir.* In this section, contributors bring to the table the social and economic relations embedded in the struggle to define and codify the concept of *terroir.* In Chapter 1, Sarah Daynes gives an overview of the academic literature on *terroir* and then goes on to look at the production of collective knowledge based on locality. Daynes's ethnography of Bordelais winemakers offers insight into local understanding and articulation of the concept of *terroir.* In Chapter 2, "The Things that Count: Rethinking *Terroir* in Australia," Robert Swinburn explores the tensions between how wine critics and academics have defined *terroir* in Australia and the lived experience of *terroir* of new winegrowers, recent transplants from urban areas. Chapter 3 also looks at questions of *terroir* in the New World. Nicolas Sternsdorff Cisterna looks at how the Chilean wine industry is mobilizing notions of *terroir* as it attempts to change the reputation of its wines from good value to quality, premium wines. More specifically, Cisterna investigates how *terroir* turns vineyards into spaces of capitalist production. In this chapter, *terroir* is used as an analytical tool for examining the power relations mobilized in the construction of spaces, in this case vineyards. In the same vein, Robert Ulin considers the ways in which the concept of *terroir* naturalizes human relations in wine production. In Chapter 4, Ulin explores the tensions between *terroir*'s ability to create specificity and distinction by tying wine to a specific place while at the same time leading back to a mystification of the social elements necessary for the production of wine.

The second section, "Relationships of power and the construction of place," carries over many of the themes developed in the previous chapters. At the same time, the chapters in this section engage in discussions of place, distinction, and labor through broader discursive frameworks. The first two chapters consider the changing place of wine in postsocialist Europe and the power dynamics embedded in wine production and consumption. In Chapter 5, "Tasting Wine in Slovakia: Postsocialist Elite Cultural Particularities," Juraj Buzalka focuses on the changing meanings of wine consumption in Slovakia, and how for young, middle-class Slovaks wine tourism and wine drinking has become a mark of distinction. In Chapter 6, Ewa Kopczyńska explores the role of wine as a component of emergent collective memory and as part of public rituals. Echoing Buzalka's ethnographic research in Slovakia, Kopczyńska uses wine production to investigate regional power structures in Western Poland.

The next two chapters in this section turn toward Western Europe and look at the ways in which wine can tell us more about changing patterns of consumption and social power. In Chapter 7, Christina Ceisel uses wine production and consumption to consider how globalization has shaped local, regional, and national symbols. Using Galician wine as an example, Ceisel looks at larger social questions related to labor, land, commodification, and nostalgia. Chapter 8, "'Local, Loyal, and Constant': The Legal Construction of Wine in Bordeaux," takes a closer look at the Appellation d'Origine Contrôlée system in France. Erica Farmer uses both ethnographic and historic sources to investigate the social relations and power structures embedded in this system. Next, Yuson Jung's chapter also looks at the bureaucratization of wine classifications and the role they play in legitimating production in some places while excluding other production areas in Bulgaria. Drawing on ethnographic examples, Jung shows how the European Union classification systems for food and beverages actively recreate established global hierarchies, particularly with reference to wine.

Section three, "Labor, commodification, and the politics of wine," looks at wine as a global commodity. By applying anthropological theory, this transnational commodity reveals both local and global shifts in consumption and the cultural meanings of wine drinking. In Chapter 10, "Following *Grands Crus: Global Markets, Transnational Histories, and Wine*," Marion Demossier applies ethnographic methods and theory to the study of *Grands Crus*. She argues that these wines offer a unique window onto the transnational processes of commodification as well as the global market forces that shape the place of the *Grands Crus*. Adam Walker and Paul Manning's chapter looks at the ways changing political and production regimes have reshaped the cultural practices surrounding wine production in Bulgaria from the socialist to the postsocialist eras. In particular, the current focus on quality wines in Bulgaria has had a significant impact on traditional Bulgarian drinking rituals that tended to focus on quantity. Ethnographic and material culture sources offer insights into the changing relationships between wine production, consumption, and cultural practices. Chapter 12 rounds out this section with a look at the ways in which small family farms in the Languedoc region of France deal with the problem of the reproduction of the family farm. In this chapter, Winnie Lem focuses on questions of labor and gender relations and the ways in which "regimes of regulation" on winegrowing family farms shape and attempt to ensure the reproduction of labor.

The last section of this book is entitled "Technology and nature." It includes three chapters that explore the tensions between technology and nature found in the culture of wine production and consumption. Chapter 13, "Pursuits of Quality in the Vineyards: French Oenologists at Work in Lebanon," looks at the hierarchy of winemaking in Lebanon and the importance of French winemakers and foreign technical knowledge in the making of quality wine. This postcolonial tendency to privilege French winemakers and expertise is indicative of a larger project of French hegemony that is deeply embedded in the commercial agendas of local actors. Chapter 14, "The Artifice of Natural Wine: Jules Chauvet and the Reinvention of Vinification in Postwar France," takes a largely historical look at the work of French *négociant*, winemaker, and chemist Jules Chauvet. Paul Cohen explores the ways in which Chauvet began to define a modern concept of "natural wine," and how this did not always mean opposition to technology and science. In Chapter 15, Rachel Black offers a contemporary exploration of the tensions between technology and nature that can be found in the Italian natural wine movement. Based on fieldwork with producers in Italy and consumers in the United States, Black looks at the ways in which nature is perceived in wine in the cellar and vineyard versus in the glass.

Many areas of wine and culture are not covered in this book, but we hope that this volume will be a call for further research and inquiry and that it will stimulate conversation among academics, students, wine professionals, and enthusiasts.

Rethinking *Terroir*

ROBERT C. ULIN AND RACHEL E. BLACK

Terroir has become arguably the most commonly referenced and controversial concept in both the popular and academic discourse and literature on wine. While having its origins in France with respect to agricultural domains most generally, *terroir* is used today worldwide to emphasize the unique character of wines with respect to the soil and climate under which grapes are cultivated in specific locales. It is commonly believed, therefore, that the taste of wine is specific to the soil and climate from which the grapes are harvested. In fact, if we follow James Wilson's (1998) influential book, it is argued that *terroir* refers to microclimates and to the deep soil conditions of often small and circumscribed parcels of land. According to Wilson, who made use of seismic technology to determine deep soil conditions, rows of vines in proximity can differ considerably with respect to the ideal nutrients that support the growth of quality wine grapes. This helps us to understand, argues Wilson, how a single winegrowing property can produce grapes and wines of differing qualities. In the past, this was largely a matter of speculation.

A book on the anthropology of wine can hardly ignore the importance of *terroir,* and so we have devoted an entire section to exploring some of the principal assumptions, arguments, and implications of this influential concept. The reader will note that we are less interested in exploring the empirical and scientific arguments associated with *terroir* and more so in evaluating how *terroir* has been used and represented historically, socially, culturally, and politically to support the reputedly unique characteristics of particular wines in particular places. Our effort is therefore a social science of *terroir* and thus distinct from much of what one can read from oenologists, winegrowers, marketers, and wine writers in general.

Sarah Daynes's chapter on the "Social Life of Terroir among Bordeaux Winemakers" takes us right to the issue of the representation of *terroir* in a region where it is highly articulated. Moreover, Daynes's contribution has much to add theoretically in that she, following Arjun Appadurai (1986) on commodities, looks at the concept of *terroir* as having a life of its own and therefore not as a derivative process. She is especially interested in how *terroir* is operative in wine production and the representations of wine and winemaking. *Terroir* is regarded as an "ensemble of knowledge" particular to a place. Daynes illustrates, furthermore, that less prestigious regions allow winemakers to be more "playful" and inventive as there are no rigid standards to which they must strictly adhere. Daynes compares the use of *terroir* in the Médoc to Burgundy where parcels of land retain their name regardless of change in ownership, thus exhibiting how physical *terroir* has an importance not quite equaled in Bordeaux. Finally, Daynes shows us how winemakers disrupt the conventional dichotomy between tradition and modernity by using *terroir* to explore science, technique, and art.

Robert Swinburn takes us to Australia to evaluate the multiple uses of *terroir*. His chapter is quick to point out that there is no precise definition of *terroir*. Rather, he maintains that the concept is evocative, having multiple meanings. His winegrowing informants are former city professionals who have moved to the countryside to engage in the making of premium wines. While many of these growers use *terroir* when talking about their wines, it is commonly held that they operate outside of *terroir* because their winemaking entails intervention with nature. For these growers, *terroir* suggests what is natural. Swinburn uses this as a departure point for evaluating the tension between the uses of *terroir* on the part of the Australian wine industry and how it is embodied in the lives of Australian winemakers. Contesting the association of *terroir* with what is natural entails, argues Swinburn, a reexamination of the environment. Swinburn provides us with an experiential or phenomenological grasp of *terroir* in maintaining that the concept of *terroir*, apart from its commercial value, entails a philosophic and spiritual belonging to a place and the reverence for place.

Nicolas Sternsdorff Cisterna explores the concept of *terroir* among Chilean winegrowers. He argues that Chilean wines are known more for their value in terms of low cost rather than overall quality. Cisterna shows how the concept of *terroir* lies at the heart of a concerted effort to improve the worldwide reputation of Chilean wines. That is, he outlines the important relation between perceptions of quality and the construction of space. The challenge for Chilean winegrowers is to construct a narrative about *terroir* that is compelling. Cisterna identifies a tension between the physical properties of a locale and what he describes poetically as the "human effort to coax land into the bottle." Cisterna's narrative is not, however, simply romantic in that he also focuses on how physical environments are turned into spaces of capitalist production, which he identifies as both material and symbolic, thus foregrounding questions of power. Cisterna reminds us that place and food argue against the anonymous, a good segue into Ulin's chapter on *terroir*.

Like Marion Demossier (this volume), Robert Ulin (1996) is by no means a newcomer to the *terroir* theme and the anthropology of wine more broadly. In a 2008 essay, Ulin argued that the concept of *terroir* was often employed in such a manner as to both fetishize and anthropomorphize nature. He pointed out the contiguity between circumscribed nature implied in the *terroir* concept and circumscribed culture that owes its origins to a Western colonial past. For Ulin, *terroir* conceals historically fashioned social relations of power and difference. Here, in his "Terroir and Locality: An Anthropological Perspective," he pursues a somewhat different strategy that is less dismissive of the uses of *terroir* through showing its considerable virtues in the age of nondistinct mass production. Ulin discusses the tendency in the winegrowing literature to focus on the commodity at the expense of the labor and social relations employed in its production, an issue common to capitalist production. Ulin argues that the popularity of *terroir* is its capacity to link wine to particular places and particular producers in light of the general anonymity of commodities under late capitalism. With the concept of *terroir*, it becomes much easier to imagine the labor embodied in the cultivation of vineyards and production of wine, not to overlook the aesthetic appeal important to the consumption of wine. Ulin thus preserves the unique appeal of distinction associated with wine through *terroir* but without abandoning the critical anthropological perspective that regards *terroir* as a narrative as much about us as about the physical environment that it reputedly depicts.

Taken together, these chapters do much more than explore particular wine regions around the world with respect to *terroir*. Rather, the particular ethnographic and historical examples explored here point beyond themselves to major themes of power, politics of representation, concealment, commodity fetishism, contested meaning and culture, and globalization that cross-cut the humanities and social sciences. *Terroir* remains, we believe, an extremely important lens through which to explore both differentiated locales and wines and differentiated social relations.

CHAPTER ONE

The Social Life of *Terroir* among Bordeaux Winemakers

SARAH DAYNES

"Let's go see the vines!" the Médoc winemaker said as I came in. As we drive on the small curvy road, rows of vines everywhere around us, she keeps pointing, describing what she sees: to the left a very good parcel used for her first wine, a few rows of very old vines she owns in the middle of somebody else's land, a large area that rolls down toward the river and that now belongs to a famous vineyard owner. She remarks on unkempt vines or wood left to rot in the rows, and makes sure I notice how well tended hers are. When we stop here and there, she cannot help it: she touches the vines, removes a shoot that should not be there, shows me precisely why it should be removed, or, if it was left and allowed to grow, how the grapevine could then be lowered next year by removing what this year is a cane. In her touch on the wood, I can see at the same time what seems to be love or tenderness, and the disinterested efficacy of a farmer's gesture repeated a thousand times.

What she sees so easily, I need to be shown and explained: the quality of the soil or the exposure of a slope as much as the way in which human hands have sculpted the vines, tended them, or neglected them. I am in my first year of fieldwork, and what I thought I knew about winemaking is shaken up, starting with the notion of *terroir:* she sees in her vineyard a landscape both given and transformed, a combination of physical and human dimensions, pointing to Brunet's definition of *terroir* as the human "reading" of a given natural milieu (1995, 7). In fact, as my visits in the field intensify, a whole series of clear-cut oppositions, common in the media and in the literature, is disrupted: science and artisanship, nature and culture, innovation and tradition. My decision to focus my inquiry on the production side was originally motivated by the strange absence of Bordeaux's small winegrowers[1] in the social sciences literature.[2] In the vein of Doug Harper's monograph on an upstate New York mechanic (1987), I was interested not in representations of wine and winemaking as they unfold in wine consumption, tasting, or marketing, but rather in how they play out in production practices: to put it quite simply, I wanted to document the craft. I thus started ethnographic fieldwork with winegrowers and winemakers on the left and right banks of the Bordeaux winemaking region. All exploit areas of land small enough that they retain control of the production from the vines to the bottle.[3] They work both in the vineyard and in the cellar, with permanent and seasonal help in the former; some of them also use a consultant in oenology for the postharvest process. As the reader might have noticed, I opened this chapter with the introduction of a woman: she is not the only one among the winemakers I work with, an accurate reflection of the 2005 census. As it turns out, almost a third of *"chefs d'exploitation vinicole"* in France are women (Taleng 2008).

This chapter focuses on the uses of the notion of *terroir* by winemakers in their professional activity.[4] In particular, I look at the sometimes complicated cohabitation of the two dimensions the notion of *terroir* takes: on one hand, it is understood as a physical ensemble; on the other hand, it is also a human construct. These dimensions have increasingly been recognized as equally important by scholars,[5] leading anthropologist Marion Demossier to speak of a "paradigm shift...from the geological argument to the recognition of the wine-grower as the mediator in the expression of *terroir*" (2011, 685). Interestingly, the experts of the viticulture section of the International Organization of Vine and Wine (OIV)[6] recently drafted a definition of *terroir* that resonates with the Médoc winemaker with whom I opened this chapter, as well as with Demossier's argument. It was passed as a resolution stated as follows:

Vitivinicultural *terroir* is a concept which refers to an area in which collective knowledge of the interactions between the identifiable physical and biological environment and applied vitivinicultural practices develops, providing distinctive characteristics for the products originating from this area. *Terroir* includes specific soil, topography, climate, land-scape characteristics and biodiversity features. (Organisation Internationale de la Vigne et du Vin, resolution OIV-VITI 333–2010)

In addition to recognizing both the physical and human dimensions of the notion of *terroir,* the OIV definition emphasizes an ensemble of knowledge[7] specific to a place and born out of the interactions between *this* place and the human practices adapted to it, which together produce a *unique* outcome: wine. Implicitly, this ensemble of knowledge is considered homogenous from within *as well as* heterogenous from without: it is suggested that it is unique and never exactly similar to any other ensemble on the other side of the road, or across the ocean.

In the context of an increased recognition of the sociocultural dimensions of *terroir* by scholars and experts, how does the notion of *terroir* play out in the professional activity of Bordeaux winemakers? Do physical and sociocultural notions of *terroir* cohabit, and if so, how are they reconciled? In this chapter, I present three ways in which *terroir* is used by winemakers.

MAGNIFIED *TERROIR*

The vineyard is so close to the village that the rows of vines reach the stone walls that encircle it. The small four-hectare property is cut in two by a narrow road that climbs up gentle hills and bumps into houses. Sitting at a table under a linden tree, our backs to the cellar with the vines almost touching our feet, we are facing most of the vineyard, bordered by a forested hilltop on one side and the village on the other. The view is a postcard-perfect expression of the Saint-Emilion winemaking region: green, hilly, busy, populated, with undulating rows of vines everywhere it was possible to plant them. The owner is talking about visitors from California who showed up one day. She is wary of American wine amateurs, because she often gets the impression that they find the vineyard small, the cellar dirty ("and yet I swear it's clean!" she adds), and her wine not "technical" enough. But as she is telling her story, a large smile lights up her face: these visitors from California pointed out the uniqueness of her land, noting that hers was a *terroir* "they could never have." She continues, "I was happy that they recognize the great advantage that *terroir* gives. Everything else, it's work."

This Saint-Emilion winemaker acknowledges the importance of *terroir* as a physical object: a poor or average *terroir* cannot give an outstanding wine, no matter the level of expertise of the viniculturist. Yet she also acknowledges the importance of human work: an exceptional *terroir* will not automatically give an outstanding wine either. Three hundred years earlier, in his treaty on taxation, Vauban made a similar argument,[8] emphasizing the idea that the land is pregnant with possibilities that can only exist and be revealed through the work of the viniculturist. Furthermore, the idea that a good winemaker reveals the possibilities offered by a specific *terroir* does not apply solely to a distinction between poor and rich land. Perhaps speaking of "friendly" and "unfriendly" *terroir* would be more accurate. Some locations make it easier to produce good wine because of the combination of soil, climate, and topography they present, just like it is easier to cook good food with good produce. The winemakers I work with all primarily use a physical notion of *terroir* that they often equate first with soil quality and that they apply parcel by parcel. Walking through their vineyard or driving down small country roads, they keep interjecting that these ten rows to the left are "really good"; they show how a slope faces the river or why the soil there is different and better than on other parcels. Yet the art of winemaking is thought to be found not in the land itself, but in how it is transformed and reflected into wine: good wine is made *both* in the vineyard and in the cellar. Several winemakers, of course, expressed a tinge of envy at the "*terroirs* of exception" that lie sometimes just a mile or two from their own land yet remain inaccessible. Still, what matters to them is what they can do with what they have, how well they can adapt to the land they work, and how they can excel at working it through their labor, creativity, skills, knowledge, and, perhaps above all, their affectionate understanding of the land they work all year long.

In other words, winemaking is thought of as a magnification of physical *terroir*. Just as the winemaker who opened this chapter could "read" the landscape, a good winemaker is thought to be someone who can "read" the physical *terroir* and transform it into wine: a good wine is a distinct wine that reflects the specificity of the *terroir* it comes from, qualities and weaknesses included. The attention to practices and techniques in the vineyard is not solely a scientific process. Winemakers know that the varieties planted, viticultural practices, harvest, and vinification all determine what the final product will be, and they also know that specific varieties and techniques are better adapted to specific physical *terroir*s than others: continuous scientific research, from crop protection to the interaction between water levels and the vines to pruning techniques to the control of sugars and acids during fermentation, is widely disseminated and made available to them through publications, agricultural extensions, winegrowers' associations, and so forth. But beyond scientific inquiry, which proves and disproves the effects of techniques on wine, the idea is to express, in the product and as well as possible, the qualities not only of a specific place, but of a specific year of production, with the notion of vintage. If irrigation is not permitted in Appellation d'Origine Contrôlée (AOC), it is because the normalization of productive years that results from irrigation would make vintages disappear. A bottle of wine, therefore, is not just an expression of a place: it is thought to be the expression of *a place in time*. Like an object of art, a wine is thought to be unique and impossible to reproduce (Benjamin 2008).

This notion of diversity in quality, or of difference as inherent to wine quality, is the backbone of the French understanding of *terroir*, and is helpful to understand why French winemaking abides by laws that tend to conceive of wine production as a holistic process. The AOC system indeed regulates not only geographical origin, as the American Viticultural Area (AVA) system does;[9] it also prescribes "everything else"; that is, winemaking practices, including the varieties that can be grown, pruning techniques, plantation density, canopy height, maximum yields, sugar content and alcohol level, the use of irrigation, soil amendment and addition, various vinification practices, and even the earliest date at which the wine can be bottled or sold.[10] Indeed, the increasingly common understanding that the quality of wine (or its character) depends not just on postharvest practices, but also on viticulture, becomes central when winemaking is understood as a magnification of *terroir*. This idea is, of course, at the basis of organic farming, and is especially important for those who practice biodynamic agriculture, as in the case of one of the winemakers I work with.[11] But the importance of the way in which wine is made (and therefore of the practices implemented in the vineyard) and the idea that wine does not start with grapes have become common well beyond organic or biodynamic vitiviniculture. Certified organic or not, all the winemakers I work with give a central place to pre- and postharvest practices, although they do so in varying ways.

Furthermore, the cultural dimension of the production process is expressed not just in what is done, but in how it is done. There is what could be called an aesthetics of practices, which is not thought of as simply a nicer or more beautiful way to do things, but rather as having a direct effect on the quality of the wine produced. Harvesting by hand, for instance, is equally justified rationally (as it limits damage to the grapes and allows for more efficient sorting) and irrationally (in terms of intimacy with the vines and care or as a humane process in comparison with the use of machines). The attachment to the period of the harvest is also due to its intensity: to see the grapes finally off the vines, safely on the sorting table, is a relief for the viticulturist of an intensity that is difficult to imagine. Months of patient care (viticulture necessitates year-round work in the vineyard, even during the winter season) and mounting anxiety (regarding pests, freezes, hail, storms, droughts) culminate in this couple of weeks, and until the last moment anything can happen. It is no wonder that such an important moment in the life of the viticulturist occupies such an important place in his or her mind, as several of the winemakers I work with have shown. Almost a year of mostly solitary labor by the viniculturist in his vines peaks in the "dense concentrations" of the harvest period, in a way similar to the rhythmic oscillation of the Eskimo society described by Marcel Mauss in his classic monograph (2004, 76). Workers, often the same from one year to the next, arrive and gather at the vineyard: the harvest is a period of intensive work and collective life punctuated by little sleep and shared meals. Once it is over, the viniculturist returns to solitary life, this time not in the vineyard, but in the cellar, for the crucial moment of the first and second fermentations. Were the viniculturist to decide to harvest mechanically, therefore reducing the human help needed for the task, the harvest would lose some of its celebratory quality, embodied in the social gathering.[12]

The winemakers I work with conceive of winemaking as an activity bound by the natural world, yet akin to a work of art and therefore eminently human: *terroir*, as a physical notion, is only a point of departure, albeit one that has to be contended with. There is no question they can assess the possibilities offered by a given place and judge of its quality. Yet physical *terroir* is not all there is: it is up to the viniculturist to reveal it. And there again, things are not always what they seem. Earlier, I used the terms "friendly" and "unfriendly" to talk about *terroirs* that are more or less propitious to viniculture. But a discussion with Olivier, a winemaker on the right bank, complicates the matter: high-quality *terroir*s are not necessarily the "friends" of the viniculturist.

FRIENDLY *TERROIR*

Olivier used to work in the wine trade. One day, he decided he had had enough. He bought a property with vines and a limestone house and cellar along the lazy Dordogne river, in the large Bordeaux Supérieur AOC, where he and his family now reside, and he started making wine. He now works two additional parcels in more prestigious appellations: a tiny one in Pomerol, and another in Saint-Emilion. As I drove in, I noticed a section of the Bordeaux Supérieur vineyard was being uprooted. Olivier told me that they were old vines from the volume-oriented 1960s, which he did not want to keep. Instead, he is about to plant some Cabernet Franc, his favorite variety as well as a common complement to Merlot and Cabernet Sauvignon, but also some Carmenère, a much less obvious choice.[13] Newly planted grapevines must mature for four to five years before a full harvest occurs, and so getting rid of a whole section of old vines and replacing them with young plants means that space will be lost to production for several years. For a winemaker, especially one on the right bank where properties are much smaller than on the left bank, losing a substantial part of the harvest for several years is a considerable decision to make. Furthermore, the land is so critically limited that it becomes very difficult to innovate with a new variety, as opposed to simply replacing the old vines. This is a risk that Olivier is willing to take in his least prestigious location, but that he just cannot afford in his other more prestigious ones:

> Here I have less economic pressure let's say, I can afford it, because I can easily lease one and a half hectare [to compensate for the loss of the uprooted section on his own land], which I cannot do in Pomerol nor in Saint-Emilion...In Pomerol I cannot afford it. But here I can, and so I'm having fun, I try to make a garden of sorts out of it, of the things I love, and, and yes, to use it to make the wine I love, that's the idea.

His least prestigious location hence becomes the friendlier one, despite the fact that the *terroir* is not as good. He speaks of it as a "garden" in which he has the opportunity to experiment, to innovate, and, most important, to make the wine he loves. With a less prestigious *terroir*, where land is not as limited in size and financial losses less important, winemaking becomes playful, and the wine produced really personal, "the wine I love," a wine of dreams and pleasure. This is something one would expect from the large vineyards, such as those found in the Médoc,[14] and in particular from the wealthy ones:

> But yes, these large wineries...there is that too, there is the size, you don't manage ten hectares like you manage one hundred hectares, it's not possible...what is too bad is that...these people often have money and they don't make their garden, I understand there is an economic project, profitability, but okay you can do it on 95 hectares and then have fun, make pleasure wines...there is no place for dreams, or for pleasure, for the pleasure to make your own wine.

Not many winemakers in the Bordeaux area experiment and try new varieties. There is a "recipe that works" and no real desire to change it. The famous "Bordeaux blend," which mixes Cabernet Sauvignon and Merlot with a secondary addition of Cabernet Franc or Petit Verdot, is such a recipe. Why experiment with Carmenère or Malbec when the vines are already planted (and not easy to replace), the wine selling easily, the business running? The same is true, albeit to a lesser extent, concerning techniques: the oak barrel, for instance, is so ubiquitous that few would think of not using it, even if alternatives exist. As Olivier emphasizes, innovation is to a great extent limited by business: while winemaking can be considered a labor of love, or a vocation in the Weberian sense, it remains that it is also a *productive* practice and a business. In the end, the wine produced has to be sold and the winemaker has to make a living. Hence for small vineyards, it is often impossible to risk a part of the harvest or to lose some land for four or five years without the certainty that it will pay off.

At the same time, it is precisely with smaller vineyards, in less prestigious AOCs, that innovation now predominantly takes place in the region, because the *terroir* is "friendlier" there and open to experimentation. The large, prestigious *grands crus classés* possess the wealth that would allow for limited financial loss, and therefore for weighted-risk experimentation, and at least on the left bank they usually also have enough land to allow for experimentation on a few hectares. Yet they also have boards of directors (since few are still family owned) and a high division of labor (because of their size), which preclude innovation partly for financial reasons and partly for organizational reasons. The board, ultimately in charge of decisions, has few business reasons to listen to the various persons who share the production process and often have innovative ideas, such as the *maître de chai* (responsible for the postharvest period) or the person in charge of the vineyard (preharvest period).[15]

Discussing innovation in winemaking practices is a complex endeavor because science, business, and tradition interlock in a very close manner. If winemakers are not prone to stray from the typical Bordeaux blend, it is not just because they are not curious, and neither is it only because they focus on business goals. It is also because they have been making *good wine* this way, better wine than when using just one grape variety. It is well known, indeed, that the reason for blending varieties is found in the specific effects each brings: combining them gives more complexity and balance to the wine. Similarly, the use of new oak barrels is not just a marketing decision to satisfy what some call the "parkerization" of taste and wine consumers,[16] and neither is it solely because of tradition: new wood brings roundness to the wine while old wood brings dryness.

Furthermore, innovation and tradition are not necessarily antinomic. Olivier, for instance, is a curious winemaker with a strong desire to "try new things out," but he also conceives of innovation as ascribed within tradition. This is evident with his choices concerning aging:

Now, I am at a turning point, I don't feel like using barrels anymore... barrels bore me... but I am in full thinking mode because... I know that commercially it's going to be a problem because customers are used to them... So I'm going to keep on making [one of my wines] like before and then I'm also going to make my wine... it's going to be aged in cement vats, natural to the highest point, and very very little sulfur, and here it is, early bottling, I'm going to make my own wine, you see.

His decision to stop using new oak barrels for aging is innovative in the sense that it goes against commonly accepted practices. In the Bordeaux area, especially in prestigious AOCs, the practice is so ingrained that it is difficult to even think about abandoning it, as he emphasizes by joking about being "the only one in Pomerol not using barrels!" His decision was not taken hastily; in fact, he fought against it for a long time:

Pomerol I stop using barrels too... And so I have the desire to do that now. Well, I've always had the desire to do that, but at the beginning I didn't want to use barrels but gradually I let myself be influenced by the wine world.

Yet this strongly innovative decision is also related to a desire to go back to what he calls "simplest things" and to more traditional winemaking. Indeed, oak barrels have not always been the norm: they were, in the past, used only for specific wines such as Saint-Estèphe and Saint-Julien in the Médoc, or Burgundy *grands crus*. And Olivier is not switching to a newer container, but to an older one; and he modifies his vinification practices toward simplification to avoid what he calls the "artifices" of aging:

I'm going to work like we worked back in the days, in fact... we used to stock in big wooden containers that are like gigantic barrels, and I'm going to vinify and age in there... So I don't make wine to, I make wine to... well... to, quotes, "fulfill myself," I don't make wine to make a living, to make money and stuff, I make wine because I like it and, so I try to listen to myself, yes, and so the barrel bored me, I started being fed up with it, it didn't please me anymore, well, it pleased me less, I felt like doing... like evolving, and in fact evolving often means to go towards simplest things, to go into simplicity, to make the purest thing, the most essential rather, essential, and so it means to get rid of the artifices of aging, even during vinification, to let things be, and... You see right now my malolactic [fermentations] are not done and they're going to happen on their own calmly, and…and so the wine is in vats, without sulfur, it's perfect, it's going well, you have to watch it, you have to be careful, but, but it works.

Hence his "boredom" with barrels is linked to a broader path; unrushed malolactic fermentation and sulfur-free aging,[17] as well as minimal filtration, are other practices that participate in his desire to make wine differently, to get back to "simplicity." The choices he makes, whether in terms of additives, filtration, or barrels, are all oriented by his conception of "good" winemaking, which can be summarized by his own words: "let things be." This general conception concretely translates into practices that are simultaneously innovative and conservative. This is a direction I found not only with Olivier on the right bank, but also with another winemaker on the other side of the river.

BORROWED *TERROIR*

The first time I met Stéphane, I was surprised to hear him mention Burgundy several times. It is a long drive from Bordeaux to his vines in the Médoc appellation. If you continue down the road, the muddy waters of the Gironde estuary lie in front of you, so wide it is hard to see the bank on the other side. The road curves to the left, along the water, and if you keep driving all the way to the tip of the large peninsula, the landscape soon appears, almost desolated, with scanty houses, low, lonely trees, and cows grazing on salted pastures. At the end of the road is the Atlantic Ocean at the mouth of the river and a salty wind. A sign says, "Royan," but what it really means is that you'll have to get on a ferry to get there. We are a long way from the rolling hills of Burgundy.

Stéphane's vineyard is an ode to tradition: "This is the Médoc!" one thinks, far from the touristy areas from Margaux to Pauillac, where the river is narrower and the city much closer. The grapes are harvested, sorted, and destemmed by hand; a wooden sorting table with a mechanical wheel sits in the interior courtyard, and it is here because it is used, not just there for nostalgic decoration. Rows of Bordeaux 225-liter wood barrels and large concrete vats line the cellar, which is an old, beautifully renovated limestone building in the middle of the village. Yet this most venerable setting is also home to various experimentations: small barrels with this or that modified during fermentation wait to be tasted in a year or two; a large, potbellied Burgundy barrel is sitting there, too, and looks almost incongruous. And the first time I visited, Stéphane spoke at length and eloquently about the Burgundian conception of *terroir* and how it differs from that found in the Médoc. How are we to make sense of this patchwork of "traditions"?

The Burgundy and Médoc winemaking traditions are distinct not only in the gestures, practices, tools, and objects they use, but also in the general idea of winemaking they reflect and put forward, which in turn indicates different conceptions of *terroir*. As Stéphane explains, in the Médoc, a good winemaker is someone who expands by buying his neighbors' land. And the acquired land will lose its former identity by becoming a part of the buyer's vineyard, usually called a *château*.[18] The most successful châteaux of the Médoc all added land as time passed; hence vintages of the same property not only were made by different winemakers and with the juice of different generations of grapevines, but the grapes might not even come from the same land.[19] Good winemaking is thought of in a completely different way in Burgundy: there is no question of expansion as a result of commercial success. Each parcel retains its name, no matter who owns it or whose hands it might pass into: such a parcel is called a *climat* and its name appears on the bottle.[20] If the same winemaker owns several parcels and works them all, he or she will not mix their grapes, but make one wine per parcel. The contrast with the Médoc is striking: there, the goal is to acquire as much adjacent land as possible in a desirable AOC and mix all the grapes together under one single name. In fact, as Stéphane points out, the notion of physical *terroir*, which he and several other winemakers primarily use in their understanding of their vineyard, is therefore more important in Burgundy than it is in Bordeaux.

Traditional practices in both areas have become such through the passing of time.[21] The gestures, tools, and techniques used in each area have evolved and solidified as the result of a gradual accumulation of collective knowledge as understood in the OIV 2010 definition. In both cases, distinct winemaking traditions have resulted from science and technique, from cultural specificity, and from social exigencies (for instance, the switch to "quality wines" in Bordeaux in the eighteenth century was largely due to the commercial challenges posed by Iberian wines to exportations to the English market (Enjalbert 1953). The crystallization of certain practices into "tradition" has led to what could be called cultural closure, precluding the emergence of new practices on a practical level, but also, more important, on the symbolic level. Olivier's reluctance to stop using oak fermentation barrels despite his desire to do so is a good example of such cultural closure: practical and commercial exigencies (such as the risk of losing customers used to oaked wine) influence his choices, yet a crucial factor in his decision remains what he calls the "wine world," in which both knowledge and symbolic norms circulate, solidifying some practices and precluding others. So his original desire to do without barrels was first repressed and only acted upon after several years of winemaking, once his technical knowledge and professional assurance had grown. In fact, he later pointed out to me that he has a tendency to "go against the grain," which is itself a witness to the importance of the symbolic norms that define a winemaking region.

Furthermore, traditional practices are also the result of nearly two thousand years of continuous experimentation: it would be foolish to understand the restrictions placed by AOC regulations upon vine varieties *solely* as the result of cultural specificity and tradition, and therefore irrational choices. Several winemakers point out that, if Bordeaux grows Cabernet Sauvignon and Burgundy Pinot Noir, it is also because they are varieties well adapted to the physical characteristics of each area. Yet it does not follow that winemakers blindly abide by the prescriptions of both the symbolic and physical dimensions of the winemaking regions they work in. As a matter of fact, the winemakers I work with negotiate *terroir* in different ways. In the Médoc, Stéphane's desire to grow Syrah is tempered by his acknowledgment of cultural specificity, and not acted upon. Syrah is not among the varieties allowed by Bordeaux AOC regulations, yet it can be grown, and the wine thus produced could be sold as *vin de table* (outside of the appellation). But he is reluctant to do so because he believes in the importance of Bordeaux's cultural specificity and would not want to see the region grow "just about anything." On the right bank, Corinne has no desire to try new varieties, and quotes Montaigne to justify her position: "Each custom has its reason." She emphasizes the specificity of Bordeaux wine and asserts that if one wants to make a different wine, one should do it elsewhere. This is what Olivier is doing: with a friend, he is going to make wine in the Corbières area. In fact, this most innovative winemaker (and most reluctant to follow the symbolic and cultural norms associated with a wine region) is also a traditionalist. Indeed innovation remains within the specificities of the area: he might plant varieties underused in Bordeaux, yet they remain recognized as traditional; or he uses, for common Bordeaux varieties, grafts that come from the Loire valley. In all cases, winemakers understand *terroir* both in a physical and cultural way, and innovation is taking the form of a careful navigation between physical limitations, symbolic prescriptions, and individual desires.

FROM *TERROIR* TO THE VALUE OF LABOR

The winemakers I work with use the idea of *terroir* in both its physical and sociocultural dimensions. Primarily, for them, *terroir* is a physical notion: it refers to the specificities of place, in particular to soil. Parcel by parcel, physical *terroir* directly impacts on the possibilities for wine production, making it more or less propitious. *Terroir* is therefore a crucial element, seen as a canvas that limits further human activity as well as the product in which it results. Human labor acts as a magnification of *terroir*, rather than aiming at transforming, changing, or bypassing it. Secondarily, they also use *terroir* as a social notion: it refers again to the specificities of place, but as a cultural ensemble. There, *terroir* has to do with a commonality in the ways the physical environment has been magnified over time, the dimensions labor has taken, the kind of wine produced in a specific region, the manner in which winemaking and wine are "thought" and represented.

Despite being located in what is often thought to be the quintessential French winemaking region and thereby the bearer of a national tradition that considers wine as a cultural specificity, the winemakers I work with disrupt the opposition between two clear-cut ideas, commonly found in the literature on *terroir*. The first contends that *terroir* is everything: there are absolute and insurmountable qualitative differences between different *terroirs*, and a mechanical relationship between physical *terroir* and the wine produced. Social practices are embedded in this relation in the form of techniques, gestures, ways of doing and thinking that are specific to a given place and thought to impact on the wine produced. Thus reproduction is impossible. The second idea contradicts the first, by arguing that *terroir* does not matter at all: with sufficient science and technique, the "kind of wine" produced somewhere can be reproduced elsewhere, bypassing both the physical and sociocultural specificities of place.

It is well known that the two aforementioned positions intersect with two distinct ways to conceive both of winemaking and of wine, often referred to as an opposition between old and new worlds (Remaud and Couderc 2006) or *terroirists* and modernists (Bohmrich 1996). Banks and Overton have called for a reconceptualization of these "flawed" categories, which they argue are disrupted by "globalization" (Banks and Overton 2010, 58). On the basis of my work with winemakers in the Bordeaux area, I make a slightly different claim: the distinction between these two categories is pertinent, yet it is more complex than the way it is presented in the media and used in marketing practices. Certainly, the winemakers I work with disrupt a clear-cut opposition between tradition and modernity: they are tinkerers who use experimentation and a knowledge of the senses as a basis for the decisions they make, as much as they are innovators for whom scientific knowledge primes over tradition. They acknowledge the role both of science and culture in their activity: they claim that while physical *terroir* defines the possibilities for the wine they produce, it is human labor that makes the wine. They assert the importance of tradition yet do not understand it as static and neither do they view it as a prescription that cannot be navigated. In fact, these winemakers provide an illustration for a reconceptualization of tradition, as put forward by several scholars, in particular sociologists of religion (Hervieu-Léger 2000). Wine production and consumption are often described as centrally defined and informed by claims of memory and by the importance of authenticity, as evidenced by Guichard's interesting analysis of bottle labels (2000). Yet these claims of memory are not simply about practices frozen in time. The winemakers I work with, including "newcomers" (who bought land to make wine and/or had another career before winemaking) and individuals who exploit a property that has been in the family for several generations, demonstrate an acute awareness of participating in a tradition as well as innovating within it, albeit in different ways. A return to "older" practices, which I encountered regularly in the field, should not be seen simply as a nostalgic process: it can be a simultaneously revolutionary and traditional decision in the Weberian sense, akin to innovative claims of tradition found in religious movements (Weber 1978; Daynes 2010).

The weight of science and technique in winemaking only makes an analysis of tradition more interesting. The ways in which winemakers understand and use the notion of *terroir* reveal more than the complex construction and uses of authenticity and tradition, which have been thoroughly analyzed by social scientists in the past couple of decades.[22] Indeed, they also speak to the difficult arrangements made between science, craft, and experience in modern societies. Echoing Willie, the mechanic and main character in Doug Harper's book *Working Culture* (Harper 1987), winemakers meaningfully arrange the world around them by contending with *things* that exist outside of them: the soil they work, the vicissitudes of the weather, the tools they use. Physical *terroir* is the first of these: in their eyes, it is the most important external limitation, the "thing" that not only defines possibilities but also has to be adapted to and taken into account in daily labor. Harper describes quite beautifully in his book how Willie, when he fixes engines or welds metal, uses an intimate and sensual knowledge of the "thing" that also implies an acknowledgment of its radical externality and therefore an adaptation. In the same way, through their labor, winemakers work *with terroir* and cannot ignore it. It is not a coincidence if Harper emphasizes that "without such [kinesthetic] knowledge, a mechanic fights materials rather than communicating—reading their messages" (1987, 133), echoing the winemakers I work with who touch the vines, look at them, and say they listen to them. Both the mechanic and the winemakers have to contend with an external object; they are users of a technology embedded in science and, primarily, in experience (Feenberg 2010). And like Willie, winemakers are confronted with other ways to work in their profession, in which human activity loses some of its intimate knowledge: the distinction made between the mechanic and the "parts exchanger" (Harper 1987, 131) could very well, by analogy, apply to a distinction between vineyards and wineries.

By focusing on understandings of *terroir*, I provide a basis for further analysis, pointing to the intersections between technique, science, and art in winemaking as they appear via the question of innovation in the vineyard and in the cellar. Hence, *terroir* is, in the context of my fieldwork, a point of departure rather than of arrival. As happens so often in ethnographic inquiry, the field displaces and disrupts the ethnographer's expectations and goals. The complicated representation of *terroir* found among the winemakers I work with has done just so in my own research: in particular, the idea of winemaking as a magnification of *terroir* is leading me toward an analysis of work and its value: at the crossroads between the material and the ideal, winemaking provides a window to inquire into "work" and the complicated formation of what Harper calls a "working knowledge."

NOTES

1. Strange because they form the majority of the 6,150 vineyards (*exploitations viticoles*) in the Bordeaux winemaking region (Lamoureux et al. 2011).
2. The excellent works published by Ulin (1996) and Chauvin (2010) respectively focus on cooperatives and on reputation in the Bordeaux wine market.
3. Which was an important criterion in population selection: I wanted to avoid the large vineyards in which there is a high division of labor, and focus on winemakers who directly work and take decisions at all levels of the production process. The contrast with larger vineyards would be, of course, interesting to further explore, as is the comparison with cooperatives, already studied by Ulin (1996). For more details on the different

forms of vitivinicultural production in the Bordeaux area, see the typology used by Lamoureux and colleagues (2011).

4. I thank the winemakers I work with for sharing their knowledge and dreams and for patiently showing me the work they do. Some of them have also read this chapter and provided invaluable feedback.

5. Regarding the sociocultural dimensions of *terroir*, see in particular Demossier (2011). In recent years, the scholarship on *terroir* has broadened to include several products; see in particular Trubek (2008), as well as Cavanaugh (2007) on salami, Meneley (2008) on olive oil, Bowen and Zapata (2009) on tequila, or Paxson (2010) on cheese. Studies of physical *terroir* abound; most are published in scientific journals devoted to vitiviniculture and enology, such as the *American Journal of Enology and Viticulture* since 1950, the German *Vitis-Journal of Grapevine Research* since 1957, the French *Journal International des Sciences de la Vigne et du Vin* since 1967, the British *Journal of Wine Research* since 1990, and the *Australian Journal of Wine and Grape Research* since 1995. The biannual international conference on *terroir*s (see the website of its ninth edition at http://congresdesterroirs.com) provides a good glimpse of the current research; interesting, for the past couple of years, there has been a strong push to include more social scientists in the conference.

6. The OIV is an intergovernmental organization with forty-five members that together amount to more than seventy percent of the wine production in the world. Notably absent from this list is the United States. The OIV is a scientific and technical organization with a mission of observation, information, and advising. Its experts are grouped in four main areas: viticulture; oenology; economy; health and safety. OIV resolutions are passed unanimously and in five languages: English, French, German, Italian, and Spanish.

7. As Michel Foucault (1982) emphasized, in French, *knowledge* translates into two different words: *savoir* and *connaissance*. The former refers to a unique ensemble of knowledge that results from learning and experience, whereas the latter refers to a narrower knowledge thought to lie outside of the individual, and is often used in the plural form. The etymology of the two terms is distinct. *Connaitre* comes from the Latin *cognoscere,* like the word *cognition*. *Savoir* comes from the popular Latin *sapĕre,* "to know" or "to be wise," itself from the classical Latin *sapĕre,* "to have taste," like the words *savor* or *savory.*

8. "Car c'est une vérité qui ne peut être contestée, que le meilleur terroir ne diffère en rien du mauvais s'il n'est cultivé" (Vauban 1933, 26).

9. **AOC:** Appellation d'Origine Contrôlée, classifies wine as well as agricultural products such as cheese, poultry, honey, peppers, or butter. Appellations are regulated by the INAO (Institut National des Appellations d'Origine), created in 1935. Bordeaux also uses a simultaneous system (*crus classés* and *grands crus classés*), mostly inherited from the classifications of 1855, 1953, and 1954 (see Markham 1997). **AVA:** American Viticultural Area, since 1980. The AVA system is based on geography, while the AOC system regulates both the origin and production process; see Moran 1993 and Zhao 2005.

10. For instance, Saint-Emilion AOC wines must satisfy the following requirements among others (see the decree for more details): five principal varieties (Cabernet Sauvignon, Cabernet Franc, Carmenère, Cot/Malbec, Merlot) and one secondary variety (Petit Verdot); the latter cannot exceed ten percent of the total vineyard; at least fifty-five hundred plants per hectare; row spacing below two meters; three pruning techniques; twelve grape bunches maximum per meter; alcohol level between eleven percent and thirteen and a half percent; maximum yield sixty-five hectoliters per hectare... (Décret n° 2011–125 du 28 janvier 2011 relatif à l'appellation d'origine contrôlée "Saint-Emilion").

11. Biodynamic viniculture, based on Steiner's anthroposophy, understands the vineyard (e.g., the vine and soil but also the climate, fauna, and flora associated with the space) as an ecological system of energetic and spiritual equilibrium in which all lives interact.

12. And the use of machines limits the interaction between the viniculturist and the vines, although the machinery used in viticulture is not as extreme as it is for other crops: wheat, for instance, can now be harvested by auto-guided, man-free machines.

13. The Bordeaux Supérieur AOC allows the following red varieties: Cabernet Sauvignon, Cabernet Franc, Merlot, Petit Verdot, Carmenère, and Malbec. The latter two are uncommon. Most Bordeaux wines are blends or *vins d'assemblage,* in which one variety is dominant, usually Cabernet Sauvignon on the left bank and Merlot on the right bank.

14. The average vineyard size is forty hectares in the Médoc but only around eight in the Saint-Emilion area.

15. This is not to say that innovation does not exist among prestigious vineyards: for instance Pontet-Canet, one of the largest vineyards in the Médoc, has been gradually switching to organic and biodynamic winemaking practices, including the introduction of horses to replace tractors. See www.pontet-canet.com.

16. See Chauvin 2005 for an analysis of the influence of wine critic Robert Parker on the Bordeaux wine market.

17. Sulfur dioxide is widely used after malolactic fermentation, in particular as a preservative.

18. In Bordeaux, it is customary to associate the term *château* with a wine-producing estate and especially with the wine it produces, despite the fact that there are very few actual castles in the area. Roudié (2000) emphasizes that this practice, which emerged in the middle of the nineteenth century, is typical of Bordeaux, but he also shows how it has been exported in France and beyond.

19. Although the grapes in both bottles come from the same appellation, since the law does not permit the addition of outside grapes within an AOC wine. Hence a vineyard in one AOC cannot add grapes that come from the neighboring AOC even though the land might be adjacent.

20. A Bordeaux bottle indicates the appellation (e.g., "Saint-Estèphe") and the vineyard (e.g., "Château Montrose"). A Burgundy *premier-cru* bottle indicates the "village" appellation (e.g., "Nuits-Saint-Georges") and the parcel or *climat* (e.g., "Les Cailles"). On prestigious *grand cru* bottles, the *climat* alone is indicated, because classified as AOC (e.g., "Romanée-Conti").

21. Records exist of both areas producing wine during the Roman Empire in the second century A. D. Bordeaux wines were imported to England as early as the eleventh century. In Burgundy, the history of winemaking has been closely associated to monastic orders, in particular the Benedictines and Cistercians.

22. See, for instance, Peterson's analysis of country music (1999).

CHAPTER TWO

The Things that Count: Rethinking *Terroir* in Australia

ROBERT SWINBURN

INTRODUCTION

Most books on the topic suggest that the French word *terroir*—pronounced "tair-wahr"—has no English translation. Attempts to define *terroir* in Australia usually refer to the influence of the site, with its unique physical characteristics, on the taste of agricultural produce. The idea is particularly well suited to wine because winegrowers seek distinction rather than uniformity in their product.

For over 200 years now, people have made wine in Australia. Australian wine histories (Beeston 2001; Cox 1967; Gent 2003; Mayo 1991) usually begin with the story of the arrival of the First Fleet in 1788 and of the exotic plants, including grapevines for wine, carefully planted next to Governor Phillip's tent. The day Governor Phillip took formal possession from the original hunter-gatherers is still marked annually with the Australia Day holiday.

Over the past fifty years, wine production in Australia has increased exponentially. Much of the momentum has come as city-based professionals have moved from cities to rural fringes to engage in small-scale premium wine production. These winegrowers[1] increasingly use the French term *terroir* when they talk about their wines despite the fact that most struggle to explain exactly what it means. A tension exists between the widespread use of the term and the general agreement that the term has no precise English translation.[2] This chapter explores this tension around *terroir* and calls for a distinction to be made between *terroir* as it is generally understood in the Australian wine industry and a *terroir* that has a definition that comes from a wider reading. The latter *terroir* is more "lived" than discussed. This tension was highlighted when I visited winegrower John Eason, a retired hospital doctor originally from England. Together with his partner, Janine Ridley, a nurse and CEO of the local hospital, he produces Pinot Noir from their 2-hectare vineyard on the banks of a spectacular mountain river. Fires, smoke, droughts, frosts, and wasps have limited their production over the past decade. They hope that one day their winegrowing enterprise might, in their own words, "wash its face," but thoughts of profit are distant. Carved into the stone of their winery (and fire shelter) are the names of those who erected the building and the Latin words, "Ne Quid Nimes," which translates as "Nothing Too Much," a dictum that seems to sit comfortably with the place and the people who live there.

Despite the fact that John seemed to embody many of the ideas of *terroir* discussed later in this chapter, he regarded himself as being "outside" *terroir* because of the physical modifications he had made to his vineyard to improve drainage and adjust soil pH. This intervention, he thought, precluded him from representing his wines as true wines of *terroir*.

The idea that wines of *terroir* are simply an expression of the site is a contested one. Another winegrower informant, Michael Glover, suggests that people are necessarily a part of *terroir* and that intervention cannot be avoided. As he points out, grapevines don't just come out of the ground and get trellised on sticks by themselves. People have to be part of it from beginning to end. Michael relates the story of how a winemaker he was working for in Sardinia sent wine to New York that contained both yeast and sugar. The wine subsequently refermented and spoiled in the bottle. Glover accused the winemaker of letting his *terroir* down, of failing the vineyard. For Glover, people are central to enabling wine to come together.

In the process of exploring this tension, I draw from the literature on the historical, political, philosophical, and spiritual aspects of *terroir* and from direct interviews and work experience with Australian winegrowers. My own experiences will also be discussed. The reason for the analysis is to demonstrate that the tension that exists in the concept of *terroir* resides in the different ways the meaning of the term has evolved across time and space. From this analysis I argue that the concept of *terroir* is an important idea in the Australian winegrowing landscape for two reasons. First, it goes some way toward explaining why so many people are drawn to an industry with a troubled economic outlook. And second, an exploration of the idea of *terroir* offers an opportunity for those who feel the need to reexamine their relationship with the environment.

OLD WORLD—NEW WORLD

The concept of *terroir* has been used in different contexts across time and space and for reasons not always benign.[3] When Australian winegrowers use the term, they are usually referring to the soil and subsoil, the slope, the aspect, the altitude, the climate and microclimate, all of which, combined, go toward making their produce unique. With wine, it has been said that while factors such as weather can affect the personality of the wine and that winemaking technique can affect the quality of the wine, only *terroir* can give wine an individual character that remains identifiable year after year (Johnson and Halliday 1992, 20). By claiming *terroir,* winegrowers are implying their wines will be unique.

Michael Glover is a career winemaker employed at Geelong's iconic Bannockburn winery, established in the 1970s by supermarket pioneer Stuart Hooper. In his teens, Michael helped plant a family vineyard in New Zealand after his father, troubled by talk among his Australian colleagues of the possibility of "winning" a nuclear conflict, fled the world of weapons systems design. Michael later studied winemaking. He has worked around Australia as well as completing more than ten vintages across Europe. While making wine with his father in New Zealand, Michael noticed that, year after year, the wine from two adjacent vineyards produced wines that were "chalk and cheese." Both were good wines, but they were consistently different in character. In addition, he noticed that when those wines were blended, the quality of the wine was compromised. He noticed the same thing while working with Dr. Loosen in Germany's Mosel region, but here there were no oak additions or maceration. As a result, it was easier to see the character each vineyard demonstrated, year in, year out. From his experiences, Glover has come to believe that a truth lies in *terroir.* He says that if you have a bit of dirt and it consistently produces a quality wine, it can't be the winemaking because winemaking can be copied. The "site," however, cannot be copied. He says that what you have that is different is a bit of dirt, and if you can get that bit of dirt to sing, then you won't have any competition.

The idea of *terroir* moves consumers beyond simple issues of wine quality by providing them with a symbolic connection to a specific piece of land and even to the people who live there when they consume that wine. This is a powerful idea for wine producers and consumers, and it lies at the heart of booming wine tourism. But while *terroir* is a powerful idea with its roots dating back to preindustrial times, it is not an idea embraced by everyone. There are winemakers, especially but not exclusively, in the "new world" who reject the concept altogether. These winemakers call on science to provide beneficial characteristics to their wine rather than accepting what nature has delivered. The privileging of science over nature has been embraced in places that developed their wine industries after the advent of the industrial revolution (Charters 2008, 58; and see Loubere 1990), and the manipulation of wine by wine scientists is particularly suited to an age where self-expression is considered an inalienable right (Kramer 2008, 229). There are "old world" winemakers too, who see the privileging of *terroir* as an expression of a peasant past better dispensed with. One particularly spectacular example is powerful French consultant winemaker Michel Rolland, who appears in Nossiter's documentary *Mondovino* (2004). He encourages his clients to embrace new science-based technologies such as micro-oxygenation, which speeds up the aging process of wine and enables it to be consumed upon release rather than matured in a cellar.

The debate that emerges around science and nature in winemaking leads the discussion on to the historical and political aspects of *terroir,* and even beyond, to considerations of a philosophical and spiritual nature. Kramer has gone as far as to suggest that to gain a full understanding of *terroir* requires a recalibration of the modern mind (2008, 225). This recalibration is alluded to when Michael Glover suggests that *terroir* is more about honoring the vineyard than it is about business or ego. He points to the Burgundian vineyard of Chambertin, which has existed for nearly ten centuries. He suggests that the winemaker has no right to impose his or her own will on such a treasure when he or she is there for such a short period of time. He draws an analogy with Da Vinci's *Mona Lisa* and suggests that nobody really owns it. They simply look after it. To do otherwise would be an outrage, he says.

TASTE, POLITICS, AND *TERROIR*

David Miller, with his partner, Sylke Rees, produces biodynamic wine from their eight-hectare vineyard. David is the founding publisher of a popular magazine devoted to environmentally sustainable living. On their website they state their commitment to making their farm healthier for future generations. As a result, no commercial chemicals are used on their vineyard for fertility or disease control and only indigenous yeasts are used in their winemaking. There is also a quote from Goethe on their website. It states that "matter is nothing, what matters is the gesture that made it." David told me he was drawn to winegrowing because of the involvement with the seasons and the local community. He has found the slow process of learning how to make wine particularly satisfying. He believes that *terroir* lives in us even if we are unaware of the concept. The proof, he says, comes from seeing the types of wine many people choose to buy, and those are wines associated with place.

The idea that taste is associated with place has a long history beginning with the Greeks and Romans over two thousand years ago (Brillat-Savarin [1825] 1994, 247–256). The notion of *terroir* has become associated with France, in particular Burgundy, because of the disciplined attention to detail of the Benedictine and Cistercian monks that attended the vines there for nearly a thousand years. The emphasis on quality has been attributed to geographer Paul Vidal de la Blache. In 1903, he published *Tableau de la geographie de France.* One of his main concerns in this work was the relationship between humans and their environment. He believed that the rapport between the soil and the people was imprinted with an ancient character (Trubek 2008, 23). The assumption on which Vidal de la Blache's analysis of *terroir* is made is that the environment determines the way of life. As Trubek points out, this is an idea that is not unproblematic in anthropology (23). From there "tastemakers" intervened and guided the relationship of the French people in particular to taste and place (19–20). If the notion of *terroir* was ever organic, it was the "tastemakers" who propelled the idea into the political realm.

In France, the notion that products are entwined with place was formalized through the concept of "geographical indications," the best known of which is French wine's *appellation d'origine contrôlée* (controlled appellation). The protection of products that demonstrate a distinctive character because of their origin poses problems for international trade and is indicative of the problems of translating the term *terroir* to "new world" policy and outlook (see Daynes, this volume).

For European countries, the label of origin "belongs" to the region and is seen as a type of collective property. What is produced cannot be separated from the environment and the history that produced it (Barham 2003, 129). When the *vignerons* of the region of Champagne wanted to reclaim the name—at one time widely used elsewhere for sparkling wine—they turned to the grapes and the soil and, by valorizing them, successfully laid claim to the name and legitimized the idea that Champagne as a region was fundamental to the identity of champagne as a beverage (Trubek 2008, 26). Other examples of the politicization of *terroir* are less benign. Trubek draws attention to a large body of literature that emerged in France between 1910 and 1930 and focused on a regional gastronomy based on *terroir* (2008) (see Sternsdorff, this volume.) This emerged, not as a natural evolution, but, in part, as a strategy by companies such as Michelin Tires that had a financial interest in promoting car journeys into the countryside (Trubek 2008, 37).

In another study, Robert Ulin demonstrates how the concept of *terroir* has been used to maintain class and power divisions. He does this by highlighting how, in Bordeaux, "differences in soil and climate [have been] invoked rhetorically to conceal the historical construction of class privilege" (1996, 8). For Ulin, when wine is presented as a product of *terroir* rather than one of industry, the claims of those associated with its production are presented as natural too (Demossier 2010, 210).

Demossier, too, shines light on the constructed nature of the idea of *terroir* (2010, 50) and suggests that "one of the French wine industry's greatest achievements has been to persuade the public and politicians that wine was a national drink sanctified by the work of generations of wine growers toiling on the sacred *terroir*" (49). And Barham points to a resurgence in the popularity of the term *terroir* from 1980 when President Giscard d'Estaing declared that year the "Year of Patrimoine" (2003). As a result of this declaration, landscapes and foods were swept up in a frenzy of revived interest in history (Barham 2003, 131), resulting in, in some cases, a "Disneyfication," or in its worst manifestation, an inward-looking xenophobia that failed to recognize the contested nature of the "authentic" and the "true" (131).

While the concept of *terroir* cannot be removed from its politics, the idea, I suggest, still has integrity. Contemplation is necessarily a part of identifying with the land, and with contemplation comes responsibility. The "rich *terroir*" (Geelong Wine 2010) of my fieldsite, Geelong, was the home of the Wathaurong people for at least twenty thousand years before the British hoisted the Union Jack there on a short visit in 1802. If you want to look carefully to the ground, there are shell middens, flint stone remnants, the occasional ochre, and grain-grinding stones around the place to act as reminders of Geelong's pre-European past. In 1835, the Europeans made their first permanent settlement in the district. Within thirty years, the local indigenous people had been almost wiped out by disease, and the few who remained, removed from their lands (Boyce 2012).

I was born into my fieldsite, the traditional land of the Wathaurong, more than fifty years ago. My father was among the first of the city-based professionals to purchase a farm there. It was the beginning of a movement that transformed a quiet landscape of small and mostly run-down mixed farms to one of tidy hobby farms, vineyards, and dressage arenas enveloped on still days by the sounds of ride-on lawn mowers. Rural coffee shops serving light lunch to local mothers during the week and Lycra-wearing cyclists and four-wheel-drive tourists on the weekend have now replaced the farm gate stalls where you could purchase apples and potatoes by placing your money in an "honesty tin." The slightly mystified old farmers who remain are directed by the council to put their green waste into bins so that it can be trucked off and turned into mulch, and helicopters spray their wetlands to control the mosquitoes so they won't pester their increasingly entitled neighbors.

I come to the topic of *terroir* with some interest. I sell wine grapes from my own small vineyard. I have a winemaking qualification, and I continue to work with a number of winegrowers who have arrived in the Geelong region to establish vineyards. The opportunity to work for these newly arrived professionals has been a way to supplement my own farm income and the income of many traditional farmers who remain. In the past, my main income came from growing "new" potatoes. For many years, local potato growers were paid a premium price to supply immature potatoes to the local market, and in the springtime people rushed to their "green grocer" to buy them. A number of things put an end to what was a sometimes lucrative industry. Not least, the supermarkets, having rapidly gained a large percentage of fresh produce sales,[4] demanded potatoes with a longer shelf life. As part of this process, the supermarket chain we supplied purchased the patent on a new variety of potato. As a result, the chain, rather than the general market, determined the price paid for those potatoes. The local industry died within a decade.

I have known and worked with many winegrowers. Those I have chosen to include in this chapter are not a random sample. I chose them because of their ability to articulate a view of wine production that resonates with my own experience. Not all small-scale winegrowers identify with the land as the informants here do, but many who do combine this deep identification with a commercial imperative. Kevin Bell is one example.

Kevin is a Supreme Court judge based in Melbourne. With his partner, Tricia Byrnes, a barrister, he makes individual Pinot Noirs from his three small adjacent vineyards totaling 3.4 hectares. On their website, Kevin and Tricia say they aim to make wine "with gentility and respect and which expresses the pure truth of its *terroir*." The winery opening in 2001 was marked by a smoking ceremony conducted by the elders of their local Aboriginal people, the Boonewrung. Their vineyard is named in honor of the Hurley family, who settled on the land in the 1870s and lived there for over a hundred years.

When I visited them to discuss their ideas of *terroir,* the extended family was busily relabeling case after case of wine with export labels to meet the requirements for a contract they had just signed to supply wine to Qantas International. This was a lucrative contract by all accounts. Kevin was more interested in talking about the ideas behind his wines and his life than the new Qantas contract. In the context of a discussion about the competitive and adversarial nature of his work as a judge, Kevin said he needed to have an organizing principle that was abstract and meaningful, not just in terms of production and activity, but also in terms of reflection and contemplation, the emotional values. Without it, he said, he would get lost. He continued, "What keeps me on song is *terroir* and the extremely firm belief that I am the custodian of this land and that it's my privilege to grow something here that expresses the inherent qualities of the land." Australia is an old and fragile continent, and by any account, it has been severely damaged by a short period of European occupation. Contemplating *terroir* has provided some with an opportunity to re-view how they relate to our environment.

THE AUSTRALIAN WINE INDUSTRY AND PERSONAL MOTIVATIONS

Ray Nadison, with his partner, Maree Collis, began establishing their four-hectare vineyard and winery in 1996 while working in medical research. In 2003, having completed their winemaking degrees, they left the city behind to devote their working lives to making biodynamic wines. Their mission is to make "real wines which reflect their unique *terroir.*" I asked Ray why he left the security of a well-paid job. He explained:

> I was working in neuroscience. I asked myself, is this all there is? Is this what I do? In neuroscience one person can never know everything. I arrived at the conclusion that I needed to make something, from the beginning to the end. With wine you can do that... It has prestige for sure but it requires an exploration that is enjoyable. And you can have pride in the finished product.

As we talked, Ray showed me the rocks that lay beneath the thin layer of soil that fed his vines. Those rocks, he explained, were the reason his vines struggled through the long summer and produced small but intensely flavored berries. But, he added, he thought *terroir* was more than just site. He said:

> My idea of *terroir* involves people and their minds. There's a real connection between soil and site and the sort of people who are drawn to it. We have four qualified winemakers here producing small amounts of wine. We want to be a culture here. All equals. And we want to develop a wine label that reflects the truth. Handwritten notes from the winemaker reproduced on each bottle so that we can provide each wine with a context.

Ray and Maree are part of the reemergence of wine production in my fieldsite of Geelong over the past forty years. This reemergence has been accompanied by a sustained period of economic growth.[5] There has always been a link between wine production and periods and people of prosperity. Cox, in his account of a nineteenth-century wine boom around Melbourne, suggests that "the rush to plant vines almost rivaled the rush to find gold. Lawyers, doctors (always plenty of doctors) accountants, journalists, artists, academics and others made it a fashion to have a vineyard..." (1967, 67; original emphasis). This wine boom was all but extinguished by the end of the nineteenth century. It took the best part of eighty years for the industry to regain momentum.

During the last fifty years in which the local landscape has changed so dramatically, the Australian wine industry has also gone through a major transformation. Large wine companies have swallowed each other up to the point that now only twenty companies produce a remarkable eighty percent of Australia's wine. Paradoxically, however, during the same period, the number of wine producers rose from less than 300 to nearly 2,500. A large majority of these twenty-five hundred wineries crush less than a modest 100 tons of grapes (Winebiz 2011). The wine industry has evolved into two discrete industries,[6] one producing commercial wine and the other fine wine (Croser 2010). Most of the new small wineries are within easy reach of Australia's cities and nearly all aim to produce premium wine. The people who own these wineries have usually had successful city-based careers. Many of them are, to cite Bourdieu, "beyond necessity" (Bourdieu 2007, 372).

The movement of city-based professionals into wine production has been so dramatic that it has resulted in a major oversupply of both wine grapes and wine in Australia, and by all accounts the industry is in crisis. Recently, a Western Australian business newspaper labeled the wine industry as "a hot contender for the title of Australia's worst industry." Citing a Citigroup report, it pointed to the fact that seventy percent of winegrowers rely on other income to support their loss-making vineyards. The report stated that, in a rational environment, grape growers en masse would be leaving the industry (Treadgold 2011). Some critics have gone further, with the national media suggesting that doctors, lawyers, and wealthy retirees who compete with seasoned generational growers for reasons of tax or fashion should never have entered the wine industry (White 2010).

A number of studies focus on the motivations of winegrowers and consumers. Accounts from the social sciences generally point to the symbolic value of wine and its wider role in society (Unwin 1996, 356). Wine is a symbolically charged product (Ulin 1996, 26), and as such has both social and ideological importance (Unwin 1996, 8). Unwin suggests that social structure has been manipulated throughout history by the use of symbols such as wine and the vine, and that to understand this process it is important to understand the different meanings people attributed to these symbols at different periods in the past (1996, 8). This is because "each generation has used wine and the vine as expressions of its own culture, building up layers of changing meaning" (Unwin 1996, 357). In the same vein, Demossier highlights the religious use of wine and suggests, "by consuming wine we are consuming space, time and symbols" (Demossier 2001, 3), and Guille-Escuret argues that "wine is a food for hierarchy and consequently it contributes to the hierarchization of society" (Guille-Escuret in Demossier 2001, 3).

While Demossier and others have drawn attention to the symbolic nature of wine and winegrowing, discussions about why city-based professionals are so drawn to the industry in Australia have been limited. In one local newspaper article, a number of local small-scale winegrowers addressed the issue of why there is an "emotional urge" to "take on a vineyard." Dr. Peter Parker, a Melbourne psychologist, said he was looking for an experience opposite to being intensely involved with his patients all day. He also noted the connection he had with his family when working in the vineyard. Ian McKenzie, a pharmacist, talked of the need for a creative outlet. Jenny Houghton, a commercial pilot, cherished the relaxation brought about by the mindless routine. And Wayne Scott, a surgeon, highlighted the contrast between his day job and the "therapy" of working in a vineyard (Port 2004, 10–12).

A discussion of America's Napa Valley winegrowers suggested that winegrowers are drawn into their new lifestyle by a number of powerful forces (Barron 1995). For some, the powerful pull comes "from an ageless set of symbols going back to the primal lure of the land" (23). For others, it is an ambition to establish a dynasty (25). Some have an aversion to fast food and shopping malls (25), while for others, making wine, or having someone make wine for them, is like producing art (33).

Rather than draw into question any of the previous analysis, I would instead like to add another layer to the discussion by moving the notion of *terroir* beyond the physical interpretation. I suggest that a philosophical and spiritual understanding of *terroir* can provide us with an understanding of what lies at the heart of why those who can sometimes feel compelled to engage in small-scale wine production.

THE PHILOSOPHICAL UNDERPINNINGS OF *TERROIR*

In 2010, I worked during vintage in a small village near Chablis in France's Burgundy region. I stayed with the owners of the winery and I took them, as a gift, two bottles of Australian wine to which I had a connection. I placed them on the kitchen bench when I went in for my first meal. At the end of vintage, the two bottles remained on the bench, unopened. Coincidentally, when winemaker Michael Glover was explaining to me how the French conceive of *terroir* he said:

> When you travel to Burgundy and you take a couple of bottles of your own wine, only the polite ones will be interested because, in Burgundy, they're not making a Pinot Noir or a Chardonnay. They're making a Clos de Vougeot or a Corton-Charlemagne. They're making a vineyard. Your wine means nothing.

American geologist James E. Wilson suggests that, apart from the measurable dimensions of the ecosystem, we need to add to our definition of *terroir* "the spiritual aspect that recognizes the joys, the heartbreaks, the pride, the sweat and the frustrations of history" (1998, 55). This extra and essential dimension of *terroir* is mostly disregarded in English wine literature (55). With that extra dimension, the culture and the history of the winegrower become enmeshed in the term. Kramer's essay on *terroir* provides the first steps in understanding what lies in the problem of translating *terroir*. *Terroir,* he suggests, is a foreign idea at odds with both science and commerce. It prospects for difference rather than seeks replication and it calls for a susceptibility to the natural world that is almost unfathomable today (2008, 228).

Kramer claims that ambiguity lies at the heart of *terroir*. *Terroir* can be presented but it cannot be proven, and doubters are blocked by their credulity in science and its confining definition of reality (2008, 228). Where the modern winemaker inserts himself between *terroir* and the wine, the traditional winemakers impart only the smallest of signatures on their wines. For the best, "the self-effacement of these producers in their wines is very nearly Zen-like: their 'signature' is an absence of signature" (232). In Nossiter's *Mondovino* (2004), winegrower Aimé Guibert argues against letting American wine giant Mondavi develop a vineyard and winery in Aniane, France, by suggesting simply that a great wine springs from humility, implying that no American company could ever embrace such a notion. This idea is built on by Scruton, who suggests that wines of *terroir* are "the very distillation of the virtue that the Greeks called *aidos,* the candid recognition that the other is more important than yourself" (2009, 35). It is here that the spiritual dimension of *terroir* emerges.

Scruton suggests that wine has been allotted a sacred function because its intoxicating nature allows it to symbolize an inward transformation where a god or a demon enters the soul (2007, 7). Wine, for Scruton, also symbolizes the act of settling, where people not only belong to each other but to a place (18). As part of his argument, Scruton (2007; 2009) identifies two strands of religious consciousness. The first, emphasized today, is belief. The second, now often overlooked, is membership or cult, where customs, ceremonies, and practices renew the sacred. The pagan religions of Greece and Rome were strong on membership but weak on belief. It was through the cult rather than the creed that one proved oneself. Citing Wagner and Levi-Strauss, Scruton argues it is through the cult that people learn to pool their resources. Land is settled, the earth is turned, temples are built, days are set aside for festivity, and then, the gods come quietly to inhabit the place, only later to be clothed in the transcendental garments of theology (Scruton 2009, 136–137).

Wine, Scruton suggests, is symbolic of that original cult where the land was settled and the city built, and what we taste in wine is not just the fruit and its ferment but the flavor of the landscape in which the gods have found a home (2009, 137). As a result, Scruton is suspicious of Australian wines, sourced from a landscape once consecrated by people who lived there as hunter-gatherers but whose culture has since been destroyed. He talks of the violence of the million-strong armies of bottles that clank their way to the city, on the first leg of their journey to nowhere, from the nowhere they have been made, "often with labels boasting their desecrated origins" (2009, 82), and with only a small possibility of redemption (82–83).

The notion of redemption is addressed by Germaine Greer in a 2003 essay on Australia's nationhood. Greer has argued that nationhood can only be achieved when we find a new way to think about the land. Rather than knocking down mountains, grinding up trees, diverting watercourses, and creating endless suburbia and the accompanying spiritual desolation (2003, 2–3),

Greer calls on us to recognize that the continent is an Aboriginal one and for those who reside here to learn, as the indigenous people have always had to learn, an Aboriginality (15). She suggests that all of us can discover "a new kind of consciousness in which the self is subordinate to *awelye*, the interrelationship of everything, skin, earth, language" (22–23). She says that, while it might be too late to reverse the devastation caused by 200 years of white settlement, any attempt should start with the recognition of the land as a sacred trust (72).

Similarly, Jefford suggests the possibility of producing wines of *terroir* in Australia requires first an acknowledgment of "the clash of cultures that followed the arrival of the vine-carrying Europeans...[with their] different philosophies of land use and possession" (2010, 101). He suggests that "the respectful attention of those who tend vines by nourishing rather than exhausting their land, and who take its fruit and make of it a unique sensual object unduplicatable in any other place, might make the start of a long restitution" (101).

The ideas represented by the concepts of *awelye* and *terroir* are not new to at least some winegrowers in Australia. Tasmania's first winegrower acknowledged, in his memoir, those people removed from the site of his vineyard by suggesting that "abstract concepts evolved by our culture, such as 'development,' 'progress,' and more pertinently 'property' were unthinkable. The concept of land ownership would be obscure: if grasped it would have seemed contrary to the natural order. Land could not belong to people, it was people who belonged to the land" (Alcorso 1994, 145).

MODERNITY AND RENEWED MOTIVATIONS

When I interviewed John Eason, he told me he felt a terrible foreboding about the future:

> I'm worried about the fact that the young are jaded by politics. I'm worried about a new fascism. I'm worried that with climate change or an economic breakdown, liberal democratic governments will crumble, and the young will be attracted by a new strong man offering solutions. I don't feel so much disillusioned as helpless. I've headed for the hills to live my life in a way that does no harm.

The concept of *terroir* often resonates with winegrowers as they emerge from the cities to engage in small-scale wine production. Rural sociologist Elizabeth

Barham links the traditional understanding of *terroir* to Polanyi's (1960) concept of economic embeddedness. Polanyi demonstrates that traditional "embedded" markets operate within environmental and economic constraints or run the risk of destroying themselves. Social motivations, Polanyi argues, are more fundamental than rational self-interest. This places the idea of embedded markets in opposition to neoliberal economics where neither time nor space interferes with the free flow of goods and capital (Barham 2003, 129). Polanyi examines ethnographies of a number of preindustrial societies to demonstrate the social embeddedness of economies and to question the neoclassical economic assumption that exchange is entirely driven by the optimizing, economizing behavior of preconstituted rational individuals. At the heart of Polanyi's argument is that land, labor, and money are fictitious commodities and could not be subject to market forces like true commodities because they require the state to manage their supply and demand, increasing rather than reducing the need for regulation.

Disembeddedness is also a central theme in the work of Anthony Giddens. Giddens has argued that modernity is characterized by a personal meaninglessness (1991, 9). He highlights the separation of time and space that are characteristic of modernity. "In pre-modern times," Giddens argues, "time and place were connected *through* the situatedness of place" (16; original emphasis). With the advent of the mechanical clock and its correlate symbol, the global map, social relations were transformed. Time and space were then reintegrated in a way that coordinated social activities to occur without reference to place. As a result, social institutions became disembedded and people lost skills.

For Giddens, modernity is a posttraditional order. The Enlightenment's mission was to prepare the way for securely founded knowledge of the social and natural world and to overcome the dogmas of tradition; however, the reflexivity of modernity, in which aspects of modern life are constantly revised in the light of new knowledge, is disturbing for ordinary individuals (1990, 20–21). More and more, the world seems out of control: "Everyone living in conditions of modernity is affected by a multitude of abstract systems, and can at best process only superficial knowledge of their technicalities" (22). With modernity, the connection to the earth, to processes, to knowledge, and even to the gods is lost (27). While traditional societies had rites of passage to facilitate psychic reorganization, with modernity a new sense of self has to be constructed. Part of the process of rebuilding the self involves reaching back to one's early experiences and selecting the new building blocks (33).

The stories of the winegrowers whose ideas have charted the direction of this chapter demonstrate the need by some to reembed themselves into the economy. Michael Glover talks of finding truth in *terroir*. David Miller argues that *terroir* is an attractive idea because it speaks to our primitive nature. For Kevin Bell, there is a need to connect with the land. Ray Nadison wants only the winemakers at his cellar door when people come to buy his wine. And John Eason "headed for the hills" when he became disillusioned with the British health care system. When people "live" their *terroir,* they reembed themselves into the economy. Accounts that point only to the politics of *terroir,* or its socially constructed nature, fail to explain why people who already have abundant cultural and economic capital feel moved to undertake long hours of seemingly monotonous work, often in extreme environmental conditions, to produce wine.

THE THINGS THAT COUNT

David Miller suggested to me that he thought personal fulfillment didn't necessarily come from success but from doing what humans evolved doing. He said:

> Winegrowing involves aspects of craft which is not necessarily dependent on the achievement but on the process. If there's anything wrong with modern life from my perspective, it's that people want a result...they think that by acquiring things they'll be happy...But happiness comes from giving and receiving service. If you find that sort of happiness, it liberates you...The essence of meaning, the demonstration of our primitive DNA, is often expressed in people when they go out in to the bush camping, lighting a fire, looking at the night sky, singing, catching a fish.[7]

I would like to use the last section of this chapter to distinguish between a *terroir* as it is spoken about in the Australian context and a *terroir* as it is lived by an increasing number of Australian winegrowers. Borrowing, with respect, a term coined by Arne Naess in 1973 to refer to the alternative mentality of environmentalism known as deep ecology (Naess 1992, 27), I would like to label the second form of *terroir* a "deep *terroir.*" Most environmentalists have a set of values that generate ideas about the right and wrong actions to take toward natural things. They act to protect nature out of a moral duty. This has been described as "shallow environmentalism." It "advocates continuous economic growth and environmental protection by means of technological innovation (such as catalytic converters), 'scientific' resource management (such as sustained yield forestry) and mild changes in lifestyle (such as recycling)" (Drengson and Inoue 1995, xix). Arne Naess, and other deep ecologists, regard morality as a treacherous basis for ecology because it requires people to act unselfishly, something they might not always do. Instead, Naess, drawing on Kant, suggested that people should act, not because they "ought" to, but because they feel "inclined" to. Feeling inclined to benevolent action comes through identifying with nature (Milton 2002, 74).

Deep *terroir* doesn't argue against the scientific and the economic as much as it looks past them. It is this that makes *terroir,* as it is lived, untranslatable. Bateson has suggested that sacredness, the things that matter most to people, depends on them remaining hidden from the rational, calculating, purpose-oriented left hemisphere of the brain (Bateson and Bateson 1987, 80–81). The sacred is processed through that part of the brain that processes emotional responses.

Deep *terroir* is untranslatable by necessity. Despite this, the idea might not be as foreign as it first sounds. Disembeddedness is an idea that appears to resonate with many winegrowers. And many winegrowers who live their *terroir* identify with the notion that people belong to the land, and not the other way around. A *terroir* "lived" in Australia shines a new light on a landscape damaged by 200 years of European occupation. With deep *terroir,* we necessarily acknowledge that the assumption that the original hunter-gatherers of Australia failed to manage the land in a rational way and therefore forfeited the right to its ownership was mistaken (Greer 2003, 3). And with this acknowledgment the notion of a deep *terroir* can move beyond the explanatory to provide a powerful model for some.

One of the first of the new winegrowers who moved from the city to engage in small-scale wine production was Claudio Alcorso. In 1962, Alcorso planted grapevines on the banks of the Derwent River, just upstream from Hobart. It was Tasmania's first vineyard and it grew to become something of note. From his Australian beginnings as an Italian immigrant in the 1930s, his long internment during the Second World War as an enemy alien, his remarkable success in the textile industry, and his leadership in the embryonic stages of both the arts and environmental movements in Australia, Alcorso had something substantial on which to focus his memoir. In that memoir, he said he wanted to be able to describe a few episodes that mattered. "But," he said, "when I closed my eyes to let the recollections emerge, the images that appeared were always related to emotions: the dreadful first sight of Long Bay Gaol, the beauty of the young vines at dawn, stomping on the grapes with the laughing Caroline, walking up the steps of the Sydney Opera House, a moment of love, pieces of silk, walking on the beach at Lake Pedder. None were achievements, yet they surfaced so easily it meant that they were the things that counted in my life, and so the ones I should write about" (Alcorso 1994, 2). For Claudio Alcorso, things relating to emotion rather than achievement were the things that counted. This provides us with a clue to the motivations of the many who have ventured to the rural fringes of Australian cities to become small-scale wine producers.

For the advocates of a deep *terroir,* globalization runs the risk of depleting the material, geographical, social, and spiritual local human resources (Scruton 2009, 29–30). The central idea of a deep *terroir* is that truth lies in the reverence of place. This is not just a physical place, but a place inhabited by people and gods. Truth is found by letting that place express itself through what is produced there. Science and commerce are mistrusted because they inhibit that expression. The notion of a deep *terroir* relates, not to achievement as it is generally understood, but to difference, to process, to humility, and to emotion. It relates, for some at least, to the things that count.

NOTES

1. *Winegrower* is a term chosen by many small-scale wine producers. It implies that the production of their wine includes growing the grapes.
2. I would like to acknowledge Nigel Rapport for pointing out that this tension might be fertile ground for my research.
3. The concept of *terroir* has been used beyond agricultural produce. One academic at a French business school lamented a system of journal rankings that privileged journals published in English, thus reducing the value of what he called "*terroir* journals" (see Torrès 2006, 147).
4. Today, two supermarket chains, Coles and Woolworths, sell nearly fifty percent of Australia's fresh produce.
5. Geelong had a vibrant nineteenth-century wine industry, but a combination of difficult economic times and the arrival of the devastating phylloxera vine root parasite saw every vine in Geelong's one thousand acres of vineyards grubbed out and burned (see Dunstan 1994).
6. This polarization is sometimes billed as globalization versus patrimonialization (see Charters 2008, 107).
7. The idea that some knowledge is innate rather than learned is discussed in Milton 2002, 34–35.

CHAPTER THREE

Space and *Terroir* in the Chilean Wine Industry

NICOLAS STERNSDORFF CISTERNA

In 2006, *Wine Spectator* magazine published a column on the destiny of wine nations that recounted the opening party of the cellars of Casa Lapostolle, a premium Chilean winery. At the event, a local attendant told the author that Chile had finally arrived to the world ranks of wine production, to which he replied that "it was really only the beginning of the beginning"(Kramer 2006). A couple of years later, in 2008, the same *Wine Spectator* magazine bestowed Clos Apalta 2005, made by Casa Lapostolle, with its wine of the year award. This was the first time a Chilean wine received the award. Thomas,[1] a journalist for the magazine, told me that the idea was to announce the arrival of premium Chilean wine and to signal to the world that they are worth seeking out.

This is in contrast to the more common perception that Chile is a land of good value wines. A Chilean saying holds that things should conform to the "three Bs" rule—that is, *Bueno, Bonito, Barato*—good, pretty, and cheap. This was also the guiding philosophy for most of the Chilean wine industry until recently. The wines are known internationally primarily for their friendly price point and good quality for price ratio, but as a Chilean wine executive put it to me, "if you're trying to impress someone, you're not going to order a Chilean bottle." Chile, the thinking goes, offers the best twelve-dollar wine around, but is not the place where you look for premium wines. Viña Errazuriz, for example, is one of the pioneer wineries in Chile that pushed for quality,[2] but found that the international perception of Chilean wines hampered its efforts. Juan from its marketing department told me:

> As a winery, we have chosen to be a premium winery, but we hit a wall. The Chilean wine industry is internationally known for the three Bs. Everyone will tell you that for so many dollars, you will never get anything better than Chilean wine. From any other country, a ten dollar bottle is horrible, but the Chilean one will be good. And this is tying us down to grow value.

The Chilean wine sector is in the midst of a campaign to change this state of affairs and add further value to its wine by telling a story of quality and *terroir*. In order to coordinate these efforts, the big hitters of the Chilean wine industry formed a trade association in 2007 called "Wines of Chile," whose task is to promote and enhance Chilean wine globally. With ninety-three member wineries representing ninety percent of bottled exports, Wines of Chile's roadmap is enshrined in the 2020 strategic plan, where it outlines a vision that increases Chile's market share globally and raises the average price paid for it. By 2020, the industry hopes to raise the price per case from USD$26.80 to USD$37.10, while almost doubling export volumes from 42.5 million cases to 80.9 million (Wines of Chile 2010), and becoming the New World's most important wine-producing country.

If Chile has made most of its business thus far selling six- to ten-dollar wines, a shift in production and marketing strategies is needed to raise value. The 2020 strategic plan argues that Chile does not have an image as a wine-producing country that international consumers recognize. People are purchasing Chilean wine in spite of its lack of message or based on the perception that it delivers good value for reasonable prices. However, according to the 2007 and 2009 Vinitrac surveys run by the market research company "Wine Intelligence," there is no solidified story attached to Chilean wine. The strategic plan goes on to argue that consumer studies show that, given the large number of wine brands, consumers are more easily moved by origin, especially when deciding to purchase premium wines. That is to say, even if consumers are not familiar with all the wineries in Bordeaux, France, the image of quality projected by this region is powerful enough to influence purchase decisions. Thus, the strategic plan concludes, "our possibility for continued growth greatly depends on how successful we are in positioning and strengthening both the Country Image as well as the category of 'Wines of Chile'" (2010, 53).

In this chapter, I think through how perceptions of quality and constructions of space become intertwined as Chilean wineries strive to change their international reputation. At the heart of this story is the recent push to put *terroir* at the heart of the quality turn; Chilean winemakers have become enamored with the concept of *terroir* since approximately fifteen years ago, and they are in the process of figuring out what to do with it. This is a question not only of finding the many micro-*terroirs* available, but also of telling a story about them that enables the industry to raise its international profile and shed the image of a value country. I argue that *terroir* is best understood as capturing the tension between the physical properties of a given location and the human efforts to coax certain aspects of *terroir* out of the land and into the bottle. Nonetheless, *terroir* also exists within a capitalist economy (and most Chilean wineries are huge compared to other wine regions), and for *terroir* to be a useful category of analysis, it must incorporate how environments are turned into spaces of capitalist production, be it material production as in the growing of vines, or symbolic production as in the representations of the Chilean landscape and its potential for world-class wines.

The rest of the chapter is divided into four sections. The first looks at the question of *terroir* and outlines in more detail how I think it can be turned into a useful category of analysis. Following that, I focus on the Chilean wine industry and sketch out some of the transformations in the way grapes are grown and wine is produced in the last twenty years. Then, I turn to symbolic representations of space and show how the Chilean wine industry is trying to change not just the material practices of how wine is grown, but also the way in which it is symbolically represented. Finally, I consider the growth of small-scale winegrowers in Chile and the vision they are advancing. In the conclusion, I turn back to the question of *terroir* as a category of analysis.

ON *TERROIR*

Kolleen Guy places *terroir* historically and looks at the story of champagne, which was one of the precursors to the protected designation of origin system that later arose in France (2007). Winemakers in the Champagne region proved adept at carbonating wine to distinguish themselves, and their wines became symbols of luxury across Europe. However, as a method of production, other winemakers quickly incorporated this technique and starting selling so-called champagne wines. The crux of the problem was whether champagne wines were unique because of their production method or because of their provenance. In a struggle to protect Champagne farmers who were revolting, the state agreed to a definition for champagne that did not rely on the method of production, but on the source of the grapes. In other words, one can make sparkling wine anywhere in the world, but to make champagne, one needs to use Champagne grapes. The uniqueness of the product comes from (or the state decided it came from) the unique attributes of grapes from the region. A similar logic works now for a number of products with protected designations of origin: one can make Parmigiano Reggiano-like cheese anywhere, but to be the real thing, it must be made with milk from cows that grazed in geographically designated areas (de Roest and Menghi 2000). Much the same, Comté cheese, or wine carrying the Bordeaux appellation, have strict rules as to where their source materials can come from. The French system of *terroir* was first turned into law in 1919, known now as Appellation d'Origine Contrôlée (AOC), and in 1935, an institute that regulates the awarding of protected designations of origin was established. Many countries in Europe and elsewhere have used the AOC system as a reference point in developing their own protected designations of origin.

Scholars see much promise in bringing geographical protections to food production. Elizabeth Barham brings a Polanyian-inspired argument to geographic protections and argues that they counteract the anonymizing effects the market has on food commodities (2003).[3] By keeping the connection between place and product alive, consumers can engage with the producer and not purchase foods as a commodity on its own terms. Amy Trubek's book *The Taste of Place* (2008) is an ardent proponent of the promises of *terroir*. She argues that the United States is a place where food is purchased as if it were any other commodity, as if it did not have a provenance. Instead, she looks to France as a place where the concept of *terroir* links place with consumption in a virtuous cycle, and offers examples of how *terroir* has begun to make inroads into American cheese and maple syrup production. Other scholars who have engaged with *terroir* have sounded notes of caution at the extent to which we can read political potential into it. In her study of cheese makers in the United States, Paxson cautions us against fetishizing *terroir* for its own sake (2010), while Demossier reminds us that we need to attend to *terroir* historically and not treat it as a given (2011). Guthman in particular has argued against reading political potential into protected designations of origin (2007). She sees them primarily as market mechanisms that work to differentiate products, but the real work needs to happen in the political sphere.

My intervention in this debate is to shift gears in the way *terroir* is marshaled for analysis. I do not use *terroir* as that which needs explaining, but rather as the lens through which to explain. This analytical orientation forces us to think about *terroir* as a worldview, a sensitivity with which one looks at the world of wine (and potentially other foods). This is by no means something restricted to academic analysis; in fact, I drew my inspiration by talking with winemakers whose worldview was tinted by *terroir*. *Terroir* is a way of going about producing and marketing wine.

In order to use *terroir* as an analytical category, space—how it is used, constructed, and represented—is a central feature. Amy Trubek finishes her book with a story about an Haitian immigrant who works in a New York wine warehouse (2008). He recalls a mango tree back home that received more sunlight on one side than the other, and thus the mangoes tasted different. With this realization, he finally gets what *terroir* is all about, and gives Trubek hope that *terroir* can be mobilized to bring more attention to the foods we eat beyond wine. *Terroir,* she says, can be found anywhere.

To a certain extent, this point is true; virtually every location will have characteristics that make it unique. On the other hand, just because a location has unique features does not mean that it merits being brought into a *terroir*-based system of production. There is no one "taste of place" or *terroir* that resides in a location. Rather, *terroir* is a latent possibility of the environment, and it is in the interaction with humans that a form comes to light. Depending on the agricultural management, a farmer can grow a mass product, farm to highlight uniqueness, or somewhere in between. At the same time, humans looking for expressions of *terroir* need to be cognizant of what makes a location unique. In talking with agricultural managers of Chilean wineries, they told me that it takes time and experimentation to learn how to work with the micro-*terroir*s in their fields. Just because they are shooting for a certain yield and flavor profile does not guarantee they will get there. A certain form of *terroir* emerges from the interplay between agricultural techniques and the environments where they are applied, keeping in mind that production must occur in sufficient yields to be profitable. David Harvey reminds us that capitalist economies generate spaces suited to the accumulation of capital (2006). In thinking about *terroir,* we must think about the kinds of economic imperatives that govern the way the land is rebuilt for agricultural production. Producing unique wines is not just a matter of letting the land speak, but also producing in yields and cost-performance ratios that allow the winery to subsist economically as well.[4]

Terroir comes to life not just in the interaction between farmer and environment, but also in the stories told about it. In his discussion of space, Henri Lefebvre tells us that societies are generative of spatial practices, but that space itself also has generative capacities (1991). For the purposes of *terroir,* a given location is both an enabler and a constrainer. Winegrowing regions are not blank canvases upon which winemakers create out of thin air; they present physical challenges and opportunities such as water availability or temperature fluctuations. Likewise, they help give form to the stories told about them by virtue of their natural or human-made features, and by the histories of the countries and other political entities in which they are located. As Manu Goswami argues, space is both a "field of action" as well as a "basis for action" (2004, 34). Space has a material dimension but is also represented and filled with meaning by humans. As a system of production that places value on the uniqueness of location, the ways in which *terroir* is symbolically represented exist in a dynamic tension with the physical attributes and previous representations of winegrowing regions, in addition to the competing claims that may arise on how to represent a region.

To summarize, to use *terroir* as a category of analysis entails paying attention to the interplay between the latent physical potential of a location, the farming techniques deployed, the kind of economic system in which these products will circulate, and the contested stories told of this process. By looking at the conjunction of these elements, an analytically strong form of *terroir* emerges that sheds light on how products gain their perceived uniqueness in today's globalizing production systems. In what follows, I show how certain regions of Chile are being reimagined and remade to produce wine at a premium level that is reflective of *terroir*.

CHILEAN WINE PRODUCTION

Chile's geography is dominated by two mountain ranges that span the length of the country from north to south. To the east, the towering Andes separate Chile from Argentina, while a second and much smaller range (*cordillera de la costa*) runs on the western side along the coast. In between these two mountain ranges lies Chile's central valley, where most agricultural production takes place, and where traditionally wineries have been located. The northern and southern ends of the country are largely unsuitable for wine production—the north is a desert, and the south is a temperate rainforest followed by Patagonia. On the other hand, the central part of the country enjoys Mediterranean weather and is ideally suited for growing grapes. Within this range, as a general rule of thumb, vines planted in the central valley face the hottest conditions, while those closer to the ocean or on the foothills of the Andes see cooler temperatures.

Chilean wine production dates back to the mid-sixteenth century, when Spanish colonizers brought vines and established the first wineries. Chilean winemaking changed in the nineteenth century, when the uva pais grape grown since the Spanish arrived was slowly replaced by French varieties (Foster and Valdes 2004). Viña Santa Rita, for example, changed its plantings from the uva pais to the French varieties in the nineteenth century with investments that came from the prosperous mining industry, a pattern common for wineries of the time (del Pozo 1995). Traditionally, Chilean wineries consolidated their plantations in one location, and a 250-hectare winery might have had 50 hectares of Cabernet Sauvignon, 50 of Chardonnay, 50 of Merlot, and so on and so forth in the same location. Prior to the revolution that shook up the Chilean industry later on, wineries planted grape varieties without carefully considering whether those were the best locations for each variety. Likewise, there was little interest in exploring locations outside of the central valley. Chilean wine exports fluctuated in value during much of the twentieth century, and not until the 1980s did wineries begin exporting in earnest and foreign investment trickle in (Foster and Valdes 2004).

Virtually everyone I spoke to in Chile pointed to the 1990s as the moment when a new consciousness emerged in the industry. If the pre-1990s era was characterized by mass plantations that produced value wines, the changes that began at this time set in motion processes that allowed Chilean winemakers to imagine themselves as capable of world-class production. The first change in the industry was perhaps the easiest to accomplish. Until the 1980s, the Chilean industry lagged behind the rest of the world in terms of technology. The entry of large business groups brought capital and allowed for upgrades to the equipment. During this period, stainless steel vats, French and American oak barrels, labs, and up-to-date pumps became commonplace in the Chilean industry. *Wine Spectator,* in a 2003 review of Chile's wine industry, said that "the seeds of the past decade's investment—in new technology, modern vinification techniques and high quality, low-yielding vineyard sites—are now coming to fruition" (Molesworth 2003, 109).

Once the technology was in place, the next step was to upgrade the human capital. Patricia, an oenologist, wine educator, and marketer who has worked for some of the major Chilean wineries, reflected on this period after the technological changes were implemented:

There was a time when we were in love with the idea that we were the best in the world, but that is because not many of us winemakers had international exposure. We could not tell how our wines fared alongside an Italian or French one. During this decade, winemakers traveled and realized that there are excellent things out there and in which other countries were far ahead of us...As a winemaker, if I want to be worth anything in the market, I have to travel and do seasons in France, Italy, Australia, New Zealand, and us winemakers understood that before looking for work, we had to go abroad first.

Soledad worked in California, and most of the winemakers I met had worked in other wine-producing countries. Alongside this push to widen the exposure of Chilean winemakers, foreign wine companies began investing in Chile and bringing their expertise. The Mondavi family from Napa Valley and Baron Rothschild from France are among the more famous foreign investors that brought their know-how to Chile.

Finally, the third stage was finding *terroir*. Twenty years ago, according to Patricia, nobody spoke of *terroir*. These days, you cannot speak of wine production in Chile without reference to *terroir*. Patricia told me that traveling abroad made a big difference in how winemakers approach *terroir*:

> That [international] exposure makes something click in you...You start out in your country, and do all these trips abroad only to realize in the end that the only thing that can give you that jump in quality is to find what makes you unique...What makes some of these great wines unique is that they found their *terroir*. We are just beginning to see what we have here, and we then begin with the more existential question of who we are, what is *terroir*. Chile is all over *terroir* now. That is the topic. It is no longer the oak barrel, the latest pump. It is *terroir*....We wouldn't have been able to have this conversation without improving the barrels, the stainless steel vats, the skills of the winemakers. We had to take that tour so that we could arrive to *terroir*.

Fernando, who has overseen agricultural management for several Chilean wineries and now runs his own, concurred with this view, and thought that international exposure has helped winemakers come back to Chile to find what is unique about the land they work on. Furthermore, "we know now a lot more about what we already had ten years ago. These days we have hillsides planted all over the place, and every time you do that, there's a new *terroir* to learn."

Alongside the push to update the equipment and the international exposure of winemakers, the Chilean government created protected designations of origin in 1995 that demarcated what have today become some of the most emblematic production regions in Chile. The map located Chile's wine regions and *terroir*s by valley running from north to south. With the benefit of hindsight, many now recognize that the north to south distinctions were inaccurate. Pablo is in charge of the agricultural division of Viña Errazuriz and has over twenty years of experience managing vines for three major Chilean wineries. When I asked him how he experienced the introduction of *terroir* from the agricultural point of view, he said:

> *Terroir* in Chile started out messy, or at least today we can say it began that way. At the time, everyone thought we were doing awesome. They did the designations of origin by valleys—Limari, Aconcagua, Maipo, Cachapoal, Colchagua, etc. In the last few years, say fifteen or ten or so, we began to realize that the differences are not from North to South, but the more important differences happen from East to West. That is to say, how close to the mountains or the ocean you are. We are far from understanding our *terroir* like the French, but we were savvy enough to figure out that the real differences happen from East to West.

Pablo then told me how he had recently found a new *terroir*—Aconcagua costa—inside the hundreds of hectares he manages. Even though Viña Errazuriz has operated in the Aconcagua valley for over 100 years, only in the last five has its agricultural team realized that areas close to the ocean presented unique conditions and merited new attention. Pablo said the team started measuring temperatures, soil conditions, and so forth, and found significant temperature oscillations that led to unique wines. "We have changed where we plant as we better understand what we have. If you understand what you have, and what you are looking for, it is easier to reach your goals. We started out looking for volume, and it was only later that we realized we had the quality to put up a fight."

Still, Pablo insisted that not every location is capable of premium wines. Part of his job is to assess the potential of each sector and balance that vis-à-vis the needs of the winery to produce set amounts of wine in each quality category. The company has asked him to focus more on quality, and then he has to see what he can do with the resources available and if some sectors can be upgraded to premium production. "This thing is not for free, and the vine will not go up in quality just because. Usually you have to invest more in managing the vines, doing soil and foliage analysis... We have had some wines that are world-class, and when that happens, you quickly start analyzing how that happened: what kind of soil and management produced that wine so that you can replicate the performance." Enrique Tirado, a winemaker for Concha y Toro, echoed Pablo's thoughts: "Perhaps the biggest challenge we face is how to achieve optimal quality from the different sectors of the vineyard, which demands ever more detailed vineyard tracking" (Molesworth 2007, 74).

Fernando concurred with Pablo's assessment that new management techniques are a recent phenomenon. "Technology changes happened in the mid-1900s," he said, but "the big changes in the last ten years are also how we manage the vines, and that's a lot more important than the cellar. You can make excellent wine with good grapes in your bathtub." Part of the new management was to move production away from the fertile valley floors and toward lower-yielding hillsides, which in addition to the potential *terroirs* available because each hill has unique geographical characteristics, were also usually cheaper to purchase than flatland. The Montes winery, which makes some of Chile's most famous premium wines, planted premium Syrah on land so steep, the winery was not sure how it would harvest it. Alongside moving production to the hills, winemakers stressed the vines by irrigating less. This leads to lower yields, but the fruit ends up more concentrated and capable of producing higher-quality wines. Finally, wineries decentralized production and began to recognize that different grape varieties thrive in different environments. Therefore, whereas the prototypical Chilean winery would have had 250 hectares of concentrated production in one location, today it is much more likely to have 50 hectares of Cabernet Sauvignon in the Maipo valley, while Sauvignon Blanc has moved to the Casablanca valley, and wineries are experimenting with Syrah grown in cooler climates close to the ocean.

Earlier in this chapter, I proposed to use *terroir* as an analytical category that traces the tensions between environment, economics, and human physical and symbolic intervention in the production of wine. The Chilean quality turn shows that in the pursuit of highlighting the uniqueness of place, a wide range of processes had to be set in motion. On the agricultural side, Pablo's example shows some of the intricacies in producing quality and uniqueness out of the land. His team has to strike a balance between the economic needs of the winery, the yields needed to produce set amounts of wine in each quality category, and what the land is capable of. Not every location is unique enough to produce grapes that lead to premium and *terroir*-based wine. And those locations that are capable require care and management that makes them more expensive, and it is up to the agricultural team to balance the resources it has vis-à-vis the yield and quality requirements asked from these locations. *Terroir* is not a straightforward reflection of place, but rather a certain form is constructed as the aforementioned factors come together and shape how winemakers approach the vines.

On the other hand, the development of a group of Chilean winemakers with international exposure was a crucial step in the quality turn. Their exposure to what the rest of the world was doing, and how they engaged with *terroir,* was the foundation upon which they later set to find the uniqueness of Chile. Even with the best technology at their disposal, the international exposure was necessary to push Chilean winemakers to consider what they would bring to the global market.

Common usage of *terroir* highlights how the connections between taste and place are established and managed, but marshaling it as a category of analysis allows us to bring into the conversation crucial steps like the internationalization of the workforce that in the end affect how the taste of place is expressed. Likewise, it brings into consideration how economic imperatives play a role in deciding how much quality and uniqueness to coax out of the environment, and when to push for quality over quantity. In what follows, I turn to the symbolic dimensions of *terroir.*

SYMBOLIC REPRESENTATIONS

Alongside the technological and agricultural changes that have occurred in Chile, the country is also trying to reinvent its international image. Juan Somavia, the manager of Wines of Chile, said: "If the industry experienced a technological revolution in the 1980s, followed by an exports revolution in the 1990s and a *terroir* revolution in the 2000s, now is the time for a marketing revolution" (Miranda 2010). The 2020 strategic plan outlined a strategy for Chile that boiled down in essence to "The best of the New World for the entire World," and chose "Wines of Chile—the natural way" as its tag line.

The strategic plan makes a case that Chile has a story yet to be told. I asked the marketing director of Viña Errazuriz about it, and he told me that when people say Chile has no story, it really means that to be known for the three Bs (good, cheap, and pretty) is not a good story. In other words, there is a perception internationally that Chile is known for value, and the surveys of Wine of Chile show that, but the depth of this perception does not go much deeper, and it is this blank space that Wines of Chile wants to fill with a new story. This new image emphasizes the country's sustainability efforts, its premium wines, and above all, diversity and *terroir.*

Many New World countries have become famous for producing a particular grape variety: Australia is known for Shiraz, New Zealand for Sauvignon Blanc, and Argentina for Malbec. On one hand, this helps with brand visibility and to develop a unique style of winemaking associated with the region. New Zealand, for example, is known for producing citrusy sauvignon blancs, which helps the wines stand out in the crowded marketplace. On the other hand, this runs the risk of variety going out of fashion and puts pressure on producers to make wines that fit the regional style.

There was much hope for Chile in the 1990s when Chilean winemakers finally found a signature grape around which to build a country image. Carmenère was thought to be a lost French grape variety, but was discovered in Chile in the 1990s where it had been mistaken for merlot. The wine industry embraced the new variety, and wineries started growing Carmenère, which would become Chile's ambassador to the world. The problem is that promoting Carmenère as the signature grape of Chile carries the same risks other wine countries face. One winemaker put it to me this way: "When was the last time you ever heard someone say that they really want to drink a New Zealand red?" And, while Carmenère might be the new kid in town, Chile is best known for producing high-quality Cabernet Sauvignon.

Instead, many people told me the real goal of "diversity" is to become like France. When one thinks of French wine, there is not a single variety that dominates over others, but rather regions within France best suited for them. Thus, Bordeaux is synonymous with Cabernet Sauvignon, the northern Rhone for Syrah, Chablis for Chardonnay, and so on and so forth.[5] The spatial imagery of France as a wine country is not dominated by a grape variety, but organized along smaller subregions considered best suited for certain grape varieties or styles of wine. Along similar lines, the Chilean wine industry is pushing for an image that showcases Chile as a place capable of multiple varieties. Carmenère will still hold a special place as Chile's unique addition to the wine world, but the real hope is that the Maipo valley will be synonymous with Cabernet Sauvignon, Casablanca with Sauvignon Blanc and Pinot Noir, Leyda with refreshing whites, Colchagua with reds, and so on and so forth.

The efforts by Wines of Chile, however, are recent, and some wineries began working to change the image of Chilean wine prior to the current campaign. Among these efforts, the Tasting of Berlin stands out as one of the boldest attempts to redefine the capability of Chilean wine. In 1976, the famous judgment of Paris took place. It was a blind tasting that paired some of France's most famous wines against Californian wines. The prevailing wisdom at the time was that Old World countries, such as France or Italy, were capable of world-class production, and wines from the New World lacked sophistication. However, the tasting, much to the surprise of some experts, came out in favor of California. American producers showed they could make wines *de terroir* comparable to the best of the Old World.

Viña Errazuriz decided to organize a similar tasting that would pair its premium wines against some of the most respected wines from the Old World. In contrast to the Tasting of Paris, which featured several Californian wineries, the tasting organized by Viña Errazuriz featured its wines exclusively. The event was held in Berlin in January 2004; sixteen wines were tasted blind, including six Chilean, six French, and four Italian. The tasting panel consisted of thirty-six journalists, wine buyers, and writers. The results were a resounding success for Viña Errazuriz: it won both first and second place (Viñedo Chadwick 2000 and Sena 2001, respectively), edging out famous wines such as Château Lafite, Château Margaux, and Château Latour. Jancis Robinson, from the *Financial Times* in the United Kingdom, was one of the tasters, and said: "The single event that conferred international respectability on California was a wine tasting in 1976...One enterprising Chilean wine producer, Eduardo Chadwick of Viña Errazuriz, has managed to organise a similar evolutionary milestone for the Chilean wine industry—or at least of his own wines" (2004). She goes on to praise the event because the Chilean wine industry "really, really needs to export, to polish its image, and to shrink the proportion of wine shipped in bulk." Other journalists also praised the Chilean wines and declared them ready to enter the legions of the best in the world.

What Viña Errazuriz did next, however, was to turn this event into a marketing strategy that could be deployed around the world. The tasting of Berlin has now been done fourteen times in places like Tokyo, Beijing, London, New York, and Sao Paulo. The setup is always a blind tasting of the top wines of Viña Errazuriz vis-à-vis big hitters of the wine world. Depending on the location, the organizers change the lineup of the other wines to include premium wines known locally, such as in New York when two Californian wines were included. Tasters often include prominent wine buyers, journalists, and sommeliers. The results change with each tasting, but for the most part at least one of Viña Errazuriz's wines has taken one of the top three spots.

When I discussed this event with people at Viña Errazuriz, their perception was that replicating this event was a useful way to convince important wine buyers that Chilean wine was worth looking at again. Their experience was that they faced a wall of preconceived ideas about wine that this event helps shatter. The fact that the tasting is blind helps them make their case that their premium line of wines is as good as any, though some of the participants have noted that they could identify the Chilean wines, and that given the high proportion of Errazuriz wines, it was likely they would capture some accolades.

A DIFFERENT VISION

If Wines of Chile is pushing for a vision that expands the reach of Chilean wine, an alternative vision is brewing in the country that aims to take production in a different direction. As I mentioned earlier, Wines of Chile is in the midst of creating a marketing revolution, but for some new and emergent small winemakers, what is needed is a return to making wine on "a human scale." If Wines of Chile brings together the big wineries, Movimiento de Viniteros Independiente (Movement of Independent Vintners) (MOVI) is its counterpart. This association, founded in 2009, brings together some of the smaller-scale projects emerging in Chile that are shooting for a different vision of small and quality-oriented wineries that reflect a particular vision of *terroir*.

One of the challenges of being a small producer in Chile is that the big wineries are enormous. When I spoke to Pablo from Viña Errazuriz, he had just returned from a trip to Bordeaux and he told me that when his counterparts found out that he managed several hundred hectares of vines, they looked at him in amazement. Whereas small wineries with just a few hectares or less are more common in Europe, Chilean wineries are often many times their size. One of the challenges this presents is that the big wineries can marshal their economic power to buy up suitable land before smaller winemakers can get there, and this results in less diversity and more concentrated ownership.

Fernando, one of the founding members of MOVI, produces Syrah in the Colchagua valley, and the biggest difference for him is that wine is more than just business—it is agriculture and culture. He agreed that many of the elements in the 2020 strategic plan are good for the industry as a whole. It is good to have a concerted effort to promote a country's image, and it is good to have economic goals, but to him that is all they are—economic goals, not wine. The real way of improving Chile's offerings, he told me, is to increase diversity and quality and to treat wine as more than just a commodity. His vision is to acknowledge that wine is ultimately a form of agriculture with a label on it, and that it can be done on a human scale that allows for personality and difference. As an example, he told me that he does not like blind tastings because they remove the story from the wine. Instead, he said that many times he enjoys the wine better after understanding why it tastes the way it does, even if there are some flaws. For Fernando, and his fellow winemakers at MOVI, the next stage for Chilean wine is not the marketing revolution of Wines of Chile, but a shift to featuring the people and families behind wine with the belief that this will also raise the wine's value. As Fernando put it: "Extra value comes from people. You can have a normal wine, with a real story—not some marketing story—and that raises the value of wine...You can achieve that with real wine; not with coca-cola, cornflakes, tomato sauce or industrial wine."

One of the interesting things about MOVI is that its main emphasis is not on the size of the vineyard, but on the worldview of the winemaker behind it. To be sure, the wineries associated with MOVI are extremely small compared to the average Chilean winery, but they are articulating a different view of how to proceed. Their emphasis is to move away from a corporatized and business-first approach to wine and to embrace the stories of the people and places behind the wine that make it taste the way it does. In contrast to a blind tasting, which shows that without prejudices Chilean premium wine is as good as any, these wines are betting that it is exactly their stories that will make them stand out. The story is what moves a wine from being a mass commodity to a product with *terroir* reflective of place and the human intervention on it. I do not wish to suggest that MOVI and Wines of Chile are completely at odds with each other. In fact, MOVI wineries can take advantage of Wines of Chile's campaign to reposition Chilean wine internationally, and some of the winemakers of MOVI either used to or still work for the larger wineries. MOVI highlights the possibility that more diversity will emerge in the Chilean wine industry; this diversity will not be just about geographical *terroirs* and quality standards, but also the production ethos that lies behind a wine. *Terroir* becomes entangled with a critique of corporatized wine production, and MOVI's vision of what makes a wine unique comes both from place and from the alternative vision under which it was produced.

CONCLUDING THOUGHTS

At the beginning, I outlined a way of marshaling *terroir* as an analytic concept. *Terroir* is not just what needs to be explained, but can also serve as an entry point into the dynamics winemakers face. To think of *terroir,* we must think of the intersection of the physical environment, the agricultural techniques, the economics behind production, and the symbolic representations. The Chilean case shows that the quality turn in Chile's wine industry went hand in hand with an embrace of *terroir,* but that it is not an automatic switch. *Terroir* as an analytical category allows us to explore a wide range of dynamics that come together to produce a wine reflective of place. However, place is not just the geographical location where wine was produced. Place is a way of thinking about the contingent ways in which spaces are imagined and acted upon and how they constrain and condition the choices for their users. It is in the intersection of these forces (which need not be all equal) that a form of *terroir* emerges that can then stand as the central feature of a wine. Space is not a given; it does not simply exist, and food cannot be a straightforward reflection of it. Space is a contested process full of choices, pitfalls, and contingencies, and the taste of place is part of the dialogue as these forces come together.

The Chilean wine case shows that for *terroir* to emerge as a central feature of Chilean winemakers' premium production, changes in physical as well as symbolic production methods were necessary. Chilean winemakers revisited their vines from which they produced value wines to see if with different management some of those plots could produce higher-quality grapes. At the same time, the way vines are planted has changed, away from the valleys and into hillsides, and their management has become a lot more focused. Together with these efforts, the wineries have banded together to fight the perception of Chile as a source of value wines, and to grow value for the industry. Viña Errazuriz has been particularly aggressive in its use of blind tastings to make this point. In order to make *terroir* the central attribute of Chilean wine, agricultural practices, human resources, and marketing strategies have realigned. At the same time, the process is not closed, and there are contested versions of what constitutes *terroir* in Chile, and how it might increase the wine's value. Whether the efforts pay off remains to be seen, but there is an undeniable sense of optimism that Chile can reinvent itself as a world-class wine producer.

NOTES

1. All names have been changed to pseudonyms.
2. *Quality* in this context refers to wines that fall within the *reserva* and *premium* ranges of Chilean wine production. Chilean wines are divided into four categories: *varietal, reserva, gran reserva,* and *premium,* with quality going up as they move from one category to the next.
3. Barham bases her analysis on Karl Polanyi's concept of the "double movement," which argues that as economic activity seeks to detach from the other sphere of life, society resists and tries to reembed social relations that respond to imperatives that are not purely economic. For more, see Polanyi 2001.
4. Of course products can circulate in alternative economies, but I am concerned here with products such as wine that mobilize the uniqueness of production as a form of differentiation in a global economy.
5. Even though regions of France are associated with particular grapes, the final wines are often commercialized based on their region of provenance rather than the variety behind them.

CHAPTER FOUR

Terroir and Locality: An Anthropological Perspective

ROBERT C. ULIN

INTRODUCTION

Wine historians, geographers, and contemporary wine writers have tended to employ the concept of *terroir* so as to unwittingly conceal and marginalize the historicity of social relations upon which the production and consumption of wine is based. Consequently, their wine narratives all too often contributed to naturalizing wine and its associated social relations (see Ulin 2008). Naturalizing social relations in the wine sector coincided, moreover, with the uses of nature in the development of industrial capitalism, European statecraft, and the process of nineteenth-century nationalism. While this is an argument to which I remain committed, I now believe it requires some modification to account for the nuances of "distinction" as applied to the winegrowing sector worldwide, especially mass production. I argue here that amidst the mass production of commodities of every sort that typifies late capitalism, or what Lash and Urry term *disorganized capitalism* (1987), *terroir* offers a partial but nonetheless important corrective to the ubiquity of separating commodities totally from the social conditions of their production, circulation, and consumption. I conclude, therefore, somewhat paradoxically, that although the concept of *terroir* assists our critical understanding of wine as a commodity through associating wine with a specific geographical domain and an imagined culture of production and consumption, it nevertheless contributes simultaneously to its enduring mystification.

THE MULTIVOCALITY OF *TERROIR*

The concept of *terroir* originated from the French *terre*, meaning land, earth, or soil, and initially had significance for a number of French agricultural products besides wine. However, in the early twentieth century, *terroir* came to predominate in the wine sector through associating wines with particular properties and regions, an association especially important to the *appellation contrôlée* legislation of the 1920s that, among other things, sought to combat fraud by guaranteeing the regional and proprietary authenticity of wine.[1] The concept of *terroir* has evolved today worldwide to denote the special qualities of soil and microclimates from which grapes obtain their uniqueness and quality. There is much symbolic capital, in the sense of Bourdieu, associated with *terroir* in that grapes produced from circumscribed terrains, in comparison to those that are generic, bring much renown and commercial value to their proprietors (1984). *Terroir* and quality have become nearly synonymous in the broad winegrowing literature.

James E. Wilson, in his *Terroir: The Role of Geology, Climate and Culture in the Making of French Wines* (1998), arguably adds much to any scientific consideration of *terroir* by showing empirically that within single winegrowing properties are significant differences in the deep geological formations that nurture the roots and ultimately can contribute to significant differences in the quality of grapes. Such an assertion moves the concept of *terroir* from reference to single proprieties to subdivisions within winegrowing estates.[2] Prior to Wilson's novel use of technology, the claims for quality soil in particular were largely suggestive and difficult to prove conclusively as there was no easy way to test the underground conditions that support grape plants without potentially harming the plants. Wilson solved this problem by employing seismic techniques conventionally used in oil exploration to determine the condition and composition of the earth far beneath the plants without having to disturb the soil in the least. He discovered beyond doubt that even on elite estates, rows of vines in relative proximity can have very distinctive subsoils and thus produce qualitatively distinct grapes. That is, the better the deep soil conditions, the more favorable the conditions for growing better quality grapes. Wilson takes us far, therefore, in understanding the geologic formations that in combination with microclimates contribute to qualitatively distinct grapes used to make wine. Much of this is in accord with the claim shared by my Médoc winegrowing informants that great wines are made in or attributable to the vineyards and not, as many people believe, through the vinification process.[3]

I discussed Wilson's remarkable and influential book in the aforementioned publication toward the end of challenging, or at least provoking, the substantial claims associated with climate and soil with respect to the quality of grapes. My intention was not to reject the importance of climate and soil, but rather to illustrate how an emphasis on so-called natural conditions can veil conditions that are more fundamentally social and historical. I argued, moreover, that there is a tendency in much of the academic and professional literature on wine to anthropomorphize grape plants and wine by associating certain terrains and their wines with such noteworthy historical themes as French blood, soil, nationalism, and the cultural identity of the nation-state. This was evident with respect to grafting phylloxera-resistant American stocks onto French plants during the infamous phylloxera blight of the last quarter of the nineteenth century. Pierre Viala, a professor of oenology at Montpellier, argued against grafting the phylloxera-resistant American plants of Texas biologist Thomas Munson onto French vines—Viala asserted such a course of action would threaten the "purity of French vines" (Ulin 2008, 48–49). An analogous view of tacit but unacknowledged naturalization was also evident in the universal expositions that became selective icons for French national culture through the Bordeaux classification of 1855. These naturalized historical examples are not all that distinct from social evolutionary theories of the late nineteenth century where peoples were likewise classified in association with colonialism along racist lines often suggesting relations between climate and temperament. The "mixing of blood" resulted in anxieties not entirely distinct from the blending of vines—miscegenation toward the end of agricultural purity. This may seem remote and a rather fantastic claim to associate with the importance of climate and soil, but it is not in error to consider the contiguity between thought about distinct peoples and thought about distinct vines. There is a symbolic interconnection here that is easily overlooked when social relations are veiled and commodities are made into a fetish, an object in itself of adoration and desire. I have come across very little in the years that I have researched wine until recently that begins to explore in any critical sense the relationships between wine and the diverse communities through which they are historically, culturally, and politically constituted.[4]

I pursue a strategy here that is somewhat different from the 2008 essay. I continue to believe that there is a strong tendency of which the *terroir* concept is suggestive to naturalize agricultural products and production and thus to veil the historically acute social relations upon which both the production and consumption of wine are based. With that said, there is also a complexity to the concept of *terroir* that eludes a simple effort to regard special claims to soil and climate as ideological or singularly hegemonic. To the contrary, there is much likewise in the notion of *terroir* that speaks to the special case of commodities in late capitalism and their antihegemonic symbolic potential of distinction. In this regard, my comments here will complement those of the early essay by developing a more nuanced and dialectical understanding of *terroir* as multivocal or polysemic. That is, the concept of *terroir* generates a multiplicity of meanings that incorporate a social terrain that is both challenging to the idea of mass-produced commodities or nondistinction and a concept that accentuates privilege and the marginalization and concealment that account for the historical and social production of privilege.

It may seem a bit unusual to turn to Karl Marx in discussing the symbolism or culture of wine given his emphasis on material conditions of life and modes of production that have a tendency to regard culture, in the form of super structure, as derivative of social labor (see Ulin 2001). However, few theorists other than Marx have better understood the historical nature of commodities. Marx argued that commodities have a dual nature in that they have both use value and exchange value. Although admittedly utilitarian, for Marx, use value is not simply a given or natural in that he regards needs as socially produced.[5] I will not dispute the utilitarian value of wine other than to emphasize that throughout history and across cultures wine has served a range of important purposes from ritual, to the medicinal, to the social more generally, and today the demand for and uses of wine are increasing worldwide. Strictly speaking, exchange value has to do with the quantitative dimension of commodities, how much of a certain commodity one can exchange for another, such as coats for cabinets or wine for cheese. However, in *Capital* Volume 1, Marx applies a critical version of the labor theory of value toward arguing with significant implications that commodities should be grasped and measured by the amount of social labor time they contain rather than price as an independent function of market demand. Under capitalist social relations, and here we mean a system where wage labor is dominant, workers are paid less than the full value of their labor objectified in the commodities they produce. Moreover, under certain conditions of production unique to the nature of capitalist social relations, the assembly line in factories as illustrative, workers, compared to artisans, no longer identify with their own labor embodied in the products of their labor. Once labor is abstract and fragmented, lacking a personal mark, it is very difficult to recognize ourselves in the products we fashion. Such a social condition is one of alienation and Marx argued strongly that the conditions under which workers produce in capitalism is typified by alienation.

The previous point concerning alienation pertains more to large-scale wineries than it does to smaller-scale enterprises that rely largely on family labor. However, the division between vineyard labor and the vinification process overseen by technical experts or oenologists at locations sometimes remote from the vineyards often is sufficiently specialized and fragmented so that vineyard workers are alienated from the final product. This was even true for some of the cooperative growers with whom I worked in the Médoc in that these growers often did not like the fact that their grapes were vinified independently at the cooperative. One informant thus decided to leave the cooperative, even though he had a leadership role, so that he could vinify his own grapes. He related to me that he experienced greater satisfaction and a stronger identity with the wines he produced.

Commodities produced under conditions of alienation appear to take on a life of their own, that is, they easily lend themselves to fetishization, a point that has its analog in Adam Smith's "invisible hand of the Market," where market forces operate independently from human agency and social relations. One may wonder what alienated labor has to do with wine or agricultural commodities more generally. I maintain that wine along with other notable food commodities such as chocolate and coffee are objects of fetish in our society in that we associate such food commodities with distinction, aesthetic value, and even the art of living that leaves the condition of their production and the critical analysis of their consumption in the historical and social margins.[6] With few exceptions (see Mintz 1985), scholars have tended to write about the commodity without telling much about the broad social and historical conditions under which commodities are produced and consumed. We know, for example, a great deal about the wines of the world, including their qualitative ratings by aficionados or wine writers like Robert Parker. However, we do not know nearly as much about the people who labor in the vineyards during the harvest, especially migrant workers (see Street 2005), or other workers apart from those with status, such as oenologists, who work at wineries year round. Consequently, wine appears to have a life of its own, and thus the general social and historical relations—in Marx's terms, the social relations of production—that inform its production and consumption live in the shadows of the wine trade. I have often been asked, for example, about the wines in the areas where I have conducted field research but not nearly as often about the families and workers engaged in various ways with wine production and even wine marketing.

Once the focus is on wine as a fetishized commodity and not the social and historical relations that give rise to wine, it is much easier to assert that the reputations of noteworthy wines are simply a consequence of their favorable climate and soil. This is in part what one concludes with respect to Wilson's aforementioned research on *terroir*, even though he does make a modicum of effort to discuss culture, although regrettably in stereotypical and natural terms such as in his representation of the original Alsatians as "barbarians" or his "orientalizing" of Gewürztraminer wines, not to mention his view of the countryside and its people as timeless (Wilson 1998, 90–94), what Fabian regards as the denial of coevalness. Take any renowned wine and study the geological formations that support the wine plants and we will arrive at empirical conditions that account for the distinctiveness of the product. This is not to say, though, that knowledge applied in the vineyards is unimportant, for surely the tending of the vines is essential to the quality of the grapes. However, if we accept that favorable soil and climatic conditions are paramount, we are not encouraged to take a more time-sensitive or historical perspective that is reflexive and able to identify both the assumptions that inform our discourse on wine or the conditions of differentially positioned human subjects engaged in its cultivation, production, and consumption.[7]

My own research in the southwest of France is highly suggestive of this point. When I first commenced field research on wine cooperatives in the Dordogne in the early 1980s, the growers in that region often asked why I was there to conduct research when the renowned wines of Bordeaux were only ninety kilometers away. I had to emphasize that I was not exclusively interested in the wine per se but rather the historical narratives that could be reconstructed to explain the development of the wine cooperative movement in the 1930s and the challenges small-scale winegrowing faces today inclusive of globalization. My attempts to grasp these historical dynamics from archives and the stories growers themselves told led me to examine why it is that Bordeaux wines have a much stronger reputation than those of the Dordogne and how that came to be.

What I discovered, and I have discussed this in detail elsewhere (Ulin 1996), is that it was not always the case that Dordogne wine was secondary in reputation to that produced in Bordeaux. In fact, wines produced in the southwest French interior were more highly regarded than those of Bordeaux before the English occupation of the twelfth to the fifteenth centuries. Nobles and church elites controlled many of the winegrowing estates in the Dordogne valley during this period, and their wines were highly regarded. By comparison, prior to the twelfth century, the Médoc, now renowned for the quality of its wines, was an area north of Bordeaux known for its forests and boar hunting (Roudié 1988, 14–16).

The marriage of Eleanor, heiress to the Aquitaine, to Henry Plantagenet in 1152 set the stage for the English occupation of southwest France as Henry succeeded to the English throne. This would in turn precipitate conflict with the French king, Louis VIII, resulting in the fall of La Rochelle to Louis in 1224. The fall of La Rochelle had significance to the English in that La Rochelle was the principal port through which the English shipped southwest French wines to England. At the time, La Rochelle had a more robust wine trade in that as a coastal city on the Atlantic Ocean it was a more suitable port than Bordeaux, which had access to the Atlantic Ocean by way of the Garonne River.

To summarize what ensued, the English king negotiated a favorable trade agreement with Bordeaux town councilors in exchange for their acquiescence to English rule. It did not take long before Bordeaux benefited from this agreement through augmenting the marketing of wines destined for England from nearby vineyards. Henry would later negotiate a similar agreement with the Bergerac town councilors in the Dordogne, although favoritism in terms of taxation was maintained for Bordeaux. As a consequence, forests in the Médoc were cleared and vineyards were planted.

The example of the English occupation is important because it provides us with historical and commercial factors central to the expansion of Bordeaux as a significant French winegrowing region. Again, this is not to deny that climate and soil may be favorable in the Bordeaux region. However, such factors do not detract from the fact that the ascension of Bordeaux over the southwest French interior in terms of the importance of its wines had more to do with social and historical circumstances that can be easily overlooked by focusing on what is natural. This is an important component of the life of commodities once they are regarded as "natural" or separate from the social condition from which they arise.

More recent examples and equally important are the universal expositions popular toward the middle to end of the nineteenth century. Universal expositions were important in that at a time of European nation building, they stood as experiential icons of national culture. This was, though, a national culture that was selective, in the sense of Raymond Williams (1977), in that often it was elite culture that came to represent the nation state. We can see this in the celebrated 1855 classification of Bordeaux wines, a classification that remains

today with only a modicum of change. The 1855 classification followed from a
request on the part of Napoleon III with respect to the Paris Universal Exposi-
tion of that year. A request went out to growers in the Bordeaux region to classify growths from first to fifth with first growths the most esteemed. It should
not come as a surprise that classified growths came from the elite and noble estates. Those growers without aristocratic roots or wealth accumulated through
banking, industry, or trade were left to the historical and social margins of
the classification.[8] What I find interesting in this example is the association
of elite wines with national culture, a symbolic move that resonates with the
aforementioned association of French wine with French blood in reaction to
the grafting of American vines. Again, it is the taken for granted and apparent
naturalization that seems to predominate.

It could be argued, perhaps, that wine is an exception to what is typically
regarded as alienation under capitalist production. After all, we often think
of vineyard labor and wine production as an art or craft, the very opposite of
impersonal assembly line production. This, though, is controversial in itself
and has implications for generational differences. When I worked with growers in the Médoc who were members of wine cooperatives, the older members,
generally in their late fifties or sixties, told me consistently that you "learn at
the feet of the vines." All of these growers, many of whom had only a sixth
or seventh grade education, learned how to tend the vines, and in some cases
how to make wine, from the senior generations in their families. This was,
for them, practical knowledge that could be readily applied and not something that could be learned from books. However, the younger generations in
winegrowing families more often attend schools of oenology and therefore are
well equipped with the latest scientific knowledge. While the younger growers
do apprentice in the vineyards, the significant emphasis is on the science they
bring to their practice.

Wine, though, is potentially subject to the same mystification we can attribute to any other commodity. While we may want to imagine an artisan tradition associated with every bottle of wine, this has not often been the case.
First is the controversy that emerged in the early part of the twentieth century
regarding what constitutes wine itself, a sometimes puzzling concern in that we
generally think of wine as a "natural product," a point taken up specifically
in the last section of this book. The very *appellation contrôlée* legislation that
contributed to the maturation of *terroir* in the wine sector also marginalized
peasant wines made from dried fruits inclusive of apricots, pears, and apples.
As one can imagine, the wines were inexpensive to make and well suited to
small-scale farming households. However, by defining wine as made from

naturally fertilized grapes, peasant wines could no longer be sold or represented as "wine." Peasants retained, though, a continuing involvement with *piquette,* grapes pressed several times with water with sugar added, thus suggesting that the commercial loss of wine did not undermine its enduring cultural importance.

The development of the *grands crus* is also an interesting story in its own right for what they disclose about distinction and "invented tradition." The *grands crus* were developed during the eighteenth and nineteenth centuries as a strategic response to the flooding of French markets with less expensive wines from Spain and Italy. Rather than seeking to undercut the price of these foreign imports through producing less distinct wines of their own, French growers sought to improve the quality of their wines by favoring grapes harvested from older plants. It is well known that older plants produce smaller harvests and thus are often preferred in the making of quality wines. The markets for French quality wines were sufficiently robust that the *grands crus* were a success, although *grands crus* estates would on occasion change ownership and sometimes suffer from neglect. For the purposes of the argument concerning distinction and naturalization, it is the culture and symbolism associated with the *grands crus* that are of special interest. Proprietors of *grands crus* estates sought not only to make distinctive wines, but to distinguish their lifestyles from the lot of small-scale and peasant proprietors as well. Consequently, proprietors of elite estates, some of which, like in the Médoc, had fallen into ruin at one point and were acquired by nascent bourgeoisie, sought to replicate the opulent lifestyle of the nobility by building their homes as small-scale replicas of the famous medieval *châteaux.* Not only were their wines distinctive, but also so were their lives in the total social round. This has some implications for *terroir* in that the associations of the wines with a particular locale also resonated with the symbolism of social class, and, as we have noted, the French nation-state as a materially embodied cultural or symbolic icon in the late nineteenth century.

The idea that distinctive wines marked by their connection to specific locales and thus reaping the benefits of commercial success is not unique to quality wines. The Listrac cooperative wines, where I also conducted ethnographic research in the late 1980s, enjoyed the reputation more generally associated with the Médoc, but with a market that was anything but distinctive. The Listrac cooperative contracted with the French national railway (SNCF) to sell its wines as the generic brand in dining cars and onboard concessions. Having such a contract was lucrative for the cooperative and a very good way to enhance the recognition of their wines. However, being the wine of the rail was anything but distinctive and thus could likewise challenge efforts to advance the reputation of cooperative wines as distinctive and qualitative.

Although French cuisine as a whole is generally renowned for its aesthetic appeal and quality, the reputations of French wines are far from uniform. While the Listrac cooperative may not have received much in the way of accolades from wine critics and writers by virtue of its association with the French national railway, its overall reputation in terms of its locale, *terroir,* broadly conceived far exceeds the reputations of the cooperatives I studied in the Dordogne. Even though virtually all French cooperatives produce some château label wine by vinifying grapes of their larger grower proprietors separately from the membership as a whole, cooperatives are regarded as producing acceptable—in some cases good—wines that in comparison to wines produced by elite estates are thought to be nondistinct.[9]

Terroir plays a very large role in the diminished value of cooperatives' wines in that they are often rightly accused of combining the grapes of their numerous members, as exemplified by Bégadan in the Médoc or Sigoulès in the Dordogne. The membership at both cooperatives exceeds 300. The stigma follows from the scientific claim that grapes originating from different proprieties are of uneven quality because the *terroirs* are themselves very distinct. The differences, in turn, are a reflection of notable dissimilarities in soil even though the general climate in a region may be identical. Cooperative growers are well aware of these criticisms but still believe that the collective vinification of their grapes and collective marketing of their wines gives them significant benefits over past periods when they were at the mercy of unscrupulous middle men that often paid them unfair but ostensibly market-driven prices for their grape harvests. However, as I have argued elsewhere (Ulin 1996), the cooperative growers in the Médoc have taken a very interesting and significant permutation on the meaning of *terroir* to their considerable symbolic and political advantage. While realizing the benefits of the individualization of grapes with respect to particular properties, if not specific parts of wine-growing estates, they think of their collective harvests as the authentic wines of the Médoc.

This claim fascinates not because it is a misunderstanding of the meaning and application of *terroir,* but because of what it suggests about the particularization and individualization of a commodity that is surely symbolically and culturally charged. In other words, my cooperative informants were arguing that distinction should come from the collective efforts of the cooperative that are socially self-evident rather than the particularization of land and soil that can conceal the class privilege and social relations the production and consumption of wines entails. It goes a long way toward challenging the alienation of labor and the fetish of products Marx has associated with capitalist production.

It would be wrong, however, as stated earlier, to dismiss *terroir* as univocal and thus suggestive of naturalization of the social and nothing more. At the very least, *terroir* is evocative and takes on multiple meanings of employment with respect to differentially placed growers and consumers. Apart from the particularization of land parcels and the emphasis on deep soil conditions, *terroir* emphasizes the link with identifiable regions and particular estates, and thus with individual proprietors and their artisan traditions. This is especially important in an era of late capitalism when commodities are generally nondistinct, resonant with manufacture in distant places with a faceless labor force. In fact, when we are made aware of the identity of workers, such as in the infamous case of Nike running shoes documented in *The Guardian* and *The New York Times,* we are often shocked to discover that employees are too often treated with abuse or utter disregard for their health. Real images of actual workers disturb the detached symbolism we associate with valued commodities meant to highlight a style of life—they are the very negation of joie de vivre.

When considering the symbolic play of commodities, Walter Benjamin and Arjun Appadurai come very much to mind, and both are relevant to the concerns here. Long associated with the Frankfurt School, Benjamin was well known for addressing the culture of capitalism and by extension the representation of commodities. Benjamin understood well, as did Marx, the very close association between human bodies and commodities. His image of the sandwich board man presages the notion that people themselves can be treated or represented as commodities, their humanity reduced to a mere object among others. The sandwich board man, a more common phenomenon in the past than it is today, involves a person "sandwiched" in between an advertisement front and back, a novelty for the 1920s and 1930s. More telling, though, in terms of our consideration of wine is Benjamin's celebrated 1969 essay on "Art in the Age of Mechanical Reproduction." Benjamin's essay is about the then remarkable ability to make reproductions of famous artworks and what reproductions convey about the very important idea of authenticity.

This theme has substantial meaning for wine and the inimitability of *terroir* in that fraud has been a long-term concern of wine growers. In fact, as noted, the *appellation contrôlée* legislation was originally designed to assure consumers that particular wines actually came from the estates or properties that bore their names on the labels. Even corks were marked with estate origins as yet another assurance against unscrupulous merchants that on occasion were known to combine grapes from a multiplicity of properties and then to market them as the authentic wines of a particular estate. Counterfeit thus has its origins in wine before making its presence all too ubiquitous in print. The *terroir* concept thus builds upon winegrowing legislation designed to protect the reputations and commercial values of renowned wines.

There are other ways in which Benjamin's idea of mechanical reproduction can provoke the qualities we associate with wine. While it is the case that great wines are assumed to be linked with remarkable soil, the technology of winemaking has improved immensely, and it is not beyond possibility that technology can challenge, or nearly so, standards that we regard as inimitable. However, this also begs the whole question of the standardization and naturalization of taste. Some consumers prefer aged wines while others clearly have a preference for younger wines that can be consumed immediately. It is also the case that there is tremendous variability in the preference for dry versus sweeter wines. The existence of wine-tasting classes also illustrates that appreciation for variety and distinctiveness of flavors, aromas, and taste are taught and therefore cannot be presumed natural. It is, therefore, conceivable that technology in the lab can produce wines that are widely appreciated, or at the very least improve less distinct ones to replicate existing social standards. The replication of distinction may transcend Benjamin's original reference to art in terms of a range of different food commodities and beverages.

Building upon a semiotic theoretical tradition reminiscent of Baudrillard (1975), Appadurai critiques Marx's association of commodities with the singularity of social labor. Rather, Appadurai argues that commodities as they are drawn both into systems of production and consumption take on a life of their own in that commodities also have a material embodiment as systems of signification and cultural representation. Appadurai's intention is to broaden our understanding of commodities with respect to systems of exchange, such as barter, where Marx's idea of social labor reputedly falls short. Most important to our concerns here, Appadurai is, like Marx, focused on the idea of value but, unlike Marx, he maintains that value operates in arenas of social life independent from production. That is, value is multivocal and thus differentially constituted. This is consistent with Appadurai's views on globalization as a process that plays out in differential and semiautonomous areas of social life and, following Lash and Urry (1987), that capitalism itself is a disorganized rather than a consistent and uniform social process. While his views on commodities flirt with fetishism and potentially contribute to its reproduction, they have merit in pointing to wine as profoundly interwoven with a system of representation, albeit one that is humanly fashioned even when cloaked in the

symbolism of national sentiment and blood. There is no doubt a reasoned allure to viewing wine, and perhaps, other commodities, as having a life of their
own, one that is as much in need of acknowledging as it is in need of demysti-
fication. One example that comes to mind and appears to emphasize well the
participation of wine in a system of cultural representation as independent of
labor strictly speaking is the introduction of screw caps in place of corks. There
are substantial practical advantages to screw caps in terms of the preservation
of wine. However, corks have a long-standing association with both the aesthetics of wine consumption and the practical matter that quality corks keep
the wine from oxidizing and thus turning to vinegar. Two of my informants
from the Listrac cooperative expressed this well in praising the cork from a
bottle of California wine that I had brought as a gift while having little to
say about the wine itself. This may of course, eventually change as consumers
begin to appreciate screw tops in terms of preserving and transporting bottles
that have only been partially consumed.

Another example is the now popular bulk wines in the United States that
are purchased in a box. Some people remark that they are surprisingly good
and that they are an excellent value, especially for parties. Again, there is the
potential for social class in this assessment and, if not, surely the impression of
unrefined taste. There is so much cultural capital invested in the ritual of wine
consumption that wine in a box affronts the senses of the wine aficionado,
much as did jug wines in the past or drinking wine from plastic or paper cups
in the present. None of this should be underestimated in spite of the apparent
current commercial success of wine in a box. How wines come to be represented, and here advertising and wine writers are collectively important, is
paramount to how they participate in systems of cultural representation and
exchange. In fact, Appadurai argues, perhaps with some irony, that consumers
have become a fetish because in being acutely subject to manipulation from
advertising they have unknowingly abdicated their agency (2008, 41). Consequently, we may conclude that not only do commodities participate in systems
of representation, but so do their consumers.

While the point of cultural representation appears to give commodities a
relative independence from what Marx called the social relations of production, the assertion that they participate independently in systems of representation is not without its problems in that questions of authority and power are
overlooked. Not to take us too far astray here, I maintain that the circulation and consumption of wine is largely driven by influential wine writers,
advertising firms, and large marketing firms such as Grand Metropolitan or
Constellation Brands. The role of marketing is fairly direct as I had numerous

informants among my Michigan winegrowing informants who complained that the marketing firms determined which wines would end up on the lists at restaurants, thus making it very difficult to place Michigan wines in restaurants where they would perhaps be most appreciated. On the side of media, anyone familiar with *Wine Spectator* will immediately recognize the influence of this publication's ranking system whereby scores of ninety or higher on a 100-point system offer substantial rewards of reputation and commercial success. The playing field, however, in such circumstances is not level, and it is clear that smaller wineries in less "renowned" regions do not have the same capacity to advance the reputation of their wines commercially in a manner that makes them serious competitors to the large firms that also have the capital to advertise. It is also the case that the large firms and wine writers are critical to the reproduction of winegrowing knowledge, especially what counts for the standards of excellence and taste one associates with wine as a commodity. This takes us back to the importance of the concept of *terroir* as a critical marker of distinction.

THE PARADOX OF *TERROIR*

Of all the associations we attribute to wine—corks versus screw tops, mechanical harvesters versus handpicked grapes, traditional winemaking versus oenology, wines sold in bottles versus wines sold in boxes—*terroir* has the most significant cultural and material associations. *Terroir* is invoked nearly worldwide to explain the ever-important distinction between ordinary "table" wines and wines of distinction. While the symbolic and cultural associations of wine make it a commodity somewhat distinct from many others, it is the case that there is significant demand for wines that are bulk and generic because of price sensitivity and the considerable influence of advertising. Each year, for example, there is much made about the arrival of the Beaujolais Nouveau although admittedly young Beaujolais wines do not stand up to aged wines—or so the conventional wisdom suggests. Australia has certainly produced its fair share of bulk wines, of which perhaps Yellow Tail is the best known and most popular. None of these wines are heavily invested in *terroir,* as the kangaroo on the label is a playful symbol that suggests the exotic nature of "Down Under" to consumers in America and Europe. In fact, with some exceptions, many labels seem to have exchanged their one time reference to serious wine for references that are comedic, playful, or artistic. It is a marketing strategy meant to capture the attention of consumers in a commodity sector resplendent with choice.

Although novelty may be an effective strategy to bring attention to wines, there are enough cultural associations and ritual associated with wine that reputedly more discerning and even neophyte consumers find mass commodities uninteresting. This is surely the case with tourism that attracts many visitors to wine regions globally with a keen interest in imbibing local wines. Local wines are often accompanied by personal and local narratives on the part of proprietors and winemakers, thus adding significantly to the pleasure and knowledge of wine tasting. I conclude, therefore, that the strong associations of wine to particular places, even micro-terrains, and their growers is from the part of consumers a reaction to generic commodities that even when well packaged and marketed add very little to imagined distinctions that have become such an important component of the pleasures and aesthetics of drinking wine. Consumers do not drink box wine to connect with a specific terrain and what that terrain has to offer in terms of its uniqueness. However, Konstantin Frank wines from the Finger Lakes region in New York State or a renowned Médoc wine like Château Lafite bring the consumer close to the place of origin, although in the case of the Finger Lakes, loyalty to local wines may also be a factor in choice.

Wines tied to particular places or terrains and their producers allow us to participate in both the imagined sensorial and artisan qualities of wine production and consumption. I maintain that wine is not alone in such associations, as the United States has also experienced a tremendous demand for other distinctive food and beverage commodities of which microbrows are illustrative. It is important, though, to recall, and Bourdieu was well aware of this, that distinction itself is socially produced and constituted and not remote from "invention" itself. What we can learn from the French *grands crus* is that the proprietors of those wines sought to set themselves off from the majority of common wine producers. This is also the case with consumers who, likewise, self-identify with a set of cultural standards reputed to be anything but uncommon. Distinction, as Bourdieu has shown us, is marked by social class, as are consumption patterns more broadly.

This point takes us back to the multivocality of *terroir*. There is an intimate connection between our individual and collective selves and representations of that which we consume that is often more opaque than transparent. Consumption patterns are connected with lifestyles that in turn are one way in which identities are disclosed and represented. The fact that *terroir* can be invoked to link wines with place as a challenge to mass production and nondistinctiveness of commodities is also an index of human subjects that are positioned rather than universal. That is, the consumption of wine itself, especially wines regarded as unique and distinctive, is itself *suggestive* of class distinctions, age, gender, and ethnicity. It is therefore an argument that itself is circumscribed to particular selves and particular groups of consumers. There is much evidence to suggest that in the United States wine remains largely associated with elites, although of the 784 million gallons consumed by Americans, 678 million gallons are table wines (Wine Institute data). Nonetheless, I maintain that practical and symbolic implications of *terroir* are important and help us to both understand and challenge the very sense of commodity of which *terroir* itself is a product. Let me elaborate on this point toward concluding.

CONCLUSION

The concept of *terroir* is, as I have argued, important to challenging mass-produced wines or wines lacking in distinction as part of a more general process that allows us to challenge mass-produced commodities divorced from the social and historical conditions of their production. With *terroir*, we can link wines to their specific places of origin and the soil conditions and climate that ostensibly speak to questions of quality. Moreover, place also enables us to connect wine to a specific proprietorship and those engaged in both the science and artisan traditions of their production in vineyards and through the vinification process. By linking wine to place and persons, *terroir* avoids the issue of alienation that, as Marx argues, is at the heart of capitalist production.

This claim to challenge alienation would seem to suffice in itself were it not for the fact that this same concept of *terroir* also contributes to the mystification and fetish of wine by naturalizing that which is social. As I have argued elsewhere (Ulin 2008), it is common among both popular and scholarly wine writers to argue that quality wines come from especially favorable soils and climates. Consequently, the social and historical conditions under which wine regions and particular properties obtain their significance are rendered to the historical margins, and so wine as a commodity seems to take on a life of its own. Under such assumptions, we fail to raise questions about the social production of representations of wine and the assumed symbolic connections with nation, national culture, and as we have seen in France of the nineteenth century, French blood. This is not extraordinary as there is a long history of either ignoring the social, cultural, and historical altogether or simply attempting to explain difference based upon "natural" endowments that can be applied to commodities as extensions of our collective selves.

The corrective to this oversight may indeed be more political than it is epistemological. That is, it could be argued that only through changes in the means by which social labor is embodied in commodities will commodities be defetishized and appear with a greater sense of transparency. However, my task here is more epistemological than political in that I am suggesting that a more nuanced perspective on *terroir* than I have previously presented will enable us to appreciate both its contributions to distinction in the age of mass production or mechanical reproduction, and the always-present possibility of mystifying the social articulations of commodities.

NOTES

1. Authenticity has become a widely explored theme in the humanities and critical social sciences, ranging from questioning the authority of authorship in the writing of texts (Clifford and Marcus eds. 1986) to challenging authoritative accounts of the past through the "invention of tradition" literature (Handler and Linnekin 1984; Hanson 1989; Ulin 1995).
2. The fact that there are such demonstrable differences between the deep soil conditions on single estates comes very much as a surprise and challenges the supremacy of wines associated with the totality of a single estate.
3. There has been considerable scientific and technological development in the labs that has done much to improve the quality of wine, especially the stability of the vinification process. However, winegrowers themselves know very well that there is no substitute for the labor and knowledge that goes into the vineyards in terms of making excellent wines.
4. All of the popular writers, such as Johnson and Parker, who both write about and evaluate wines, focus almost exclusively on the product. In some cases, they may say something about the families engaged in wine production insofar as elaborating the history of winegrowing estates is part of the story they wish to tell. Power as it plays out in the representation and social relationships of wine are not factors in their accounts.
5. This is a really important point as it opens up the process of human development and change to the process of historical self-fashioning. It comes as no surprise, therefore, that both products of nature and humans alike can be seen in reductive natural terms.
6. The fact that food and drink are so inextricably intermeshed with power and the historicity of social relationships makes their deconstruction—the socialization of the naturalist perspective—so important to both historical and contemporary research. The largely interdisciplinary emergence of food studies is making important strides in this direction.

7. For a very interesting analysis of the discourse of wine from an anthropological perspective, see Michael Silverstein's essay in the 2006 *Annual Reviews of Anthropology*.
8. It is commonly thought that nobles lost their estates as a consequence of the French Revolution. However, it is well documented that some noble families were able to reacquire their winegrowing estates through the disguise of intermediaries. Some of the noble winegrowing estates did not prosper and were abandoned or neglected until purchased and restored by a nascent nineteenth-century bourgeoisie.
9. Strictly speaking, to market a wine with a château label, all the grapes must originate from a single property. Each cooperative has a small number of members with this capability. It is widely thought that grapes from a single property are superior to those from a multiplicity of terrains. Consequently, cooperatives are berated for combining the grapes that originate from their membership at large.

Relationships of Power and the Construction of Place

RACHEL E. BLACK AND ROBERT C. ULIN

The introduction of local products to global marketplaces has in many cases displaced and reshaped the local meanings and values of these products—this is particularly true for wine. In some cases, wine starts off as a local product produced by individuals for personal consumption and small-scale trade. Historically for agricultural workers, wine represented an important source of calories and was part of their daily sustenance. The introduction of small-scale wine production to larger markets changes the social dynamics of wine as it moves from being a part of daily alimentation to becoming a commodity for trade. Once just another agricultural crop, wine can become a lucrative cash crop. In these cases, growers become specialized and they often gain prestige within their communities because of their new economic standing. In many cases, wine then becomes dislocated from daily life and local cultural practice. Local people no longer drink local wine with their meals, as it is too expensive for everyday consumption. Vineyard lands are valuable, and locals often sell out to larger interests and outside investors. This leads to the dislocation of local cultural practices. In other cases, wine may have long been a lucrative agricultural product. This is the case of Bordeaux, an area with a long history of growing wine for rich export markets. In this case, the presence of foreign capital has had a long-standing influence in the construction and reproduction of local social hierarchies (Ulin 1996). Producers of Bordeaux and Burgundy wines have been careful to protect their economic interests by creating complex systems that carefully delineate the place of production and production methods (Demossier 2011). As the importance of *premier cru* wines continues to grow thanks to new markets in China, producers and importers continue to promote not only the prestige but also the authenticity of these wines. Both prestige and authenticity have become deeply embedded in the concept of place. In each of these cases, the value produced through exchange transforms wine into a commodity with a social life shaped by politics (Appadurai 1986, 3). More specifically, the politics of place play an important role in shaping the value of wine.

Building on the focus on place in the previous section on *terroir*, this section looks more specifically at the relationships of power embedded in wine production, consumption, and regulation. Debates about *terroir* underline the importance of place and the power it holds. As Marion Demossier has pointed out, labor can be reproduced, but the unique qualities of place hold a potentially exclusive value (2011). In this sense, how space is delimited becomes very important for drawing lines of power; this also tells us a great deal about who is included and who is excluded from production areas and where certain groups sit in the hierarchy of power created through this process of exclusivity. Erica Farmer's exploration of the history and laws that make up the AOC in France looks at how these regulations create exclusivity through the process of defining place. At the same time, Farmer argues that the *cahiers des charges* (production regulations) leave space for the negotiation of cultural processes that are part of winegrowing and winemaking. Farmer calls this process "the social construction of Bordeaux wines"—legal power and regulations connect geography, notoriety, and tradition. At the same time, these systems of codification reproduce hierarchies of power within a specific community of producers, and this is not without its problems.

This place-based construction of regulations and heritage preservation poses unique problems for wine-producing regions that have a history and traditions not centered on geographic origin. Yuson Jung raises this point in her chapter on wine production and consumption in Bulgaria. Jung focuses on the current attempts to bring Bulgarian wine production into the European

Union systems of protected designations of origin. What happens to local and national traditions when they are forced into supranational frameworks that potentially dislodge local practices? Jung notes that the EU system is designed to protect member state economic and political interests; however, Jung highlights the disconnect between EU policies and local customs. Attempts to preserve local wine culture, which do not necessarily mesh with the realities of the global market, are challenged by increased bureaucratization of the wine industry.

Heritage preservation is also a concern in other wine-producing regions of Europe. This is not a straightforward process, and the very concept of heritage is often deeply contested and nearly always negotiated. Christina Ceisel looks at the performance of place carried out around wine in Galicia. Ceisel investigates the impact of globalization on the wine industry in Spain. On one hand, global markets reify local, regional, and national symbols. Wine, an everyday staple in Galicia, becomes a valuable commodity on the global market. Assurance of authenticity plays a major role in creating value in this unanchored market: this is where savvy producers reappropriate local traditions and perform them for a new global audience of wine consumers. On the other hand, Ceisel argues that the global marketplace also allows for Galician wine producers to bypass the stronghold of bureaucracy in Madrid, giving Galicians direct access to the EU fund and global markets.

In many Eastern European countries, wine regions are in the process of creating or reconstructing traditions and a taste of place that underwent major upheaval during the socialist period. In her chapter, Juraj Buzalka focuses on the ushering in of the free market system in Slovakia and how this economic change has created nostalgia for the rural past. This is particularly true for the group most engaged with these new markets and processes of globalization—the middle class. Ironically, these same people also see the importance of developing a fine wine trade in Slovakia. Buzalka looks at the ways in which wine tastings and wine tourism articulate relationships of power between the rural and economic elites. There are two competing desires: one is to develop a lucrative wine tourism industry associated with social distinction; the other is to maintain the practices of amateur winemaking and the conviviality of sharing wine that occurs outside of market exchanges.

The social and cultural value of sharing wine has also come under attack from commercial interests in Poland. Ewa Kopczyńska looks at the ways the history of wine in the Lubuski region is being reconstructed as a way to deal with a history of displacement. German winemaking traditions are naturalized and become part of a Polish narrative and tradition. The local wine festival has become a symbol of regional identity; yet at the same time, it is co-opted by commercial interests that have moved the focus away from wine. Like in the case of Slovakia, larger market forces have marginalized amateur and small-scale wine producers who are unable to sell their wine at the festival for bureaucratic reasons. Kopczyńska shows the importance of wine in the postsocialist era. Wine has become an important part of selectively excavating the past and constructing a sense of place in the wake of socialism. At the same time, this is not an easy process—larger market forces risk undermining local winemaking practices and, in turn, changing the cultural significance of wine drinking.

The chapters in this section explore the relationships of power manifested in the growing of grapes, the making of wine, and its consumption. In all of these cases, power is associated with place—being able to control the construction of place and the economic value of this exclusivity that manifests itself through the limited production of wine. Moving beyond the taste of place, these chapters explore how wine defines place and the connections this beverage creates not just between people and the land, but also between rural people and global markets.

CHAPTER FIVE

Tasting Wine in Slovakia: Postsocialist Elite Consumption of Cultural Particularities[1]

JURAJ BUZALKA

"Being a rightist I can tell you wine does not need any special protection by law or via taxation; as a consumer I have to admit it does, as it represents our culture since ages..."

Jan, wine-tasting tourist, age 33

"[T]he higher the position one holds, the better chance one has of getting good wines...people doing manual jobs have fewer chances to drink high-quality wines, and to learn how to differentiate it..."

Pavel, wine-tasting tourist, age 41

In this chapter, I discuss the development of elite distinctions in wine consumption through observing wine-tasting tourism of the younger generation of Slovak managers in the late 2000s. I argue that wine-tasting tourism becomes one of the distinctive indicators of how market forces unify production as well as consumption. The introduction of *terroir* as a value system, marketing strategies, and new technologies of winemaking indicate that the globalization of wine has successfully entered Slovakia and differentiated consumers on the basis of class. Wine tourism takes place locally, and models of "culture" based on heritage preservation, multiculturalism, and the promotion of regional specificities shape wine consumption, depending on power relations on a much smaller scale than the global level. While global forces have changed the way wine is produced and consumed, the same elite that is otherwise celebrating the achievements of the global market has learned to fiercely defend and enjoy the cultural particularities of winemaking and wine tasting. This celebration of *terroir* cannot be seen without considering the market's ambivalent influence on the reemergence of practices and representations of rurality after socialism. These romantic attitudes do not only result from the market's call for tradition, but they also depend on what I call the post-peasant social base in postsocialist Eastern Europe.

In the following section, I first offer a brief overview of the history and the current state of winemaking and consumption in Slovakia. I attempt to show first how a group of successful managers with strong promarket opinions with regard to economy and society argues for the nonmarket value of wine. I also present the activity of managers who, together with amateur winemakers, decided to organize a noncommercial wine competition, questioning the commercial status of wine consumption. In the concluding section, I discuss the relationship between market and value in what I call post-peasant Eastern Europe after socialism. This chapter relies on fieldwork carried out in the most developed and largest Small Carpathian winegrowing region, located in the vicinity of Slovak's capital, Bratislava, in the country's southwest. Additional data were gathered in a region with continual small-scale winemaking, namely in the historical region of Hont, south of central Slovakia.

WINE IN SLOVAKIA

While beer brewers in the early 2000s still expected the consumption of their most popular beverage to exceed 100 liters per person annually (in 2002, it was 92 liters per person), ten years later, the consumption of beer decreased to 70 liters.[1] The economic crisis, an aging population, and high taxation of beer were considered the major reasons behind this declining consumption. Wine consumption, on the other hand, has grown.[2] In addition to the import of cheap wines under the European Union (EU) market, fine wines consumed by more affluent consumers have also contributed to the growth.

Although Slovakia had about sixteen thousand hectares of vineyards, fewer than two-thirds of those vineyards were actually under production in the 2000s. Nonetheless, wine consumption has been gradually growing since Slovakia entered the European Union in 2004. In 2009, eighty-seven percent of wine produced in Slovakia was of high-grade quality (inspired by German terminology, these are so-called wines with an adjective—selection of grapes, late harvesting, ice wine, and so on), indicating an increasing success of new technology and marketing techniques.[3] Approximately one-half of all wine consumed in Slovakia is of domestic origin. As a result of law 313 of 2009 on viniculture and winemaking, the German terminology based on sugar content in grapes has been replaced by French *terroir* practices (wines are denominated according to appellations and *terroir,* that is, geographical origin), even though the German-style nomenclature was still used to orient consumers. Among the wine varieties produced in Slovakia, the dominant ones consist of Grüner Veltliner, Müller Thurgau, Olaszriesling, Blaufränkisch, Saint Laurent, and Cabernet Sauvignon. Since the early 2000s, the trendy varieties also include Merlot and Chardonnay. As the representative of the winemakers' association claims, "Consumers demand higher quality every year…we are happy to see the culture of quality wines consumption is increasing."[4]

The new generation of consumers does not drink as much beer as its parents and grandparents used to drink twenty or so years ago. Some of the younger people have embraced new habits of fine wine tasting promoted by winemakers, especially in the Small Carpathian and south Slovak winegrowing areas. Being the most traditional and largest of the Slovak winegrowing areas and making profit from the vicinity of the affluent capital, Bratislava (unemployment under five percent in 2011 and GDP per capita above the EU average), the new trend of wine consumption was promoted in historical Small Carpathian wine towns like Pezinok, Modra, Svätý Jur (considered valuable for growing white wines), and Skalica (famous for its red wine).[5]

After the autocratic and protective policies of Prime Minister Vladimír *Mečiar* (1994–1998) were defeated, the new Slovak generation of "yuppies" has grown under the liberalization regime of the two-term governments of Prime Minister *Mikuláš Dzurinda* (1998–2006). Under Dzurinda, major changes with regard to foreign investment, privatization, and liberalization of the economy took place. Slovakia entered the EU, NATO, and OECD, respectively, and became fully open to the EU common market and to EU regulations. As an effect of these changes, wealth in Slovak society grew more unequally distributed, both regionally as well as among social groups. At the same time, new models of regional development, not least with regard to tourism, have been introduced in new EU member states together with subsidies schemes for agriculture and regional development (see also Buzalka 2009). New cohorts of managers, often with foreign experience and language competences, entered recently privatized enterprises. New trends in wine production technology and consumption habits followed these economic changes. Younger winemakers began developing their businesses after returning from abroad and/or establishing their private enterprises using the infrastructure left over from socialist cooperatives. Wine symbolically replaced beer and distillates as a fashionable beverage, being served more frequently as a marker of distinction of those who could and were allowed to afford it (Bourdieu 1984). It has also been served more often to the official state guests who began to visit formerly isolated Slovakia.

Slovakian wine has enjoyed a lower taxation rate compared to distillates and beer. Wine has benefited from the lobbying of wine-producing associations and the consumers of their wines. The special treatment of wine has been explained as an "economic paradox" among the economic analysts who dominate the public discussions in Slovakia and who follow a neoclassical economic model. These analysts maintain that there is no economic reason for wine's tax exemption. Rather it is well known among wine tasters of all political affiliations that the wine industry benefits from friends in power who love wine and wish to support its consumption as a distinct "product of Slovak wine culture" that is too weak to resist the globalization of wine. Some successful campaigns by winemakers' associations against planned taxation of wine were directed at wine consumers who agree that Slovakian wine deserves to be treated as an exception. For example, stickers and leaflets against the introduction of taxes were distributed along with tickets at the major annual wine event in November 2011, attended by several thousand wine enthusiasts. These people—most of them consistent followers of market ideologies and strong critics of EU agricultural and regional policies who live in the Slovak capital—showed that, when it comes to "wine as a product of ('their') culture," free market rules count less. Because of an attachment to specific regional origins of fine wine and the consequent need to preserve Slovakian wine as a heritage product, most wine lovers think it should be allowed to correct the market's "invisible hand." To proceed with analysis of this nonmarket value of "rural idyll" based on wine, the topic of socialist and postsocialist wine needs to be addressed.

WINE TRANSFORMATIONS

Apart from a few socialist cooperatives and wineries producing limited varieties of quality wines for socialist state power holders and for export, most of the Slovak population consumed uniform wines untouched by any form of marketing, regional, or class distinction. Small-scale family winemaking on plots inherited from parents or rented from the cooperative for one's family needs characterized the winemaking of southern Slovakia. Some of this production found its way into the black market under an informal socialist economy, but most privately produced wine was exchanged among family members and friends.[6] In socialist times, wine was not considered as prestigious a beverage as it has been deemed since the fall of socialism. In some circles, especially among the descendants of presocialist vineyard owners and traders, the consumption of good-quality wine had been present. Ordinary consumers by that time asked for red and white wine only while dining in a restaurant or shopping for Sunday lunch. Only a few individuals cared about the particular variety, bouquet, or regional origin. Handfuls of wine retained their regional names when served in pubs such as *modranské* or *skalické,* but this was an exception originating from the presocialist reputations of the most developed wine towns rather than from the actual characteristics of the wine. From today's perspective, the wine publicists present uniform socialist winemaking and consumption in the following way:

> Grapes in wagons were carried out to the state winery where blended wine was produced out of them. This wine was filled into one liter universal bottles. It was a simple-minded time for wine...This wine did not demand much passion. It remained ferociously egalitarian, as wine was imprisoned in the same bottles as vinegar was.[7]

In contrast, after 1989, the wine publicist argues, modern Slovak viniculture was waking up from a major transformation. After a while, "Slovakia was impressed by new wines that subjugate people with an unknown variety of tastes and aromas."[8] This change came with the introduction of new technologies, privatization, and marketing strategies. In addition to a new generation of winemakers, the strong agents of change were the consumers, who as a social group benefited from the liberalization of the economy since the early 2000s. Slovak fine wine became the distinct beverage of this new generation.

The accent on the distinct character of wine today in public opinion thus contrasts with the "egalitarian" mass wine of the socialist past. The reality of the winemaking transformation, however, was far less contradictory. I talked to a former top-level manager (age 71) of the largest socialist winery in Slovakia about winemaking under state socialism:

> Most of the grapes went to *coupages* in order to make average wine for mass consumption. That wine was supposed to keep its average quality

for one or two years while it was expected to be sold out in shops. The consumer was not educated about high quality wines...the graduates of wine schools began to change the consumption habits of ordinary people only slowly...Most of the vineyards consisted of three to four sorts of wine varieties planted next to each other. Today, nobody wants this mix.

Although no technology was available for the preservation of wine, vineyards were of mixed varieties, and socialist consumption demanded quantities rather than quality. The winemakers' importance in the process of winemaking had been strengthened already in late socialism (see Walker and Manning, this volume). Young, university-educated *pivniční majstri* (cellar masters) unhappy about uniform mass production took responsibility for winemaking in socialist cooperatives using traditional and new varieties, currently celebrated as "post-socialist" cultivars such as Devín, Hron, Rudava, and others, which had been cultivated in the state-owned institute for viniculture.

State subsidies for agriculture were reaching peaks in late socialism, and winemakers belonged to the most privileged from among the agrarian producers. The similarity with contemporary lobbying favoring winemaking at the expense of other sectors of agriculture is a case in point. My informant remembers the contacts with socialist power holders in the following way:

> If something was not agreed upon during the office meeting, it was solved in the cellar afterwards...When a minister came, there was a wine archive opened in the monastery cellars for him. The car drove him to the backyard, so people did not see him coming, and there was a party. For these kinds of people there was always older vintages and variety wine available. We negotiated successfully the limited resources needed for purchasing Western technology and new sorts of plants with these people.

At the same time as the late socialist wine production was advancing, individual members of cooperatives were renting vineyards from their employers. By selling grapes to the cooperative state-owned winery or making their own wine, they contributed to their family income while supplementing their regular jobs. With some minor exception of imports from Bulgaria, the Soviet Union, and Hungary, the vast majority of wines were of domestic origin. Only a handful of people had all grapes of the same variety in their vineyard. Most homegrown wine remained part of local tradition. Consumption of fine wine nevertheless remained restricted. In the traditional Small Carpathians wine region, a sixty-eight-year-old winemaker remembers socialist wine consumption in the following way:

> Variety wine was consumed with friends...At home—in the afternoon or in Sunday—home-made wine in the cupboard used to be ready for drinking...The small producers did not know how to keep wine for longer and usually wine was consumed within one year until new wine was poured into barrels.

My friend who was a child during late socialism remembers also the transformation of consumption habits after socialism collapsed:

> Traditionally in our family wine used to be made at home and we drank it all there. Today we also drink it all, but due to the increasing variety of fine wines on the market, house wine is rather supplementary, especially for those from among our numerous family members who can afford professionally made brands.

Some older wine experts, such as a former cooperative manager who used to visit socialist wineries all around Slovakia, criticized the trap consumers seem to have fallen into today:

> I do not like this mentorship! You come to the winemaker. He says to you: "This is Veltliner! You have to smell this, you have to taste that!" He tells you in advance what you should feel like about wine you drink. Wine today is a matter of prestige. It used to be a little bit like this also under socialism, especially when it came to producers of other liquids, but today it is prestige only. You need to tell a fairy tale about wine, pretend you made everything by hand, even though everybody knows you need advanced technical equipment and technology in order to produce such wine. This is just marketing! I do not have much to discuss with these winemakers, many of whom I knew when they preferred cultivating peaches at socialist cooperatives instead of wine. Today they cultivate pompous wine brands and many of them did not see vineyards the whole year!

With the widening of class differentiation after socialism, fine wine received profound attention from the new middle classes. The reputation of wine as a beverage increased thanks to marketing, the traditions of wine regions were reinvented—not least because of the new rules of the EU that gave a lot more power and money to the regions compared to the almighty socialist state— and the special taste for and qualities of wine began to be celebrated. There was also continuity with the elite status of wine drinking. Like socialist cadres twenty-five years before them, new elites, financial managers, property agents, IT experts, lawyers, show people, and other businesspersons began to invite their business partners and customers to wine cellars, and some of them began to invest in collecting wines. After their initial enchantment with imported wine, elites and better-off middle-class persons in their thirties and forties living in the Slovak capital were attracted to Slovak fine wines. Wine began to represent "symbolic dominance" in consumption—in the way Bourdieu (1984) defined it—more than it did under socialism. Although distinct wine tasting existed among communist power holders, only with the introduction of capitalism did fine wine drinking became a legitimate "symbolic mastery" of postsocialist elites.

Authors Gil Eyal, Iván Szelényi, and Eleanor Townsley applied Bourdieu's work on postsocialist transformations. As they emphasize, the education system allowed individuals who went through it to get better-paid jobs and "positions of influence by appropriating the mechanisms of 'symbolic mastery'... In their quest for cultural prestige and distinction, the elites create credentials and titles for themselves" (Eyal et al. 1998, 61–62). Wine consumption after socialism thus creates legitimate social distance between those who know how to appreciate good wines and those who do not. This distance has a clear class basis and reflects the privileged position of the managerial elite under capitalism. The questions that remain to be answered are what kind of processes have been behind this gentrification, and how have they been legitimized?

Especially after joining the EU in 2004, Western companies purchased former socialist wine production facilities and started to market newly acquired brands. Tourism, especially Westerners traveling to Central Europe and Easterners venturing to wine destinations in nearby Austria as well as France and Italy, enriched the popularity of wine tasting. Of crucial importance was a particular group of middle-class consumers who entered the alcohol market in the 2000s as successful managers and specialists. While winemaking for one's own purposes and wine-related socialization of families had been waning because of the decline of agriculture and growing outmigration from rural areas, this new urban middle class began to follow the sophisticated marketing by professional winemakers and to learn to enjoy new tasting habits of what came to be considered top-quality wine. Slovakia was catching up with the global trend of a growing service sector in the economy. Tourism, folklore, catering, and other "authentic" services elsewhere have been closely connected with romanticized images of the past and of the countryside (see Stronza 2001).

Wine marketing and consumption became one of the boldest examples of this revival of the "good old days." Many feudal elements, such as wine being the "drink of kings," castles, and noblemen's names have been added to the marketing of wine as an elite product. The tradition of fine wine production has been reasserted via rebranding of old trademarks and the developing of new ones. Among the most famous trademarks is J. E. Hubert (currently owned by German company Henkell & Co.), presented as the first sekt factory outside of France. According to its advertisements, its sparkling wine has been produced in Bratislava since 1825. The recognition of Slovak wines by marketers has also built upon the reinvention of the presocialist past.

The achievements of Slovak winemakers in international competitions contributed to the popularity of this "invention of tradition" and have significantly increased the popularity of fine wines in recent years. The first evaluation of Slovak wine made by Robert Parker in a 2001 edition of *Wine Spectator* (Rheinriesling 2001 from Château Belá) was considered particularly valuable. For marketers, this accolade brought Slovakian wine global recognition. Wine publicists characterize this wine as being the "first really great, aristocratic Riesling made by a Slovak wine maker." The success story of the prestigious Château Belá wine restaurant, hotel, and winery where Parker's chosen Riesling originates has been narrated in the following way:

> One beautiful day in 2000, Petrech's [now the chief winemaker, once a socialist cooperative manager, J.B.] mobile phone was ringing. On the other side of the line there was Countess Ilona von Krockow who asked whether he would be willing to meet with German wine maker Egon Müller. The countess wished to re-establish wine production in castle cellars. Fortunately, Petrech was fluent in German and his wine pleased Mr. Müller very much. A unique co-operation emerged from this wine courtship. Rivel [Petrech's company established soon after 1989] became the grape provider for Château Belá and Petrech its wine-maker, the spirit of new trademark (Sedlák 2011, 24).

The wine from Château Belá is sold as an elite product. Connected with the castle that under restitution law was returned to its precommunist owners, its trademark links what is considered the best wine restaurant and *terroir* in Slovakia (southern Slovak winegrowing area) to a classicist castle.

Other stories reinvent recent presocialist traditions. These usually include the personal story of wine trader Palugyai, who was the first to introduce a wine pipeline from his winery to the train station in Bratislava. Famous personalities who tasted Small Carpathian wines included composers Beethoven, Liszt, and Rubinstein; Hungarian revolutionary poet Petőfi; and even cosmonaut Gagarin. Wine producers and advertising experts have not only invented all these stories, the stories have also became part of the everyday discourse of wine tasters. Their popularity reflects a wider revival of nostalgia under capitalism. This nostalgia, on one hand, reflects the legitimization processes managed by elites after socialism who by appealing to presocialism distance themselves from what came to be considered an unfashionable socialist past. On the other hand, as I convey toward the end of this chapter, this nostalgia encompasses both the reproduction and reinvention of particular post-peasant class relations and representations.

In addition to rustic imagery of winemaking and consumption, marketers have introduced new sophisticated stories about distinct Slovak wines. These, for example, present the value of Slovak wines grown in the northernmost, economically efficient wine production region. They also stress that the variety of soil and climate in a relatively small area of the country purportedly adds value to wines from Slovakia. The temperature difference between summer and winter of twenty degrees Celsius makes Slovak wines, according to these narratives, "unique, fresh, bouncy, aromatically rich and expressive." According to the director of the leading winemaking company, *terroir* is nothing more than "the taste of soil one was born upon," and this move toward an expression of *terroir* can equally hold marketing value and advocate an antiglobal quality. As he says, "wine, in comparison to other beverages and food…successfully resists globalization," and the marketing potential of Slovak wines is "borderless."

For many marketers, the similar geographical latitude of Cote d' Or in Burgundy and the Slovak wine production areas makes wines from Burgundy and Slovakia comparable, especially given the recent introduction of *châteaux* labels for more expensive Slovak wines, which reflects not only the calls for an agrarian past, but also the neocolonial dominance of French-style quality measures.

Winemakers, advertisers, publicists, and state officials expect that Slovakia will become better known not only for its rich wine tradition and for the technological advancement of its winemaking, but also for some geographical distinctions, similar to those of Tokaj wines.[9] While Slovakia has a climate that does not favor the growing of high-quality red wines, the climate is well suited for producing acidity that refreshes red varieties of grapes, which is ideal for producing high-quality rosé. For marketers as well as winemakers, rosé is poised to become one of Slovak's brands. The introduction of the market and EU regulations made fine wine consumption an ideal field in which to mix the romanticism of the rural nation, class distinction, and market globalization. Who actually buys this wine-culture mix in the Slovak context?

CONSUMERS OF SLOVAK WINE BRANDS

Although the average monthly salary in Slovakia approached 800 euros in 2011, the good quality varietal wines costing 6–10 euros per bottle remained unaffordable for the average Slovak consumer. However, since the liberal transformation changed postsocialist Slovakia in late 2000, an increasing number of new middle-class consumers entered the Slovak fine wine market. The majority of these young, successful consumers live and work in the capital, Bratislava, and have jobs in finance, information technology, the real estate sector, and at the headquarters of private and state enterprises.

My key informants were from among the professionals I met during my university studies in the mid-1990s. We used to drink beer and other beverages in a fairly egalitarian way in student pubs and dormitories. Some of my friends already had good jobs while doing their studies. Their income allowed them to drink Western beverage brands considered prestigious in early postsocialism. We largely purchased inexpensive wines for student parties at the grocery store or from petty private winemakers near the dormitory rather than higher-quality wines that only very slowly entered our drinking scene. Most of my friends did not drink wine at home, and the vast majority did not come from regions where wine had been produced. Companies do team building exercises at wine cellars, they have meetings over wine with business partners, and maturing middle-class professionals have begun to acquire tastes, including for wine, considered appropriate among their peers. My friends distanced themselves from their fathers who did not drink wine, from older-generation fellows who preferred more egalitarian beverages such as beer, and from all those who could not afford fine wines. Their age offered them a chance to gradually occupy mid-level management positions in private businesses as well as better-paid jobs in state or service sectors. By 2012, roughly half of this group had small children who on occasion were taken to wine-tasting events. They, as well as the winemakers, considered wine tasting a family and social event combined with a visit to the charming countryside. Their financial situation, university education, age, and permanent address positioned them as members of Slovak society who benefited most from the change of the regime after 1989 and from the economy in the early 2000s. As a generation, they did not bear the major burden of the postsocialist transformation. Thanks to their language skills, they even managed to find work and study abroad. Sophisticated marketing of wine in Western Europe—particularly in winegrowing countries—made it easier for them to adopt new consumption habits. With some minor exceptions, the vast majority of these "benefactors of the transformation" characterize themselves as right wingers. They belong to the generation that refused to support the national populist and isolationist rule of Prime Minister Vladimír *Mečiar* (1994–1998) and who very critically assessed the period of state socialism, especially its egalitarianism in consumption and welfare.

The supporters of center-right parties backed promarket reforms, and the representatives of these parties did not hesitate to consider their supporters as society's elite. The majority of the thirty to forty people with whom I participated in wine tastings over the past six years gradually moved to more neoliberal positions. One of the key periods of my fieldwork took place in mid-November 2011, during the annual wine tasting in Small Carpathians. Some weeks earlier, the center-right government coalition failed to keep a majority in the parliament. The reason for its failure was the bailout of the EU finance mechanism that the Slovak parliament was expected to support as a way to solve the debt crisis in the Euro zone. My friends widely supported the populist arguments of the neoliberal party, were critical of the EU plan, and supported the ideas of market fundamentalism responsible for the government's fall.

Although politics was not the major issue discussed at the annual wine tasting, the ambivalent position of my promarket friends with regard to wine shows how their beliefs in the market are questioned by what they celebrate as national wine heritage. My free-market-oriented friends happily follow this "call of *terroir*," speak about the support of national food producers, and resist megastore shopping. My friends stress the value of community, trust among people, and authenticity with regard to wine and food. The wine-tasting events offer this illusion of community informality. The preferences my friends claim today certainly depend on their coming of age. At the same time, the impersonal market urges their desire for "natural" and "authentic" foodways. It is, however, also important to link their reaction with the history of uneven development in Eastern Europe. The parochialism this threefold combination of community, market, and particular power relations brings into being might well be illustrated through the example of wine routes.

SMALL CARPATHIAN WINE ROUTE

The most famous and well-established wine-tasting event in Slovakia that my friends attend every November is *Malokarpatská vínna cesta* (Small Carpathian Wine Route). It starts in Bratislava and ends forty kilometers away in the city of Trnava, located northeast of the Slovak capital. The event started at the beginning of the 1990s with seventeen open cellars. Since then, the winemakers who were known only to their neighbors have become famous all around Slovakia. Additional events complement this annual tasting: Open Cellars at St. Urban's Day in mid-May; Pig Sticking and Wine in January; the Wine Ball in February; the Wine Market in April, Lavender and Wine in July; the Day of One Wine Maker, the Day in the Vineyard, the Grape Picking Festival, and the Hubert Feast of Wine in September; and St. Catherine's Wine Festival of Young Wines in autumn. Advent with Wines and many other events have also enriched the wine taster's calendar in recent years. Wine and related products are on sale at these events, contributing to the livelihood of hundreds of artists, craftsmen, and catering specialists.

In November 2011, six and a half thousand wine lovers visited 130 cellars in the Small Carpathians. The tickets were sold out months before the event took place. More than twenty thousand people took part in the event. A single ticket cost forty euros, considered expensive for the average consumer. The official webpage of the association organizing the event states:

[T]he Small Carpathian Wine Route has helped to put local wine on the map and contributed to good sales. The wine route also shows how Slovak society is changing and how people's taste for wine has grown: the younger generation tends to prevail among the visitors. All of which goes to show that Slovak wine has a proud tradition and a promising future...What most attracts visitors...is its atmosphere. Adding the greatest allure to the tasting experience are the cellars...drinking wine is a true sensation.[10]

Every year, the members of the Small Carpathian Wine Route association, an organization that includes winemakers, municipality representatives, and regional entrepreneurs, gather to continue building its brand. Claiming to be an apolitical association, the organization aims to support the development of tourism in the Small Carpathian region and to preserve what it considers as local traditions. The majority of wine tourists appreciate the visits to wineries and the tastings of local delicacies. Coziness, a rustic, excellent atmosphere, and hospitality in family-owned cellars are among the top reasons for repeat participation at the event. Similarly, Gmelch and Gmelch describe the growth of this new form of elite tourism in Napa Valley, California (2011). In the case of Slovakia, local peasant delicacies gain status, becoming gourmet products (Cavanaugh 2007). As with other areas that have faced the development of a heritage industry (see Bunten 2008), the locals in Small Carpathians consciously share aspects of their culture with tourists. Wine tourists appreciate this communal atmosphere of sharing and small-scale exclusivity in this era of global impersonality.

Experts and economic analysts argue that private entrepreneurship changed old socialist winemaking into a new form of craft. Wine is today bottled in fashionable bottles with labels designed by the best designers. It became popular to take part in wine tasting every year and to celebrate the culture of *terroir* in what has grown to be the richest part of postsocialist Slovakia. For my friends, wine is a "unique beverage, with vast variability of tastes." For some, it "evokes memories of France" and achieves the position of "the most noble alcoholic beverage with several thousand years of tradition." Some wine "provokes thoughts and interesting ideas." It is a "relaxing beverage" and even "a healthy drink that accompanies a good meal" because it is, so they say, a "pure, natural product...the only one that does not need fire in order to become alcohol." My friends think wine consumers represent a minority of alcohol drinkers. According to them, "most consumers belong to the middle and upper middle classes. They are not looking for immediate intoxication, but inspiration and a chance to have a cultivated conversation in a relaxed atmosphere."

All these opinions about wine that I gathered during my fieldwork connect three important elements of wine consumption. As the result of global influence on technology and marketing, wine in Slovakia remains strongly tied to local production; it crosses the urban-rural divide and provides the sense of community tied to land and heritage. At the same time, drinking fine wine is a matter of elite distinction. As I would like to show in the next section, this distinction is more complex in the postsocialist setting than the ideal distinction theory shows. Some members of the new elite sometimes actually cannot and do not want to be "distinct" wine drinkers.

LITTLE BARREL IN HONT

In 2010, some of my friends and I who had been meeting at the Small Carpathian Wine Route began to support wine tourism in the significantly less developed region south of central Slovakia. The Hont region is approximately a two-hour drive east from Bratislava and a one-hour drive north from the capital of Hungary, Budapest. In the mid-eighteenth century, the Hont region (including the southern part that now belongs to Hungary) was the third largest winegrowing area in what is now Slovakia. The wine diseases that affected Europe in the end of the nineteenth century such as phylloxera and peronospora changed much of the wine landscape in this area, and wine cultivar hybrids—so-called *samorodák* or *polodivô* (literary translation: "self-producing" or "half-savage")—proliferated in what is now south of central Slovakia. The popularity of wine cultivars continued in private vineyards even during socialism. Unlike in the Small Carpathians, where German settlers began to cultivate *vinifera* wines long before the nineteenth century, in Hont, vineyards were planted with *vinifera* wines only in late socialism. Especially in the late socialist 1970s and 1980s, the south of central Slovakia belonged to the most prosperous agricultural areas of Czechoslovakia (see Drábiková 1988, 75).

The production of *samorodák* characterized homemade production in the Hont region until the 1990s, when wine production elsewhere in Slovakia was on the decline. Family vineyards remained a source of pride until then. As the numerous abandoned vineyards in the region after socialism testify, not all inheritors continued cultivating vineyards after socialism collapsed. This was in part a result of the deep decline of agriculture and the consequent outmigration from the depressed rural regions. Another reason behind this decline was that *samorodák* remained unknown to most middle-class consumers and, supposedly unsuitable for fine wine production, it has never entered the market. It is expected that one-quarter of wine in Slovakia remains unrecognized by the state, and this is also the ratio of a black market in wine.[11]

The tasting event and competition *Hontiansky súdok* (Hont Little Barrel) aimed to attract winemakers who produce wine for their own consumption and who eventually sell their wines to close circles of friends and family members. Established in 2010 in the small spa town of Dudince, the event gained a regional reputation among amateur winemaker competitions.[12] In 2011, the attendance of participating winemakers rose by one-third. In 2012, the event broke the 2011 record and the organizers managed to gain public support for covering some of the costs of their competition.

Following weeks of collecting wine samples and thorough tastings, the public wine tasting took place on May 18 and 19, 2012 in one of the spa hotels in Dudince. In addition to amateur winemakers, local power holders and businessmen were present. My friends from the Small Carpathian Wine Route also took part in the event, claiming their interest in developing the region of Hont into a known wine area. Except nostalgia and meeting with old friends, the desire to make life for people in their native region more bearable was given as the major reason for their support. Discussions of wine distinction recalled the ones I had heard in the Small Carpathians. Even the discussion on Château Belá and its famous winemaker was brought to the table to contrast the region's winemaking with the way "professional winemaking has progressed in Slovakia." The next day, dozens of participants visited a historical winegrowing village, Sebechleby, and its wine cellar area (*chyšky*) at Stará Hora to taste local wines, in particular *samorodák*. My wine-tasting friends from among the wine tasters who were not native to Hont were surprised by a cordial invitation from the local winemakers, who offered their wine for free. This contrasted with the image of the hard-working, calculative winemaker from Small Carpathians whose aim is to attract the capital's elites. My friends from Bratislava advised the winemakers to start thinking about making some financial profit from their wines.

The amateur winemakers who have already invested in higher-quality equipment and begun to follow modern winemaking technology hope that Hont Little Barrel will take a more commercial direction. Taking inspiration from the Small Carpathian Wine Route and coordinated through the help of regional development agencies, the first wine trail was organized in Dudince in August 2012. The opposite opinion is held by those who embrace an old-fashioned *samorodák*, at least in some quantities in addition to reputable varieties, and would like to remain removed from commercial wine tourism. They have no intention of selling their wines and rather prefer to socialize with friends and neighbors while tasting it. This conviviality from Hont is nowadays harder to find in the Small Carpathians.

The Hont Little Barrel is organized thanks to the voluntary work of a handful of amateur winemakers and their friends living in the capital. Their contribution to the festival and consequent conviviality over tasting their own wines makes this event a success. Discussion over wine in Dudince and Sebechleby included also the critiques of commercialization of wine in more advanced Western regions. In southern Moravia, my friends from Hont recall, they were not only asked to pay an entry fee but also to pay for wine samples. To their surprise, after sitting in the cellar, they were additionally charged for live folklore music performed at the tasting event. In Hont, the local winemakers and event organizers still prefer to provide folk performances as a part of the tasting, and do so for their own pleasure. In 2012, they themselves even sang and played. Considering the significant presence of managers from the capital who likewise came to enjoy the local *samorodák* atmosphere, this generosity shows that the noncommercial and egalitarian value of wine matters for them.

The reason is that the elite described in this chapter have not managed to distance themselves fully from "the people" since socialism collapsed. Virtually all my friends come from families that were part of the socialist intelligentsia where the grandparents used to be peasants. Their personal wealth is greater than that of the average Slovak citizen, but the difference between them and ordinary citizens is smaller than the one between classes in Western Europe, especially when considering their loans and debts for purchasing property in capital. Distinction based on more commercial tastings such as the one in Small Carpathians, therefore, has not always found the same resonance among the new middle classes as the direct economy-centered analysis shows. Although the social distance between visiting professionals and locals remained, more egalitarian post-peasant conviviality overcomes the commodity value of wine.

As I showed in the two cases of the Small Carpathians and Hont, various values of wine have coincided with postsocialist power relations. The call for community trust represents a reaction to impersonal capitalism among promarket managers as well as professional winemakers. At the same time, the development of class distinction—well represented by fine wine tasting in Small Carpathians—has actually been questioned by the revitalization of community tradition in Hont with the central role of noncommercial, community wine sharing of wine enthusiasts.

VALUE OF WINE AFTER SOCIALISM

Considering the nonmonetary value of wine, it is necessary to look at the wider implications this has in the context of postsocialism. My elite informants participated regularly in the Small Carpathian Wine Route, and some attended Hont Little Barrel. In the 2010 and 2012 elections, many of them voted for the neoliberal Freedom and Solidarity Party and supported the view that the market should be the dominant distributor of wealth and justice. When it came to wine, however, the majority of my friends argued that wine producers should enjoy favorable taxation and that the "culture of wine" must be protected against the global market. As my longtime friend underlined:

> [T]here should be no excessive duty put on wine as it would ruin small winemakers...low tax is one of the few available protection tools for domestic production...as wine cultivation represents a hundred years long tradition, it should be protected by the state. We should be interested in promoting the country—that a good wine is connected with Slovakia. This way we support our producers and quality...we should learn more about our wines, protect them, drink them more and be proud of them.

More elaborate explanations for the special value of wine were offered by one of the biggest wine collectors from among my informants:

> There should be some protection as there is protection for cultural heritage and local specificities that includes wine...we should create a system of sustainable national production of wine, some tradition of viniculture exists here that might be endangered by the global wine market... Everything made in this country deserves protection, as we are a community sharing currency, taxation system and culture...there should be a program explaining to people why should they buy local products, including wines.

As Jeff Pratt argues, the paradox arises from the capitalist economy that puts value on monetary exchange (2007). By using money, however, most people buy the opposite of monetary exchange; they buy products considered personal, local, and authentic. The marketers thus create the added value of products by expanding their market value by nonmarket means, exactly by adding symbolic value to products, making them local and authentic. Wine is an excellent product that shows how nonmonetary value in late capitalism might take over the commercial value, even in social groups that otherwise praise the ideology of "the invisible hand."

Wine tourism is used as a key indicator of how market forces after the fall of state socialism coincide with projects of heritage preservation, multiculturalism, and the promotion of ethnic specificities (see Buzalka 2009). It thus demonstrates the ambivalent relationship between public representations of commodity value and social change influenced by EU policies and discourses.

The increasing popularity of rustic practices and representations in contemporary Eastern Europe—of which elite consumption in the Small Carpathians and egalitarian wine tasting in Hont are excellent examples—must incorporate capitalist calls for tradition (see Pratt 2007) as well as the effects of uneven development. I call these combined effects of global capitalism and postsocialism in contemporary Eastern Europe post-peasantism.

As I aimed to show in this chapter, winemakers and the new postsocialist middle classes allied to manage these parallel processes of valuation and distinction in opposition to the market. As Andre Czegledy shows through elite "urban peasants" in Hungary, despite living in cities such as Budapest, many people retained their rural practices, identities, and memories through their leisure activities and through sociality around their hobby plot or allotment (2002). His examples and those presented in this chapter show that boundaries between the rural and the urban have remained porous in Eastern Europe, as they were under state socialism. My argument does not simply concern how wine has been represented between agrarian and modern, rural and urban in Slovak late capitalism as a distinct, healthy, traditional, and cultural product of and for the elites in opposition to mass commodities. Rather, my argument is that socialist economies reproduced and at the same time generated social bases that became sensible to practices and representations of the agrarian past after socialism fell apart (see Buzalka 2007). At the same time, the ruptures and insecurities of the postsocialist and ongoing capitalist transformations and crises have fueled new attitudes based on a romanticized, nostalgically imagined past.

Stephen Gudeman's valuable model of economy's dialectics of the community and market, especially the market's cascading into nonmarket realms where it did not exist earlier, might be modified by this post-peasant alternative (2008). Most of Eastern Europe has departed from agrarian times quite recently through state socialist modernization. Despite its modernist attempts, state socialism managed to reproduce and even strengthened many elements of rural life, such as the role of kinship and religion, and these elements became crucial for postsocialist development, including current transformations resulting from the integration of Central and Eastern Europe into the European Union. My argument, however, also is that socialist and postsocialist economies reproduced and at the same time generated social bases that became vulnerable to radical appeals after socialism fell apart. Gentrification of postsocialist elites visible in support for "national culture of winemaking" that is close to ethnic exclusivity reflects the ambivalent effect market forces have had in Eastern Europe.

NOTES

1. I would like to express my gratitude to all my wine friends and colleagues who helped me make this chapter empirically valuable. I also am thankful for the support of the Seventh EU Framework Project MEDEA (project No. 225670 *Models and their Effects on Development Paths: An Ethnographic and Comparative Approach to Knowledge Transmission and Livelihood Strategies*), which made me begin thinking about wine as an elite beverage in the Slovak context. For thoughtful comments on this chapter, I am very thankful to the editors of this volume.

2. http://peniaze.pravda.sk/spotrebitel/clanok/25296-slovensko-starne-a-pije-menej-piva/, accessed May 30, 2012.

3. The consumption of wine per person in France reaches sixty liters a year. In Hungary or Austria, the countries bordering Slovakia, the annual consumption is thirty to forty liters per person, double the amount of Slovakia www.domnarodnychvin.sk/clanky/agenturne/slovaci-zacali-uprednostnovat-kvalitne-a-slovenske-vina/, accessed May 30, 2012.

4. www.vuepp.sk/Komodity/r2009/II.polrok/vino2.pdf, accessed May 30, 2012.

5. http://ekonomika.sme.sk/c/3683758/slovenski-vinari-pokryju-viac-ako-polovicu-domacej-spotreby-vina.html, accessed May 30, 2012.

6. For more information about the history of winemaking in the Small Carpathian region, see, for example, Popelková 2007.

7. For more on the wine shadow market under Kádarism, see Hann 2006.

8. See Sedlák 2011, 23.

9. Ibid.

10. The Tokaj wine region is located in northeast Hungary, but its minor part also belongs to Slovakia. There has been an ongoing diplomatic dispute between Hungary and Slovakia over the size of the Tokaj winegrowing area that stands in the territory of Slovakia.

11. www.mvc.sk/the-day-of-open-wine-cellars, accessed May 30, 2012.

12. www.strava.sk/showdoc.do?docid = 2041, accessed May 30, 2012.

13. Participation is restricted to winemakers who do not produce wine for commercial purposes, that is, it is not possible to buy their wine in a wine shop. For more information about the event see www.vinohradnik.sk.

CHAPTER SIX

Wine Histories, Wine Memories, and Local Identities in Western Poland

EWA KOPCZYŃSKA[1]

Drinking wine in Poland is definitely constructive drinking (Douglas 2003). Wine tastes and habits are classified in social, economic, and cultural categories. They are categorized in terms of social structure and in terms of hierarchy (upper/lower tastes), oppositions (usual/outstanding drinks, simple/sophisticated), or development (basic/refined) (Unwin 1991). Wine drinking and wine producing can also be seen as a process of distinction (Bourdieu 1984; Gade 2004; Silverstein 2006). The Eastern European political shift in 1989 was a catalyst for reconstructing and restabilizing new social and economic relations. Food habits, as everyday practices, embodied and always under construction, not only help to unravel identities (Wilson 2006), cultural dynamics (Counihan 2004), and narratives of territorial ties (Bell and Valentine 1997, 14–15), but are also identities themselves—after all, "we are what we eat." Mary Douglas argues that "the drive to achieve consonance in all levels of experience produces concordance among the means of expression, so that the use of the body is co-ordinated with other media" (1996, 71). Mutual conformity can be traced to food habits and social position or between beverages and identity patterns.

When trying to understand wine producing in Poland, economic justifications are not sufficient. The motives and legitimation of this practice refer to issues of tradition, continuity, and national and local identity. But there is more to it than just constructing a narrative of legitimacy. Following Mary Douglas, I argue that wine is a language or code that expresses controversies concerning crucial ideas, taboos, boundaries, myths, or just, as Durkheim would say, collective representations of society itself. In this chapter, I focus on the idea of wine's naturalness in Lubuskie and on objectified wine culture. This is material objectification, becoming a component of collective memory, and behavioral objectification, when public ritual becomes an arena for the creation of social self-definition and a space for ideology (national/locality). I also depict the processes of winemaking as reshaping regional political power structures.

Poland is not a well-known wine country. Nevertheless, wine has been and continues to be produced here. Subject to climate change and historical and economic turbulence, the inhabitants on the Vistula river have long planted grape vines and vinified their grapes. Some regions have had an old and almost continuous tradition for many centuries: Sandomierz, Zielona Góra (Lubuskie province), Malopolska (Lesser Poland), Wielkopolska (Greater Poland), and Dolny Slask (Lower Silesia). Other regions in Poland have had their own wine only occasionally during climate warming in the late Middle Ages and also today. Despite the diverse regional meaning of wine production, it has never become a part of Polish national heritage.

For geographic, economic, and cultural reasons, Poland is considered a vodka culture (Fogarty 2009), although today beer seems to be replacing vodka (CBOS 2010). Current annual consumption of wine in Poland is 2.7 liters per capita (International Wine and Spirits Research 2011), whereas in 1996 it was just 1.06 (Fogarty 2009). It has, therefore, doubled in the last ten years and increased systematically. The majority of wine is imported. The domestic market is dominated by Bulgarian (Sophia, Fresco) and Hungarian wines (Tokaj, Egri Bikaver) (Euromonitor International 2012; Prange-Barczyński 2009). Sophia is the Eastern equivalent of the Western European "one-euro wine," and its popularity is analogous to the miracle of Two Buck Chuck in the United States (Veseth 2011). Furthermore, wine itself is associated with special occasions, with celebrating important events, days, or successes, and with raising toasts (Fogarty 2009). Moreover, wine in Poland is regarded as a feminine drink, one of few feminine soft alcoholic beverages (wine, beer, other alcoholic drinks), and it is most often women's preferred choice of alcohol (thirty-eight percent of women versus six percent of men) (CBOS 2010). Polish consumers clearly prefer red (two-thirds of all wine consumption) and sweet wine, while dry and white or rosé wines do not receive much recognition (Olejniczak 2004; Prange-Barczyński 2009). The Lubuskie winemakers stress that there is no developed local wine culture, meaning that white, dry, sometimes tart regional wines do not find many enthusiasts. This is why some winemakers produce local wines that are sweetened or have honey added for tasting purposes at food fairs. The characteristic local wines are produced for a more limited circle of guests of vineyards, enotourists.

Despite the modest consumption of wine in Poland, interest in winemaking is increasing. Poland has been acknowledged as a wine country within the coldest European Union winegrowing zone A (with Germany, Luxembourg, Belgium, the United Kingdom, and northern countries). Even in the northernmost areas of Poland and those areas with the most severe climate, small-scale private producers try to produce quality wine accepted by critics, consumers, and winemakers themselves. The great majority of vineyards do not exceed five acres, and only a few are more than ten acres. The total area of Polish vine cultivation is roughly a thousand acres, a figure that increases continually (Burkot 2010). Polski Instytut Wina i Winorośli (the Polish Institute of Vine and Wine) estimates the number of vineyards in Poland at around 500 (2012). Winemaking is mostly a semi-amateur practice based on limited experience and self-taught knowledge, and all of the production is for consumption by family, friends, and guests. Except for the largest holdings, nonprofessional winemakers, hobbyists who earn their living as teachers, journalists, clerks, small businessmen, and sometimes farmers run vineyards. Most of them belong to groups and classes whose position is ambivalent and who are between social strata (e.g., farmers with small-scale but high-qualified food production or positions that are low-paid, but play an important role in local communities, such as journalists or officials). This cross-section of winemakers is an argument for the evident effect wine has in creating distinction.

There are also economic and legal reasons why winemaking is a hobby. Until recently, it was practically impossible for small producers in Poland to release their wines to the market, and today, following the introduction of the new "wine act" (July 10, 2008), it is still difficult or unprofitable. At the very beginning of the winemaking process, the producers are obliged to obtain many permits to confirm their status as entrepreneurs, which results in considerable expense. For small producers, from an economic point of view, this activity is unprofitable in the short run, and in the long term it entails high risks. Therefore, a substantial proportion of such wine producers, and the clear majority in the Lubuskie region, have not put their products on the market. In 2010, two relatively large vineyards produced and sold their wines on the market, and thirty more officially registered as wine producers (Burkot 2010). All the others sell their production surplus (usually a few hundred bottles a year) through informal channels.

Although most Polish vineyards are no more than ten years old, and only a few were founded twenty or thirty years ago, wine regions are becoming more and more recognizable. Polish wine is taking part in the process of constructing new relations between inhabitants and the place where they live, and also between specific provinces or regions of the country. Wine is becoming a component of group identity, a new interpretation of tradition, and a key to understanding the past. The differences among Polish wine regions come down to climate and historical and organizational issues. These characteristics define relations between regions and, to a considerable degree, determine the politics of the subjects of local wine. Climate conditions decidedly limit the scope of varieties of vines planted in Poland, yet all regions become more and more specific in their selection of grapes. *Vitis vinifera* is cultivated in the mildest western and southwestern regions only, while hybrids predominate in central and southeastern areas. The traditions of producing wine are also different: in the Malopolska and Sandomierz regions they are rooted in the deep Middle Ages, but have been broken and forgotten for centuries, whereas elsewhere they were vivid until the twentieth century. Additionally, the changing borders of Poland and the disappearance of the state for 150 years in the eighteenth and nineteenth centuries add even more confusion to the current discussions on national or ethnic identities of wine. All sorts of wine institutions, associations, and individual producers are leading these discussions. Meetings such as the annual Polish Winemakers' Convention, wine magazines, websites, Internet forums, and, last but not least, dozens of blogs, are an arena for interchange and sharing ideas. One of the key elements determining the force of historical or "soil and climate" arguments is the level of institutionalization in a particular region. Strong regional associations gathering individual winemakers together, active leaders, people in high places engaged in wine issues, with the "voice of *terroir*," are conditions of the strong cultural and political position of the region. National and European grants supporting the development of local winemaking further institutionalize bonds within several regions (Podkarpacie, Malopolska), strengthening regional wine identity. Developed viniculture is a distinctive feature, and it raises the cultural status of a region at the national level. These factors also locate regions in the structure of being central or peripheral on the cultural map of Poland. While the term *terroir* is central to the locality and uniqueness in the discussion of European wine (Crenn 2007; Morlat 1998; van Leeuwen 2006), it is not yet crucial in the Polish wine debate. The reason is probably that vine varieties and types of wine are not yet unambiguously assigned to particular regions. The merit of Polish wines' status enters into the *terroir* disputes (Bohmrich 1996; Gade 2009), mainly with the advantages of favorable climate and soil or with arguments of history and continuity (Barham 2003).

WINE HISTORIES

A characteristic of the Lubuskie region in Poland is its very long and continuous winemaking tradition. It was incessant from the Middle Ages to the Second World War. Except for the early Middle Ages, this region for centuries belonged to a German population, who were almost entirely displaced at the end of the Second World War. This leads to a contradiction: on one hand, the wine tradition is uniquely continuous, a key asset for the region in its rivalry with other Polish wines. On the other hand, this tradition contains radical breaks and replacements of one culture by another. Reconciling incoherent historical narratives constitutes a challenge for the contemporary winemakers of the Lubuskie region. The followers of continuous wine tradition can refer to Slavic winemakers of the Middle Ages or to German prewar culture. There is a break in time or a break in population. Daniel Gade reflects on a similar lack of continuity of wine communities when researching the case of Cassis in southern France. The tradition referred to dates back to the ancient past and then to contemporary practices (Gade 2004, 862). Invoking the distant past helps to legitimize old or quite new traditions (Hobsbawm and Ranger 1983; Ulin 1995).

As a result of the Potsdam Agreement after the Second World War, the borders of Poland shifted westward, and mass population transfers took place, which had a big effect on Poland's geographical structure. A characteristic common to new Polish regions is the appearance (still very dynamic) of a new society, the so-called indigenization of the lands. There is a new social fabric that does not possess a uniform, common identity. The tearing apart of old, prewar neighborhood relations, old borders, and old divisions into *theirs* and *ours* made the continuation of definitions inherited from ancestors impossible. For this reason, a crucial aspect of the process of settlement turned out to be the construction of a new model of locality. In the case of the Lubuskie region, winemaking was an important narrative. Because of geographical and economic factors, wine was produced here continuously, in spite of worse (beginning of the twentieth century, late 1920s/early 1930s) and better (1860s) periods, in spite of a temporary worsening of the climate at the turn of the century, in spite of difficulties with fighting diseases (peronospora) and recultivation of the soils (Kuleba 2005). The decisive blow in the breakdown of winemaking traditions did not come until the Second World War, or, in fact, its consequences in the form of the displacement of the Germans, that is, almost all the previous inhabitants of the region. Attempts were made to maintain the vineyards and wineries they left, which were handed over to the Polish Lubuskie Wine Manufacturing Company, the heir to the prewar Grempler Factory.

Unfortunately, political-economic conditions of postwar socialism and the break with the cultural continuity proved destructive for Lubuskie winemaking, leading to a gradual neglect of vineyards, a decrease in the acreage, and complete abandonment in the 1970s. The incoming population, acclimatizing to its new homeland with difficulty, did not take up the prewar cultivation, preferring to concentrate instead on reconciling its own farming traditions with the circumstances it had been given. The tragedies of the displacements, such as difficulties associated with adjusting to the new reality, daily painstaking efforts to gain new family and economic stability, different, weaker, more demanding soils than on the farms left in the east, the need to resume the education neglected during the war, and fast acquisition of professional skills, had an overriding and urgent status. Furthermore, the hostility to Germany precipitated by official state ideology generated attitudes far removed from concerns over the material and nonmaterial goods acquired. Vineyards and domestic vine cultivation were therefore treated as a given element, a natural characteristic of the landscape, worth exploiting, but not necessarily maintaining. It appears that this approach meant that we can today sometimes find single specimens of vines, climbing up the walls of prewar "post-German" houses. They have been growing for decades, untrimmed, but bothering no one, their fruit feeding animals and sometimes used by people, similar in status to wild rose or elder.

LOCAL IDENTITY: NATURAL WINE OVER TROUBLED HISTORY

Polish society is made up of a multitude of identities. Poland entered the European Union (EU) in 2004, lending even greater complexity to the issue of Polish identities. There are at least three levels of affiliation: one of them is European, particularly stressed during the process of joining the EU; another one is national, legitimizing Polish sovereignty in past centuries as well as after 1989; and there is also a regional and local community level, the basis of the public administration structure and civil society activities. Food habits are the parts and the expression of identity issues (Galasińska and Galasiński 2005; Jansen 2001) and political and moral discussions. The model example is a debate on the Slow Food movement (Leitch 2008), which can be treated as a "quality turn" (Goodman 2003) of food models, but also of the concept of community. The ideas of relocalization, reengagement, the return of *homo geographicus,* and "idiotope" (Pascual-de-Sans 2004) in the new global context, typical in most Western countries and increasingly influencing their economies and food supply chains, are shaping the Polish social landscape as well.

After the communist system collapsed in 1989, Poland's administrative structure underwent an increasing decentralization. The provinces (*voivoide-ships*) and districts are acquiring ever-greater autonomy, and to an increasing degree becoming truly autonomous entities. This is not only expressed at the institutional and economic levels, but is also manifested in cultural policy and changes at the level of group identity. The contemporary interest in winemaking is part of the changes associated with the emancipation of local histories and identity narratives, undermining the previously dominant national narrative. The severing of rigid formulas linking a national community to a political institution and a given geographical territory (Gupta and Ferguson 1992) opens a whole range of alternative identity narratives. Winemaking in the Lubuskie region is the arena for disputes between rival definitions of community. The local history and winemaking traditions can be defined by affiliation to a place and relations with temporally (the prewar German community) and spatially (other regions of Poland, other winemaking regions of the world) distant groups.

Although over half a century has passed since the events of the Second World War and the tragedy of the displacements, questions connected with responsibility, moral legitimization, and simple human decency in civil Polish-German relations continue to arouse vivid emotions. In opinion polls, and also in the interviews I have carried out, the problem of Polish-German relations at the time of the displacements is treated as taboo: avoided or spoken of in terms of the friendly, conflict-free realization of administrative management (Borodziej and Hajnicz 1998). For years, the trauma of war and displacements blocked the building of symbolic bonds between the former and present residents. The anti-German ideology of the communist Polish state was consolidated by unjustified, yet still very real, fears of the return of German estates and lands (Sakson 2003). It was hard for the Polish arrivals to feel safe in their new home, which is why the Piast myth was so strong. Today, as the old myths have lost their power, legitimization takes place through identity narratives, among which the wine discourse, thanks to its "naturalness," plays a special role.

The ideology of communist Poland stated that the Recovered Lands were originally Polish, invoking the times of the old Piast dynasty (the first historical dynasty to rule the Polish state). Moving Poland's western border was therefore interpreted as an act of historical justice, with the Poles settling on the former German territories treated as pioneers returning the correct national identity to these lands (Dmitrów 1998). After the fall of the communist system, this kind of legitimization ceased to fulfill the sentiment of belonging. The reactivation of winemaking is therefore a way of solving the paradox of the German-Polishness of these lands. The vineyard, seen as a means of signaling belonging to a place, is supranational in character. The Lubuskie winemakers can refer to the "naturalness" of this tradition, connected to the climatic and soil conditions of the region. The "natural" tradition is found in the earth, as it were, and not in the inhabitants. So the Polish winemakers are taking up a challenge bestowed upon them by nature, not by the generations of the old community.

Focusing on wine quality itself is reflecting the supranational, "natural" character of wine. According to many winemakers, while tradition might be an additional factor motivating or increasing the attractiveness of local wine, it is absolutely not its legitimization. For these winemakers, wine has value in and of itself, to which all others are subordinate. This is why producers sometimes prefer new, more resistant grape varieties to the old ones, and why they strongly prefer modern methods of cultivating vines, considering records from prewar chronicles as nothing more than a curiosity. Only some risk allowing old vines into their vineyards, while the majority find that sentiment must come second to pragmatic concerns over the health of their remaining plants. They maintain that wine is more important than tradition, and that the capriciousness and unpredictability of these varieties require them to look for newer, easier grafts. One female vineyard owner commented when asked about historical varieties: "I'm a tiny bit skeptical, because it's like with tastes from childhood, we remember the taste of...bread with sugar well, but if we ate it now, it would turn out that it's not that good" (KiNS-VI2010). Despite modern skepticism about traditional farming and production, winemakers have similar attitudes toward historic populations—friendly and full of interest. They know a lot about local history, historic architecture, and people. All of them are familiar with the typical varieties of the region cultivated before the war (Traminer, Sylvaner, Pinot Noir). Some of them attempt to seek out and identify old vines.

Wine, perceived as a natural resource and a challenge put out by soil and climate, stands above national conflicts and permits difficult historical subjects to be tackled relatively painlessly. Wine is not Polish nor German—it is not any nation's property—so it opens a common space of communication. Prewar and contemporary winemakers can share their wine experiences, knowledge, motives and aims, emotions, even some physical artifacts (like tools, buildings, or plants). Being between two national tracks of history is no longer a threat to the existing political order and sense of security. In contemporary images of the region, historical elements are all the more frequent and more direct. Nineteenth-century figures, places, and events are becoming an important issue for the local press, activists, or artists, and are also employed as a feature of marketing, for creating the image of clubs or restaurants. This is a new phenomenon, and winemakers are one of the forerunners of this nostalgic trend.

Perceiving wine as a natural resource permits producers to also cross the boundaries made by the changing political systems. Winemakers stress that the cultivation of vines did not end with the displacement of the German population. In particular, the statements of people involved in interregional disputes abound with the topic of the continuity of this tradition. The vineyards that fell into the hands of Poles were treasures that needed developing. Wine professionals coming from the prewar eastern borderlands of Poland took up the interrupted work on the Lubuskie wine, with publications made and new winemakers educated at the Fruit Farming and Winemaking Technical School (in the 1990s, many of the winemakers, by then elderly, established the first local winemaking association). Despite these activities, the vineyards ultimately collapsed in the late seventies. There were many reasons for this: from unfavorable climatic conditions, to lack of experience and competence of the immigrant population, to political and economic factors (the abolition of private property, nationalization of land). A remnant of the old tradition was the Lubuskie Wine Manufacturing Company, as well as the annual riotously celebrated and widely popular Grape Harvest Festival. Today's vineyards are therefore deriving directly neither from postwar tradition nor a material continuation of the German vineyards. However, many threads of varying thickness connect these three traditions. While the transition connected with the war and displacements created a fissure in the social fabric, culture, and tradition, a comparative material continuity was preserved. The vineyards, vine bushes, architecture, and machines remained virtually untouched, and at least some of them remained in use. Meanwhile, between contemporary winemaking and postwar attempts to maintain the region's wine status stands a generational bond. The knowledge, experiences, and memories of the "pioneers" of the 1940s and 1950s today take on fresh meaning as a legitimization on a nation-wide scale of the status of the winemaking region.

CONTINUITY: WINE MEMORIES MATERIALIZED

We are witnesses to changes in the social image of the past. At the same time, several ways of perceiving history are in operation. Each of them cultivates different social bonds and places a different community in the center. The past takes on meanings in them, becoming a cohesive narrative based on contemporary social structures and forms of consciousness (Halbwachs 1992). In this way, it constitutes an element forming and strengthening the identity of the group and the sense of belonging to it. Memory, the subject and object of national community, is losing its monopoly in the Lubuskie region. The local wine cannot be national property because this would mean taking someone else's property. Worse still, the central myth of such national wine memory would have to be the moment of the exile of the former winemakers and the plunder of their property. Regardless of the historical rights, and the political and moral judgment of this event, this narrative would weaken the status of contemporary winemaking.

Family memory, which includes household wine production, also does not fulfill the function of authorizing contemporary winemaking. Unlike Slovakia, for example, where family traditions constitute a strong root of wine (see Buzalka this volume), the nature of the relationship between contemporary wine and domestic fruit wine is weak or even hostile. Fruit wines have very low social status in Poland; winemakers contrast these types of practice on the amateur-professional or primitive-vintage axis. Furthermore, family stories comprise collected memory more than collective memory (Olick 1999). These two approaches identified by Olick allow us to identify the perspective whose subject is community. Family memory is autobiographical memory (Halbwachs 1992; Olick 1999), and the relationship with remembered events has the character of experience. However, these collected family and individual histories, containing direct motivations for winemaking, do not constitute collective memory, are not owned by the larger community. The reason for this is that they lack the elements needed to comply to the contemporary idea of wine: vintage, uniqueness, connection to the region, *terroir,* historical continuity (see Farmer this volume). However, each of these elements is contained by local history. This is collective memory, although the group that is its repository and object is not continuous. This type of collective memory, thanks to its material representations in social landscape, can be taken up and continued by the community that replaced the former residents. In this way, the Polish winemakers, both the postwar ones and those of today, can feel a bond with the old German winemakers and view themselves as carrying on their work. Although the topic of continuation of prewar traditions is often played down by small wine producers (collected memories), it takes center stage in the stories of larger, more organized entities: the representatives of associations, larger, more institutionalized producers, and people involved in local politics. In their accounts, the issue of historical legitimization plays a greater role.

The material culture of winemaking was always important in the identity discourse of the region, especially evidence of the "wine industry" in the architectural fabric of the town. Vine leaves and bunches of grapes are practically a ubiquitous decorative component. They can be found on the façades of buildings, on twisted elements of gates and fences, on stained-glass windows, paintings, tableware, municipal and private documents, and on small architecture—benches, lampposts, hydrants, or even memorials. These details of prewar heritage largely survived the communist period and the eradication, of varying degrees of intensity, of everything German. The motifs of vines and the wine identity of the town were accepted and positively valorized by the new settlers. The postwar tearing down of signs, painting over German notices, changes of German place names to Polish ones, and erasing other clear traces of German presence did not affect the signs of viniculture. They were sometimes neglected, but not deliberately destroyed. Furthermore, acceptance of this component of the space was shown by cultivation of its symbols and placing them on new buildings. This phenomenon continues today. The wine grape is a generally accepted decorative element, a kind of symbol of Zielona Góra, the capital of the wine region. We can find it both in official documents and in private buildings and commercial objects. This part of the material culture therefore assures the continuity of the winemaking tradition. The depictions of leaves and grapes filling the public space comprise figures of memory (Assmann and Czaplicka 1995). They are a medium for cultural ideas and to a great degree constitute the historical identity of the place as it functions in the consciousness of its inhabitants. This objectified collective memory, although widespread and accessible, is not a subject of interest on a day-to-day level. Only in moments of reflection, when there is a need for collective self-identity for political or economic goals (e.g., creation of a tourist image for the city or region) do they become important. Thanks to these islands of time, it is possible to suspend time and refer to another temporality (Assmann and

Czaplicka 1995, 129). This other rhythm is the natural cycle of vegetation of vines, combined with the continuity of the efforts of generations of winemakers. The decorative vine motifs, architecture connected to winemaking and old vines, are visible, material elements of a space characterized by continuity and comprising a cultural basis for the contemporary winemakers, irrespective of their level of traditionalism.

POWER AND POLITICS: WINE HARVESTING
WITH AND WITHOUT WINE

An objectified culture, fulfilling mnemonic functions, contains alongside it material products, rites, and customs (Halbwachs 1992). The annual grape harvest festival in Lubuskie has taken place regularly since the mid-nineteenth century and was adopted immediately by the postwar residents of the region. Traditionally, this was a typical harvest festival during which there was rejoicing at the successful harvest, celebration of the winemaking tradition, and consolidation of the community with the yield in the background. In the postwar period, when wine production took on the form of nationalized farms managed by the Lubuskie Wine Manufacturing Company, the traditional formula of this festival lost its raison d'être. Some of the elements of the ritual survived, but its participants and the meaning of the individual acts of the drama changed. Instead of private vineyard owners, the participants in the ceremony were now local high-ranking Party officials or the "grape harvest committee," alongside representatives of selected institutions, dancing groups, and theaters. The local wine became scarce with the collapse of winemaking traditions.

The postwar grape harvest festival was a celebration of the "Recovered Territories," the Polishness of the city and region, while wine, not necessarily the local variety, was an additional attraction and catalyst for popular entertainment. During this festival, an intensifying of the narrative legitimizing the relationship between the new inhabitants and the city took place. In the local press, during shows and other mass events, the question of tradition, Polish history, and the process of domestication of space itself was especially visible. The grape harvest, also known as the Zielona Góra Days, was at the same time a cyclical confirmation of the legitimacy of the new, post-migratory society. The apotheosis of Polishness and Polish traditions was connected with the continuation of the topic of winemaking, which was, after all, the main motif of the whole festival. The idea of the natural, "primeval," native Polishness of these territories repeated, so to speak, the topic of the naturalness and localness of wine production. These stories—that of wine and that of the nation—were consolidated mutually. The grape harvest, then, was a cyclical public ritual during which the myth legitimizing the community, its origin myth, was played out. Despite the light and frothy and decidedly secular nature of the event, free of any grandeur and maintained in the tone of a carnival, it had the character of a ritual. The categories used for describing the event made reference to the mythical beginnings of the community. The language of the press for the occasion was stylized Old Polish, using terms such as "the townsmen and townswomen" and "noble beverage." The aesthetics of the decorations and stage for the event also showed evidence of a "nostalgia for origins" (Eliade 1960).

Simultaneously, the festival was accompanied by the socialist idea of modernity, technological and social progress, and moral renewal based on the values of the communist order. This mythical-utopian narrative left no room for history, especially the most recent variety. Eliade's "terror of history" (1971) was here the terror of the German history. The escape from linearity that was, according to Eliade, characteristic of the ancient man, allows one freedom from the suffering associated with transience. The community that came about as a result of the great postwar displacements tried to liberate itself from the pluralistic vision of the place, which was unacceptable for psychological and political reasons. Winemaking tradition was, therefore, an element of the escape to myth and utopia. From the point of view of today's winemakers, the socialist grape harvest festival, on one hand, ensured the continuity of the region's wine status, but, on the other, it had lost this status. The continuity concerned the image of the place, which was known as a wine city and region both by its inhabitants and by guests, even despite the lack of local wine in the 1970s and '80s. However, the break in this tradition came with the departure of the "harvest festival" idea of the grape harvest and with the event's lack of roots in local agriculture. For years, the "grape harvest" took place without vineyards, grapes, or winemakers.

Following the end of the old order in 1989, the situation gradually started to change. First, the political-ideological layer began to crumble, that is, the narrative concerning the reacquisition of the native Polish space. The communist ideology in many countries of the Eastern Bloc had long lost its power, and the fall of further communist governments sealed its fate. In the case of the Polish Recovered Territories, this meant an end to anti-German discourse, which had in any case long before lost its currency as a result of the increasingly widespread political, economic, touristic, and personal contacts between Polish and Germans. The cyclical grape harvest festivities continued to invoke medieval traditions, but the myth played out by them lost its power. In the conditions of a fledgling market economy, economic functions grew in importance, and the festival turned into a huge fair lacking any regional character. With time, greater significance was assumed by carnivalesque sideshows, concerts by pop stars, fireworks, and shows. Today, these are still important elements of the festival, lasting several days.

The growing popularity of wine production in the first decade of the twenty-first century has led to increasingly vociferous calls for its greater participation in the "grape harvest." Grouped in new associations, the Lubuskie winemakers have become visible participants in the debate over the festival's format. Increasing numbers of advocates of the winemakers' work have been expecting a change of the mass event toward a celebration of the unique character of the region. Alongside the existing deciding entities, such as local authorities, businesses with a local or wider focus, and the region's inhabitants and tourists, an important subject has appeared whose interests and values are taken into account in the debate over community identity and social space. However, this led to local winemakers making an appearance at the "grape harvest" a few years ago without their wines. Because of legal and procedural factors, they did not offer their wine for regular sale. Their role in the whole event was marginal, and in fact they were practically unnoticeable. The last decade has comprised a succession of discussions, conflicts, and agreements made and relinquished one after another between the winemakers and the municipal authorities responsible for the Grape Harvest Festival. The direct object of the disputes is the participation of local wine in the city's wine market. The fundamental issue, however, goes considerably deeper, concerning the meaning of the new-old wine tradition in the official image, economy, and cultural policy of the city. This is, therefore, a question of redefining the collective identity, the rights and responsibilities resulting from living in a culturally defined space, perception of one's own history, and that of the place. It is important to consider the relation between the cultural heritage of the former inhabitants and the architecture left by them: their cemeteries, churches, memorials, parks, and industrial heritage. After the fall of communism, the public space was bereaved of its ideological symbols: names of streets and public offices were changed, the symbols of subordination to the Soviet Union were removed and replaced by symbols of independence (the eagle on the Polish emblem regained its prewar crown), and national heroes replaced Lenin, Felix Dzierzhynsky, and Soviet soldiers on monuments. National emancipation bloomed. Nowadays, postnational identity (Hedetoft 2002) has become a factor and is supported by the ideas of the European Union, globalization, and new regionalisms; it has introduced a new dynamic to identity politics (Deflem and Pampel 1996). The contemporary

Lubuskie winemakers are, whether intentionally or not, representatives of a new understanding of the culture of the place.

The contestation of the existing interpretation of community is an attempt to disturb the axiological center connected with the subjects in power (Shils 1961). Important, the people involved in contemporary Lubuskie wine production do not want to function on the cultural margins, but are instead trying to disturb the structure of the center. For the last few years, they have demanded an ever greater part in the Grape Harvest Festival, a better site for the "wine town," and treatment as distinguished subjects of the event, and not one of the minor attractions. In the last two years, however, a trend is developing toward withdrawing from participation in the city festival. The irreparable contradictions between the event and the format of the wine harvest have become increasingly evident. The lack of general wine culture and mass demand for regional wine, the considerable contradiction between the urban space—bureaucratized, commercialized, and institutionally managed—and the vineyard—private, individualized, and dependent of the whims of nature—undermines the sense of the grape harvest in the city. The winemakers are therefore concentrating on enotourism and inviting guests to their vineyards, offering them wine there. The result of several years of disputes and compromises is a clear change in the structure of power. The status of the festival has become a value for which the organizers of the festival must compete with the winemakers. "Grape harvest at the vineyard" has been placed against the mass urban party.

CONCLUSION

The symbolism of wine is used in the cultural and identity policy of the Lubuskie region, which is a marginalized area in comparison to the rest of the country. With a lack of cultural distinctiveness for historical reasons, and because of the fact that it is economically and politically weak, it is given an opportunity to distinguish itself through wine and the enotourism connected with it. It is very well placed in the interregional rivalry of Polish wines. While its vineyards are dispersed, and suffer from low levels of industrialization, organization and investment, this wine constitutes a "cultural token" of exceptional value, marked by its historic status and record of continuous production. Its narrative emphasizes naturalness and originality (Demossier 2011). As a result, wine is becoming a medium that permits appreciation of the region and the formulation of higher, more refined cultural aspirations.

The emancipation of the community takes place on the basis of the relationship of the individual winemaker with his or her vineyard. Wine production is seen as a unique, distinguished activity, contributing to a higher level of existential quality of life for the producer. A winemaking society differs from an ordinary agricultural society because the work on the vineyard itself and its results raise social status. "You know, I explain it this way: some people, as you know, escape to the countryside, don't they? People move to the country, buy land and...and what now?...They won't plant potatoes, right? Corn neither, nothing to boast about. They won't say: this year I had these great cobs. It's [wine,] kind of a bit snobbish" (KaZG-VI2009). The grapevine is a plant that has a unique, almost totemic nature—it becomes part of the social system and an element of social relations. "It's like this, it's difficult to explain...You certainly won't find this kind of relationship with potatoes" (BaSt-VI2010). This relationship has an effect on the psychological and social nature of the winemaker. An analogous process takes place at the community level. Winemaking traditions raise the status of the community and of the region. In the region I have presented, wine advantages are still not fully exploited as a result of the lack of consensus between the various actors in the local power structures, yet in the more established or institutionalized areas wine is an obvious tool for collective cultural advancement.

The Lubuskie winemakers are in many respects the vanguard for cultural changes. They are aware of their special role in contemporary economic processes and see themselves as a showpiece of the region, even though it took time for the local authorities to comprehend their significance for the image. Although the group is small in numbers and lacking political power, the context in which they operate makes them a representative of locally important ideas. Furthermore, one of the winemakers' proposals is education of the society in matters of the taste and culture of wine. Winemaking for them is a kind of mission, whose aim is not only a new style of consumption, but also a new manner of participating in social reality.

NOTE

1. I wish to thank Grażyna Kubica-Heller for her constructive and significant feedback on my writing.

CHAPTER SEVEN

El Sabor de Galicia: Wine as Performance in Galicia, Spain

CHRISTINA M. CEISEL

INTRODUCTION: ENTERING EL PAZO DE GALEGOS[1]

As I left Santiago de Compostela, I followed the autopista (AP)-53 through the countryside toward Ourense. I was on my way to meet farmers of *la pataca de Galicia* (the Galician potato), and planned to visit vineyards along the way as part of my larger research project on Gallegan foodways and culinary tourism. My maps pointed to a promising prospect; however, the disjuncture between the Spanish of the map and the Galician of the road signs made navigation somewhat more complicated. A humble sign guided me through twisting roads lined by houses with small gardens and family vineyards intended for personal consumption or sale to larger bodegas and local cooperatives. As I arrive at Pazo Galegos—the edifice itself an imposing manor, which I am later informed had belonged to the man who discovered the corpse of Santiago de Compostela, the patron saint of the region—the young proprietor, Pablo García Cebeiro, greets me and takes me on a tour of the property. Close to the house, recently converted to an inn, stands a strong, twisted vine. With pride, Pablo explains that this vine can be traced back to the Roman times.

In the cellars, an ancient, still functional, wine press sitting awkwardly atop a stone square is a demonstration of masonry, tradition, and heritage. The ancient wine press ties the land and vineyard to Galicia's history and predates the formation of the nation-state of Spain. Upon asking, I am assured that it is still functional—a few years ago, they pressed some grapes in it for a demonstration.

This vignette foregrounds many of the tensions between heritage and modernization that characterize much of contemporary food culture and commodity culture in general. Globalization has led to a reification of local, regional, and national symbols. Yet, while these symbols are reinforced, they also are sold on the global market as valuable commodities. States and individuals have commodified authenticity and heritage as entry points into global markets (Chan 2008). As such, there are opportunities for direct investment from supranational bodies such as the European Union (EU), as well as protection schemes from organizations such as the EU and UNESCO. The contemporary moment, marked by shifts in capitalism termed *neoliberalism* (Harvey 2005; Massey 2007), is also characterized by the increasing commodification of identification markers—on ethnic, racial, national, and individual levels (Hall 1996; Halter 2002; Slater 1997). As these signifiers circulate, they carry symbolic meanings and expectations. Across the globe, connected by transnational flows of commerce and people, individual citizens and governments are advancing identities performed through foodways as a means of seeking representation in the global marketplace. Galicia provides a microcosm through which we may view these processes, and the cultural practices of vinification—the social and political efforts surrounding the production and circulation of wine—provide avenues for consideration of larger social questions regarding our relationship to the land, labor, and nostalgic memory.

El Pazo de Galegos uses these representations of authenticity and cultural heritage in its applications for financial aid from both the Xunta de Galicia— the autonomous state of Galicia—and the European Union. The label depicting the Roman wine press for the 2007 Albariño extends the emphasis on Galician tradition and heritage. Throughout their advertising, marketing, and production, Galician vintners, viniculturists, and tourism officials draw on a local Galician identity to construct their difference from Spain as a nation-state. As transnational commodities with localized origins, wines—particularly those from a *denominación de origen* (D.O.) region—perform a nostalgic identity for consumption on the local level and for export to markets abroad.[2] Examination of the complexity of this phenomena reveals tensions of late consumer capitalism, particularly as it engages with questions of authenticity, nationalism, and heritage.

GALICIA: A NATION WITHIN A STATE

Galicia makes up the northwest region of Spain, due north of Portugal. After the democratization of Spain in 1978 (when the constitution was approved), a decentralization process began (Encarnación 2008). This process, as described in the constitution, recognized Spain "as an indivisible state comprised of several 'nationalities' and cultures" (3). After Catalonia and Pais Vasco, Galicia was the third autonomous community granted in the new democracy, and is included in political discussions as constituting a nationality within the Spanish national territory (103).[3] Although the region is associated with strongly conservative politics (as represented by the Partido Popular [PP]), the past thirty years have seen a dramatic growth in the Bloque Nacionalista Galego (BNG), a populist coalition of various leftist political families, and nationalist sentiment in general—partially attributable to the 2002 *Prestige* oil tanker disaster (Magone 2004; Núñez 1997). Twenty million gallons of oil coated over 400 kilometers of Galician coastline, halting the fishing industry, one of the main economies in the region, for six months. Galician citizens mobilized and demonstrated before receiving assistance from Spain or the European Union. The environmental group Nunca Maís formed in the wake of the disaster continues to mobilize around environmental issues in Galicia (Font 2003; Young 2002).

Galician nationalism, on the right and the left, manifests itself as a resistance to the Castilian[4] influence of Spain, as well as a tradition of small family farms and viticulture that comprises the region's Albariño and Ribeiro production. The people I encountered in my research emphasized the connections between the wine and the *terroir* of Galicia. Broadly speaking, *terroir* refers to the particular qualities the land provides to the grapes grown on it. As Ulin (this volume) describes, *terroir*'s definition extends to contain a cultural meaning bestowing an elevated Bourdieuian symbolic capital to grapes grown in lands culturally recognized for their soil and microclimate, and legislatively designated apart. These grapes—such as those grown in *denominación de origen* (D.O.) regions like the Rias Baixas—are worth more money. Linkage to the land generates a particular value, which is malleable as narratives are developed.[5] Demossier (this volume) further argues, "the *terroir* story fossilizes social relations, work and landownership." As Farmer (this volume) notes, tradition is a central component undergirding the appellation system. To these insights, I add that within today's transnational marketplace, wines—particularly those from a D.O. region—perform a particular nostalgia, providing a voyeuristic journey either to a primordial past (via the ancient processes of vinification as preserved in legislation) or through familiarization with *terroir* from travels around the globe.

PERFORMANCE, AUTHENTICITY, AND HERITAGE, NOSTALGIA

I approach these questions through a performative lens. As a theoretical and methodological approach, *performance* refers to the ways meaning is enacted in everyday life. Its use in the social sciences and cultural studies aims to draw attention to the constructed nature of social life as well; rather than a distant, objective observer, the researcher is embedded in the texts and social fabric being studied. As Norman Denzin writes, "We cannot study experience directly—we study it through its performative representations" (2003, 112). In theorizing performance as part of our understanding of culture and social interaction, ethnography creates a scholarly text intersubjective in voice. Navigating between the personal and political, it links stories to larger structural formations that inform our understanding of the past and possibilities for the future (Denzin 2003; Ellis and Bochner 2005; Holman Jones 2005).

As a response to the perceived threats of globalization, citizens are reasserting regionalist and nationalist identities. Appadurai notes that this is the result of the "disjunctive and unstable interplay of commerce, media, national policies, and consumer fantasies," and the resultant focus on ethnicity and primordia is a global force—"slipping in between borders"—and "turning locality into a staging ground for identity" (1996, 41). This staging ground takes the form of "authentic" and "heritage" products in terms of commodity culture. Lionel Trilling (1972) theorizes that the condition of modernity has pushed "authenticity" to the forefront of our social capital—we are unsure of who people are and where they are from, and so a great value is placed on being who one claims to be and knowing where something is from. This extends to objects and cultural artifacts as we have become a consumer society—we seek refuge from the uniformity of large-scale mass production. Heritage, meanwhile, "produces something new in the present that has recourse to the past" (Kirschenblatt-Gimblett 1998, 149). Kirschenblatt-Gimblett underscores the importance of the newness—the "processes of protection, of adding value speaks in and to the present, even if it does so in terms of the past" (150). To meet the demands of transnational capital, modernization initiatives are undertaken—such as the processes encouraged by government bodies at the local, state, and supranational levels to increase production in terms of "economic development" within a neoliberal framework (Harvey 2005).

I use the term *globalized nostalgia* for the performance of authenticity and heritage that emerges from these pressures. This term refers to the socially constructed and performed concept of an essential identity that can be recovered and enacted through our legislative policy, consumption habits, and promotional efforts. Nostalgia is the overdetermined, "scripted" relationship between the present memory and the imagined past (Denzin 2006). McCarthy and Engel note that nostalgia operates as an "ethnic and nationalist myopia" (2007, 10). Nostalgia within commodity culture functions such that "the viewer need only bring the faculty to the image that will supply the memory of a loss he or she has never suffered" (Appadurai 1996, 78). Modernity supplies the condition for nostalgia, and our cultural landscapes supply the memory to fill the voids of perceived loss. Nationalism and nostalgia converge, particularly around the category of foodstuffs and viniculture, to create a sense of longing for homelands past—both of the actual, diasporic past and of the romantic imagined past. These homelands are recreated via invented traditions as "heritage" (Hobsbawm and Ranger 1993). As neoliberalism has encouraged "the commodification of everything" (Harvey 2005, 165), products such as wine enjoy the cultural capital provided by particular forms of legislation, nationalist mythology, and transnational circulation.

The motivations behind the representational regimes are varied, but visible throughout Galicia. By linking their wines to a primordial past, influenced by the wording of the European Union legislation, Galicia's vintners receive funding from both the Xunta de Galicia and the European Government—which in turn reinforces nationalism's presence. While funds from Madrid, the seat of the Spanish government, are sometimes available, they were not mentioned often. Europeanization has in many ways allowed Galicia to supersede the Spanish state as it seeks to assert itself globally. Somewhat paradoxically, this has strengthened Galician national identity within the confines of Spain. This is visible in the signifiers chosen to represent the wines and the region in advertising and at festivals.

PERFORMING THROUGH THE GRAPEVINE

I focus on the foodways of Galicia for several reasons. A country with many strong and long-standing regional identities, Spain serves as a window into the complexities of national identity recuperation, the search for authenticity, and the commodification and sale of identities and ethnicities on the global market. Galicia has a tradition of regional autonomy and a strong separatist movement. Many of its traditions—including foodstuffs and wines—are omitted from the Spanish imaginary, which privileges gazpacho, paella, and Rioja wines as signifiers of the nation. As a counterpoint, the European Union's appellation system contributes to the development and branding of Galicia's wines, encouraging local producers to modernize production processes and increase exports. Consortiums aimed at promoting the wine varieties' prominence adopt marketing strategies stressing the wines' historic ties to the *terroir* and culture of Galicia. Claims to Galicia's Celtic history abound in the literature promoting the region.

One example of this is the Paco & Lola bodega's wine named for Galicia's heroine poetess, Rosalía de Castro. Sold primarily within the region, the wine is less expensive than the bodega's flagship Paco & Lola. It is also, as described by the Carlos Carrión, a nod to the women working in the vineyards. As Carrión and his colleague Diego Garcia Santiago described de Castro's work, it was "about the living and the dead, immigrants, melancholy, and weeping."

Rosalía de Castro is an ever-present figure in Galicia. As my language instructor told me, "Every town has at least one street named after her." She was an intellectual leader of the nationalist moment and the author of the first book published in Galician after the Dark Ages. As such, she is a national hero, and in the post-Franco era, was embraced as an icon for the nation. The holiday Dia de las Letras Gallegas celebrates authors and poets of the Galician language and honors the day de Castro's *Cantares Gallegos* was published— May 17, 1863—ushering in a renaissance of Galician culture. De Castro's poems were part of a larger political struggle against Madrid. During the Carlist Wars (1873–1876), Galician nationalism grew as a reaction against Carlos V's efforts at state centralization. As Lecours (2010) writes, this resulted in the formal articulation of a regional identity, led by the intellectual elites. Through their efforts, they resurrected Galicia's Celtic history, put "into practice the 'reconstruction' of a Galician nation as part of a 'recuperation' of a popular peasant culture and folkloric traditions, above the popular culture and against the official culture of the Spanish state: the Castilian culture" (Souto 2000, 424). Then as now, efforts at homogenization are met virulently with nationalist reactions, at both the national and supranational levels.

The globalization of the Galician wine market roughly coincides with the development of Spanish democracy and late consumer capitalism. While Spain lacked the traditional Keynesian welfare state that characterized much of the West, in the post-Franco era, the Spanish state embraced the decentralization and democratization models demonstrated by its European neighbors.

As Engel points out, these processes included "major power shifts away from the central government to local levels. The focus is on democratic participation, local control, and community decision-making" (2007, 221). This model was supported by the European Union, whose methods of neoliberal governance throughout the 1980s emphasized regional governance (Jeffery 2002, 239; in Engel 2007). I put these social developments in conversation with the European Union's policy imperatives and the current economic crisis's pressures. Ultimately, the twin processes of modernization and heritage marketing result in the simultaneous localizing of the wines within Galicia's cultural and political heritage, while exporting "Galicia" to the global community.

GLOBALIZED NOSTALGIA: MARKETING
CULTURE AND AUTHENTICITY

Advertisements created and distributed by the regulatory bodies—the Denominación de Origen (D.O.)—of Galicia's wine regions encompass the nation within the culture of the vineyard and wine-drinking. Figures 7.1 and 7.2 were created and distributed by the D.O. Rias Baixas, whose primary product is Albariño, and D.O. Ribeiro, where a variety of grapes are grown (including treixadura, torrontés, and godello). In the case of a recent Ribeiro ad, the embodiment of Galicia's history within wine culture is represented literally: a wine bottle encapsulates the Cathedral of Santiago as we are told, "Try it. [It's] the flavor of Galicia." The sticker distinguishing the bottle as from the Ribeiro region is visible on the bottle (obscuring part of the iconic Cathedral of Santiago de Compostela), and the text below the image reminds us that the Ribeiro was the first area to attain the status of Denominación de Origen (in 1932).

A similar ad contains the Galician landscape at the bottom of the page, with the image of buttery yellow wine pouring into a glass filling up the otherwise blank page. Here we are told to ask for it by name: "Rias Baixas"—when we drink Albariño from the Denominación de Origen Rias Baixas we drink the best of Galicia. In both advertisements, the stamps of Xunta de Galicia, EU agricultural funding (FEADER), and Spain's Ministry of Environment, Rural, and Marine Development appear.

As Stuart Hall notes, "national identities are not things we are born with, but are formed and transformed within and in relation to representation" (1996, 612; italics in original). In these ads, as in the actual products themselves, a natural Galician heritage is presented through imagery, text, and policy. These combine to form a national identity around foodstuffs. However, rather than a primordial or essential identity, it is a construction contingent upon the twin

FIGURE 7.1: *El Sabor de Galicia* ("It's the Flavor of Galicia"). Seen at a bus stop in Santiago de Compostela and on a bus.

processes of modernization and heritage recuperation. This speaks to a global-ized nostalgia for an "authentic past"—one tied to an articulated knowledge of the production of artisanal products and their territories. Consumers experi-ence these wines as authentic through the knowledge that their origins are veri-fiable (such is the rationale for the D.O. scheme) and also from the knowledge of the historical and personal story behind the production or genealogy of the

FIGURE 7.2: *Pídelo por su nombre* ("Ask for it by name."). Ad in an activity guidebook provided by a hotel. C.R.D.O. Rias Baixas

wine—its story, so to say. This knowledge functions as cultural capital, driving the touristic interest in wine country.[6]

Thus, cultural capital is associated with personal knowledge of the locality of the products we consume. In these cases, a product is commodified for global export, at the same time that local heritage is drawn on for political, economic, and cultural purposes. The labeling and naming practices of the region bypass Spain in favor of a completely Gallego identity. The consumer's knowledge of Galicia prior to the purchase may or may not matter to either the producer or consumer—the legislative incentives, regional/national character, and heritage labeling provide enough incentive; it is possible that the education might occur later. Carrión of Paco & Lola was quite explicit when asked about the relationship between the nomenclature of his bottles and global marketing strategy—"we want people to remember the image, not Spain. No one knows Spain." Echoing that sentiment and underscoring the importance of Galicia as a nation within the imagination of the producers and consumers, Manuel Paz of the bodega Valdamor emphatically dismisses the idea that Albariño is known as a Spanish wine, declaring: "Gallego! We are recognized as the star."

Both historically and in its contemporary iteration, politics motivate the interest in linking food, place, and taste. Arguably, the legislation of *terroir* was initially a labor issue—the agrarian workers in the Champagne region did not want to be marketed out of a job, as consumers recognized the labels over the region. Today, we have gone back to the land for the many reasons *terroir* was initially codified: the preservation (or reinstitution) of small agriculture, an interest in craftsmanship. It is the global sense of nostalgia that is (ironically) new. The spatial relationships constructed as a result of the forces of global capitalism and globalized nostalgic identity bear further investigation, because they produce new affiliations even as they take "recourse to the past."

PERFORMING TRADITION: THE FIESTA DE ALBARIÑO

August 2, 2010

The sixty-eighth Festival of Albariño is in full swing. On the outskirts of the festival, ladies sell traditional Galician desserts and lottery tickets. Carnival rides ring the perimeter of the main plaza. A large tent with people hawking traditional Galician crafts sits off to the side, while by the parked cars women and men sit on blankets offering costume jewelry. The main thoroughfare is converted into the thoroughfare of the festival with tents; as you exit you go past the large cathedral and through beautiful parks. Throughout the festival, you see groups of young and old people in matching t-shirts (groups called *penas*), perhaps being overserved. Souvenir tasting glasses are sold; wines by the bottle and glass are available.

The annual festival, the oldest wine party in Galicia and the second oldest in Spain, attracts over one hundred fifty thousand people. While other food festivals in Galicia draw mostly local, working-class attendants, this is an international festival that attracts a very upper-middle-class audience and sells out hotels in the city and throughout the neighboring towns. Cambados is the heart of the wine region, and a lot of energy, organization, and money go into the festival. The festival lasts an entire week rather than just a weekend. There are conference talks, tasting seminars, painting classes, and photography exhibitions. The festival has expanded beyond wine to encompass a range of cultural interests.

The Festival de Albariño, and Albariño wine, are explicitly associated with the *terroir* of the Rias Baixas. Albariño is a distinctly Galician grape. It produces a white wine, an "aromatic and zesty wine with characteristics varying from subzone to subzone—more 'melony' qualities from Val do Salnés, peachier and softer notes from O Rosal and earthier styles from Condado do Tea" (http://www.riasbaixaswines.com/about/what_albarino.php).[7] Within Spain, Albariño (and white wine in general) are primarily consumed within Galicia—outside of the region, it is more popular as an export product. Within Galicia are five subzones, each with distinct characteristics that have gained traction in the international market, and recent modernization efforts have been adopted with an eye toward expanding export potential.

Thus, this is an important event for wine producers. While there are other wine festivals, they are smaller and more local in character. The Festa do Albariño (the festival's Galician name) is the premier local festival for gathering a cosmopolitan audience.

The Albariño festival goes to great lengths to distinguish itself as Galician, in contrast to Spanish. There is no mention of the Spanish state. Instead, we are greeted by Gallego music and served a menu that eschews iconic Spanish dishes such as paella, tortilla Española, and gazpacho, in favor of empanada, mussels, and navajas. Similarly, the wine labeling presents iconic images of Galicia and explicitly links itself to a Galician past. This often invokes a Celtic history, which itself was recuperated as a political project from its romantic period in the nineteenth century (Souto 2000).

As Kirschenblatt-Gimblett reminds us, neoliberal formations have enabled and required local sites to use heritage as a way of making space profitable. Localities are able to reinvent themselves under the auspices of "preservation," transforming "a location into a destination, produc[ing] 'hereness'" (Kirschenblatt-Gimblett 1998, 153). At the Albariño festival, this happens at three levels.

First, the festival provides a venue for the stories citizens "tell themselves about themselves" (Geertz 1973). The stories are about the locality, its history, and traditions, providing a sense of connection to the space, regardless of the actuality of the "thrown togetherness of place" (Massey 2005). Festivals' stories sort through the various narratives and provide a streamlined narrative for both visitors and local citizens—albeit based on a fixed, static identity.

The second level exists for those who travel to see it in its locality—Spaniards, other Gallegos, and summer vacationers. In these cases, we have examples of "community-based festivals' selected dishes thought to be familiar to the crowds but also fitting of a particular public identity, one that was usually based on an imagined past" (Long 2004, 43). In this case, these dishes might disappoint a traveler not familiar with Galicia and its customs, or someone expecting more exotic fare. The foods of Galicia rely on the quality of the ingredients and not their preparation—freshness and subtle seasoning (with the exception of the healthy use of olive oil and salt) are the dictums cooks and chefs work with. This simplicity might be mystifying, or even boring, after a long trip. However, within the context of the festival, and, working within the logic of heritage marketing and globalized nostalgic consumption, it is the very traditional and "simple" nature of the dishes—and their unerring "authenticity"—that marks them as desirable for display and sale as festival items.

The third level is international—expanding the knowledge and cultural capital beyond the local or national. Heritage not only transforms the local into a destination in the sense of "here," but it also "produces the local for export" (Kirschenblatt-Gimblett 1998, 155). These efforts are encouraged by government tourism agencies, funded by European Union initiatives, and explicitly linked to notions of historical difference and a primordial authenticity.

Thus, in producing and reenacting an authentic Galician identity, these festivals create and circulate an imagined past that connects them to contemporary consumption habits—such as the focus on consumption as the means of cultural expression, and commercial culture as an indicator of modernity (Miller 2007). Constantly recirculated and exported, in these instances *terroir* is capitalized upon. We also see a commitment to Galicia and the land as a means of remembering a community's history and developing a future. It is this duality—our interest as consumers in supranational high-end food marketing and our increasing awareness of the ethics of consumption (Davidson 2007)—that is reconfiguring our relationship to the rural. As sociologist Isamu Ito (2011) noted, this sort of urban interest in the rural has become a global phenomenon, often promoted as an idealized haven from the frenzied pace of the city.

PACKAGING GALICIA: OLD WINE IN NEW BOTTLES

To the rest of Spain, Galicia has remained somewhat remote. Until about ten years ago, the roads between Madrid and Santiago de Compostela were "so bad that what is now a six-hour drive would take about twelve hours." This isolation led many Spaniards to think of Gallegos as old-fashioned, rural, and backward (Jose Coton, interview, August 2010). As such, Galicia is omitted from the Spanish imaginary, instead signified by the gazpacho, flamenco guitar, and dancing of Andalucía or the modernist architecture of Barcelona.

In the absence of such recognizable landmarks and cultural icons, Galicia has begun to rely upon its wine culture, particularly Albariño, as a means of expanding its national identity and economy as a response to its exclusion from Spain's larger economic plans. As mentioned earlier, Europeanization has in many ways allowed Galicia's government to bypass Madrid and petition Brussels directly for funding (Nielsen and Salk 1998, personal interviews). Furthermore, local citizens return to ancient identities, such as their Celtic past, for legislative protection, marketing, and tourism. Their motivations and outcomes are felt in very individual ways, yet configurations of global capitalism continuously shape these experiences.

The spatial relationships that globalized nostalgia constructs bears further investigation. While there are many productive avenues for political intervention, there are likely many potential pitfalls for the revival of potentially volatile nativisms. To the latter point, I offer the EU legislation regarding the appellation system, which produces narratives that obscure the historically transnational nature of food. (The potato is from "the new world," which was old to someone else).

To the former point, Robert Davidson develops *terroir* in conjunction with our increasing interest in "space" and "place" and argues that the appellation system creates a "new relationship to the rural that, while directly connected to supranational practices of contemporary high-end food marketing, also points to an awareness of new discourses regarding the civics and ethics of consumption" (2007, 40). In this instance, the *tourismos* (tourism offices), and their presentation of the vineyards as areas of historical and touristic importance, provide a window into the marketing of space as place. In light of the European Union's appellation policies and the pressures of Europeanization on the agricultural sector—and just as much enabled through EU and regional investment—Galicia showcases its territory as the land of cheese, honey, and wine. The maps and booklets provided at the *tourismos* offer histories of the products, local sources, and road maps to stores, vineyards, and restaurants. Entering a tourism office in Santiago de Compostela at once situates and dislodges our sense of space. The vast collection of books of maps, pamphlets with fold-out maps, county maps, and maps of the city at once tell me where I am, but provide endless documentation of where I may go, where the nation has been. The numerous maps focus on the gastronomy of the region, the most prominent of which feature *rutas de quesos y vinos* (routes of cheese and wine). Along the highway, the Respol gas stations feature fliers and billboards that assure us we are receiving "original" products. And, taking a cue from the famed Michelin guides, Respol also provides guides with hotel and restaurant information, as well as a supplemental wine guide.

ALONG THE ROUTE: RELATIONSHIPS BETWEEN THE BODEGAS, THE STATE, AND THE EUROPEAN UNION

It is here that the performance of Galician soil becomes tangible. Despite the general belief that Spain's ascension to the European Union shortchanged its farmers, the EU provides money through the European Agricultural Fund for Rural Development (FEADER in Spanish). The imperatives behind these include a modernization of technologies, an increase in production, and a diversification of rural sectors. The modernization and increase of production implied therein are interesting given the simultaneous restrictions on the EU's labeling laws, but it offers a means to reiterate the importance of the land.

A narrow vertical sign announces the presence of the Bodega Gerardo Mendez, which is presented as a "bodega Antigua" from 1973. Asked about the description, Encarna laughs and explains that the vines are ancient, even if her family isn't. The bodega is family run—in addition to the five-person family, it employs two people, and contracts more during harvest. Harvest begins September 15, but because of the weather in 2011 it might be sooner. In addition to the grapes on the property, the bodega rented three parcels and has a group of viticulturists it works with. The bodega also selects grapes from other properties while the fruit is still on the vine. Both the Xunta and the EU have given Gerardo Mendez money to upgrade its equipment. When asked about promotional efforts, such as advertising, Encarna laughs and tells me "you're looking at it! We are very small!" This is a common experience in the bodegas—very few staff and little attention paid to marketing and promotion. Those efforts fall to the D.O. Rias Baixas.

The Albariño grape is an important tie between the region and Europe. Popular lore traces the grape's ancestry to that of Riesling. It is said that the monks of Cluny brought the grape to Spain as they made their pilgrimage to Santiago de Compostela. This narrative ties Galicia to the larger European project. Similarly, ascension to the European Union has also allowed Galicia the ability to bypass Madrid and access funding from the EU as it grows its export industries.

For example, Paco & Lola exports more wine to the United States alone than is consumed in the country (Carlos Carrión, interview, July 2, 2011). The cooperative opened in 2005 partially with funds from the European Union and the Xunta de Galicia (the autonomous government of Galicia). The cooperative possessed no vineyards and thus vinified the Albariño grapes that came from the small vineyards of local growers. Support from the EU also included subsidizing the purchase of new equipment and bringing sales and marketing executives from abroad to the region to learn about the product. As Encarna Gerardo Mendez of Bodegas Gerardo Mendez explained to me, these initiatives helped a lot with the expansion of the business: "We present how much of the machine we can pay for, and then they will help pay for a certain percentage, generally up to twenty. They also bring people here, or send people there from the Chamber of Commerce, to talk to each other."

The machines are designated on each property with a sign bearing the various flags and emblems of the supranational, national, and regional initiatives that contributed to their purchase. Shiny and silver, they stand in marked contrast to a studied, rustic wine country—stone walls, creeping grape vines mounted above the ground on wood frames and chickens often roosting underneath—forming a picturesque, idyllic countryside. What becomes important, Encarna noted, is that the machines macerate the grapes appropriately. "We have to maintain the form of work of the ancients without the physical work."

The European Union's interest in this sector is twofold. In part, the EU has had to respond to the discontent its citizenry has displayed at the prospect of their "Europeanization." This has taken the form of promoting "unity in diversity"—a policy of promoting the regional identities that have been reasserted. In 2002, the European Commission stated:

The aims of the EU's cultural policy are to bring out the common aspects of Europe's heritage, enhance the feeling of belonging to one and the same community, while recognizing and respecting cultural, national, and regional diversity, and helping cultures develop and become more widely known. (Commission 2002, 3)

This statement reflects a decidedly multicultural, pluralistic view, one that is a response to charges that the European Union presents a challenge to national and regional identities, or seeks to erase them in the name of pan-Europeanness.

On the other hand, these initiatives seek to provide an economic base to modernize these same regions through the development of their "heritage" products. The EU's appellation system has been key in implementing this. Achieving this status requires tying one's agricultural product to the land and to patrimony. An agricultural sector must convince the European Union's regulatory body that there is an inherent and historical tie to the land—one worth preserving for the sake of heritage.

I met Carlos Carrión, the president of Paco & Lola, on a Saturday afternoon as I visited its facility near the town of Meaño in the Salnés Valley, near Pontevedra. A young bodega, it opened in 2006 as a cooperative. Rather than owning its own vines, it relies on local growers to bring their grapes in at harvest, generally between September 15 and 30. The grapes are analyzed and sorted on site, and the growers are paid accordingly. In addition to being certified as Albariño grapes by the Consejo Regulador (Regulatory Council), the parcels are visited regularly by Paco & Lola staff to assure quality during the growing season. Four hundred thirty-four families make up the cooperative, contributing their grapes to the production of Paco & Lola wines. The bodega's publicity documents boast that their

> recent creation has allowed them to use the most recent installations of technology in the world of wine…The combination of the ultimate advances in oenology and the experience of the winegrowers allows us to create the best wine possible from the raw materials. (Press Dossier 2011)

The bodega further emphasizes its handpicked grapes, selection processes that rely on rigorous quality control, and the subsequent pressing, racking, filtering, and bottling practices, which rely on the technologies described earlier.

Its flagship bottling, Paco & Lola, was envisioned as an international wine. In my conversation with Carlos Carrión, he mentioned that the name of the company was chosen explicitly for the ease of pronunciation in any language. Even the use of the ampersand, rather than the "y" (and) to connect the names allows for an open interpretation. Meanwhile, Paco, and to a lesser extent, Lola, are explicitly Spanish names. The labeling is very modern, black-and-white polka dots, in contrast with the traditional tan labels of the estate bottles. As the press dossier describes the wine:

> A Divine Duo…Paco & Lola is the bet for a special moment, singular
> and sophisticated…This Albariño has been conceived with a global vi-
> sion and a cosmopolitan style, but at the same time authentic and close to
> the lifestyle of our consumers. People without complexes, with an open
> mind, and willing to try new experiences. (Press Dossier 2011)

While Paco & Lola presents itself as a global wine, the bodega nevertheless
goes to lengths to mark the wine and its consumers as "authentic"—they know
their lifestyle and crave new experiences. The wine's image matches the lifestyle
of the consumers and allows them to perform an authentic identity while also
performing a new Galicia—one that is contemporary and cosmopolitan while
adhering to tradition.

Upon its founding in 2005, the bodega received funding from both the
Xunta de Galicia and the European Union. The funding helped buy equipment
and provided support for the salary of an employee through the association
IGAPE (Galician Institute for Economic Development). Sixty percent of production is exported to the United States, its main importer. Maintaining the
balance between technology and tradition, it boasts a model of sustainable
production. The third largest producer in the region, it comprises 200 hectares
in the Salnés Valley and is the largest cooperative.

Wines bottled by the bodega Paco & Lola reflect a similar blend of marketing cosmopolitan optimism and localism as seen in their namesake bottling.
Lolo is a lower-end wine, featuring two dogs on the label, aimed at the youth
market and sold in supermarkets. Their "iWine" is macerated over dry ice at
low temperatures. The bottle is an obvious spin-off of the iPod—a sleek, silver
label covers the bottle completely, with a play button on the label.

The production facility for Paco & Lola is a sleek, modern facility sitting
atop a hillside among the sweeping patchwork of the green hillsides of the
Salnes Valley. I had arrived there on my first foray into the field. A large tour
bus sat parked in front, partially blocking the view. The tour group, consisting
of about forty guests from the Madrid area, had just entered a large seminar
room, with a glass wall overlooking the steel casks holding the 2011 harvest.
As the Paco & Lola staff poured wines for a tasting, a video was projected on
a screen detailing the harvesting and fermentation processes, as well as a recent
visit by the vice-president of Kendall Jackson, Paco & Lola's U.S. importer.
Walking in slightly behind the group, my colleague and fellow wine enthusiast,
Stephanie, and I were encouraged to join and were introduced to Carlos and
Diego. I explained my interest in Albariño wine and my research project, and

they offered to speak with me after the presentation and tasting with the tour group. In the interim, the cellar master, "Chema" (a nickname for Jose Maria), took us on a tour of the cellars, detailing the ways the grapes are brought into the facility during harvest and showing the equipment used to measure the sugar content in each grape—thus assessing which wine it will contribute to and how much the grower will be compensated. The bodega has an association of winegrowers that tries to ensure that the growing conditions are as ecologically sensitive as possible. Chema used the term *parece ecologia* (it is done in an ecologically sound manner, without having the proper paperwork), which was echoed at other vineyards. As is found in the United States and elsewhere, the organic or eco-friendly certification process is lengthy and at times very costly. Paco & Lola found that its oversight of the growing practices of its participating parcels and the interests of the growers (whose plots of land were in its backyards and often accompanied vegetable gardens and chicken coops) converged to encourage ecologically sound practices. During the harvest and bottling stages, the Consejador comes to analyze the wine and make sure it is Albariño. In addition to a chemical analysis, they also taste the wine for its subjective qualities.

The neighboring bodega, Valdamor, presents a much more traditional image. Hacienda-like in appearance, the bodega features ornate wrought iron gates, dark wood, and a small showcase of ancient winemaking tools. Valdamor also relies on local growers, for whom growing is "*cocina de autosustencia*" (self-sustaining cooking). For these small farmers, viniculture is a part-time job that supplements income from other work. The bodegas and viticulturists agree to contracts stipulating official prices, depending on the grade of the grape set by the Consejo Regulador. In this manner, the D.O. manages the market setting the norms for labor, production, and the subjective values of the wines carrying Denominación de Origen.

In addition to the mark, the D.O. Consejo Regulador also provides promotional support. As the D.O. has been promoting the wine and the region, they have been winning awards. During my conversation with Encarna, whose father is a member of the Consejo Regulador, she notes that the element of traceability the label provides instills confidence in the product. The maps, *rutas de vinos,* have sent more people to her family's bodega, but the translation to sales depends on the person—generally three bottles. She finds the D.O.'s public relations efforts more helpful—such as bringing in journalists and wine importers from Brazil and China.

Thinking more broadly, we see this through the idea of the vineyard and rural as a respite from the harried pace of the city, and commodity export, where the commodity has been imbued with the significance of the local and a touch of the exotic—or the ordinary (see also Swinburn, this volume). Either way, these products are explicitly territorialized, "invested in the territory of the nation, the attendant language of nationalist identification" (Nguyen 2002, 20). In the case of foodstuffs entering the global market, we see the confluence of the traditional and modern, the popular and the folk. This is often articulated through marketing efforts and legislation seeking to "protect" an area's "heritage." All too frequently, these efforts and trends codify and reify the ideas of a folk culture and heritage, rather than appreciate the "dynamic process by which culture is created as well as its relationship to constantly shifting experiences, changes in technologies, and commodification" (Kelley 1992, 1402).

These processes, as currently articulated, legitimate global structures of domination through an invocation of what Weber calls an eternal yesterday (Weber 2004). Ultimately, these representations of heritage identity within the transnational marketplace call into question tensions between hybridity and purity, modernity and tradition, and claims to primordial identities and borders. Commodities and consumption are central to understanding social and cultural arrangements under late consumer capitalism.

However, insofar as qualitative research is an activist project (Denzin and Giardina 2011, 13), we can work to connect these iterations to larger interruptions in the historical present. Some of these might include environmental and economic movements that articulate a politics of space as inclusive and civics driven—such as Nunca Maís (Never Again), the Galician environmental group that formed in the wake of the *Prestige* oil tanker disaster and now advocates across a range of environmental issues. Tying this moment's interest in authenticity, heritage, and *terroir* to larger interests in land and community—thus moving from questions of "place" as a bounded entity towards questions of community and environment—provides promising avenues for thinking our way through the circuits of capital, culture, and territory in the historical present.

NOTES

1. *El Pazo de Galegos* translates to the Palace of Galicia/Galician People.
2. I refer to products that reside on store shelves and labeling and naming practices conceived therein, as well as the advertising and promotional campaigns that often accompany these exports.
3. For this reason, I will refer to the nation of Galicia when speaking of the citizens or politically, and to the region of Galicia when speaking geographically.

4. *Castilian* (*castellano*) refers to Spanish as spoken in central Spain.

5. For example, Ulin notes the historical, rather than strictly geographical, factors that played into the Bordeaux region's reputation for excellence (1996).

6. For a comparative perspective, Walker and Manning (this volume) provide a detailed description of the development of the Georgian wine industry in relationship to EU regulations and investment from NGOs and government bodies for economic development into international trade networks.

7. http://www.riasbaixaswines.com/about/what_albarino.php (accessed January 14, 2013).

CHAPTER EIGHT

"Local, Loyal, and Constant": The Legal Construction of Wine in Bordeaux

ERICA A. FARMER

The wines of Bordeaux have a very ancient reputation, it made sense to safeguard the traditional characteristics of the culture and of vinification; from there the recourse to "usages locaux, loyaux, et constants" allows one to determine if this commune, this parcel, this grape variety, this cultural practice...conforms in terms of tradition. The delimitation of appellations is not, prior to anything else, anything more than the juridical consecration, founded on scientific bases, of an ancient state of being.[1]

The concept of *usages locaux, loyaux, et constants* (local, loyal, and constant usages) is at the heart of the *appellation d'origine contrôlée* (AOC) system for wine regulation. Serving as both a legal balancing test and an approximation of untranslated sociocultural values and je ne sais quoi, this set of linked factors serves to connect geography, notoriety, and tradition within Bordeaux wine culture in fundamental ways, while simultaneously creating an enforceable legal framework that allows for the interpretation of culturally based evidence.

The phrase defines a set of necessary but not sufficient conditions that together constitute a synergistic marker that stands as a proxy for socially constructed meanings about Bordeaux wine. In a technical way, the formulation acts as a means to simultaneously allow for the type of predictability required by the strictures of law while preserving a certain amount of space that allows for the flexibility and negotiation that sit at the heart of all social practice. As a consequence, the role of social construction and policing sits at the heart of the legal regulation of AOC, and I would argue that the strength and enforceability of the system comes in large part from the attendant ability of the AOC system to allow for variation within boundaries, which allows legal and sociocultural frameworks to align in productive ways around the regulation of traditional knowledge in the realm of Bordeaux wine.

The legislative formulation acts as a marker for a variety of factors about place, history, heritage, and the construction thereof. The first prong, *usages locaux,* creates a link to a particular, definable locality. The second, *usages loyaux,* requires recognizable links between the wine and the defined locality, recognizable not only by insiders, but neighbors and outsiders as well. Finally, *usages constants* asserts the time-honored nature of wines already defined as unique, recognizable, and locally linked. Through the combination between these elements, these components combine into a juridical test that stands in for a set of qualitative values about what differentiates an AOC wine from a particular place from that of its neighbors and others for sale in the wider market, simultaneously allowing for a degree of predictability and an intense connection with sociocultural practice within the region.

This chapter will consider the way these linkages are constructed around wine in Bordeaux through an exploration of the ways in which the "local, loyal, and constant" test simultaneously works to fix the outer edges of practice while also serving as a proxy for a group of qualitative sociocultural factors that often remain purposely vague or undefined. The next section will look to the historical roots of the AOC system and "local, loyal, and constant usages," before proceeding to consider the interplay between fixed limits and internal flexibility in the ways legal and social structures interact with AOC protections. From there I turn to a case study around the region of Sauternes to show a historical example of how the analysis and extension of *appellation* works in practice via the use of these factors. Finally, I conclude with a discussion of the concept of *typicité* in relationship to variations within and around regional wine styles. This will show one of the very real spaces in which the flexibility of the system matters, in the social construction of the cultural meanings of what it means for a wine to belong to a particular AOC, even as it highlights the fact that such questions are never quite as settled as they may seem.

CONCEPTUALIZING AOC

> In Gironde, admitting that our wines benefit from a worldwide renown, it is beyond doubt that the origin of the product is always the principal cause of its market, the consumer not having any interest in coming to Gironde to buy wine from Burgundy or from the Midi (letter 23 avril 1908, Gironde Archives 7 M 169).

Functionally, AOC protection marks wines and other foodstuffs by protecting their names from misappropriation by producers outside a delimited region of origin. Typically classed as a form of intellectual property,[2] these rights in France also link into other types of law as well, notably in the case of fraud and labor law (Gangjee 2012, 96; Visse-Causse 2007). Historically, *appellation d'origine contrôlée* as a legal system grew out of a number of preexisting social antecedents, and it is from this relationship to earlier structures that the strength of the system derives. That said, however, the idea of *appellation of origin* as a marker of regional connection preexists the existence of the AOC law. At the time of the creation of the legal regulations at the turn of the twentieth century, production syndicates and other actors had established local reputations linked to various locations in Gironde and elsewhere in France. *Appellation d'origine simple,* as opposed to *appellation d'origine contrôlée,* serves as a historical antecedent, with the earlier concept based around a stated, geographically based link used to identify products originating from particular places (Visse-Causse 2007, 5). There were no officialized standards or checklists or formal controls in place, but there was a level of recognizable usage of certain regional names and styles in certain communities that long predated the beginnings of official AOC legislation. In codifying them, AOC connected with a long accepted cultural conception of the link between products and place, particularly aligned through the idea of *terroir.*

The shift to a more controlled protection of product names came out of the phylloxera crisis of the turn of the early twentieth century. Brought unwittingly to the Old World from the United States in the late 1860s, the parasite decimated European grapevines, which had no resistance to the insect (Kehrig 1886). After the major declines suffered by the industry as a result, as production began to recover, overall quality of wine declined as all manner of fraudulent activities occurred, from adulteration to falsification of labels to misrepresentation of origins. As the new century dawned, in the words of a prominent regional wine historian, *"tout le monde fraudait"* ("everyone was committing fraud"). Additionally, because of the prestige of the region, Bordeaux wines were often the ones producers chose to impersonate—leading to cases where five or six times the number of bottles actually produced at particular *châteaux* were sold on the market under the name of the property (Gironde Archives, 7M169). Fraud statutes enacted in 1905 and 1907 were used as early means of combating such activities, but proved incomplete in their effectiveness. Championed by the producers and legislators of Bordeaux, the creation of the 1919 AOC law was seen as a way to combat the problem and to safeguard reputations under threat from unpredictability and consumer confusion. AOC protection sought to allow greater oversight and to regularize production practices while preventing imposters and inauthentic products from entering the marketplace under certain names.

At a basic level, for a regional wine to gain protection under the law, several conditions must be met. Applications must come from a group of producers, who create a document called a *cahier des charges,* which lays out the boundaries of the region and the appellation name, while also putting forth a set of specific qualities that include permitted grape varieties, sugar and alcohol content, yield, and any specialized methods of production used (Loi du 22 juillet 1927 modifie la loi du 6 mai 1919 (Protection des appellations d'origine) (July 27, 1927) (Official Journal 7762). Each of these defining factors is meant to combine into a stylistic construction of a particular wine that differentiates it from wines produced under other AOC designations.

The factors of the *cahier* delimit the technicalities of the "local, loyal, and constant" formula in a less qualitative, more testable way. Boundaries of local communities are defined socially in connection with protection and give their names to the relevant appellations. Many of the early court decisions end, after analyzing data about reputation and style within a particular community, with assessments of these loyal and constant usages by appealing to a shared (though often nebulous) sense of what area wine styles are. For instance, in a case where interested parties attempted to extend the appellation for Pomerol to the neighboring community of Néac-Pomerol, the court weighed evidence about the usage of the term *Pomerol* to designate wine produced there and found such usages wanting. Thus, the court held that the reputation of the Pomerol name did not extend as far as this particular community, which was ultimately a failure of the reputational, "loyal and constant" prongs of the balancing test. Although these are clearly questions of interpretation, evidence from the local and neighboring communities, particularly around ideas of the resonance held by certain names and the associations linked to them, are exactly what these factors stand for. Use of the name as a marker is not enough, even if it is consistent. Instead the social perceptions of the product in connection to it are just as important. The court rather matter of factly notes that the wines connected to Néac-Pomerol "are much inferior to those of Pomerol, and only some of them can even be compared to the second growths (*deuxième crus*) of Pomerol. It is only by a usurpation of the name [of Pomerol] that they can sell these wines" (Feuille Vinicole, January 19, 1922, Gironde Archives 7M195). As this case shows, reputation is both taken for granted and dispositive in defining what AOC is and stands for, and precisely what the "local, loyal, and constant" balancing test seeks to define.

Given this give-and-take interrelationship between the legal system and localized ideas about reputation, consensus, and best practice, the AOC system aligns very much with Bourdieu's sense of habitus as simultaneously "*structure structurante*"(structuring structure) and "*structure structurée*" (structured structure) (Bourdieu 1979, 191). The AOC legislation enshrines preexisting practices and social structures just as such practices are reinforced by the additional power that comes from the legal system. Thus, the social meanings constitute the raw material of the law even as they define its contours.

Yet even as they provide strong connections, such definitions are far from crystal clear and uncontested. Although nearly all of my informants shared a sense that AOC was of value, its linkages with other elements, such as quality and prestige, can often complicate precisely what AOC signifies in a broad-based way. Even in the face of differing opinions about precisely what the designation meant in a broader sense, however, my interviewees did largely agree that in the end, much of the value of the regulation stemmed from the possibility of knowing what you were going to get, a certain stylistic predictability in the designated wines. As one of my informants, a trained oenologist and wine educator, told me:

> It gives you some information along the six AOC criteria—area of production, grape varieties, vineyard technique, yield, winemaking technique, and alcohol level. The value for the consumer is that you get what you expect. If you order champagne, you know it's going to come with bubbles. For consumers it is a marker of a certain kind of reliability.

As Trubek notes, "Taste then, in France, resides as a form of local knowledge"(2008, 44), and AOC in some ways stands in for that kind of distinction and distinctiveness.

Early proponents of the AOC legislation were quite explicit in the role they saw for the "local, loyal, and constant" factors, both in the context of prestige as well as stylistic predictability. When asked about whether the newly created system was solely meant to aid the more elite properties in the region, although he did acknowledge that when the AOC was more celebrated it was bound to be more limited than in the case of less prestigious regional names, Capus, the legislator who created the AOC legislation, noted that to claim the system was intended only to protect the most high-profile properties

> is a profound error; the *grands crus* do not need this law to be defended; this law is above all for the small and medium-sized proprietors from regions and appellations that do not have an abundant enough production to sell under their own names, but where the primary appellation is the local or regional appellation. What would be the value of the designation Bordeaux...if the designations Médoc, St-Emilion, Margaux, were considered without value? ("Conférence de M. J. Capus sur les appellations d'origine" November 7 1927, 7M195)

Although this statement admittedly comes from a very interested politician, something of the way the system functions in practice is in line with his sentiment.

This type of construction is another of the ways in which AOC, the balancing test, and other related structures map onto existing social hierarchies. AOC is constructed in a tiered way, with the largest appellation, AOC Bordeaux, encompassing all wines produced within the borders of the Gironde region, which centers around the city of Bordeaux. Within that broader region are subregional appellations, such as that for the Médoc, which further subdivide around regional identities and communal appellations, such as AOC Margaux, which conform around even tighter connections to local, loyal, and constant usages. As the cohorts become smaller and more clearly defined in the case of these appellations, you gain greater consistency of *terroir* due to the smaller scope of the space and more clearly defined regional styles as well, due to commonalities in grape varieties planted or similar traditions of *assemblage*. The smallest of these appellations are often the most prestigious ones, and sometimes certain *châteaux* can also act as special cases—as the case par excellence of a regional style. A number of my informants noted that, as Capus alluded to, the real value of the system was for producers on the fringes. Smaller, less prestigious producers gain more incrementally from being able to use the name of the AOC than elite producers, who have access to other kinds of markets more keyed to the name recognition of their particular *châteaux*, for example. "The best of the AOC will always get the benefit," one oenologist told me. "It's the periphery—the folks on the outside—where it matters more. It really doesn't affect the Latours." Situated within such a system, the value of the ability for variation within the wine AOC may become clearer. The breadth of the construction of the *cahiers des charges* allows for a number of properties to conform to a recognizable style of production while still permitting a range of producers to take advantage of the economic and social values of the distinction derived from the protected name.

The formalized *cahiers des charges* required under the law sets up a series of parameters through the construction of regions of production, varieties, and techniques. The system thus allows for variations within limits, providing a degree of predictability while maintaining some space for differences in practice among members of the protected class. The parameters themselves are where the cultural knowledge lies, and as a consequence, facts about best practices, hierarchies, methods, structures, and promotion are inbuilt into the system itself. Although constructing the *cahier des charges* does necessarily set outside limits of what does or does not constitute a protectable wine, it does not create an absolute recipe for the product, in terms of setting precisely the combinations of elements that come together in the wine. For example, although the documentation does include a list of permitted grape varieties a producer may use, it does not define which of them might be chosen from within that list, or in what proportion they are combined. Especially in a region where wine-making practice is marked by *assemblage,* which necessarily leads to a higher uniqueness among wines even of a particular category than in a monocepage system, the legal system is configured in such a way as to permit, and arguably embrace, a range of practice as well as a more broad-based idea of what an appellation stands for than might otherwise be the case. *Assemblage* refers to the practice by which wines are composed from multiple grape varieties, which are blended into the final product. This is a notable trait of Bordeaux wine, and the practice began to compensate for the vagaries of the growing seasons for the primary regional varieties, Merlot and Cabernet Sauvignon, which can be notoriously difficult to grow, particularly in the region's relatively northern latitude. By blending multiple grape varieties into a final wine, rather than relying on a single variety to grow to ideal maturity in the somewhat fickle weather conditions, producers could create more consistent wines (in terms of both quality and style). This is also one of the sources of the broader variation that can be found in wines throughout the region as well as within the individual appellations, as many of the relevant choices of *assemblage* occur at the level of individual producers. Legally, this reality is manifested in the structure of the law in large part because of the fact that protection attaches to a class, that is, a range of possible products, rather than any single product. The applicability of the law to the realities of the region would be far less if the system were premised on a less collectively based system of protection, as this would not really address the sociohistorical context (in terms of fraud and regional recognition) from which the regulation is derived. This is further reinforced by one of the particularities of the AOC right, the fact that any producer in the region who conforms to the specifications of the *cahier des charges* is granted the right to use the AOC designation. As such, the system itself reinforces this bounded spectrum of variability in the construction and protection of wines of the region.

This type of usage of AOC to protect regional wines as a broad spectrum rather than specific individual products also links into traditional roles of social arbiters—notably brokers and syndicates—in the social regulation of wine in the region (Chauvin 2010; Chevet 2009). The traditional regulation of wine in the region was (and in many cases still is) linked to particular social actors who categorized products and acted as brokers and go-betweens in relationship to wine quality. In many ways, the assurances now reinforced by the legal system came first from these social networks. An international merchant class, based around the city's docks, was for centuries the only guarantor of product quality, with the reputation of these brokers linked to the reputations of the various *châteaux* throughout the region. Such arbiters often served to consecrate perceptions about what wines from various regions were like in terms of style, as well as which regions were placed where in the sociocultural hierarchy of production. Here too, ideas about quality and predictability over time are tied to people and social practice, with brokers and syndicates creating, in human form, the connections that are doubly constructed through the vehicle of the AOC law.

USAGES LLC AS SOCIOCULTURAL CONCEPT AND IN LEGAL PRACTICE

Although the alignment between *terroir* and the boundaries of delimited AOC regions can be extremely close in some parts of France, in Bordeaux that is far from the case. Multiple *terroirs* constitute part of all the major AOC subregions, and it is through social construction via the "local, loyal, and constant" factors that the differences between the protected areas are marked. Given the tiered nature of AOCs, this can lead to real economic disparities based upon in- or out-group status in regard to a particular AOC. One informant noted that "being able to put Margaux on your label is the closest thing to a license to print your own money,"[3] and, tellingly, prices for wine categorized in that appellation can be up to three times those in adjacent AOC Haut-Médoc. In regard to AOC Pessac-Léognan in the Graves region, I was told that prices were thirty percent higher for wines that belong to the more elite Pessac-Léognan appellation versus the broader Graves appellation. Thus, the strength of this social construction has major real-world economic effects. When cases make it into the court system,[4] the means of assessment of claims has been based, both historically and today, around the "local, loyal, and constant" formulation. The parties must prove the correspondence between place, reputation, and qualities, and if the appropriate connections exist, status is extended to the property and sometimes its commune as well. Each of the elements is necessary, but not sufficient alone, and it is by proving each of these individual elements that the right to an AOC is established. Community perceptions shape AOCs by recognizing their value, defining what they are, and policing their boundaries through in-group/out-group politics. All of this makes the court inquiry one of hearing evidence of cultural practice to answer three fundamental questions:

1. Is the wine/product in question linked to a place?
2. Is there a recognizable tradition of practice linking that product with the place known both inside and outside the community?
3. Is this a time-honored linkage reinforced by the passage of time?

In many ways, the value of the "local, loyal, and constant" formulation lies in the type of clarity it brings to court determinations about status. Cultural value is always going to be difficult to define, even as it remains fundamental to such an inquiry. The test allows for the possibility to tie strongly into the types of philosophical values that led to protection in the first place, allowing the courts to serve as arbiters of practice without needing to define and dictate precisely what practice is.

TESTING LOCAL, LOYAL, AND CONSTANT USES IN SAUTERNES

By means of illustration, the next section will consider the ways in which the concept of local, loyal, and constant usages developed around AOC Sauternes in the early years of the existence of the law. This case highlights some of the

negotiations and complexities around the definition of locality, style, and reputation in regard to the wine produced there.

Specific natural conditions, in the guise of microclimates, are vitally important to both the style and quality of wines that are part of this AOC, which encompasses some of the area's most famous sweet wines. Southeast of the city of
Bordeaux, the region is within a valley whose specific weather conditions have
a fundamental effect on the grapes grown there. This is the home of the fungus
Botrytis cinerea, known colloquially as "noble rot." While in other climates
the fungus simply kills grapes, the combination of early fog and warmth found
here has a different effect—the fungus "roasts" the grapes on the vine—super
concentrating the sugars of the grapes. The consequence of this process is a
far lower yield than other vineyards and a sweet, candied-tasting wine with
a depth of fruit flavors very particular in style. The communities of Sauternes
and Barsac are located at the heart of this microclimate, and thus lay claim to
being the best examples of these unique wines.

The effects of the microclimate are considered less pronounced in neighboring areas, and as such, wines placed outside the appellation's boundaries
are forced to use the related, but less prestigious, designations for sweet white
wines, such as Loupiac and Cadillac. Thus, although linked to natural factors, regional limits are legally confirmed not by *terroir* alone, but also by the
practice-based assessment of the "local, loyal, and constant" test.

This preeminence of cultural parameters, rather than solely a "natural" or
terroir-based analysis, can be seen at once in a court decision related to the
very *terroir*-based question of whether the position of alluvial plains should
effect AOC membership for the Sauternes *appellation*. In that instance, the
court held: "The area of production imposed in order to qualify for the right
to the *appellation d'origine* should be consecrated not because of geographic
elements or the qualities of the soil or the wine, but through *usages locaux,
loyaux, et constants*" (La Petite Gironde 1932). Thus natural factors alone
are not enough, but must instead be connected to recognizable sociocultural
practices to ensure protection under the law. The individual qualities of place
are not enough, and the additional element needed is a sociocultural consensus
around qualitative factors and perceptions.

Additionally, agreement about membership in the Sauternes production
area is far less clear than it might otherwise be, in part because the political
boundaries of the town were set well after winemaking practice and custom
had been created and had begun to police the Sauternes style. The region of
protection has always extended beyond the town itself, and the legal rule states
that when a producer appeals to add wines from a particular property to an

appellation, if the court grants status, that status also transfers to the other producers of that community. This means that with each subsequent successful challenge to AOC membership, the boundaries of protection shifted in connection to the cases made by the parties about the reputational factors of the legal test. Again, shared perceptions about reputation play a key role in defining the scope and objects of legal protection. "The judges decided that usages giving rise to the appellation should be born of collective custom…and cannot be justified by habits, no matter how ancient, that are followed solely in isolated domains" (*La France* 1923).

There are over fifteen years worth of early court cases trying to define the boundaries of the region, which add segments onto the Sauternes map in this way. The year 1914 saw the accession of Château Respide in St Pierre de Mons, which was the case that ultimately led to the rule about adding communes based upon individual cases. The year 1922 saw a series of challenges brought by surrounding communities, which led to practice-based splits decided on a case-by-case basis. The neighboring communities of Sauternes, Barsac, Preignac, Forgeus, and Bommes attained AOC Sauternes status, while Pujols, Budons, Cérons, and Podensac did not. Appeals and reapplication occurred in the ensuing years, but the list of prescribed communities remained primarily the same (Gironde Departmental Archives, Bordeaux. File 7M196).

The linkages between the factors and their social meanings provide the backbone of the system, which links into social structures and hierarchies in marked and particular ways. Local, loyal, and constant usages also constitute a theme *outside* of the courtroom, which reinforces the type of importance they hold in the parameters of the law. The following section will consider the ways the flexibility within the limits of the law is expressed through a discussion of the fluidity and change around the concepts of *typicité* and regional style.

TYPICITÉ, REGIONAL STYLE, AND LOCAL, LOYAL, AND CONSTANT USAGES

Given the ways in which many key vini-viticultural concepts simultaneously enshrine both uniqueness and a type of generalizable predictability, one can further consider the role of internal and external perceptions in construction of meaning as part of the value of AOC. To consider the role of local, loyal, and constant usages in winemaking practice, I consider the concepts of *typicité* and regional style as similar constructions of qualitative social value in relationship to AOC wines in Bordeaux.

The ideas of *typicité* and *assemblage* constitute major parts of Bordeaux wine culture. The definition I was given of the former was that *typicité* "is the result of the work of man within the region." In practice, the term unites choices around the management of the natural world, such as treatment of the land or the choice of which varieties to plant, as well as the choices that combine into the winemaking process such as uses of technology or the particularities of the ways wine is blended into a final product. The concept of *assemblage,* or blending, connects to such choices as well. Because Bordeaux wines are not based around single varietals, but instead combine elements of different grape varietals (predominantly cabernet sauvignon and merlot) into a single wine, *typicité* is of broad importance in terms of defining what wine from a particular region will be like. Shared ideas about the best varietals to plant in a region or the appropriate proportions within the finished wines differ among the subregions of Bordeaux, and in the end *typicité* is part of the "style" captured under AOC.

Because of the ability of such a concept to bound the unpredictability of necessarily unique production, *typicité* and style can be seen to approximate an essence of what makes products special and "other" than similar alternatives to be found in the market. As one informant noted, "It's about knowing the style is going to be consistent. If I order a St. Julien, it should taste like a St. Julien, not a Pomerol, and that comes down to the soil and the practice and the grape varieties and all of that put together."

Regional styles in Bordeaux have historically been the basis of the definition of in- and out-groups around the various *appellations*. Even before the system was formally institutionalized, they were mobilized as descriptors of regional practice, although such a sense has always been something of a cultural fiction. Yet even as my informants and other actors questioned the continuing salience of such shifting concepts, there remained a sense of their residual cultural meaning. Perhaps the strongest way to see this at work is not in the definition of appellation styles, but through the ways in which, particularly because of the influence of international tastemakers and a broadening base of wine consumers, they are beginning to shift and change.

In an interview with a leader of the Margaux wine syndicate, I posed this question of style, asking her, "How would you describe a Margaux wine?" She responded:

The style of Margaux has changed a lot since 1995 or so. Before it was feminine. Elegant...smooth...almost too light (*trop léger*). St Julien and Margaux are about the same, and Pauillac, St Estephe, Moulis-Listrac are similar in style. Overall the new style is much more structured and powerful, and a bit more homogenous than before.

The qualitative adaptability of the region is nothing new, but at the same time, AOC seeks to hold constant something of practice that remains keyed into the social meanings of what AOCs stand for. Another informant saw the situation similarly.

> Appellation matters, but not in the way it's been twisted to matter. *Terroir* is not one size fits all in all regions—people don't realize this when they complain "appellation quality is not what it once was." Since in Bordeaux they aren't coterminous, there is no such thing as "appellation style." You can describe the style of a property, but that's it.

Yet despite being of the "I know it when I see it" variety, the concept of style still very much resonates in practice. When I visited Château Margaux, the woman leading our tasting began discussing the state of the appellation, and she clearly thought some of its peers were not really making "Margaux-style" wines—a fact she illustrated with an anecdote about ordering a bottle of "Margaux" at a restaurant that was without the finesse she had expected from it. The sentiment is also what lies behind the idea of AOC as a marker of consumers "getting what they expect" from the wines they purchase. The system is (admittedly by many) not a perfect one, but in the face of the complications of assimilating all of the relevant information to make such a determination individually, it functions as a culturally useful shorthand in this regard. Such factors are also part of the reason *châteaux* try to recreate the historical ways their wines have been described, also known as "maintaining *château* style." To highlight the fact that such concerns about style are far from settled even in the minds of producers, I end with a moment from another of my *château* visits. I was taking part in a tasting, and the *maître des chais* (responsible for the *assemblage* of the wine) was in attendance. I struck up a conversation, asking what I thought was an easy question. "How would you describe the style of your wine?" I asked. He stared at me somewhat blankly and I attempted to reframe the question. Awkward silence intervened again as he thought for a minute. "Umm...I guess it's in the style of Margaux?" he replied after a few more moments. Given that this *château* is actually part of the neighboring appellation of Haut-Médoc, perhaps this had not been such an easy question after all.

In the end, these kinds of gut-feeling assessments and qualitative associations are, I would argue, just the reason why a test like local, loyal, and constant usages can be of value for both legal and sociocultural actors. Just because cultural fictions are contested or even patently false does not mean that they do not still act as important holders of sociocultural meanings. They are precisely the kinds of lies we build our dreams upon. In the face of the potential and growing contentiousness around what style (or AOC for that matter) means, the flexibility of a standard such as "local, loyal, and constant usages" allows social practice to shape law and regulation in potentially complex ways. As these trends continue, although it is certain that what reputations and loyalty to practice mean will change, the system will be able to grow alongside such changing concepts of sociocultural practice because of the interconnections between law and society around AOC.

CONCLUSION

I would like to suggest that the interest and power of a test such as "local, loyal, and constant usages" is the ability it holds for the flexibility and negotiation of social practice to fit within the framework of the law. Going further, I would also claim that such a "best fit" connection between social practice and the elements of law is of value because, despite the very real spaces of dissent around some of the relevant definitions, the interconnections between place, practice, and reputation under the "local, loyal, and constant" formula for AOC protection aligns communal values and shared sociocultural meanings in a truly exemplary way. By looking at this system, one conceptualizes a space that reveals the intricate ways in which cultural practice can be embedded in legal practice, particularly through the use of cultural norms as legal evidence, while also illuminating some of the particularities of the relationship between law, culture, and social consensus. Place alone is not enough, even as places grant their names to the AOCs themselves, but the marriage between these elements of locality and reputation grant wider significance to winemaking sites and practice by connecting law, culture, and geography through AOC.

NOTES

1. Roudié cited in Hinnewinkel and colleagues (2008, 26). All translations from the French are my own.
2. AOC rights are considered the foundation of the international legal concept of geographical indications (GI), which protect the names of place-based products under intellectual property law. Despite their connection to intellectual property, however, GIs also problematize many of the

fundamental assumptions of such regimes, particularly around ideas of authorship, collective ownership, and originality.

3. Château Margaux is one of the big four *grands crus* from the 1855 classification, and one of the most expensive wines in Bordeaux. There is also an AOC called Margaux, a highly prestigious designation in the Médoc.

4. Under the terms of the AOC law, cases to contest appellation membership are brought to the administrative courts in the area in which the potential infringement occurs, or membership is asserted, to better allow for knowledge of local reputation in weighing the relevant claims of the parties.

CHAPTER NINE

Cultural Patrimony and the Bureaucratization of Wine: The Bulgarian Case

YUSON JUNG

INTRODUCTION

On a cloudy and chilly autumn day in 2008, I was walking downhill toward the town's center in the provincial town of Belogradchik in northwestern Bulgaria. It was around 9:30 on a Saturday morning. Unlike the weekdays, when my fieldwork routine at the winery started in the ungodly hours between 6:00 and 7:00 A.M., I noticed small and big plastic barrels displayed outside of hardware stores along the main street. A couple of families were loading the barrels in their respective cars. Having seen many such plastic barrels in the nearby village houses and at the winery where I was doing my fieldwork, I thought this was interesting and wondered whether they were for wine or had other functions such as fermenting cabbages, a common Bulgarian winter tradition.

Later that day, I overheard the tractor driver of a boutique winery, Sasho, a calm man in his fifties, asking one of my winemakers whether he could buy a little grape from the winery to make his own wine. I asked Sasho why he wanted to buy the grapes, and he answered, "I have to make *my* home-made wine (*domashno vino*), of course! Last year, I was a dummy and bought the grapes myself and, of course, the wine did not turn out that great because the grapes were bad [quality]." Puzzled, I asked again: "But Sasho, can't you just buy the already-made wine from the winemaker? You know they sell good wine in plastic bottles for the villagers and townspeople at a very affordable price." He responded, "I know... But I would rather make my own wine. It's always been like that. I know it will maybe not be as good as the specialists' [winemakers'] one, but it's *mine*... My grandfather did it, my father did it, and now I am doing it with my son. Bulgarians love to make their own wine."

Sasho was not alone in expressing his desire for making one's own wine during the grape harvest season (*grozdober*) in Bulgaria. Many winery workers also made their own wine or brandy from the grapes or pressed grapes acquired through the wineries at which they worked. Even the closest friends of the winemakers would insist on making their own homemade wine despite the realization that its quality was likely to be inferior and its production costs higher.

Sasho's comment made me realize why so many Bulgarians I had talked to have almost always brought up the topic of "homemade wines" of their family members when talking about Bulgarian wines. Wine was not simply a cultural pride in Bulgaria. More important, many Bulgarians considered winemaking a cultural patrimony, namely a cultural heritage to which they could claim a sense of entitlement. If winemaking is an entitlement for many Bulgarians, a heritage handed down over generations, then how do they negotiate such a sense of entitlement with the bureaucratic system of classification and authentication that validates cultural heritage in the increasingly competitive and globalized wine world?

Another of my interesting fieldwork[1] experiences took place at the guesthouse where I rented a room. I brought a bottle of wine from the winery and told the owner about my excitement of having participated in a bottling session. I was ready to pull the cork to try the wine, but he was quicker and called his wife to bring "his wine" that he made the previous year. His wife brought a large soda plastic bottle that contained his homemade wine. He proudly poured the wine and encouraged me to take a sip. I offered him a glass of the bottled wine from the winery. I tried his wine, and he tried "mine." Although I wanted to be polite, I could not help but cringe at the sourness of his wine during the first sniff and subsequent sip. Lost for words (it was painful to gulp down the liquid), I finally uttered, "hmm, interesting..." His wife laughed and said that I must not like it. He said that the bottled wine I brought was good, but too "heavy" for him, and he preferred to sip on his wine. His wife seconded and added that she usually mixed in some soda to make it *even more* pleasant. When I later told this experience to my winemakers and winery workers, they laughed heartily and simply said: "Welcome to Bulgaria." They further pointed out that every village house has a small plot of vines, and the "stubborn" Bulgarian peasant will always make his or her own wine and consume it regardless of its "objective" qualities.

This episode is instructive in thinking about Bulgarians' relationship to their winemaking tradition and the seeming gap between the lack of international recognition of their cultural patrimony[2] on one hand, and the strong local sense of entitlement to their heritage on the other hand. While "taste" is a subjective matter, evaluative standards such as quality and authenticity are often considered objectifiable in the popular discourse, and they are used for bureaucratic classification and authentication. The bureaucratization of "traditional" foods and drinks legitimizes the claims for exclusive entitlement in today's global market. This is commonly observed in cases with disputes over cheese names (West et al. 2012) and champagne (Guy 2007).

This kind of official classification system, or appellation, was first created in 1935 to prevent fraud and to protect specific wines of traditional distinction in France (Colman 2008; Ulin 1995, 2004). The French model has proven economically very successful and has been followed by many other wine-producing countries (Colman 2008) and extended to include other agricultural foodstuffs (such as cheese and meat products) claiming particular cultural patrimony (Trubek 2008). In other words, the bureaucratized classification of food products has increasingly become an important factor in validating distinctive place-based identity claims and commercial successes (see also Meneley 2007).

Attending to the discourse and practice of the bureaucratic classification system in the global wine market, therefore, sheds light on the often unnoticed power relations among competing identities of "place" that are hierarchically organized and bureaucratically sanctioned. This hierarchy has both symbolic and practical implications in today's globalized world: not only does it reproduce the hegemonic order of some locales (cf. Appadurai 2002), but it also limits the cultural capital in the articulation of other (more marginal) locales.

The ethnographic episodes described earlier set an interesting backdrop for the politics of wine in the global wine industry because wine as an increasingly popular commodity and index of refined taste (Silverstein 2006) is enmeshed in power relations and the identity politics of place. Simply put, a premium-quality wine from Michigan will not be perceived the same way as a premium-quality wine from Bordeaux. Wine, in this regard, is an excellent example of a global commodity that allows us to understand how the bureaucratization process affirms the essentialized constructions of "place" organized along the spectrum between important or prestigious (i.e., high cultural capital) and marginal (i.e., low cultural capital). The case of the Bulgarian wine industry, which has traditionally been heavily export oriented (sixty-five percent of its production is exported), provides a particularly fertile ground to think about not only the socially constructed nature of "place," but also the contested narratives in the local level where the "local" itself is a process (Jung n. d.). Furthermore, the complex interactions within the local context, as well as at the European Union (EU) and global levels make the Bulgarian wine case highly instructive in understanding the cultural politics of food in the era of globalization (Nutzenadel and Trentmann 2008; Phillips 2006; Watson and Caldwell 2005).

Considering the fact that the geographical origin, often resorting to the "cultural capital" (Bourdieu 1984) of a particular place (locale), is an important factor in the fiercely competitive global wine trade, interesting questions arise: what are the stakes for marginal Bulgarian wine producers who must rely on such capital for survival in the global wine market? How do they reconcile with their beloved cultural heritage that has not organized the discourse and practice of wine around the idea of geographical origin of "place" reflecting particular characteristics of the grape, soil, climate, and winemaking tradition? What are the means by which they can be *recognized* of their cultural heritage? What are the implications of bureaucratized geographical classifications for Bulgarian wine producers now subjected to the EU's wine law and whose wine-making practices are regulated for the export market?

In this chapter, I examine these questions within the context of the EU's classification system for agricultural products (PDO: Protected Designation of Origin) established to protect the cultural heritage and political economic interests of the member states. From the vantage point of the marginal Bulgarian wine producers, I explore how this classification system regulates the production of wine, offers an official sanctioning of authenticity, and privileges *certain* place-based identity claims by denying others bureaucratic and legal rights (see also Trubek 2008, 24–31). Moreover, this system organizes and reproduces a hierarchy with practical implications for international branding and sales and limits local agency in elevating the standing within the hierarchy. This system then, not only reflects the power relations within the EU member states, but also the complex workings of power within the wine industry, which reproduces a global wine hierarchy.

THE ARTICULATION AND RECOGNITION OF CULTURAL HERITAGE

Anthropological discussions of heritage have primarily focused on the diverse claims to heritage and how they are contested and appropriated in local contexts (e.g., Hirsch 2010; Karp et al. 2006). By highlighting the "agency" of the creators of these claims, however, few studies have considered the role of the "audience" who too play an important role in *recognizing* such claims (cf. Taylor 1994). While an extensive review of anthropological studies on heritage is beyond the scope of this chapter, I suggest that it is important to consider how claims of heritage *are* or *are not* recognized by the audience (bureaucrats and consumers alike) of such claims.

Bulgaria has an incredibly interesting history of wine production, as I have discussed in detail elsewhere (Jung 2011). Here, suffice it to point out that Bulgaria is arguably the oldest winemaking region in the world, tracing the history of winemaking to the ancient Thracians who inhabited the Black Sea area (Borislavov 2004). Although commercial wine production was prohibited under the Ottoman Empire, individual households could produce wine for ritual and home consumption purposes. During the socialist era, Bulgaria developed an enormous industrial base for wine production, making it the designated wine country of COMECON (the Soviet economic alliance) and exporting about sixty percent of its production (Noev 2006). To date, Bulgaria remains the country with the highest proportion of exported wine, even compared to the EU-15 largest wine-producing countries (sixty-five percent). The Bulgarian wine industry is characterized as heavily export oriented, largely occupying the price-for-value shelves in the global marketplace (Gilby 2007; Moulton, Simova, and Young 1994). This background is important to keep in mind for the purpose of the following discussion regarding the implications of the bureaucratization of wine and the significance of "recognition."

Contrary to the passion and tradition for "making" wine, as discussed earlier, there is a sharp contrast in the everyday discussions about "drinking" wine in Bulgaria. Among my Bulgarian friends and informants, the relationships between the origin of place of the grapes as well as the taste and quality of the wine were hardly central questions. In fact, while they articulated great historical pride in their wine *making* (producing) tradition, they would often refer to themselves as *not* having a "wine culture" (*"nyamame vinena kultura v Bulgariya"*) like in France or Italy, because they don't have the tradition of matching certain wines with certain foods, nor do they drink wine for its connoisseurial pleasure imagining the geographical origin of the grapes. In other words, the articulation of the Bulgarian wine heritage has largely been framed around "making" and attending to the family vineyards.[3]

Bulgarians are perhaps not unique in acknowledging the lack of "wine culture," even as they express their strong pride and a sense of entitlement as an old wine-producing country. Ulin (personal communication) shared similar tendencies among his French cooperative winegrowers, and Demossier, for example, has demonstrated how the current wine drinking culture in France

is a result of a complex process of integrating wine as part of the French national identity construction (2011) (see also Guy 2007 for similar discussions).
Whether the "wine culture" Bulgarians refer to is indeed something invented
in other so-called elite wine countries (e.g., Ulin 1995) is beyond the point of
my discussion. The Bulgarian example highlights the repeatedly articulated
ambivalence in terms of being "recognized" as a wine country with a respectable reputation of a *distinctive* wine identity on the global wine map. Given
that geographical origin (in the name of *goût de terroir,* taste of place) has assumed significant cultural capital in the wine world, Bulgarians' ambivalence
(or perhaps disengagement) toward the "taste of place" and their winemaking
practices that did not privilege this notion of *terroir* begs for local contestation against the hegemonic discourse. I suggest that the bureaucratized system
of classification, however, limits such local contestations with little room to
negotiate the local sense of entitlement of the wine heritage. For Bulgarian
wine producers, this system poses a serious challenge in developing their wine
industry to elevate its status in the global market: Bulgaria's lack of cultural
capital in the wine world hinges upon Bulgarians' lack of a hegemonic "wine
culture" that organizes the discourse and practice of wine along geographic
origins. The hegemonic wine culture in the contemporary world privileges the
notion of "*terroir,*" the taste of place that reflects the specific characteristics of
the climate, soil, and other influences from nature. According to this discourse,
a fine wine from a particular place is valued upon its specific character stem-
ming from its particular *terroir.*

Most Bulgarians do have some basic association about their white and red
wines and where those wines respectively come from. For example, white wine
is commonly associated with the northeastern region by the Black Sea and
the northern region by the Danube river, whereas red wine is believed to be
from all over Bulgaria (except around the capital city of Sofia), but particularly
from the south. For the majority of the Bulgarians, however, the more specific
association of certain wines with certain places refers to the location of the
former socialist wine plant (*vinzavod*) or to the name of the particular wine
industry (*vinprom*) in a given locale rather than the location of the vineyards.[4]
Under the centralized socialist economy, grapes were distributed throughout
the country and the final product only bore the name of the wine plant/indus-
try where the wine was made.[5] The map below reflects such an association
with the wine plant/industry rather than the actual places of the vineyards. In
other words, the listed names point to the names of the wine industry facilities
(which include wineries, warehouses, and/or agricultural complexes) rather
than the names of the regions where the vineyards are located.

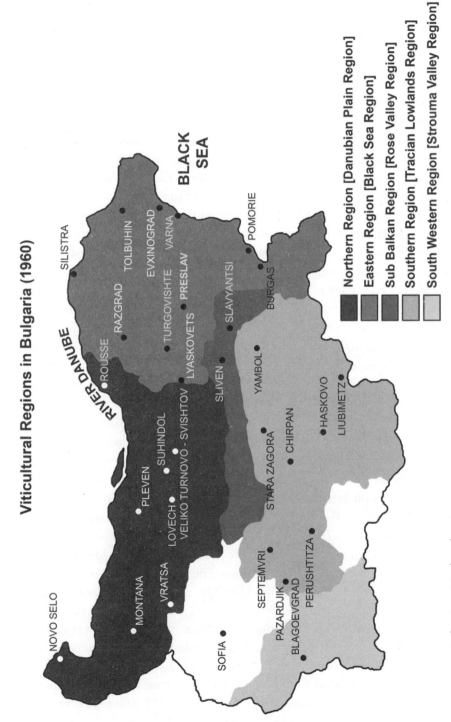

Viticultural Regions in Bulgaria (1960)

NOVO SELO

RIVER DANUBE

SILISTRA

ROUSSE

MONTANA

VRATSA

PLEVEN

LOVECH

SUHINDOL

VELIKO TURNOVO · SVISHTOV

RAZGRAD

TOLBUHIN

EVXINOGRAD

TURGOVISHTE   VARNA

PRESLAV

LYASKOVETS

SLAVYANTSI

SLIVEN

SOFIA

SEPTEMVRI

PAZARDJIK

BLAGOEVGRAD

PERUSHTITZA

STARA ZAGORA

CHIRPAN

YAMBOL

HASKOVO

LIUBIMETZ

BURGAS

POMORIE

BLACK
SEA

Northern Region [Danubian Plain Region]
Eastern Region [Black Sea Region]
Sub Balkan Region [Rose Valley Region]
Southern Region [Tracian Lowlands Region]
South Western Region [Strouma Valley Region]

FIGURE 9.1: Bulgarian viticultural regions.

As Sasho once told me as we were cleaning the barrels in the winery: "You know Bulgaria is a red wine country, even though we *do* produce white wines which are very pleasant to drink, especially during summer time...Do you know that all the folk songs on wine in Bulgaria are about red wine? But, do you know there is actually one song about white wine?" I looked at him with a smile, expecting a humorous response or joke. He started to sing: "White wine, white wine, why are you not red?" Everyone around us burst into laughter.

There is partial truth to the joke Sasho shared. In terms of international "recognition," Bulgarian wine has maintained a strong reputation with red wines since the late socialist era in the 1980s when the Bulgarian state-owned wineries successfully exported them to the Western market (Gilby 2007; Robinson 2006). In fact, the first reputation of Bulgarian wine in the Western world was primarily around its quality red wine offered at affordable prices. Furthermore, according to my informants, during the intensive period of democratic transition following the collapse of the socialist regime, the Bulgarian wine industry continued to rely heavily on its export of bulk red wine to the Western market (including Japan). Many wine countries outside of Europe do not stipulate that a demarcated wine must be 100 percent from that geographical region. For example, in California, the geographical mandate requires only eighty-five percent of the wine to come from the particular appellation. When one buys a bottle of wine from Napa Valley, for instance, theoretically fifteen percent of that bottle can be from anywhere in the world.

Some of the Bulgarian winemakers with whom I have worked closely recalled the "wild" times in the 1990s when they would ship millions of tons of bulk red wine to California to be blended with Californian wine. Bulgarian red wine was considered an excellent choice to enhance the quality of Californian reds, which often suffered from overripe grapes because of the changing climate. Similarly, another winemaker reminisced about her work with Japanese wine importers in the 1990s: while Japan's climate is not suitable to vine growing, it has a vibrant wine drinking culture, and many Japanese support the cultivation of a Japanese wine industry. The Bulgarian bulk wine she sent over would be bottled in Japan and sold as "Japanese" wine because Japanese law permitted such a practice.

These stories are surprising to those who have had little exposure to "Bulgarian" wines and wondered how these marginal wine producers could sustain themselves after the collapse of the centralized socialist system in 1989. Similar to wine production in other countries under socialism that emphasized quantity over quality (see, for example, Walker and Manning, this volume), the Bulgarian wine industry had to reorient itself and strike the right balance of quantity and quality during the period of transition. Bulgarian wine producers could not merely give up on their enormous quantity-oriented industrial base developed under state socialism. Nor could they compete with New World producers whose wine quality has been recognized as superior to the quality of wines from Eastern Europe in the global wine market, especially since the 1990s.

Additionally, in their marginal global standing, Bulgarian wines' "taste" has rarely been associated with and recognized by their geographical origins. Yet, as some Bulgarians would argue, that is not the only way to appreciate wine; wine remains an important part of their cultural heritage, as shown in the enthusiasm for homemade wine. In this regard, Bulgarian wine producers' primary struggle is to have the Bulgarian wines *recognized* as distinct cultural patrimony (and not simply articulated as such). In what follows, I examine a local debate concerning the EU wine reform as well as a "scandal" involving the categorization of Bulgaria's wine *terroir(s)* in the EU level. These examples discuss the implications of the increasing bureaucratization of cultural heritage more explicitly around the idea of Protected Designation of Origin (PDO), or what is more broadly understood as the discourse of Geographical Indication (GI).

WINE LAW AND CLASSIFICATION FOR AGRICULTURAL PRODUCTS OF GEOGRAPHICAL ORIGIN OF THE EUROPEAN UNION

Wine has traditionally been a symbol of cultural identity in many European countries. In 1992, the European Union (EU) officially recognized geographic names that carry high symbolic capital (legacies) under the names of Protected Designation of Origin (PDO).[6] Strictly speaking, because of its unique place in European cultural heritage, wine follows a separate regime under this regulation that stipulates more specifically the geographical origins and quality standards of wines from the EU. All wine-producing member states have what the EU "wine law" calls "Quality Wine psr (QWpsr)" (produced in a specified region) that follows the geographical classification (appellation) system of its country. For instance, champagne is a QWpsr under the French appellation system that is only produced in the region of Champagne, France. This system delineates geographical boundaries and specifies particular winemaking methods that qualify the product as champagne. Any other "bubbles" outside of this appellation cannot claim the same geographical origin nor could it be called champagne legally and bureaucratically.

While this kind of classification system is advantageous to the so-called elite wine producers positioned at the top of the hierarchy, it makes it increasingly difficult for the marginal producers to elevate their standing within the hierarchy. The following ethnographic example illustrates the limitations of "local agency" within the context of bureaucratically authenticated "recognition" by an international audience.

During the busy grape harvest season in mid-September, wine producers from the northwestern region were summoned to a seminar room by the government agency for wine in the region's major city of Montana. This agency was in charge of controlling and implementing the EU wine policies, including the so-called wine law. A couple of bureaucrats, including the director of the control department from the Sofia headquarter office, came to brief and educate the wine producers in the region about the new EU wine reform soon to go into effect. Some twenty wine producers attended the seminar, and many exchanged a common complaint that they were convened during the busiest harvest season. The main presentation revolved around the oenological practices the wine reform addressed.

The crux of the EU wine reform concerned the crisis distillation subsidy as well as the prohibition of further converting agricultural lands to vineyards and providing incentives to grub up existing vineyards and convert them to other farmlands. This was primarily in response to the global oversupply of wine and the decreasing competitiveness of European wines (for a more extensive discussion, see Jung 2011). The former issue had no relevance to Bulgarian producers as Bulgaria only joined the EU in 2007 and was never subjected to the EU-wide agricultural subsidy for distilling unsold wines into biofuel. While the latter issue did apply to the Bulgarian context, the focus of the briefing was the customs-related matters around the limitation of the alcohol percentage of "concentrated grape juice (must)" for the region. In other words, the bureaucrat informed the regional wine producers that they belonged to the European wine zone "B II" and that they must adhere to the sanctioned oenological practices of the zone according to the EU wine law. More specifically, he discussed that, in this zone, sugar manipulation (called *chaptalization* in technical terms) is allowed to salvage wine production in bad harvest years, but the maximum alcohol percentage of the unfermented grape juice used in such occasions has been lowered from 2 percent to 1.5 percent, so that the wine cannot exceed a certain maximum alcohol level. Otherwise it will not be considered "wine" and the producers will be subjected to the excise tax, from which wines are currently exempt.

With this announcement, the bureaucrat could not talk further because several producers became agitated and interrupted him with questions. One winemaker who turned rather red raised his hand and asked: "how can you tell us that we cannot exceed fifteen percent to be called wine and not pay the excise tax?" Another bureaucrat from Sofia who accompanied the head of the agency responded rather bluntly: "Well, this is the EU-wide regulations. If you are against this idea, then you take it to the court. That is the only way to change things in democratic governments." This comment stirred up the majority of the attendants, who started to grumble and comment sarcastically. Then another wine producer took the floor and remarked to the head bureaucrat:

"You have been in our wine business for a long time, right [he was apparently a former winemaker himself, I later found out, trained during the socialist system with some of the winemakers present in the seminar]? You must understand, then, that this is absurd. You have to be with us to change this EU absurdity." This time the head bureaucrat answered: "I know how you feel, but we can't do anything from our position. We are simply the executive control agency of the Bulgarian government. In addition, how can we [Bulgaria] go against 35 states? If you want to raise your discontent, use your professional organization to raise your voice. We, unfortunately, can't help you."

The debate, or what I would rather describe as a venting of frustration, went on among the wine producers. But they seem to know their discontent will ultimately not change anything. Especially for producers who depend on exports to the Western market, the official and bureaucratic authentication is critical for "recognition" by their global buyers. This is not to suggest that these marginal wine producers have no grounds for resistance and subverting EU wine laws. In fact, as the example of "Super Tuscan" wine in Italy suggests, some marginal producers do succeed in resisting the system of bureaucratic classification and carve out their own distinction for quality that is globally recognized. For Bulgarian wine producers, however, such an example appears more like an exception and from their marginal vantage point, they feel rather limited in coming up with viable alternatives. Furthermore, they feel increasingly deprived of a sense of entitlement from their own cultural patrimony.

"DESIGNATED" GEOGRAPHIC ORIGIN: THE POLITICS OF QUALITY, QUANTITY, AND IDENTITY

The implications of wine bureaucratization are also demonstrated in the Bulgarian wine industry "scandal" in the face of EU accession. To harmonize Bulgaria's national system with that of the EU, Bulgaria had to lobby and be recognized officially for its wine heritage at the EU level by having its wine regions classified according to the wine law. This resulted in two officially recognized QWpsr regions for Bulgarian wine: the Danubian Plain and the Thracian Valley (Figure 9.2). The classification of Bulgarian wine regions into only two areas was a consequence of crude local politics in the aftermath of state socialism. According to Bulgarian winemakers, this result pegged Bulgaria into a lower standing in the wine hierarchy than even during the socialist era, despite the overall improvement of the wine quality in the past decade.

As mentioned earlier, Bulgaria's wine industry was premised during the socialist era upon an enormous export base primarily to the Soviet Union and its allies, and later to Western markets such as the United Kingdom, Germany, and BeNeLux (Belgium, Netherlands, Luxemburg). The latter served as significant dollar income for the communist Bulgarian state in the 1980s. While quality was important for the Western market, the Bulgarian wine industry during the socialist era put its primary emphasis on the quantity of wine production. The largest export market, namely the Soviet market, was considered very undiscriminating when it came to the quality of wine, and a popular joke within the industry was that "as long as it was booze, the Soviets did not care." To date, one can easily witness huge sizes of wine tanks made of cement that can hold a minimum of ten tons of wine in many industrial wineries in Bulgaria, suggestive of the production scale of that era.

During the industrialization of the wine sector under socialism, the Bulgarian state adopted the appellation model of France and categorized Bulgaria's viticultural regions into five areas codified into state law in 1960 (see Figure 9.1). The classification of wine regions was roughly influenced by the concept of "terroir," taking into consideration the grape varieties and climate, but not so much the soil types per the French model. As mentioned earlier, interestingly and perhaps ironically, this categorization was based more on the location of the industrial wineries (vinzavod: literally meaning wine plants) rather than the vineyards, although each winery specialized in particular grape varieties. For example, wineries around Novo Selo in northwestern Bulgaria and Suhindol, part of the Danubian plains, specialized in the processing of Gamza, a native wine grape around the Danube (in Hungary, this grape is called kadarka). Some southern regions such as Perushtitza or Haskovo were known as the Cabernet Sauvignon and Merlot producers.

While this geographical classification did not go as far as establishing a kind of "wine culture" as in France with regional and national identity politics (Demossier 2011), it did create a basis for understanding the connection between a locale and grape variety for specific wine regions in Bulgaria and helped the Bulgarian public identify certain wines with certain regions, even

Bulgarian Wine Regions Recognized as EU's QWpsr

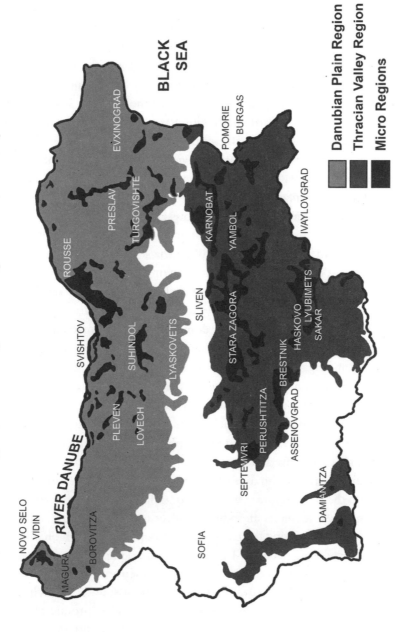

FIGURE 9.2: Bulgarian wine regions recognized as EU's QWpsr.

if the association was actually with the wineries (socialist wine industry/plant) rather than the locations of the vineyards.

How did the five geographic wine regions become two when Bulgaria entered the EU in 2007, disregarding its earlier officially sanctioned classification? According to my key informant, winemaker Alexander, it was the result of shortsighted self-interests of two major industrial wine producers. As mass producers exporting the majority of their wine abroad, these two winery owners did not want too many limitations on their wine-producing operations within a more restricted region. According to the EU wine law, one can only use the grapes from that particular region to qualify the wine as a geographical product. Because of the socialist centralized economy, wineries did not own their vineyards until the privatization of vineyards took place in the late 1990s. During state socialism, large industrial wineries always sourced grapes from all over Bulgaria to maintain the large production level. Thus, when the National Vine and Wine Chamber, the representative professional organization of Bulgarian wine producers and grape growers, had to put together the geographical indication proposal before Bulgaria's admission to the EU, the two largest wine producers exercised their lobbying power to settle for two broad regions for the quality wine label (QWpsr) of Bulgarian wines. This is what wine producers in Bulgaria call the "wine region classification scandal."

When different players in the domestic industry reacted negatively to such a result, one of these wine producers defended himself by creating an advertisement slogan for his exported wines in the UK market that stated: "Origin does not Matter." When I confirmed this story I heard from another of Alexander's wine-producing colleagues, Alexander became very agitated as he recalled this incident: "Can you believe it? What kind of stupidity and embarrassment is this? Wine is *all* about geographical origins—otherwise why would there even be a wine law and so much politics and bureaucracy around that?"

Particularly striking about this Bulgarian example is that "*terroir*," a central discourse in the contemporary wine world, especially in relation to "geographical origin," has not been an explicit concern for the majority of Bulgarian wine producers who pride themselves on the cultural heritage of wine. In fact, many wine producers (let alone the general Bulgarian public/consumers) found the bureaucratic system of classification and authentication very confusing, inefficient, and ultimately disadvantageous from their standpoint. While labeling is regulated by the EU wine law, many commercial wine producers in Bulgaria find the labeling rules inadequate for both the domestic and international market because Bulgarian wine has rarely been recognized by the hegemonic discourse of place (*terroir*).

Ironically, the Bulgarian case can be read as how the hegemonic discourse and practice of *"terroir"* has *not* become part of the story (unlike other case studies on wine production elsewhere). The gap between the articulation and recognition of cultural patrimony remains, especially as the present bureaucratization of wine authenticates only certain wine regions as premium-quality producers whereas the others are classified as table wines without a particular geographical distinction.

Contrary to the current trend in the global food marketplace to reconnect consumers and producers through the "place" of the products' origin, thereby salvaging the anonymity and lower quality of industrial commodities not valued according to particular locales (e.g., Wilk 2006), the bureaucratization of Bulgarian wine within the context of the EU's classification of products of geographical origin pegged Bulgaria into a "generic" status where specific locales play little role in *recognition* by global wine consumers.

The crude local politics as well as the savvy politics of elite wine producers in the EU make it very challenging for a marginal Bulgarian wine industry to reinvent itself as a premium-quality/fine-wine-producing country with distinctive wine regions that represent distinctive place-based wine identities. Instead, some winemakers argue Bulgaria is doomed as the "price-for-value" (cheap and decent tasting) wine-producing country with a generic wine identity in the global market. Because cultural values are often associated with distinctive identities, the fact that Bulgarian wines are only recognized as "generic" (cheap and decent tasting) becomes a frustration for these Bulgarian winemakers.

CULTURAL PATRIMONY AND THE BUREAUCRATIZATION OF WINE

The Bulgarian wine industry is still divided on its future visions. Many of the large producers with their enormous production infrastructure struggle to maintain a shelf position in the global wine market. As mentioned earlier, the Bulgarian wine industry has been structured around the export market, which poses new challenges to these wine producers who struggle to strike a balance between the politics of quality and quantity. For the smaller wine producers whose ambition is to elevate Bulgarian wine in the wine hierarchy and be recognized as a distinctive wine *from* a region in Bulgaria (as opposed to being identified as merely a *Bulgarian* wine) that *tastes* differently from other world wine regions, the bureaucratization of the wine regions has already done its damage. Under these circumstances, does cultural patrimony even matter in the Bulgarian wine case?

I suggest that the bureaucratization of wine indicates a strengthening of the hegemonic wine hierarchy in the neoliberal market milieu. It also legitimizes the claims for exclusive entitlement in the global market. In this regard, without the official sanctioning of authenticity of geographical origins, the marginal Bulgarian wine producers have limited agency in establishing *and* being recognized with distinctive geographical identities of Bulgarian wines within the wine hierarchy they are competing in. With only two wine regions recognized officially as the sanctioned QWpsr in Bulgaria, it is difficult to engage in the hegemonic discourse of fine wine premised upon a hierarchically organized and bureaucratically sanctioned classification of carefully demarcated locales. The bureaucratization of wine thus provides one of the means by which wine producers can claim *and* be recognized for their cultural heritage.

Unlike *cultural heritage,* the term *cultural patrimony* implies a sense of entitlement. While Bulgarians consider winemaking as a cultural patrimony attaching a strong sense of entitlement, their cultural politics of wine in the global market is limited by the bureaucratization of wine that establishes an officially sanctioned classification system. The highly competitive global wine market depends on these classification systems based on places. Yet, as the Bulgarian case shows, there are power relations among competing identities of "place" both in the domestic as well as international levels. The implication of the hegemonic wine hierarchy (from the vantage point of the global market) is that it reproduces a structure where certain locales are valued higher than others. More important, this hierarchy also limits the cultural capital of other more marginal locales that thrive to articulate their appropriate market value and elevate their standing within the hierarchy. The labeling rules and authentication of particular geographical origin in today's wine world, therefore, provide a fascinating case to examine the often unnoticed role of bureaucratization of wine and how it impacts the cultural politics of wine for marginal wine producers trying to position themselves in the competitive market.

By discussing the Bulgarian case, I have also suggested that the bureaucratized system of classification limits local contestations against the hegemonic discourse of wine that privileges the notion of *terroir.* Furthermore, it allows little room to negotiate the local sense of entitlement of the wine heritage that has not stressed such a notion as shown in Bulgarians' enthusiasm for homemade wine. The multiple layers of power relations within the global wine industry are deeply engaged in the bureaucratization of wine. This prompts us to rethink the commonly presumed (and often romanticized) relationships of geographical origins, taste, quality, and identity of wine in the contemporary globalized world. Who claims the relationship between a particular geographical origin and taste? Whose claim is accepted, thereby providing an official sanctioning of a particular wine identity and quality? And finally, who is the audience that recognizes such a claim?

The Bulgarian case points to the significance of paying attention to these interrelated questions to understand the mechanism as well as the consequences in the bureaucratization of wine. In the European tradition, wine has never been simply an alcoholic beverage or value-added commodity. It has been always part of a distinctive cultural heritage and ownership of culture deemed worthy of state protection. To consider the cultural politics of wine merely in relation to marketing in the era of neoliberal globalization is to miss the complex workings of power in the local, state, global, and supranational levels that grant one the exclusive right and ownership of a particular cultural heritage. The identity of a wine is not only a result of grape sort, soil type, and other technological interventions, but also a reflection of cultural politics and political economy.

NOTES

1. My fieldwork for this research occurred between 2008 (consecutive five months including the harvest and winemaking season) and 2009 (three months over the summer), as well as follow-up research in 2012 (three weeks over the summer). This chapter draws from my larger postdoctoral project supported by an IREX fellowship (IARO through a U.S. State Department Title VIII Grant), a Woodrow Wilson International Center for Scholars East European Policy Fellowship, and Wayne State University's Faculty Research Grant. None of these sponsors are responsible for the views expressed in this chapter.
2. The dictionary definition of *patrimony* is "property or legal entitlements inherited from one's father and handed down through generations" (*New Oxford American Dictionary*). Scholarly discussion of cultural patrimony has been related to the idea of "owning culture" (see especially Kaneff and King 2004; Taylor 1994).
3. One of the prominent Bulgarian national heroes, G. S. Rakovski, famously wrote: "In Bulgaria, it is rare for Bulgarians not to have vineyards. This is their favorite occupation. A peasant considers himself unhappy and feels ashamed if he does not have a vineyard" (1859).
4. For instance, there was an umbrella organization for the entire wine industry called D.S.O Vinprom (*Durjaven Spirten Obedeninie Vinprom*, State Spirit Union Wine Industry) in Bulgaria. Under this organization,

each winery was named Vinprom X (based on the name of the location of the wineries).

5. For instance, a famous Bulgarian wine from the native grape sort Mavrud is commonly associated with Vinprom Assenovgrad (Wine Industry Assenovgrad), where the wine plant is located. Similarly, Vinprom Stambolovo (Wine Industry Stambolovo) is associated with Merlot. While the majority of the vineyards for Mavrud was located around Vinprom Assenovgrad, the vineyards for Merlot have been located all around Bulgaria, and it was hardly guaranteed that the Merlot from Vinprom Stambolovo was produced from the grapes of nearby vineyards.

6. In official terms, the EU regulations mention three groups for products of particular geographical origin: PDO (Protected Designation of Origin), PGI (Protected Geographical Indication), and TSG (Traditional Specialty Guaranteed). Wine and spirits follow a separate regime under this umbrella regulation (Regulations on the Protection of Geographical Indications and Designations of Origin for Agricultural Product and Foodstuffs, EU No 510/2006), commonly referred to as the "geographical indication/appellation system."

7. The locations of the wineries marked in this map are only a partial representation of the industry. The map does not list all wineries in Bulgaria.

Labor, Commodification, and the Politics of Wine

RACHEL E. BLACK AND ROBERT C. ULIN

Arjun Appadurai argued cogently in his edited *The Social Life of Things* (1986) that theorists have paid insufficient attention to the representations and cultural mediations of commodities. It was less his intention to provide an ill-deserved autonomy to commodities than to supply a perspective on "material things" and their circulation as more than simply derivative. In arguing such a point of view, Appadurai had in mind, among others, the Marxist tradition according to which commodities were often regarded as derivative of social labor, thereby ignoring their cultural articulations and their social meanings. It was Appadurai's intention to encourage us to think more profoundly about how culture shapes the goods we produce, represent, and consume.

Appadurai's argument seems especially relevant to wine, which by all senses of value is one of the most symbolically and culturally charged commodities. One only need reflect upon the elaborated vocabulary we associate with its description and evaluation and how wine in many places around the world has become iconic for the "good life." However, and here Marx did get it right, under the conditions of late capitalism, and arguably earlier, commodities seem to take on a life of their own. Marx referred to this process as *fetishiza-tion*, whose consequence was the failure to recognize the labor embodied in a commodity's fashioning. For Marx, not only did commodities appear falsely to have a life of their own, but labor in capitalism assumed a condition of alienation.

Wine is, in particular, very much illustrative of this tendency toward both fetish and alienated labor in that most wine writers have focused on this venerated beverage without giving due consideration to the social and historical conditions of its making. Popular journals on wine, for example, provide copious details on the wine itself and its *terroir* of origin without telling us much about workers in the vineyard or, for that matter, the historical and political processes that elevate the reputations of some winegrowing regions over others. Even more serious works on wine by renowned scholars often present a narrative of local wines from the top down, thus failing to address growers and their workers who often find themselves in the historical margins.

One of the particular strengths anthropology brings to the study of wine is its focus on differential power processes inclusive of culture, political economy, and politics that underlie and inform the narratives through which heterogeneous winegrowing communities are represented locally and globally. This section of the volume speaks, therefore, to issues of labor both in terms of social class and gender. It is especially important in challenging uniform assumptions about wine and winegrowing populations by addressing how winegrowers in the concrete are differentially positioned. Moreover, the process of commodification is critically examined, as are state politics, in shaping the global reputations of wines. The objective of the following three chapters is not to tarnish the romantic image of wine but rather to challenge its potential for fetish by focusing on power, representation, and social relations in their multiplicity.

Marion Demossier's "Following *Grands Crus:* Global Markets, Transnational Histories, and Wine" exemplifies well this volume's theme to discuss wines in the particular and to make use of wine to elaborate salient contemporary issues in the social sciences and humanities. Demossier provides us with a model for studying wine that breaks with a long-standing tradition of its localization, reinforced by the concept of *terroir,* and its essentialization by being regarded, like culture, as a circumscribed object consisting of ideal characteristics. Her strategy is to shift the narrative to analyzing global and transnational processes as they conjointly shape and in turn are shaped by the local. She deconstructs, moreover, our by now familiar concept of *terroir* by showing how this concept fossilizes social relations, work, and land ownership. She points out, though, that there is an emerging slight shift away from the focus on soil to labor as the determining factor in establishing the quality of wine. Demossier shows how dominant cultural forms, in her case the *Côte d'or grands crus,* are embraced and significantly transformed in the midst of power relations that link localities to the wider world. For Demossier, the globalization of the *grands crus* is not simply a straightforward process, as their representation and employment have to respond to different and changing societal fashions. She concludes by emphasizing the importance of transnationalism to examining what she calls "scale-making projects" and the emergence of "new landscapes of wine cultures and tastes."

Winnie Lem's "Regimes of Regulation, Gender, and Divisions of Labor in Languedoc Viticulture" is very important and unique for what she reveals about the gendering of wine. Lem's long-term research has been conducted in Languedoc-Roussillon in the south of France known for its small-scale family farms and high-yielding low-grade wines. She is interested in the issue of succession among winegrowing families but also the processes through which men and women are "deliberately fashioned or reproduced as workers." Lem makes use of Marxist and neo-Marxist perspectives, especially Gramsci, in identifying two different regimes of social control, the regime of family hegemony and the regime of family authoritarianism. While both regimes involve regulation of adult children by the family patriarch, she contends that family hegemony has a component of consent absent in family authoritarianism. While Lem believes that family farming seeks to fend off the worst implications of globalization that entails problems with succession, she also argues that the unit of family production has masculinized viticulture. The end result of this male gendering process is the commodification of wine production in Languedoc and its integration into national and international markets.

Adam Walker and Paul Manning's "Georgia Wine: The Transformation of Socialist Quantity into Postsocialist Quality" looks at the politics of representation through evaluating Georgian wine as an index of transformation. Walker and Manning relate that the retrospective view of commodities under socialism is one that emphasizes quantity over quality. Consequently, the socialists are viewed as producing poor-quality commodities inclusive of wine while also having through productivist logic little regard for the environment and perhaps labor more generally. However, Walker and Manning are careful to point out that this view is ironic in that socialism built the conditions of industrialization necessary for contemporary postsocialist wine production.

Moreover, they challenge the assumption that the period of socialism entailed a simple disregard for quality wine production. Rather, attempts were made to improve the quality of Georgian wine with the intention of making it a luxury commodity available for all rather than a select class of privileged consumers. The narrative constructed by Walker and Manning is complex and nuanced, taking up the themes of resistance to socialist wine production and the integration of wine with contested identities. They conclude that quality has now become a marker of postsocialist success even though how quality is measured is "ideologically" contested.

As we can see, wine as an object of production, circulation, and consumption never operates independently from specific historical, cultural, and political contexts. It is, moreover, a commodity that enables us to examine the complexities of local and global processes in their interrelation and in the multiple and often conflicting arenas of individual and collective identities.

CHAPTER TEN

Following *Grands Crus:* Global Markets, Transnational Histories, and Wine

MARION DEMOSSIER

When I started a doctoral thesis three decades ago on Burgundian viticulture under the direction of Isac Chiva,[1] one of the founders of French rural anthropology, it was expected that a traditional ethnographic research project would focus on a single defined bounded site, clearly anthropologically conceptualized and with a strong emphasis on techniques and material culture (Marcel Maget's influence). The ideal framework for the researcher was the administrative unit of the region, in my case the *département* of Côte d'Or and the AOC (Denomination of Origin) area, as together they represented the ideal institutional, socioeconomic, and political contexts. As a young ethnographer at the time, my topic, the winegrowers of the Côte d'Or, was, however, a risky choice in the sense that the study of wine elites was largely underrepresented in the discipline of "anthropology at home," but seemed logical and unproblematic given the significance of winegrowers in the traditional field of peasant studies.[2]

Progressing into the "thick description" of the diverse deployments of what it meant to be a *grand cru* producer in this area, it became quickly obvious to me that a strict focus on wine production would only tell one side of the story. Seven years of intensive fieldwork have been followed since then by another twenty years of more fragmented and multi-sited ethnographic encounters.[3] However, throughout that time, I have felt constantly constrained by the deeply rooted social construction of wine at the local level and its essentialization as an anthropological object of study. "We have nothing to sell here" was the ubiquitous rhetorical device offered by the local *grands crus* producers when asked about past and present recessions. Global forces and the compression of time and space have had an ambiguous and paradoxical impact on expressions of Burgundian professional identification. Its entanglement with cultural complexity was above all compounded by its essentialization in public discourse with the figure of the *vigneron* as an artisan and artist dominating the field of action (Trubek 2008; Ulin 1996).

Martin Sökefeld has argued that this ambivalence and dualism is an essential aspect of the usefulness of identity as a productive element as it contributes to its refinement (1996). In the case of the *grands crus* producers, this was intrinsically part of the professional and regional discourse, which often hides the commodification of the product, obscuring the complex networks of its economic circulation and in some cases, ill-defined commercial practices.[4] The material difficulties of following wine, from the vineyard to the glass and beyond regional or even national geographic boundaries, risks becoming a quest for the Holy Grail in the context of a product constructed and studied as a closed object in professional, regional, and national terms. Through the ethnographic study of discourses and practices, anthropology has the ability to collapse a number of potentially troublesome dichotomies such as the local and global, the virtual and real, the bounded and unbounded, the universal and the particular. The *Grands Crus* thus offer an ideal opportunity to examine not only the commodification of wine in transnational terms, but also the site, which has adapted itself to global forces. As Phillips has argued, food, and wine here has been and continues to be central to the production of a global imaginary (2006, 43). In the flow of ideas and people inscribed in this global imaginary, production and consumption remain two sides of the same coin.

Starting from the premise that high-quality wine is a global commodity that could be defined at the intersection of nationalism, cultural "distinction" deployed by a wealthy group of international consumers, and Western European viticulture, this chapter seeks to engage with recent methodological debates on multi-sited ethnography (Falzon 2009). Rather than mirroring the multi-sited ethnography of commodities such as sugar (Mintz 1985), tuna (Bestor 2001), or, more recently mushrooms (Choy et al. 2009, 197), the *grands crus* story offers a new insight into the social construction of quality at the local level and its circulation as an iconic discourse of the negotiated relationship between culture and nature. Through the concept of *terroir* and its globalization, the Côte d'Or *grands crus* offer a classic example of a geographically and historically stable site and a fluctuating, but strongly culturally defined group of producers working in a particular ecological milieu. The metaphysics of sedentarism as defined by Lisa Makkhi (cited by Gupta and Ferguson 1997, 6) here is embedded in the *grands crus* story. In the overwhelming majority of cases, the families of producers have been present for at least three generations, and it is commonly said that: "You need three graves in the cemetery to belong." It is true that a small number of international companies such as AXA insurance or the Champagne house Henriot have invested in the region in recent years, but they have not affected the social configuration of the place significantly as often they provide employment for locals and "keep everything as it was." Compared to other wine regions, the Burgundian landownership structure and the scale of the vineyard has deterred any major external investments from international companies, and even the wealthiest local winegrowers had to look outside Burgundy for investments. As Andonin Rodet, a prominent Burgundian *négociant* noted during an interview in the *Nouvel Observateur:* "We are looking South because we are so crammed in our native Burgundy."[5]

In what follows, the Burgundian *grands crus* story will be analyzed against the background of globalization and in terms of transnational practices and representations by focusing on the production of culture "in place" and its translation and displacement in other cultural and social settings. Through an ethnography of *grands crus*, the production and consumption of these wines will be examined in the light of recent debates about *terroir,* "distinction," taste, and place. I will argue that transnationalism creates new meanings and representations, which disconnect the product from its original birthplace, but translate it within a new context of consumption. In return, transnationalism transforms locality while maintaining the *grands crus* story. What the producer or consumer engages with is this core set of values articulated and reiterated that bounds a place to a product through its constant deployment and circulation. Learning the grammar of the site and the language of its products can thus become integral to the experience of drinking and to the social forms and shared sociability underpinning it. Individuals engage in different ways with the place and product. Throughout my continuous and regular multi-sited ethnography of the Côte d'Or, new ethnographic vignettes have continually called into question our ethnographic analysis of the tensions between the single boundedness of the site and its wider circulation at the global level. Following Matei Candea's argument, this chapter aims to engage with the concept of arbitrary locations and the debate surrounding the second generation of multi-sited ethnography to examine the key question of the site as loci of culture (Falzon 2009). The question of the site here is considered as a bounded unit of analysis (Candea 2007, 169) crucial in ethnological terms as it is essentialized while being globalized. By following its expression and contradictory manifestations through discourses and practices emerging in the field of a bounded location, it provides the ethnographer with a fruitful way to examine wine culture at the local level in the context of globalization. Rather than Crucetta's ethnography (Candea 2007, 175), a community ethnography, that of Burgundian *grands crus* producers, is the arbitrary location that provides a window into complexity.

THE CÔTE D'OR *GRANDS CRUS:* A GLOBAL IMAGINARY OF EXCELLENCE

Wine in Burgundy is often discussed in the plural, defined as a wide and diverse range of precise geographic plots, some of them no larger than a small garden, but always clearly identified and named. The evocative power of Romanée Saint Vivant, Corton, and Puligny-Montrachet among others classifies the drinker immediately in an international common language shared by educated, wealthy, discerning, and, until recently, predominantly Westernized elites. Like Bordeaux wines, Burgundian *grands crus* reinforce ideas about lifestyle and class in a more than ever culturally differentiated world. Here in the Côte d'Or, the experience takes on a new dimension. The international resonance of the *grands crus* story not only appeals to consumers seeking distinction in the Bourdieusian sense, but has also become emblematic in the world of wine production.

This evocative and powerful construction of the place as a natural site protected from any external changes has progressively been consolidated in response to the increasing internationalization of wine supply and the growing competition in the market. It offers a counterstory to that of globalization, standardization, and industrialization as increasingly, the taste of place is seen as a challenge to the vast array of anonymous, mass-produced foods and beverages now available to the consumer (Bessière 1998; Peace 2011; Pratt 2007; Trubek 2008). If quality was not explicitly spelled out at the core of this social edifice of Burgundian wines, it is because the main story was one of a historically stable *terroir* defined as an imaginary discourse about the historical relationship between a specific place, one acquired with difficulty and through hard labor, and a specific winegrower and his family. The *terroir* story fossilizes social relations, work, and landownership (see Robert Ulin's chapter in this volume).

The Côte d'Or, as a limited area of production, is marked by the belief in the advantages of scarcity as a crucial means of adding value, which has ensured a long period of uncontested hegemony on the international scene. As Garcia-Parpet has argued, this confidence has been threatened by the increase in power of the countries that have been termed "New World" since the 1990s (2008, 238). More competitive in price, perceived as reliable in terms of quality, and appealing to young urban wealthy segments of society, these countries have impacted on the positioning of more traditional and bourgeois products such as Burgundian wines. The principle of rarity and limitation of supply was applied as a marketing technique, especially at the top of the wine hierarchy, and was even emphasized among producers of *grands crus* to construct the quality of their products in a differentiated fashion. This tendency has been reinforced in a growing and competitive market where a transnational affluent but diversified group has shown a strong demand for clearly identified wines as markers of social status and "distinction." The AOC system has effectively consecrated the *terroir* story, which has now been promoted for several decades.[6] Recent attempts by individuals to shift these boundaries have been resisted by the INAO (the institute in charge of granting rights to AOC) as exemplified by the unsuccessful fight of a Nuits-Saint-Georges winegrower to have his Saint-Georges classified as *grands crus*.

Yet what has changed at the core of this construction is the shift in emphasis toward the winegrower and his labor and away from the soil or geological characteristics as the loci and prime characteristic of quality. Over the years and with the progress of oenology as well as general knowledge about wine, the geological argument still dominates the social construction of quality,[7] but has lost some of its ability to convince consumers and producers of its unique effect in the definition of quality in wines. What we have witnessed in parallel at regional and global levels is the rise of the winegrower and winegrowing craft as one of responsible land custodianship. The slow development of organic vine growing in France illustrates this new shift.[8] This shift can also be read through the square meters devoted to individual winegrowers and their stories in the L'Athéneum wine bookshop located in Beaune, a section that did not exist two decades ago (see Daynes's chapter in this volume).

As we have seen, the Côte d'Or *grands crus* story has contained at its core a certain degree of stability, while at the same time adapting its main characteristics to the increasing modernization of our societies. Its success, so often praised internationally by wine lovers, experts, and producers, could be defined as an archetypal transnational investment terrain (Peace 2011, 251) and a successful worldwide cultural story (in Eriksen's meaning; 2001, 294). Its long-established reputation as a significant place producing the best wines in the world relies on the connections made between different imaginative discourses and experiences, which promote place, producers, and consumers in a quasi-religious encounter. The taste of place here takes on its full meaning, but is passed on in different ways from the knowledge about the place to the taste of a particular wine. On one hand, the story is about a real and authentic social experience of the wine-grower, usually the head of the lineage with his close and enduring tie to the land that is recurrent in narratives about Burgundy. But this is also about experiencing the showcase-bounded culture, the visit to the cellar, the knowledge of the producer, and the visual and gustative initiation to a particular location or plot. For some wine lovers, this visual, gustatory, and sensorial experience constituted through the encounter with this bounded culture is conducted through meeting winegrowers and their families, descending to the cellar, learning about the grammar of the *grands crus,* and by memorizing the contrasted social and emotional experiences.[9] Embedded in a specific place usually defined at a gustatory, an emotional, and a sensorial level, the encounter encapsulates a distinctive social experience of a cultural form that could be easily disseminated, translated, and shared worldwide. Many wine lovers compete to access these stories as social experiences and dream of having visited and tasted the object of their desires. As one of my Scottish wine lover informers wrote when he learned he would be invited to visit the famous DRC (Domaine de la Romanée Conti): "It includes attending the wine auction, and Andrew tells me that we will also be visiting DRC!!!!!!" As the novice and less knowledgeable consumer is often drawn to Burgundy because of its image of prestige and social affluence, he or she could, in some cases, be put off by the elitist and competitive culture surrounding it. Yet their engagement takes very different forms (Teil 2004).

Like the tuna industry analyzed by Bestor, the Côte d'Or *grands crus* story acts as a form of cultural marker for the world wine industry, and is perpetuated, disseminated, and transmitted through various connections established among agents and brokers effecting linkages. The technicians of globalization, as Bestor defines them, play an important part in essentializing the story and connecting the producers and consumers to the original experience (2003). Yet they also influence the ways wine is made and play a crucial role in creating a market niche for specific products as explained by one of my long-term informers: "This is the case for me. I have agents in Paris and in Japan, they like my wine, they encourage me to develop, they buy and pay well, this is encouraging… Behind this they create your reputation and it has a snowball effect."

Very early on, the social and historical actors of Burgundy, especially of the Côte d'Or, historically a strong center of power politics, understood the necessity of traveling and disseminating the good news. The work of the Confrérie des Chevaliers du Tastevin, created in 1934, contributed to the same kind of dissemination, but with a strong emphasis in drawing back consumers and clients to the original experience. The Confrérie has some twelve thousand knights or *chevaliers* worldwide and is devoted to promoting Burgundy—the region and the wine—in grand style,[10] and its role has been one of promotion of the Côte d'Or *grands crus* model incarnated by the Clos de Vougeot as a site of cultural encounters and a distinctive historical and social experience. Most of its members belong to highly regarded professions, and it is presented as a private club.[11]

The Burgundy wine trade is made up of integrated social systems that connect production and consumption through tightly coupled linkages across great geographical distance. One of my informants cited the example of a well-known organic wine producer who, in 1993 following a poor harvest, decided to go to the United States with her bottles and organize tastings with clients and the press. It was a great success, and she not only increased her prices tenfold but also sold her entire stock. The originality of the model is that it puts emphasis on drawing back the consumers to the original site of a culturally mediated experience through the connection to the grower. Here too the question is about the ways dominant cultural forms may be picked up and used and significantly transformed in the midst of the field of power relations that link localities to a wider world (Gupta and Ferguson 1997, 5).

TRANSLATING *TERROIR* IN NEW ZEALAND

The anthropology of wine has been dominated by a literature concerned with places and peoples and how the experience of space is socially constructed (Trubek 2008; Ulin 1996). Geographers have also contributed constructively to the debate by focusing on places and how they are marketed within the global wine chain supply. Global trade is seen as increasingly organized through ever more complex interfirm and intrafirm relationships and contracts. Thus value chain research emphasizes that firms are linked in internationally dispersed, but integrated systems of input supply, trade, production, marketing, and consumption (Gwynne 2008, 95). Yet even if geographers have endorsed the fact that the only way to show that one's wine has *terroir* is to make it and then tell people about it, very little is known about how specific cultural forms are imposed, invented, reworked, and transformed from local vantage points. As in the case of tuna, the contemporary wine market could be defined as utopian in the sense that it is nowhere in particular and everywhere at once (Bestor 2003, 301). What role do social actors play in telling the *grands crus* story to others? To what extent is the international market for *grands crus* defined more through storytelling than political economy? Moreover, how products acquire more value through their circulation is another key question.

The AOC wine model is seen by several commentators as a monopoly rent; the AOC recognition gives the *grands crus* producers a unique positioning in economic terms at the international level. While we are told everything about production, the consumer or buyer is to some extent invisible in the minds of Burgundian winegrowers. Yet the consumer's role has been central in the definition of wine as a commodity of a certain prestige and status, and wine culture with its experts has often mediatized the engagement with the product through social media and wine blogs (Demossier 2010). Product diversity goes together with strong consumer price heterogeneity that is not random but tightly linked to the French system of *appellation d'origine contrôlée* (AOC) on the basis of a hierarchical distinction among specific, limited geographical areas or *terroirs* (Chiffola and Laporte 2006, 164). Chiffola and Laporte have shown that there is still significant price variability within individual appellations (2006). They argue that a given appellation is not sufficient to define or characterize a type of quality for the set of products endowed with it. Quality depends on the technical choices each producer makes within the limits set by each appellation "decree."

Most *domaines* possess several appellations, but with a concentration on regional appellations or, at the other end of the spectrum, oriented toward the more prestigious *crus*. *Domaines* are also differentiated by how they sell; that is, sale circuits used and their corresponding clienteles. Chiffola and Laporte both note that only prices posted by the *domaines* for private customers who come to buy wine onsite may be known, and this information does not circulate extensively (2006). Meanwhile, price reached by a producer and intermediary is usually a strategic piece of information that remains confidential. In their analysis of price formation, they argue that professional relations and routines play an important role as well as networks of friendship. It should be noted, however, that a valuable appellation portfolio is only associated with prestigious status if the producer actively promotes it, and this involves production practices, business strategy, and active integration into "exchange networks" (Chiffola and Laporte 2006).

This cultural form cannot be circulated without a wider and continuous dissemination encouraged by technicians of globalization (Bestor 2003) who have themselves experienced the site. During my initial period of fieldwork in the 1990s, I stayed with a family of winegrowers who more than twenty years later remain some of my key informants. Their particular positioning in the wine industry was always associated with a *regard éloigné* and a certain distance due to the vicissitudes of life: twenty-four-year-old Elodie, a graduate student in English, had to take over the running of the *domaine* following the sudden death of her father during the harvest. She fell in love with a young bus driver, Nathan, originally from a family of farmers from the Auxois (north of the Côte d'Or) currently employed at the viticulture school, and they decided to take over the management of the *domaine* composed primarily of *grands crus*. When they agreed to open their doors to an anthropologist, they already had several students living with them and they were in a transitional stage in terms of their acquisition of knowledge and skills. This very privileged ethnographic experience was one of the richest and most successful as we were all going through the learning process.

Among the students working there, I met a young winegrower from New Zealand, Rick, who came to discover "how *grands crus* were made." Rick was the oldest of a family of New Zealand Otago Pinot Noir producers and he stayed for a period of one year to learn his trade. Following his experience, Nathan, then Elodie and years later their children went to visit Rick and to promote the Burgundian wine model. In 2010, Rick, now the president of the Central Otago Winegrowers Association (COWA), invited me to come and discuss the *terroir* strategy with local producers in New Zealand, an invitation I could not accept at the time. Asked why *terroir* was of interest to New Zealand wine producers, Rick responded that "in defining Central Otago's own viticultural path forward, it has been, and will continue to be, essential to look towards the classic model of Burgundy and its *climats* for inspiration and guidance." In a letter addressed to the Association pour la reconnaissance des climats de Bourgogne on November 26, 2010, Rick argued:

> With a truly noble variety content to grow here, along with expressive schist-based soils and a complex array of microclimates and landscapes, the region naturally looks now to seek clarity in the potential of each site and how this might be manifested in the glass. It is clear that inspiration and direction may be gained in this endeavor by considering the classical model of Burgundy and the heritage of *les climats*.

Through Rick's attachment to Burgundy and his admiration for the *grands crus* model, several strategies were promoted in Otago to imitate Burgundy's success. Rick's letter underlined the growing concerns for the relationship between a site and its concrete gustative and sensorial expression in the glass through the taste of the place.

At the core of Otago wine producers' concerns is the role of the winegrower as one of custodianship "in an ongoing pursuit of quality" as emphasized by Rick. Yet what this cultural exchange, established since 2006 between Otago and the Côte d'Or wine producers, tells us is how some of the dominating conceptions of wine and regulation of the market, traditionally defined by their relationship to nature (the Old World equals nature as a driving determining force, and in the New World, nature is seen as an enemy that must be controlled and dominated by science), can overlap in some local circumstances and lose their initial meaning in the process of transnational circulation. Anthropologist Robert Ulin has argued that the relationship between artisanship and science is a point of conflict and tension in the self-definition of winegrowing culture in southwest France, and thus a cultural view of work and self-identity that is differentiated acknowledges both the potential and the constraints of power (2002, 691).

READING AND CONSUMING *GRANDS CRUS* IN ASIA

In the sociological literature on winemaking, the work of Mary Douglas (1997) and Wei Zhao's (2005) analysis of wine classification open a fruitful debate about the concept of classifications and their implicit, but controlled understandings (Chauvin 2009, 6). The *grands crus* story is not only about the French classification system based on geographic origin rather than grape variety as in America, but it is also about how the reading of these classifications operates differently in transnational contexts, through different drinking cultures. I have argued elsewhere that wine can be described as a food for hierarchy and by choosing which wine to buy and in what circumstances to drink it, wine consumers are building identity (2005). Using Wei Zhao's theoretical framework defining classifications, I would like to examine the issue of the *grands crus* and their diversified consumers.

According to Zhao, classifications have three main functions. They confer identities on social actors or objects and inherently imply social control, they create social boundaries signifying the social standing of actors, and finally they involve political struggles between different interest groups and classifications embodying political power. In this context, the appellation classification in the French wine industry is already more sophisticated and refined than that in the American wine industry (Zhao 2005, 184). The *grands crus* in the French system express specific social values and embody distinctive beliefs. Their consumption thus creates social boundaries, resulting in differentiation in social standing among actors defining the relationship between them and describing the whole structure. As we are talking about extremely expensive wine (up to £8,000 a

bottle), this is no longer about differentiation between groups already economically distinct, but it is more about internal group definition and bounding where
new groups disturb the already existing social configuration. Wine experts have
reported several stories to me about the new social class of parvenus who could
afford such wines but "do not have the culture." I even know of a famous French
sommelier who gave up his job in the 1990s as a result of his confrontation with
this new economically wealthy group. Another wine international expert told me
of his consternation when he saw a Russian "wine lover" in Paris buying a bottle
of DRC and adding coca cola to the contents of his glass. One of my compatriots
living in London among expatriate bankers described the lack of knowledge and
the snobbery attached to ordering wine in restaurants when going out with city
friends: "They asked for the wine list and chose the most expensive wine from
Bordeaux or Burgundy, they know nothing about wine."

Using different ethnographic vignettes, I want to examine how the complexity intrinsic to the *grands crus* story acts as a global classification struggle competing to access the new Asian wine market. Bordeaux and Burgundy compete
to attract new Asian consumers to their markets and the encounter has taken
different forms with, for example, Chinese buyers investing in old Bordeaux
grands crus vintages. What they share in common is the prestige and economic
status of their products, yet they offer different kinds of engagement with their
local products reflecting their respective local and regional wine economies.
During my last visit to Beaune, several wine producers mentioned Asia and its
potential as a wine market. February 2011 was marked by the launching of the
Académie du vin de France in Hong-Kong by l'Ecole du vin (School of Wine)
and its creator, Olivier Thiénot. I previously interviewed Olivier in 2004 in
Paris a year after the creation of his school, and the Académie project was not
yet on the cards. We met with some of his collaborators, Marie-Dominique
Bradford, still with him, and Christophe Macra, who has since left, to share
wines they wanted to present to their students the day after. According to Olivier, "this is not all about *typicité* and the ability to recognize and appreciate the
quality of wines from all over the world, this is also about sociability." Their
pedagogic approach was at the time defined by the WSET (Wine and Spirits
Education Trust), and a strong emphasis was put on the knowledge acquired
and, implicitly, the performative aspect of wine tasting. Most of their *stagiaires*,
as they called them, were French, urban, young male and female professionals
who wanted to enhance their social status. Yet what was also clearly emphasized was the sociable and playful atmosphere of the gathering. However, tasting and its evaluation were central for the process of learning accompanying
the dissemination of wine culture.

Since then the école du vin de France has developed, counting today around fifteen thousand students per year (no longer called *stagiaires*), and offers tasting events in Asia, Hong Kong, China, and Taiwan. Its website claims to engage with wine culture and its stance is about acquiring culinary and oenological knowledge in a professional context: "our courses cater for any wine enthusiast, anyone who is interested in wine for personal reason, anyone who already works or wishes to work around wine." A strong connection is established with trade in luxury goods, gastronomy, and gourmet products, as well as the wine industry, hotels, restaurants, and tourism. This cultural model of wine tasting, which has grown in parallel with the spread of French culinary culture led by French chefs abroad, targets a group of newcomers through sociability, pleasure, and taste. What it tells us about Burgundy as a model and cultural form is that place matters as much for consumers as producers. The understanding of place through taste and its memorization remains a question of personal judgment, cultural formatting of your palate, and individual predispositions, and a great deal of differentiation prevails among tasters. Knowledge in this context becomes a key issue in terms of economic and social power.

Over the last two decades, Chinese and Asian consumer preferences for liquor and beverage consumption have significantly altered as per capita income has increased (Pan, Chang, and Malaga 2006, 975). Wine is largely perceived as a luxury good and the market for wine consumption is still in its initial stages, but more and more people in the emerging middle and upper classes are drinking what they define as "table wine" (interesting term in itself). One of my Chinese postgraduate students in politics told me that wine knowledge and culture is seen as conferring a high-status identity, and at a time of major societal transformations the access and acquisition of wine knowledge and culture is a way of signifying and consolidating your social standing and prestige. Wine culture has become a means of Westernizing, and she recalled her father taking her to classes in wine tasting as part of her preparation before going to study in Europe. Burgundy has also organized wine tours to present its vineyards to Chinese consumers, and last year I met a group of Chinese academics who were taking pictures of the emblematic Romanée-Conti plot in front of a clear warning sign stating in French and English: "Many people come and visit this site, we understand. We ask you nevertheless to remain on the road and request that under no condition you enter the vineyard." The globalization of *grands crus* is far from a straightforward process. It needs to mobilize consumers in different fashions responding to societal changes and the greater mobility of individuals.

Yet similarly to Europe, the *grands crus* story in Asia appeals to a wide range of consumers who cannot be reduced to a well-defined market. The son of my main informers mentioned earlier, Pierre, who at the time of my initial fieldwork was just four years of age, told me his story of working as a wine bar attendant when he was in Tokyo for a year following his three-month stay in New Zealand with Rick, my New Zealand informer. Every evening around the same time, a young Japanese male professional dressed in a suit came to the bar, sat down, and ordered a different Burgundian wine. After a few nights, Pierre introduced himself as from the area in question and asked him if he had been to Burgundy before. The Japanese wine enthusiast replied by naming each of the *crus* of the Côte, mentioning the names of some of the most renowned producers and describing with precision the tastes of some of the wines even if he declared after a while that actually he never been there, illustrating the deterritorialization of the drinking encounter with Burgundy. Pierre was impressed by the knowledge of this client and said that during his trip he met a few Japanese wine lovers obsessed with Burgundy. In Japan, the status of wine is also an important social marker and the gift culture, which is part of how business is conducted, gives a prominent place to wine as a gift enhancing the status of the donor. This kind of fascination with places and names is shared by the growing middle class in South Korea.

Interestingly enough, the Burgundian wine profession recognized that its commercial structures prevented it accessing these new markets compared to Bordeaux wines. What it has to offer, however, is the singularity of each of its *grands crus* through an imaginary story of excellence linking a winegrower and his or her work to a plot of land and a highly singularized commodity. Identifying, naming, and knowing become part of this complex commodification process, yet the consumption of these products remains highly differentiated and competitive in terms of access to knowledge and thus power. The examples of producers Georges Roumier, Marc Colin, and Michel Colin-Deléger are often cited by winegrowers as they had to face thousands of calls and faxes ordering their wines after they were cited in a Manga, *The Drops of God*, devoted to wine, which was a best seller in South Korea in 2004. *The Drops of God* was a smash hit in France (it has been translated by the publisher Glénat), helped to introduce wine to the masses in parts of Asia, and had a massive impact on the wine industry in South Korea.[12] The story is about the world of wine, its highly ritualized forms of knowledge, its critics, and Shizuku, who is summoned to the family home, a splendid European-style mansion, to hear the reading of his father's will. He learns that, in order to take ownership of his legacy, he must correctly identify, and describe in the manner of his late father, thirteen wines, the first twelve known as the "Twelve Apostles" and the thirteenth known as the "Drops of God" (*Kami no Shizuku* in the original Japanese edition and *Les Gouttes de Dieu* in the French translation). He also learns he has a competitor in this, a renowned young wine critic called Tomine Issei, whom his father had apparently recently adopted as his other son. The July 2009 *Decanter* publication of "The Power List" ranking of the wine industry's most influential individuals placed Shin and Yuko Kibayashi at number fifty, citing their work as "arguably the wine publication of the last 20 years." Without being aware of the storm happening so far away, a delegation of the BIVB (export managers of the Burgundy Wine Board) went on a visit to Korea in 2007 to discover that the Manga phenomenon had put Burgundy on the map of Korean consumers, and the delegation had to face forty companies and more than 900 people making inquiries about Burgundian wines in just twenty-four hours.[13] This episode, recalled during the opening of the first *vinosciences* launched in June 2011, provides an example of how Burgundy needs to communicate better.[14] But it is also about constructions of the local and the global that could nourish each other by being reembedded in some places with changing ideas about *grands crus* and the world reinscribed by people (Philipps 2006, 45). Here the Burgundy *grands crus* story takes on different forms and shapes, presented as an icon of Korean popular culture, but it is still about a plot, a winegrower, and a taste in the competitive world of *grands crus*. Knowledge thus plays a crucial role in enabling group identification and in including or excluding others in the competitive field of wine tasting.

CONCLUSIONS

For all its success, the *grands crus* story has not gone uncontested even in Burgundy and Bordeaux, and a few social actors have started to contest the hegemony of the system and to question their own viticultural practices as well as the value of *terroir* and the AOCs. If the new globalization process may play a role in reproducing distinct rural localities (Arce 1993), the globalization of wine also creates complex and contradictory processes essentializing further some fragments of the locality while transforming others. As part of the process, both territorialization and deterritorialization contribute to different engagements toward the imaginary world of wine. The VTFP (*Vins à très forte personnalité,* or wines with strong personalities), which were the center of the debate during the *vinosciences* of 2011, are an example of this transformation. These wines have been promoted by a new generation of ecologically minded wine producers who have decided to opt for a technical improvement of their own products, arguing that: "When you work hard and you aim at producing better wines, in one way or another it costs more, then you logically have to increase your prices and then your clientele changes as a result" (one of the VTFP producers). Behind their approach is the willingness to produce the best possible wines on the basis of a technical evaluation and a personal interpretation. In this category one might find natural wines (see chapter in this volume), but also wines with very long period of maturation or wines from sulphite macerations. As one producer remarked: "I make wines with a small amount of sulphur, but not systematically from organic grapes. One of my colleagues from Champagne is in the same boat." Most of the producers in this category are associated with biological wines and/or the biodynamie trend, which is far from unusual in French viticulture (Teil and Barrey 2009).

There is a sense that these products appeal to new consumers interested in ecological or environmental issues who are seeking other strategies to differentiate themselves from more traditional wine consumers (Demossier 2010). Another distinctive feature of these wines is that they, yet again, underline the singularity of their wines and provoke a negative reaction from experts, winegrowers, and other wine lovers already used to the taste of place (taste of *terroir*). Often the VTFP are perceived in wine tastings as having defects and containing technical flaws: "This one was sparkling, they did not like it, it did not correspond to their expectations in terms of the tastes of the AOC in this area. But you see I thought it was nice, you could drink it with your picnic on a nice summer's day," my informant told me. Changing tastes in our globalized era through the wide range of cuisines now available nearly anywhere in the world has an impact on tastes in wines. As a result, a few wine merchants and intermediaries see it as a promising niche market and encourage the producers to continue their quest as illustrated by the example of the Panthéon *caviste* (Paris).[15] The first *vinosciences* organized last June was about the VTFP, and the audience in the room was quite critical and suspicious about them as they were perceived as denying the role of *terroir*. This episode could be read as a disjuncture in relation to the *grands crus* story, but it is also about different strategies coalescing to respond to greater differentiation in parallel with the consolidation of the *terroir* and the *grands crus* story worldwide. As one of my informants explained: "If you are working very hard and you like your product and it sells, the AOC system becomes meaningless. What matters is quality..." In the increasingly globalized world of wine, transnationalization offers a fruitful platform to examine the relationship between scale-making projects and the emergence of new landscapes of wine culture and tastes.

NOTES

1. Isac Chiva's contribution to French ethnology has been outstanding. He passed away on April 30, 2012. This chapter is dedicated to him. www.lemonde.fr/disparitions/article/2012/05/21/isac-chiva-1925–2012-figure-majeure-de-l-anthropologie-sociale_1704947_3382.html.

2. The work of Charles Parain (1957) and Claude Royer (1980) inspired a trend in French ethnology that devoted its attention to the study of winegrowers as part of rural ethnology. There was already a strong local emphasis on the culture of winegrowers in France as exemplified by the mushrooming of several local museums. For example, in 1937, Beaune opened the Musée du Vin under the direction of Georges-Henri Rivière, one of the founding fathers of rural ethnology and curator of the famous Musée des Arts et traditions Populaires (MNATP) in Paris, which has recently closed down.

3. Two other periods of fieldwork took place, one semester in 1999 supported by the University of Bath, and a year in 2004 funded by the British Academy Research Grant Large Research Grant 35396.

4. Burgundy has over the years been marked by a number of major fraud cases, and recently some local wine producers have been prosecuted for cheating the AOC system and selling adulterated wines to the public with false labels.

5. *Guide Nouvel Observateur* 2000, 94.

6. A hierarchy based upon four different categories of AOCs was offered to the visitors: regional, village, *premiers crus,* and *grands crus,* and these could be easily read in the landscape. As the visitor ascends the hierarchy, the product becomes more rare and singular, not just more expensive. The *grands crus* represent just 1.4 percent of total regional production and are divided into thirty-three AOCs, while the regional wines represent 51.17 percent and include twenty-three AOCs.

7. It is worth noting that the recent application to UNESCO world heritage status was led by a geologist, a professor at the University of Dijon. However, he is a member of a research center, UMR 6298 Archéologie, Terre, Histoire et Sociétés.

8. For more information about the development of organic wines in France, see the excellent article written by Teil and Barrey (2009).

9. See the excellent review on food and the senses published by Sutton (2010).

10. See its website and the importance of the rituals in integrating new members: www.tastevin-bourgogne.com/en/.

11. See its website: www.tastevin-bourgogne.com/en/index.php?rub = 9.
12. It was created and written by Tadashi Agi, a pseudonym employed by the creative team of sister and brother Yuko and Shin Kibayashi, with artwork by Shu Okimoto.
13. See http://gestion-des-risques-interculturels.com/risques/un-manga-japonais-a.
14. The *vinosciences* were the first professional conferences organized among all the producers of Burgundy as a wine region under the headship of the BIVB (Bureau Interprofessional des vins de Bourgogne-Burgundy Wine Board). They aim at defining new directions, opening debates, and presenting the results of recent research projects.
15. See www.bourgogne-live.com/2011/11/les-vins-a-forte-personnalite-13.

CHAPTER ELEVEN

Georgian Wine: The Transformation of Socialist Quantity into Postsocialist Quality

ADAM WALKER AND PAUL MANNING

SOCIALIST WINE AND QUANTITY

Georgians like to say that Georgia is the homeland of wine. Archaeological evidence increasingly verifies this provenance: sites in Georgia, Armenia, and in the nearby Caucasus represent the oldest known sites of grape domestication and wine cultivation, stretching back as far as eight thousand years (Barnard et al. 2011; McGovern 2003a, 2003b). In contemporary Georgia, wine is the central material and symbolic element in the most ubiquitous Georgian ritual form, the *supra* (a feast characterized by ritually structured toasting and the display and consumption of large quantities of food and wine) (Kotthoff 1995; Manning 2012; Tuite 2008). With such a long history of production and central cultural value, it is fitting that Georgia became the largest producer of quality wine for Soviet consumption.

Since the fall of socialism, wine has taken on an additional heavy symbolic burden as an indicator of Georgia's postsocialist economic condition.

As one of the few Georgian commodities for which international recognition is a realistic aspiration, Georgian wine is increasingly significant for its ability to act as an index of transition, the success of which is measured in wine's supposedly emergent "quality." This developmental story depends on a widely circulated theory of the inverse relation of socialist production to quality, according to which, Georgian wine, like so many other socialist commodities (see Fehervary 2009; Manning 2009), necessarily decreased dramatically in quality under socialist production regimes that emphasized only quantity. Postsocialist wine production then, would have to convert socialist regimes of production, which emphasized quantity, into postsocialist regimes of production that would restore the quality Georgian wine allegedly had before socialism. Socialist production is represented as an unfortunate detour in the long history of Georgian wine production. Such a contention is ironic because the conditions for contemporary Georgian wine production lie in socialist processes of industrialization; as such postsocialist wine production cannot be understood without reference to its Soviet origins.

More generally, we argue that, not only are postsocialist regimes of production emphasizing quality self-consciously opposed to socialist regimes emphasizing quantity, but that the "qualitative" and "quantitative" logics of these respective regimes are matched in each case by homologous logics in regimes of consumption ("qualitative" and "quantitative" drinking). Thus, for postsocialist wine producers, transforming socialist quantity into postsocialist quality means not only producing new Georgian wines, but producing new Georgian forms of consumption for those wines. Thus, as Deborah Heath and Anne Meneley argue for comestible commodities in general, symbolic and technical categories of production inform consumption externally (providing material objects for consumption) and also internally (providing categories like "quantitative" and "qualitative" that inform and mold that consumption from within) (Heath and Meneley 2007, 593–594).

PRODUCING QUANTITY

The Soviet system notoriously privileged production as the primary domain through which communism as a social ideal could be achieved: "Relentlessly productionist, socialism represented production as the foundation of wealth, morality, and worth, with commerce and consumption presented as decidedly secondary bourgeois preoccupations" (Rogers and Verdery 2012). With the relative devaluing of consumption—in particular aspects of bourgeois consumption through which citizens achieve identities vis-à-vis their relation to commodities rather than through the productive identification with work—the Soviet system was bolstered by an ideological apparatus that greatly politicized acts of consumption. This is hardly surprising, as the centralization of production served to create a range of goods that in many ways constituted a central relationship of citizens to the state (Fehervary 2009). Consumption was invested with enormous importance because it had the potential to mediate the legitimacy of the unified system of production central to the Soviet socialist project.

Correspondingly, the Soviet state was also heavily involved in regulating appropriate modes of consumption among its citizens. Here, the sphere of consumption was not so much denigrated as ideologically managed, most famously by the promotion of *kul'turnost'*, or "culturedness," a sort of 1930s Stalinist civilizing process that regimented proper forms of consumption and comportment as well as creating new socialist "cultured" commodities to potentiate these new forms of cultured behavior. An important element of *kul'turnost'* was its distinct material culture. The *kul'turnost'* ideology sought to rehabilitate what had been considered bourgeois materialism and consumption by treating commodities as respectable symbols of "culture" *(kul'tura)* and as instrumental vehicles that could directly infuse "cultured" comportment into the socialist citizenry (Volkov 2000, 221–222).

The production of such goods as wine, champagne, caviar, cognac, chocolate, and perfume—from all of which sensuous pleasure is derived by being eaten, drunk, or smelled—was held to a high level of importance in early Soviet industrial development. Such "common luxuries" were material emblems of the ideal of "culturedness," and their circulation across Soviet space ("cultured trade") represented the achievement of socialist production to widely distribute goods that, once only available to few, could be enjoyed by all workers. These goods, according to Gronow, can be defined as mass-produced, cheaper copies of finer, expensive goods that had the aura of luxury because they had been consumed—or the Bolsheviks believed they had been consumed—by the former Russian nobility. The message these goods carried was clear: now the ordinary Soviet worker had access to a standard of living earlier restricted to members of the nobility or rich bourgeoisie (33).

The Soviet state early on designated wine—Georgian wine in particular—as a privileged common luxury slated for dramatically increased production. As Patterson has shown, Georgian wine was well known among pre-Soviet aristocratic elites: Georgian wine had been traded among nobility-run Georgian estates and elites in the empire since the 1890s. Thus, after collectivization, under the third five-year plan, Georgian oenologist Beridze conducted a survey of ecological microzones and indigenous grape varieties best suited for quality wine production within Georgia (Patterson 2007). This study affirmed that indigenous grape varieties were particularly suited to Georgian production, and organized the coordination of varieties with particular regions. The micro-zones and grape varieties established during this period have proved incredibly durable; they largely form the basis of postsocialist law on wine and vine that regulates production to this day.

The early experience with Georgian wine was undoubtedly influenced by a "cosmopolitan" familiarity among the Russian aristocracy with French wine, which was at the time gaining a reputation for its state-directed codification of estates that were to correspond to hierarchically graded quality designations. It is likely no coincidence that the delimitation of microzones of production associated with quality wine within the Soviet Union occurred at roughly the same time that France began to implement its distinctive *appellation contrôlée* laws. Since so much attention has been given to the Soviet Union's appropria-tion and emulation of America's high-modernist brand of large-scale Fordist agriculture (e.g., Scott 1998), the idea that the Soviet Union would appropriate a system mirroring the French program of *terroir* might come as a surprise. Whereas in Fordist agriculture production is undertaken by a singular pro-ducer (a firm) whose form could be appropriated by the Soviet system in which the state directly managed production, the French system of *appellation con-trôlée* assumes a collection of fairly small-scale producers whose production is protected in exchange for quality guarantees given by the state.

Terroir is a complex phenomenon that emerged historically with European—particularly French—political-economic and ideological struggles to define the character and significance of wine in international circuits of production, ex-change, and consumption. Strategic usage of the term derives from France in the nineteenth century, at a time when the complexity of wine as an object increased greatly. *Terroir* eventually came to function as a way for various groups—grape growers, winemakers, *négociants*, and wine houses—to protect their interests through the claim that a particular relationship among various factors relating to land (climate, slope, soil type, grape variety) produces place-based particularity that gives intrinsic value to wine, be it aesthetic, traditional, or cultural. Historically, regions that lay claim to possessing a unique *terroir* become aligned with state programs that grant protection to geographical in-dications by way of *appellation contrôlée* laws (for recent critical perspectives on *terroir* and geographical indications, see Cavanaugh 2007; Meneley 2004, 2007; Paxson 2011).

Ulin has argued compellingly that, in France, geographical indications emerged not as a result of any essential relation of source with quality—but instead through several historical processes through which claims about the intrinsic quality of wine produced in particular places were naturalized (1996).

For example, the reputed qualities of Bordeaux are situated not in the natural superiority of the land on which it is produced, but in the historical political-economic conditions through which Bordeaux wines became privileged for export by way of the control of ports. The value of Bordeaux wines was increasingly shored up by a relatively small cadre of bourgeois land-owning elites, who in turn achieved codification of their market share by way of *appellation contrôlée* laws. The success of the processes through which the superiority of certain *terroirs* were naturalized occurred not only as a result of the simple political and economic might of bourgeois land-holding elites, but was additionally promoted by an ideological apparatus in which the same elites laid claim to a long historical connection to the land by way of their self-association to imagery linking their estates and product to a heralded aristocratic past.

In Georgia, insofar as an elaborate system of microzones was established, they possessed commonalities with European categories of *terroir*, but were notably different. Whereas the *terroir*-like system functioned as an index of Western forms of quality, it was necessarily divested of its material basis. In practice, since production took place in state-built factories and most grape growing took place on widely dispersed collective land holdings, site designation beyond that of very broad regional-based categories was eschewed. Whereas in Western contexts, *terroirs* work through the claim of source-indexed qualities inherent within the wine produced, in the Soviet Georgian context, production zones were subsumed under the category of Soviet *"brand"* typical of the sphere of "cultured commodities" (on socialist doppelgangers of the capitalist category of "brand"; see Fehervary 2009; Manning 2009; Manning 2012, 118–147). Associated with vintage-dated wines restricted to certain production zones or varieties, "branded" wines were indicative of the ability of socialist production to attain the quality of the best European wines. Such wines corresponded not only to *terroir*-like categories defined by source, but to varietally labeled wines as well, and they were representative of the success of the socialist achievement of quality. They were heralded for their achievements in international wine competitions, often explicitly compared to French *terroirs:* "[Georgian brand table wines] resemble that of the best brands of Bordeaux and Burgundy" (Beridze and Azarashvili 1965, 14).

CONSUMING QUANTITY

Whereas industrially produced branded Georgian wine was held in very high regard throughout the Soviet Union, Georgians throughout the socialist period notoriously valued locally produced, nonbranded wines for the purposes of ritual consumption in traditional feasts called *supras*. From the perspective of the Soviet state, this was somewhat ideologically suspect inasmuch as it represented a semiautonomous informal sphere of production and consumption outside the scope of state supervision, regulation, and provisioning. In addition, the *supra*, as a central ritual event requiring the consumption of massive quantities of wine (from either state or private sources), was often considered ideologically opposed to the goals of socialist production and a form of unproductive consumption parasitic on state production, either as a wasteful or corrupt misappropriation of public goods for private consumption, or a drunken ritual associated with lowered worker productivity or hooliganism. However, the socialist state not only sought to curb the wasteful excesses of the traditional *supra* by censuring it from the outside, but also by remaking it from the inside as part of a more general Stalinist civilizing process of "culturedness." The *supra* is a ritual form that at every point involves quantitative consumption to enact social status at household and individual levels (including, of course, gender). Thus the competitive enactment of household status is realized through the largely invisible feminine labors of preparation and display of large quantities of foodstuffs (Manning 2012, 153–159), and parallel, more visible, quantitative enactment of masculinity involves displays of coerced and competitive drinking (Manning 2012, 159–162). Throughout the socialist period, the state attempted to assimilate this version of the ritual characterized by quantitative excess (sometimes called a *ghreoba* ["orgy"]), to more temperate models of "cultured" socialist consumption embodied in the ideal of the "cultured *supra*," which emphasized moderate consumption of food and wine (Manning 2012, 148–177). However, while the production and consumption of Georgian socialist wine only partially intersects with the production and consumption of wine for the *supra*, both discourses, the socialist state discourse of production and the *supra* discourse of consumption, are dominated by a single logic emphasizing *quantity*.

Almost anyone who visits Georgia for the first time will receive a fairly hasty education on the ritual importance of wine. The uninitiated often first notice the stark regimentation of wine consumption, permitted only as a part of a *supra*, and then according to a rigid toasting regimen. The *supra* is a highly venerated feast in Georgia, often promoted as central to the national and cultural identity. A series of toasts are proposed in highly regulated order and ended with a glassful (or vase, chalice, or horn-full) of wine consumed in its entirety. Wine consumption in Georgia is even today widely restricted to toasting within a *supra*, with no place for casual drinking. Sipping wine is entirely unknown, inconceivable (for perspectives on the *supra*, see Kotthoff 1995; Manning 2012, 148–177; Mühlfried 2005; Tuite 2008).

Everything about the ritual of the traditional *supra* is oriented toward a uniform logic emphasizing *quantitative* wine consumption that indexes masculinity. As Alexandre Dumas described this logic during a visit to Georgia: "The important thing is how much one can drink. Even the most moderate drinkers usually manage five or six bottles of wine, and the average is twelve or fifteen" (Dumas [1853] 1962, 189). As Dumas also noted, this quantitative logic of consumption is reflected by the elaboration of the material form of special ritual drinking vessels, which vary qualitatively in their form, but are all united quantitatively in their large capacity: "They have a bewildering variety of drinking vessels of all shapes and sizes, even the smallest holds at least a bottleful—gourds, silver-mounted drinking horns two or three feet long, bowls with the head of a stag painted inside them in such a way that the antlers seem to move as one drinks" (Dumas [1853] 1962, 189). Such "different" (*ganskhvavebuli*) drinking vessels replace the ordinary clear drinking glass for special toasts. These drinking vessels have large capacities and the interesting property that they cannot stand up unaided. Since any toast must be drunk to the bottom, and then the glass must be put on the table, these drinking vessels have

FIGURE 11.1: "Logic." "Drink this *qants'i* [drinking horn], it will do you good." "I can't, even dumb animals have a sense of proportion!" "For precisely this reason we must drink more, so that we can be distinguished from animals" (Niangi 1940, 9, Artist M. Lebeshev).

a built-in regulatory, or even coercive, ritual function in that they literally *force* the drinker to drain the glass. They are thus associated not only with quantitative drinking, but also coerced drinking (*ghvinis dadzaleba* lit. "forcing wine"). It should be noted that whereas certain other beverages are suitably substituted in less formalized *supras* (vodka, or the Georgian grape spirit called *chacha*), wine is privileged as an ideal substance for the purposes of ritual consumption, and is singularly associated with the drinking apparatuses associated with coerced drinking.

The most iconic form of special drinking vessel is the simple drinking horn (*qants'i*). As we can see from the cartoon in Figure 11.1, one of many satirizing the *supra*, which appeared in the official Soviet satirical journal *Niangi* (see Manning 2012, 147–177), the drinking horn embodies in material form the implacable quantitative "logic" of the *supra*, where the performative power of the words spoken in a toast are always measured in the quantity of wine one drinks. All toasting themes (including obligatory toasts to ancestors, children, women) are mobilized for the single goal of enforcing drinking. The immense man on the left is prevailing on the smaller man to drink from a large drinking horn (*qants'i*). The smaller man protests with dismay that "even dumb animals have a sense of moderation." The larger man parries this seeming good sense with the unassailable logic of the *supra*: "Then we must drink more, so that we can be distinguished from animals!"

During the socialist period, the *supra* was a key site where the relationship between the socialist state (as the locus of production) and private, informal kin relations (as a heavily scrutinized site of consumption) were continuously worked out. As Mars and Altman famously argue, the *supra* takes a role comparable to informal networking practices of *blat* in Russia (1991) (cf. Ledeneva 1998; for a comparison, see also Manning 2012, 153–159). Thus, during socialism, from the perspective of the state, the *supra* represented the moral face of corruption, a mixture of the public and private in which private consumption is used as a means for political ends. Therefore, the *supra*, which often entailed the consumption of large quantities of food and wine (presumably) skimmed off state property, was a highly ideological contested ritual that from the perspective of the state indexed immoderate, degenerate, or uncultured behavior, yet it at the same time indexed the material prosperity made possible by socialism. However, in certain state-fostered national-culturalist discourses, the *supra* also represented a venerated aspect of Georgian national culture, which provided a teleology for socialist production. After socialism, new Westernizing elites ironically recapitulated the main outlines of the socialist critique of the *supra* by equating the *supra* with endemic corruption and more generally treating the ritual as an index or even cause of all the various failings of Georgian public life, from socialism and totalitarianism to failed transition to democracy (see Manning 2012, 147–177; Mühlfried 2005; Tuite 2008). As a result, the success of the transition not only depended on creating new European-style Georgian wines, but also new European-style Georgian wine drinkers who wake from the socialist hangover of the *supra* and sip new Georgian wines to appreciate their taste.

POSTSOCIALIST QUALITY

In Eastern European and former Soviet discourses on transition, there is a widespread assumption (both within formerly socialist societies and without) that the "success" of postsocialism is contingent on the eventual arrival of a new era of quality for the commodities consumed and produced within formerly socialist spaces. This derives from a commonly held assertion that socialist societies failed to produce goods in sufficient proportions to the needs and desires of the populace; and insofar as they achieved some modicum of success in this endeavor, quality was almost always a necessary sacrifice. The "quality" of commodities is discursively treated as notably absent in socialism, owing to the inability of socialist forms of production to maintain quality in the long march to supply socialist spaces with the availability of widespread consumer goods. Such discourses align with an early dynamic in postsocialist spaces in which the arrival of goods from the outside was often assumed to encourage patterns of consumption that would signal increasing incorporation into the West, granting legitimacy to the self-evident superiority of Western political-economic ideologies. However, as anthropologists have long documented, insofar as Western goods materialized, they were often significant by way of their unattainability and coemergence with new forms of inequality and poverty. Further, the extent to which these consumerist discourses hold weight is more owing to the hegemonic weight of post facto pronouncements on the failure of socialism writ large, than to any serious and independent scrutiny of the way "actual existing socialism" provided a different model for the production and allocation of goods that enables and constrains modes of valuation that are not coterminous with capitalist systems of value (Fehervary 2009; Verdery 1996). Here, we would like to emphasize that the problem is not that these discourses do not have explanatory power—indeed socialist goods were materially structured in part by the conditions of the political economy of socialism, in which quantity took on great significance—but rather that they threaten to legitimize and naturalize quality as a core rubric that defines the failure of socialism and the subsequent success of capitalism.

PRODUCING QUALITY

Under postsocialism, quality comes to stand not only as a rubric with which to assess commodities produced in postsocialist space, but as a legitimate index of the success of postsocialist transition writ large. In Georgia, this tendency to equate the success of transition with the transformation of the quality of commodities is an especially relevant feature of wine, and as a result wine production has received significant state and developmental attention. We now contextualize current development efforts within the context of decollectiviza- tion, and then consider how contestations over geographical source protection and quality management have the potential to result in different forms of value protection among producers.

In Georgia, the current state of the wine industry cannot be understood without reference to decollectivization. This process occurred in the chaos of the early 1990s, in which collective farms were first pillaged by armed bands, and then whatever was left was privatized, acquired by nouveau riche Geor- gians with connections to the Ministry of Finance for nominal sums. A locally administered system of land privatization led to the highly uneven redistribu- tion of land throughout the countryside: as a recent report from Transparency International states, today, less than one percent of farmers own more than four hectares of land (Transparency International Georgia). Additionally, the nonavailability of inputs and machinery for working the land produced an impetus for large portions of the rural population to turn to kinship-based subsistence farming, a situation that mirrors what Verdery has called "forced retraditionalization" in the context of Romania (2003, 13).

Privatization, considered both as a set of enabling theories and a rather di- verse set of actual practices, strongly influenced the dynamics of the emerging wine industry. First, the process of privatization itself (and attendant enabling theories privileging capitalist forms of property) was widely assumed to natu- rally lead to the efficient and rapid integration of postsocialist spaces into West- ern market economies (for critiques of this theory naturalizing privatization in postsocialist contexts see Alexander 2004; Creed 1998; Verdery 2003). In the Georgian case, as in many others, privatization of land did not lead unprob- lematically to the countryside's transition into an efficient, market-integrated sphere. Lack of machinery and infrastructure dramatically reduced the value of the newly privatized land and farm work became a more labor-intensive process in general. Further, the privatization of wineries to politically well-connected nouveau riche Georgians at "symbolic prices" created a group of inexperienced winery owners with few previous connections to wine or the communities in which the wineries were organized. Today, a situation remains in which grievances are aired yearly by farmers whose primary source of income derives from the selling of grapes to wineries, a practice increasingly declining as there is less and less interest among wineries to source grapes in this manner. Instead, many wineries have begun to acquire more vineyard land to vertically integrate their supply chain and consolidate their production, as many others practice counterfeiting (on postsocialist counterfeiting see Manning 2012, 104–109). Pleas by farmers for state intervention to require wineries to buy their grapes have become progressively more desperate since the 2006 Russian ban of Georgian wine, which left many formerly stable wineries with stockpiles of unsellable wine and increased the poverty of rural farmers.

Counterfeiting of Georgian wine is widespread inside and outside Georgia. In 2006, amidst a long list of confrontations between Georgia and Russia, the Russian government imposed a ban on the import of all Georgian wine and mineral waters, citing contamination with heavy metals and pesticides, effectively negating the previous $60 million market that made up eighty to ninety percent of production (Dunn 2008; Joseph 2009). Whatever the specific validity of the reasons for the Russian ban, it remains that postsocialist production of wine, mineral waters, and many other goods is strongly haunted by ubiquitous counterfeiting and rumors of counterfeiting (Manning 2012, chapter 4).[1] Counterfeiting of wine produces two additional problems for the postsocialist Georgian wine producers: the sudden disappearance of a large Russian market, already domesticated to the characteristic socialist tastes of Georgian wines, and the general threat to the goodwill of Georgian wine as a whole represented by rampant counterfeiting. It was around this time that the trope of "protection" as a primary goal of the wine industry's development interests began to widely circulate in Georgia. As a result, Georgian winemakers would have to reengineer their product to produce new forms of quality that would allow them to replace their erstwhile Russian markets with European and American ones (particularly in the wake of the 2008 war between Russia and Georgia) and combat the loss of goodwill resulting from counterfeiting.

There was no question, then, that socialist production of quantity would have to be transformed into postsocialist quality, but there was little agreement on how to achieve this. Development organizations generally claim that success requires Georgia's emergence as an "Old World" producer, whose unique *terroir* must be developed and protected by laws mirroring European equivalents of the *appellation contrôlée*. However, such a model tends to clash with the recent widespread circulation of neoliberal ideology among the current Georgian governing regime, in which there is more respect for subsuming quality maintenance under market processes, and value protection to the realm of intellectual property (on semiotic differences between the former (*terroir*) and the latter (trademark or intellectual property) model of "source," see Manning 2012).

To illustrate this opposed set of tendencies with a concrete example, we briefly review a recent development project that promotes the former model, noting how it intersects with contestations from the latter. The UN's Food and Agricultural Organization (FAO) recently completed phase two of a project entitled "Protection of Georgian Wine Appellations" (2008). The project relied upon a network of "stakeholders" and "donors" of legal and financial aid toward the completion of the project, which included other international development organizations, Western-funded Georgian NGOs, Georgian governmental sectors, and large, privatized industrial wineries as well as various other private organizations such as the Union of Georgian Sommeliers.

The Protection of Georgian Wine Appellations was a multipurpose project with several activities, composed of training on model frameworks for organizing wine, wine law assistance, legal training in international civil adjudication, the writing of international treaties, and assistance for updating "technical standards" to an "international level." Of primary significance was the push to integrate Georgia by law and treaty into an international framework that would facilitate the Georgian wine industry's entrance into international trade networks.

As part of this process, key "stakeholders" drawn from public, private, and development spheres were given training on institutional wine models, as well as a "study tour" to Italy. The training and study tour emphasized the Italian structure of quality control and regulation, in which regional appellations of origin (called *Denominazione di Origine Controllata* in Italy) are managed by semipublic/semiprivate accreditation laboratories that grant export permission on the basis of tests that establish quality and conformity to local wine laws. Italy, considered an "Old World," generally *terroir*-driven, wine-producing country, is often invoked as an ideal model for the Georgian wine industry's transition, owing to numerous factors, including its relatively late arrival as a high-quality Old World region, its ancient and diverse winemaking techniques, and the importance of locally produced wine.

The "protection" of the Georgian wine industry was also promoted by encouraging the thorough integration of the wine industry into internationally recognized agreements that designate and enforce appellations of origin.

In Europe, such agreements historically align with property and trade interests to ensure the protection of value claims deriving from production within particular regions or zones, and are constructed on the basis of a model of *terroir*. There is a general discrepancy between states who sign on to appellation of origin protection treaties and those who do not, opting instead to arrange international agreements on an ad hoc basis. The former tends to be represented by countries that lay claim to "Old World" *terroir*, like France, Italy, and Portugal, whereas states with a claim to "New World" status are much more reluctant to sign on, as is the case, for example, with Australia, the United States, Argentina, and Chile.

As the name itself suggests, the FAO Protection of Georgian Wine Appellations is a project in which Georgian wine quality is slated to derive from a European-type *appellation contrôlée* system, but contestations exist that point in different possible directions. For example, there has been an ongoing effort to update wine laws to ensure Georgian winemaking techniques—including designating authorized oenological practices and prohibiting chemicals and chemical processes in the winemaking process—are up to "international standards." While, internationally, wine standards are currently guaranteed by state practices that oversee technical processes to ensure safety and source designation compliance for export wines, this form of regulation is increasingly managed alongside "voluntary standards" provisions such as Codex Alimentarius, established by the FAO and World Trade Organization (WTO). This follows a trend that Dunn has pointed out, where standards in Georgia have shifted from a Soviet model, in which standards originated in the paternalistic Soviet state, to current models in which reforms are put in place "based on neoliberal spatializing projects that claimed to create new technological zones that would allow Georgian products to circulate in international markets" (2008, 252). This model privileges "principles of audit and accountability," which align with core neoliberal values of self-regulation, the location of disciplinary authority in supranational bodies instead of the nation-state, and a situation in which "change [is] driven by the market response to consumer desires rather than by a parentified state eager to protect its citizens" (252). While voluntary standards like Codex Alimentarius have received limited application in Georgia, they represent an ideological trend that questions the need to devote state resources to regulating agricultural production. Important, such provisions theoretically place more of a burden on producers in managing standards compliance, which can be more easily met by large producers with the capital and technological proficiency to comply.[2]

Appellation contrôlée systems and *terroir* are ideologically contested on other grounds. As discussed previously, *appellation contrôlée* systems serve to solidify hierarchies of land value and are based on the argument that the value of wine derives from site specificity inherent in the *terroir* concept (Barham 2003; see also Ulin, Farmer, current volume). *Appellation contrôlée* systems are often associated with widely dispersed land ownership and production, as their primary function is to ensure that access to quality designations are restricted to communities who uphold the reputation of the appellation. While the *appellation contrôlée* system is akin to a trademark system in that it designates a source, it has key differences (see Manning 2012). *Appellation contrôlée* systems tend to apply to a delimited area of land on which the proprietors may lay claim to the use of a particular regional name within which generalizable characteristics are supposed to inhere. Trademarks, on the other hand, restrict use of a name tied to a particular "brand" to an owner of the trademark, which constitutes a form of intellectual property. As Barham has argued, *appellation contrôlée* systems constitute a special type of intellectual property that challenges "the law, culture and economic logic of American business, oriented as it is towards liberal economic theory based on individual ownership" (2003, 129). In Georgia, where the current government espouses a near fanatical reverence for neoliberal ideology, there are hesitations concerning the appropriation of *terroir*-based models for the wine industry.

Whereas the fragmentation of land ownership might reasonably suggest the potential success of an *appellation contrôlée* model in Georgia, there are severe limits to this approach. For example, the extremely unequal access to machinery and capital makes the prospect of market-oriented wine production daunting for most rural wine producers. This is due in part to the extreme loss (via pillage) of collective resources during the period of civil unrest in the early 1990s, and the privatization of all remaining machinery. Whereas other wine regions have overcome problems of lack of machinery and resources by way of the implementation of cooperatives, in Georgia, few attempts have been made to recollectivize following decollectivization, owing in part to the ideological denigration of state-enforced collectivization during the Soviet period. Georgian government officials have been plagued by the problem of how to quickly and effectively establish a system of source protection (especially to weed out counterfeiting in light of the fragmentation of the ownership of land and production facilities). Recently, Minister of the Economy Kakha Bendukidze, well known for an economic policy that aims to privatize as many state assets as possible, recommended a solution that, while it has not yet been implemented, is ideologically suggestive. According to his model, appellations themselves would be privatized, giving ownership rights of the appellations to top wineries who could "internalize" the costs of the transition toward an *appellation contrôlée* system (Patterson 2007, 11). According to this model, the *appellation contrôlée* system does not act as a framework that guarantees the reputation of the general qualities of Georgian regions and that is held collectively, but instead as a commodity that itself can be owned—much more akin to a form of intellectual property. In effect, under this model, appellations become hybrids of collective geographic designations (appellations) and something more like trademarks (cf. Manning 2012, 86–117). Such a model that assimilates appellations to the logic of intellectual property, trademark, or brand reflects an increasing interest by the Georgian state to funnel money into opening new markets to Georgian wine, and is indicative of the interest of the state in branding wine as an export commodity symbolically representative of Western integration.

Therefore, all parties agree that quality is the goal, but how quality is to be measured and marketed remains ideologically contested. Currently, quality is seen as dependent on the ability of large industrial producers to vertically integrate production processes, thus resuscitating and appropriating the decayed infrastructure of the Soviet period and converting it into a modern industry capable of supplying wines in demand in international markets. The concept of *terroir,* when transferred to the soil of Georgia, is therefore interpreted as enabling specific new owners to make an unassailable claim to quality located in the historical and cultural relation of Georgians to wine. This mirrors Paxson's claim of "reverse engineering" of *terroir* among cheese producers in North America, insofar as *terroir* is appropriated within a space semiotically and political-economically very different from that of its European origins (2010). In Georgia, which importantly has until very recently lacked an indigenous critique of industrialized agriculture (Manning 2012, chapter 5, 8; Manning and Uplisashvili 2007), *terroir* is increasingly appropriated by large industrial producers who market Georgian wine by appealing equally to its European quality standards as well as its long-standing cultural value (mirroring the much more successful Georgian beer producers, see Manning 2012, chapter 8; Manning and Uplisashvili 2007).

CONSUMING QUALITY

Having produced quality wines for export, Georgian wine producers also seek to produce domestic consumers of quality. Here, as with beer marketers before them, Georgian wine producers market Georgian wine as having "dual lineage," involving simultaneous appeals to European technoscientific standards and Georgian cultural values. In effect, Georgian wine production and Georgian wine consumption alike must be "reverse engineered" (Paxson 2010), but there the problem is not only adding a European qualitative dimension to Georgian wine consumption, but also accommodating qualitative consumption of wine to the quantitative consumption of the *supra,* without losing a *terroir*-like grounding in Georgian tradition in the process.

These themes are illustrated by the recent emergence in Tbilisi of several flagship wine shops owned and run by singular producers (such as Château Mukhrani and Kindzmarauli Marani). Such shops are interesting for the way in which they pair imagery particular to a modern internationalist aesthetic of wine (stainless steel storage tanks, degustation machines, stemmed crystal glassware) and representations of traditional Georgian wine culture (*qvevri*—clay amphorae used for fermenting and storing wine, idyllic ethnographic representations of the Georgian countryside, and Georgian drinking implements such as *qants'i,* or drinking horns). Important, such shops attempt to appeal to a hybrid imaginary of the Georgian consumer, at once cosmopolitan and traditional. For example, in Kindzmarauli Marani's flagship store, wine is sold not only in a standard 750 ml bottle, but also in bulk—poured from a modern, stainless steel tank into two- or five-liter plastic containers. On one hand, this reflects a fairly practical reality: it is still uncommon for many Georgian homes to have wine openers, since *supra* wine is most often either homemade or bought directly from the bulk reserves of factories. Yet this also serves to subsume the quantitative logic of *supra* consumption under the emerging category of "quality." Even when purchasing wine in larger quantities that facilitate the rapid-paced toasting of the *supra,* the consumer can nevertheless be assured of the superior and modern quality of the product—not the cloudy, amber stuff of most *supras* but a clear, aromatic white wine deserving of sociable sipping from European-style stemmed glasses *and* ritual toasting from Georgian drinking horns. As we have observed ethnographically, the very same wine, depending on whether it is purchased in labeled bottles or in bulk, can be consumed very differently in opposed genres of consumption. European-style bottled wine is associated with novel European forms of sociable drinking (including sociable gatherings of women, for example) that emphasize the qualitative dimension of wine; the wine is sipped for its taste without attendant toasts, while the same wine, purchased in bulk, is assimilated to the existing quantitative logic of ritual consumption in the masculine context of the *supra.*

Georgian wine producers, then, are attempting to create a domestic market for their hybrid product by creating genres of consumption hybridized between emergent quality and traditional quantity. In the *supra*, wine is drunk most often out of short, bulky crystal glasses. The point is not to emphasize taste or other qualities of the wine itself in the process of consumption, but to emphasize the process (and quantity) of drinking itself. The materiality of the glassware emphasizes the quantitative dimensions of the act of consumption. This becomes more evident when considering the Georgian practice of drinking *ganskhvavebuli*, or differently. A common component of most *supras, ganskhvavebuli* marks a moment when men show particular respect for a toast (such as to women) by draining a "different" (and much larger) glass (see Figure 11.1).

The most typical and emblematic form of *ganskhvavebuli* drinking vessel is the drinking horn, or *qants'i* (illustrated in Figure 11.1), which is symbolically synonymous with both quantitative drinking (*ganskhvavebuli*) and the related practice of *coerced quantitative* drinking (*ghvinis dadzaleba*, literally "forcing wine," essentially forcing a person to drain an especially large "different" drinking vessel). As we see in Figure 11.1, the drinking horn stands as a handy visual symbol for the whole quantitative "logic" of wine consumption at the *supra*. Hence, in the early 2000s, another wine company, Tbilvino, deployed the image of the drinking horn, shorthand for the quantitative drinking practices of the *supra* and forced drinking, as an anti-image opposed to the uncoerced, qualitative drinking appropriate for their products. The sign shows a man's feet coming out of an enormous *qants'i*, with the legend "Don't force it!" (*Nu daadzaleb!*), a clear reference to practice of "forcing wine" (*ghvinis dadzaleba*). The subtext, of course, opposes new wines to old drinking vessels as opposed forms of qualitative and quantitative consumption, with the implication being that this wine is so good there will be no *need* to coerce anyone to drink it.

FIGURE 11.2: Tbilvino ad (early 2000s) captioned "Don't Force it!" showing a man's feet emerging from inside a giant drinking horn (Paul Manning photo).

CONCLUSION: FROM QUANTITY TO QUALITY

What is notable about emerging discourses on quality is the extent to which they become self-evidently associated with the success of transition. We have shown how the increase in the value of export wine is widely associated with generalized economic success, even in the face of mounting evidence that the elite cordoning off of value derived from wine production in effect promotes the continued traditionalization of rural producers without significant vested interests in industrial production. Whereas formerly, wine produced in Georgia was slated for cultured consumption throughout the Soviet Union and the Eastern Bloc, more recently, with the disappearance of socialist markets and the absence of a domestic market, the wine industry is concerned with making wine a product primarily respected within international Western circuits of consumption. Insofar as industrial wine is domestically marketable, it tends to be so among a minority of relatively wealthy, often reform-minded, urban consumers whose aspirational forms of consumption are symbolically derived from Western forms of sociality and an ideological opposition to ritual consumption of the *supra,* a tradition (like socialism and the chaos that followed it) these new Georgian elites blame for a whole range of political and social maladies that afflict Georgia (Manning 2009; Manning 2012). Ideologically, then, the quantitative principles of socialist wine production and traditional wine consumption (the *supra*) are linked together as more or less equivalent symbols and symptoms of a debased and debilitating socialist or traditional past that must be erased in the transition (Manning 2009). Thus the push toward wine quality amounts to an ideological project often presented as synonymous with the success of transition writ large, a matter of national interest whose success is much more than a mere economic issue. At the same time, as we have shown, the project of transformation of socialist quantity into capitalist quality has engendered new quantitative and qualitative forms of economic and cultural forms of stratification and exclusion that are characteristic of postsocialist Georgia.

NOTES

The authors would like to thank Anne Meneley for her careful reading and helpful comments.

1. As Patterson has shown, wine counterfeiting in Georgia can refer to two common tendencies. Wine is considered counterfeit if it is 1) incorrectly labeled as deriving from a particular microzone (for example, if a famed

Khvanchkara wine is not actually produced within the small Rachan zone dedicated to its production), or 2) not wine at all, as in the practice of producing a hard-to-detect counterfeit by mixing grape powder and spirit, particularly effective in the production of famed semisweet red wines (2007, 10). Both are generally spurred as a result in a perceived high-market demand for wines (such as Khvanchkara or Mukuzani) that by virtue of relatively small microzones can only be produced in small quantities. It is also hotly contested as to whether these practices occur more frequently in Georgia or in other formerly socialist republics—particularly Russia.

2. As Dunn argues, Codex Alimentarius is a neoliberal project promoted by the WTO that attempts to implement unified product standards, documentation, and audit practices in an effort to produce common technological zones that facilitate successful international trade (2008, 252). While the Codex is promoted with the specific goal of ensuring public health, it serves other purposes more directly linked to the function of international markets. "Codex is thus an 'immutable mobile,' to use Latour's (1987) phrase, that claims to link far-distant places not only by being utterly devoid of the specificities of place itself but also by literally making different places, with all their peculiar facilities and habits and infrastructures, equivalent to one another. Codex claims to create new topographies of trade by flattening the particularities of place" (Dunn 2008, 252).

CHAPTER TWELVE

Regimes of Regulation, Gender, and Divisions of Labor in Languedoc Viticulture

WINNIE LEM

INTRODUCTION

Languedoc-Roussillon in the south of France is reputed to be the largest wine-producing region in the world. Characterized by seemingly endless vineyards, it is also known for yielding large quantities of the notoriously low-grade wines—*vins ordinaires*—that have flooded local and national markets from time to time. Such prodigious production of poor-quality wines combined with the volatilities of the market have meant that Languedoc viticulture has suffered repeatedly from economic crises generated by poor sales—*les crises de mévente*—since its integration into the capitalist market over the course of the twentieth century. Yet in the early decades of the twenty-first century, the wines produced in this region have been touted as having saved "France's bacon" in the competitive global market.[1] Languedoc wines have actually sold well relative to those from Bordeaux and Burgundy, whose prestigious appellations have suffered slumps due to growing competition from the emergence of New World wines on the international market. While wine magazines and business journals frequently fuel a popular image of wine production as a venture taking place on *châteaux* and splendid estates in France, in the vast Languedoc region, the greater share of the wine is actually manufactured from grapes grown on small-scale, family-owned and operated farms.[2]

A perennial concern on such farms centers on how to secure sufficient labor to keep the farm in operation over both the short and long term. This problem of reproduction persists as a structural dilemma embedded into small-scale, partially capitalized enterprises that operate by generating marginal profits. Such small farms—or petty commodity enterprises—are run using family labor and occasional or part-time paid labor. This contrasts with large farms and local estates, which are fully capitalized and operated by a permanent force of paid workers.[3]

This chapter, then, is an examination of the ways in which family wine-growers confront the problem of the reproduction of the family farm in rural Languedoc.[4] By focusing on gender and divisions of labor, it explores the practices that center on the mobilization of the labor of women and men for the daily round of production and also for the continuity of the farm over the generations. I postulate that the workforce on family farms is not spontaneously created but that men and women are deliberately fashioned or reproduced as workers. According to Burawoy, key to understanding the ways labor is controlled, managed, and secured is an appreciation of conditions through which labor is reproduced and also, particularly, the nature of specific forms of dependence in the reproduction of labor (1985). These conditions involve, inter alia, the processes of regulation that operate to control, manage, and secure labor on the unit of production. This chapter, then, examines the practices of regulation operationalized within two distinctive but entwined "regimes of regulation" in Languedoc family-based viticulture. I call these the regime of "familial hegemony" and the regime of "familial authoritarianism."[5] In a regime of familial authoritarianism, the reproduction of labor is conditioned by a series of coercive social practices. By contrast, in a regime of familial hegemony, consent is the key social dynamic that conditions the reproduction of labor. For analytic purposes, the regimes may be separated. However, as the examples will show later, the regimes are intertwined and complementary. While the practices and strategies mobilized in these regimes are dedicated toward producing and sustaining women and men as workers, decisions to engage and persist in the work of vine cultivation are also the results of choices individuals feel they have made.

In rural Languedoc, sons and daughters of farmers often say they chose to take on the *métier* of their parents. Yet the practice of the children of farmers succeeding farm parents is so common in the milieu of family viticulture it appears to be a sociological norm. As Pierre Bourdieu observed in formulating his theory of practice, human action involves choices and decisions, and at the level of individual experience, people feel they are free agents who exercise choice. Yet the accumulation of some choices, on a sociological plane, is an expression of regularity. Such choices become a norm despite the absence of a sociological principle or rule that determines such behavior. To Bourdieu, the challenge was to account for how such "behaviour could be regulated without being the product of obedience to rules" (1994, 65). In drawing on the insights of Bourdieu, I focus on how such choices are conditioned by the context in which they are made—how they are constrained by the range of choices visible to individuals; how acts of making normative choice become embodied as a disposition. In other words, this intervention is an exploration of the habitus of women and men who commit their labor to viticulture.[6] I undertake this exploration by using the conceptual schema of the regimes of regulation as a tool to help think through the process by which certain choices become embodied in the men and women who run family winegrowing farms. As my focus on practices of regulation within the institution of the family and on regulation itself implies the exercise of authority to moderate action in some way, I am adhering to a conceptualization of this kin-based form of organization as a field of hierarchy and power.

FAMILY, HIERARCHY, AND POWER

In the economy of Languedoc viticulture, the family is a key institution. Such kin-based institutions are the primary unit of organization in carrying out activities required to sustain a livelihood in small-scale viticulture. Farms are run using the labor of a range of kin including consanguines and affines. Thus the labor of fathers, sons, brothers, sisters, and daughters as well as husbands, wives, and in-laws is mobilized to sustain farm enterprises. Family relations, therefore, imply work relations, and the organization of work life and family life requires negotiation, control, and direction. The management of the various functions of the family requires the exercise of authority and power. Foucault (1979), Gramsci (1971), and many analysts have insisted that relations of power pervade all social institutions and such relations permeate kin-based institutions. The family therefore is an institution that is a field of power in which hierarchies are embedded. Divisions prevail between those who have power and can exercise control and those who must defer to authority and are controlled. In rural Languedoc, those who have power and can exercise control are often called formally the heads of the enterprise—*chefs d'entreprises*—in census material and land registers. They tend to be the oldest male work-aged individual in these enterprises. So, in a sociological sense, they may be thought of as the *patriarch*. The patriarch tends also to be the head of the family—the *pater familias*. Divisions of power on Languedoc family winegrowing farms therefore often coincide with generational and gender divisions.

Many feminist scholars have long asserted that these divisions contradict the idealized view of families as democratic institutions and havens from a heartless land. Olivia Harris, for example, observed that "the language of kinship is concerned with generosity and sharing; [but] this is only one side of the story. Kinship is also a language of hierarchy and dependency, of authority and obedience" (1982, 150). The view of the family as a hierarchical institution is now largely taken as de rigueur in analyses of kin-based forms of organization, since such institutions are infused with relations of power, domination, exploitation, and coercion. Yet it is also an institution suffused with affect and calls for commitments based on emotion, sentiment, and symbolism. As Rayna Rapp observed: "It is through their commitment to the concept of the family that people are recruited into the material relations of households. Because people accept the meaningfulness of the family, they enter into relations of production, reproduction and consumption with one another—they marry, beget children, work to support dependents, transmit and inherit cultural and material resources" (Rapp et al. 1979, 177). Rapp's comments encapsulate the ethic of familism that underpins the family as a project and family-based endeavors as a common family project.

THE COMMON FAMILY PROJECT

In rural Languedoc, the "common family project" is centered on the continuity of the family farm both on a daily basis and over the longer term. In a milieu dominated by family-based viticulture, the reproduction of each family-based enterprise is a priority. By accepting the commonness of the common family project and consenting to this priority, different categories of kin in particular—wives, sons, and daughters—consent to the prerogatives of sustaining the enterprise and commit their energies and their labor toward sustaining the farm over the daily, weekly, and yearly cycles. Such acquiescence to the common family project in Languedoc reflects the internalization of the values of familism and family farming in the body of the worker and the habituation of individuals to the requirements of work routines and priorities. Such assent, discipline, and habituation in many cases is a consequence of the practices exercised by those who have the authority and power to forge a worldview in which certain choices appear natural. Such practices prevail in enterprises and regimes of familial hegemony. The example of Gérard Barthes illustrates the ways familistic ethic became instilled through distinctive practices and actions undertaken by those who command in a regime of familial hegemony.

FAMILIAL HEGEMONY

Gérard,[7] aged twenty-three, has taken on the métier of *viticulteur* and works on the family farm alongside his father. He explained his decision to commit himself to farming by referring to the trinity of values associated with Languedoc viticulture—family, farming, and freedom—regularly cited in the ontological narratives of Languedoc growers.[8] He says:

> My parents are country folks—*paysans*—and I am the son of a *paysan*. Naturally, I love working in the fields. I love it because you are free. There's no boss looking over your shoulders, giving you orders and pushing you around. You are really working for yourself and for your family.

Gérard lives in a household with his father, Eric, and mother, Jeannette, and together they work their fifteen and a half hectares of land. As the only son in a family of four children (Gérard has three sisters who at the time of fieldwork were all married and lived in other households), he was required to help out his father on the enterprise and familiarize himself with all the tasks necessary in winegrowing. From the age of five, Gérard regularly accompanied Eric to the fields whenever he could. Eric carefully and patiently explained all the tasks involved in vine cultivation, oversaw Gérard work as a young apprentice on the family farm, and taught him to love this work as a *métier*. Eric was also a fierce defender of family-based viticulture, being one of the key figures to organize winegrowers' protests and demonstrations to defend Languedoc viticulture against the forces of globalization.[9] Gérard admired his father's commitment and determination and decided at a young age to carry on in his father's footsteps. As a teenager, he also agreed to apply to the agricultural college, which had programs to train young growers in the latest techniques of vine cultivation and wine production.

Gérard's father, like other farming fathers, played a key role in transmitting the values as well as the practices of vine cultivation that prepared sons to work on the farm and to eventually take over the enterprise. To Gérard, the virtues of working the land are simply common sense—"natural" to use Gérard's word—and he professed to have always wanted to become a grower. Gérard's reference to generation in his statement hints at one of the most serious problems farmers must confront in running family-based farms. This is the issue of succession. As my later discussion shows, the various ways in which crises of succession are managed and resolved actually reveal some of the central tensions and conflicts that govern enterprises that rely on the mobilization of family labor. However, in the case of the Barthes family, this crisis was resolved fairly smoothly. It was seen as proper by all members of the family that Gérard would take over the farm, as he was the only son in a family of four. Gérard himself accepted his responsibility to carry on farming, and this duty to succeed was expressed as a desire and a will to do so on his part. The apparent facility with which the issue of succession was resolved in the case of Gérard assimilated the ethic of a common family project. His father disciplined him to the needs and priorities of wine production by deploying strategic practices of apprenticeship in which he could direct, closely supervise, and monitor the activities of his coworker and successor. Gérard eventually became habituated—self-disciplined—and no longer needed the direction or supervision of his father.

Gérard's case evokes Foucault's (1979) ideas of panopticism and discipline. *Panopticism* is a technique of surveillance that allows continuous supervision with minimal resources and that ultimately incites states of docility and self-discipline. According to Foucault, panoptic forms of surveillance rely on the support of training techniques or "disciplines" that reorganize the body to foster "useful" obedience. The example of Gérard illustrates two of the ways in which discipline proceeds. In Foucault's work, discipline is a practice that seeks to control the activities of bodies. Gérard's parents controlled his activities at school, in training programs, and in the vineyards, and each stage of his "apprenticeship" was carefully monitored. The practices of control exercised by Gérard's father were not overt and eventually came to be unnecessary, as Gérard internalized the priorities and values of farm life. It became embodied as a disposition to take on the farming as a practice. As Bourdieu's discussions of habitus remind us, Gérard followed in his father's footsteps, but no rule obliged him to do so. Such decisions also appear as common sense and part of the natural order of things. The process of making ideas, choices, and decisions appears natural, though it reflects the agendas of dominant groups and classes of people. This process then is encapsulated in the term *hegemony*.

The concept of hegemony has been used by different scholars to explain situations of domination and the exercise of power, not as brute force but as an invitation to acquiescence.[10] While no precise definition of hegemony is offered in Gramsci's work, the most quoted characterization of the term comes from his *Prison Notebooks*. According to Gramsci, hegemony is:

> [T]he "spontaneous" consent given by the great masses of the population to the general direction imposed on social life by the dominant fundamental group; this consent is "historically" caused by the prestige (and consequent confidence) which the dominant group enjoys because of its position and function in the world of production. (Gramsci 1971, 12)

As many writers remind us, hegemony is a process and also the result of processes that involve efforts exercised by rulers to sustain power and normative orders (Lem 1999; Smith 1999; Thompson 1978). As both *chefs d'enterprises* and patriarchs, men are particularly well positioned in the world of contemporary Languedoc wine production to impose the general direction of social life. This position of men as patriarchs and the dominant role they play in imposing and defining the direction of social life appear as part of the commonsense reality of everyday life—part of the natural order of things. However, this position is, in fact, the product and outcome of a distinctive history. It emerged from the processes of capitalist modernization that altered the gendered division of labor and provoked the masculinization of viticulture. The processes of capitalist rationalization engendered men as a dominant group in the world of production while, simultaneously, they reinscribed notions of femininity and womanhood with a vision of the housewife as the embodiment of a middle-class ideal.

GENDERED DIVISIONS OF LABOR

In contemporary Languedoc, women who agree to marry winegrowers essentially offer their consent to the common family project by committing their labor to domestic work. This conjugal act affirms their role as a housewife responsible for the daily sustenance and maintenance of the winegrower. Part of this conjugal commitment involves playing a secondary and subordinate role in the vineyards, undertaking what is called "helping out" husbands in the fields by heading out occasionally and very reluctantly to the vineyards. This dominantly domestic role of women in contemporary Languedoc contrasts with roles played by women in early twentieth-century Languedoc. At that time and until mid-century, women tended to work alongside men in the fields. On the large estates and on the small holdings of the region, women and men tended and cultivated vines. On the *châteaux* and domains of the region, for example, the workforce often included women (*journalières*). As day laborers, women and men made the daily journey to the estates, usually located outside the villages where they lived. Estate workforces included women agricultural laborers *(ouvrières agricoles)* who formed part of a resident labor force on large domains. Women often performed many of the same tasks as men. *Journalières* and *ouvrières* also undertook such tasks as plowing, hoeing, and planting. Women and men drove horses that drew tillers to plough fields. Women and men also shared the task of applying antifungal treatments (mainly against oïdium—a vine mildew) to the vines, wearing atomizers on their backs while manually sprinkling powdered sulphur directly onto plants. In the past, there was, nonetheless, some differentiation in the types of tasks performed by men and women, and division of labor by gender did prevail. *Journalières* and *ouvrières* were often assigned tasks defined by owners as lighter and more dexterous. Women-specific tasks included the work of collecting vine shoots, hoeing and weeding, pinching buds, gathering and tying pruned stems into bundles for firewood, spreading fertilizer, and sulphuring the vines, as well as cutting grapes during the harvest (Frader 1991). Vineyard work for women also involved such tasks as applying treatments against chlorosis, a disease in which the green parts of the vine plant become blanched. Women often followed behind men pruning vines to paint over the surfaces of the pruned stocks with a solution of water, iron sulphate, and citric acid. While this differentiation existed, women nonetheless routinely executed many of the tasks in vine cultivation and division of labor was not hard and fast. Yet in the contemporary context, vine work and all the tasks associated with it have come to be defined as men's work.[11] Viticulture has become masculinized, and women's experience of vine work is now limited to occasional and subsidiary tasks coded in their ontological narratives as "helping out."

This transformation in the experience of work and the division of labor in the vines was accompanied by a century-long process of the commodification of Languedoc wine production and its integration into the national and global markets. Over the course of the late nineteenth century to the mid-twentieth century, Languedoc viticulture underwent a process of change from being a largely a side-line production on polycultural farms oriented toward domestic and local consumption to a monoculture oriented toward producing a commodity for sale on a capitalist market. This transformation entailed the different processes of rationalization of the organization of production as well as the introduction of capital-intensive techniques of vine cultivation. In the period before World War II, these changes took place mainly on the large estates of the region, and these changes fell most heavily on women laborers. On large estates, the arrival of such items as mechanical sprayers, tractors, vine shoot crushing machines, and mechanical harvesters rendered women redundant. Considered the least efficient and least productive members of the labor force on estates, women agricultural laborers (*ouvrières agricoles*) were often the first to lose their employment.[12] In the post–World War II period, the process of rationalization broadened to encompass smaller growers as the state initiated a drive to transform French farming from an archaic, under-mechanized undertaking to a productive venture that would produce commodities for competitive markets on an international scale. This process of modernizing Languedoc viticulture involved the rapid restructuring of wine-growing through further rationalizations and the mechanization of technologies of production.[13] Restructurings in the post–World War II period involved the elimination of small-scale units of production and regrouping lands into larger, capital-intensive, cost-efficient, and fully rationalized commodity-producing units of production. Called Malthusian in orientation, the means by which a capital-intensive form of viticulture was to be realized were many and varied (cf. Averyt 1977).[14] But together, they resulted in an accelerated exodus from the countryside to the industrializing cities of France and intensified the existential dilemma faced by those engaged in family farming.[15]

Family farmers came to be preoccupied not only with how to retain the labor of sons and daughters, but also with how to sustain family farming as a viable way of life in the face of relentless drives toward modernization.[16] The processes of modernization were aimed not only at transforming the economy, but also at creating a modern subject assimilated to the ideal of being a progressive farmer locked into the circuits of commodity production. As these developments unfolded, conditions of work and divisions of labor also transformed over the course of the twentieth century and exacerbated worries over the reproduction of family farms.

MODERNIZATION, MASCULINITY, AND POWER

Modernization has not only differentiated the experience of work for women and men, but it has also meant the reinforcement of power differentials. This has occurred not only through the simple economic process of capitalist rationalization in which machines replaced women, but it was also reinforced through a political process in which the state through its policies, subsidies, and programs encouraged the masculinization of farming. Support, credit, and financing of the purchase of machinery were offered to men. Training for the use of modern technologies and techniques in the degree and diploma-granting programs run by the state are extended to men, and many young men, like Gérard, took full advantage of them. The acquisition of such degrees facilitated loans and therefore access to modern technologies and upgraded land. As a consequence, men not only controlled the technologies, production, and capital, they also controlled the knowledge, or what Bourdieu (1977) calls "cultural capital," needed to make a living from the vine. Machines in many respects were the embodiment of capital, and men's control over machines and other means of production allowed them to occupy a privileged and socially valued position in the world of production. Men not only controlled production of the primary source of livelihood, but these activities were accorded high economic value and social prestige in an increasingly commodified economy. In these respects, the modernization of viticulture reinforced men's monopoly of power as an expression of the legitimate demands on the services of others. Men became associated exclusively with the cultivation of vines, and work in the vines once the work of *viticultrices, journalières,* and *ouvières agricoles* became the work of *viticulteurs, journaliers,* and *ouvriers agricoles.*

Women became housewives—*femmes au foyer.* In many ontological narratives, women tended to define themselves as *femmes au foyer* first and foremost. The association of *femme* with the *foyer* became galvanized as their livelihood activities became removed from the fields and centered on the home. This identification prevailed among women who continually worked in the fields on a daily basis with their husbands or fathers. This was particularly striking in the case of women like Christine Sanchez, who called herself a *femme au foyer* despite owning and operating a land holding she inherited from her parents until her marriage at the age of thirty-five.

Women consistently positioned themselves in occupational terms as *femmes au foyer* despite their work as wage earners in factories or in the service sector. Therefore, other forms of work they undertook, other activities in which they participated, were subsumed by the work associated with being a *femme au foyer. Femme au foyer* has in these respects become a hegemonic identity, seen as natural, part of the commonsense structuring of the role and position of women in Languedoc rural life.

The self-definition in terms of a *femme au foyer* prevails mostly among work-aged women. By contrast, many women of an older generation who form part of France's senior citizens (*troisième âge*) define themselves through a multiplicity of terms. Several self-definitional terms recur in their ontological narratives. Older women who no longer work in the vines or in any form of income-generating work describe themselves as *ouvrières, viticultrices, journalières,* and *fermières*—women farmers. This of course reflects the experiences of the older generation of women who worked constantly on small holdings and local estates and made their living directly from their work in the vines.

Despite the fact that farming has come to be a masculine occupation, some women saw themselves as entangled in a common family project. This entanglement was the result of coercive strategies that compelled them to work against a desire to conform to the prevailing cultural norms of appropriate women's work. Such coercive strategies were enacted by the *pater familias* and were evident in examples of women who took on the métier as a *viticultrice* in a milieu in which *viticulteurs* are the norm. Such women recount how they succumbed to the practices of patriarchal coercion that prevailed in regimes of familial authoritarianism.

FAMILIAL AUTHORITARIANISM

Conflicts and crises regularly arise as farmers attempt to secure labor for the reproduction of the enterprise over the short and especially over the long term. These conflicts are intensified in the context of Languedoc by the facility with which the transformation of labor that is "unfree" and bound by personal ties into "free" labor can be accomplished under pervasive market capitalism. In many households, the crisis of succession involves complex maneuvers and negotiations in which the exercise of power and relations of what might be called patriarchal domination prevail, particularly in families with only female heirs. In these families, daughters, like sons, were subjected to pressures to work on the farm and to take it over. Fathers offered gifts and threatened punishment to ensure that their only child, their daughters, would continue to run the holding.

These dynamics were in evidence in the example of Marie Pons, one of the few women winegrowers in the villages where I undertook fieldwork. Marie explained how she in fact wanted to escape the drudgery of a life of farming, but became trapped by a promise and a sense of duty. She stays on as a winegrower, so she claims, because of a promise made to her father on his deathbed, in which she swore never to sell a single hectare of the family property. Marie explained that during a long illness that preceded his death, he kept urging her not sell the land. He impressed upon Marie that he poured his lifeblood into the soil of the farm, and so to sell the land would mean killing him twice. So she kept her promise.

Like Christine, she married at the age of thirty-five, late by local standards, and soon afterward gave birth to a daughter. She claims to have married late in life because she was always too busy working on the farm. Marie married a man whom she says was the only man she knew who could stand to have a real winegrower as a wife. Many in the village commented that this was a marriage of opportunity as her husband was a landless migrant from Spain who worked as a seasonal worker on her farm during the harvest. According to Marie, many men did not see her as marriageable because she looked like a woman but worked like a man.

Marie talks about having suffered because of her promise. While Marie is proud of the fact that she can work that land, at the same time she is adamant that this is not really suitable work for women. She has never really been comfortable as a *viticultrice*. She explains with distaste, "Your hands are always dirty. You smell and your skin gets coarse and wrinkled very fast." "But," she carries on: "when my father was alive we really had no way of running the farm without my help. So I was forced to go to the fields with him."

By "forced" Marie meant her father used a set of coercive strategies to ensure that she would not sell the land. As a young girl, whenever she expressed reluctance or doubt about taking over the farm, her father used threats to cut her off and disown her. Marie's dependence on her father and her family for her own material reproduction gave her father's threats real force. In this context, where the family is central for the organization of moral and material well-being of individuals, the threat of disowning children serves as a powerful force for exercising control. Marie's unhappiness at being "kept down" is manifested in her distaste for farm life and feeling humiliated by her presentation of self to the public world as a woman who seldom conformed to the prevailing norms of femininity. One of the norms of femininity is to be supported, dependent on a male who works in the masculine world of farming. These forces therefore have reinforced the dependency of women on men by promoting the masculinization of farming. This also means male control over the most important livelihood source. Women's dependence on men for their sustenance and material reproduction is pervasive and has rendered women highly susceptible to being controlled by men in a regime of familial authoritarianism.

According to Foucault, the exercise of force and coercion represents frustrated or failed forms of discipline in institutions (1977). In the context of Languedoc wine farming with only female heirs, these frustrations resulted in fervency in asserting the commonness of the family project. Fathers were forced to work against the hegemony of appropriate work for women.

Fathers and husbands tended to try to control the course of the lives of both male and female children to guarantee the continuity of the farm. The most commonly used tactics were gifts of land. Once those gifts were accepted, it often meant binding the relationship of the person to property. In this sense, the gift given is actually poison; as Fred Bailey pointed out years ago, a gift poisons one's independence. Marie was given this gift as soon as she turned sixteen. It was also given to Albert Martinez as one tactic in a series of very forceful tactics deployed to ensure the continuity of the Martinez family vineyard.

SONS AND SUCCESSION

Albert was the second and youngest son in a family of five. Both Albert and his brother, Marcel, were plucked out of school by their father to help on the farm as soon as each of them turned thirteen. Their sister, Hélène, was allowed to continue in school. Marcel always resented being forced to quit school for work on the farm, and it was determined that he would quit farming as soon as he could. Albert was less antagonized by the idea partly because he witnessed many long and bitter battles between his father and brother over the issue of succession.

Marcel was quite open about not wanting to carry on the family farm and this honesty enraged the father. The huge confrontations between Marcel and his father often ended with the exchange of blows and the meting out of a series of punishments. With Albert, the *pater familias* employed a rather different tactic. Long before his retirement, Albert's father initiated a campaign to exert pressure on this less determined son to take over the holding as he represented the last and the surest hope for the survival of the family vineyards. Albert recounted how his father managed to persuade him to stay on the farm by offering rewards instead of punishments:

> When I turned 18, in 1958, my father gave me a "gift" of 1.6 hectares of vines and he said that from that point onward I was a winegrower, in my own right, no longer just a helper to him. This gift was really part of my inheritance. It was given to me early, before my father retired, as a way of keeping me interested in farming. Because my brother had always said that he would leave farming if anything else came along and because I was the youngest son and I didn't have such strong feelings,

my father saw me as insurance against the farm failing. I hesitated for a while over whether to accept this gift, for I knew that accepting it meant that I would be tying myself to the farm and to the land and that I would not be able to do something else with my life. For a while I did want to follow in my older brother's footsteps and leave this life of drudgery and uncertainty. But I couldn't face the prospect of endless fights with my father, seeing how he and my brother were always going at each other. So in the end, I accepted the gift and gave in to my parents' pressure for me to stay on the land.

In 1972, Albert's father died and the entire family holding was divided up among the three children. It was significant that, in the same year, Marcel finally left the farm and broke his links to the land by selling his share of his inheritance to Albert and moving to Lyons to work as a mechanic. He only managed to escape from the farm after the death of the patriarch and ties of patriarchal power were extinguished. Mothers fail to exercise the same authority. Hélène also lived in Lyons and worked in a nursery school. She had left the village much earlier and rented her land out to Albert. Although Albert took over the farm as head of the enterprise, he saw this undertaking as a form of submission to parental will and in some respects an act of defeat. By capitulating to parental pressure, Albert felt he had committed himself to a way of life rife with crises and that this had led to hardship and economic insecurity.[17]

These sentiments, supported by prevailing ideas of modernity, are in fact common among heirs to family farms and fuel the reluctance of children to take up farming. In light of the state of permanent crises in which viticulture seems embedded, many children equivocate and finally refuse to commit themselves to farming, a way of life beset by economic crises and hardship. Moreover, the presence of a highly developed market for their labor provides an easy means of escape, since, in principle, employment in industry is readily available. In practice, however, the availability of employment has varied according to economic developments in certain historical periods. For example, the situation of high labor mobility was stimulated in the post–World War II era. However, the economic downswings of the "post-Fordist" decades of the 1980s and 1990s have reduced the possibilities of employment in industry, and continuing recessions in urban economies have altered the profile of rural to urban migration.

Among the family wine producers, the highly developed market in labor presented itself as such a field, and calculations were made by all members of the household about the value of labor and the virtues of taking up forms of work outside farming. Thus, the labor market can exert powerful pressures that can threaten the continuity of the household and the enterprise and undermine patriarchal authority experienced and exercised in these cases as the rule of parents, usually the father, over children. In many cases, fathers exercised their power to restrict their children's access to those alternative cultural fields and sustained the practice of withdrawing children from school to get help for the field, finally withdrawing them altogether to begin apprenticeship as winegrowers. In this way, the vision of choices is limited. Young children are thoroughly dependent on their parents for sustenance, Albert had little choice but to yield to his father's authority and to what his father defined as the family imperative, that is, maintaining a viable unit of agricultural production.

In situations in which filial duty was challenged, parents employed a variety of means to compel children to devote themselves to the common family project. Bribes were offered, threats made, gifts given, and exhortations wielded to compel children to assume what was defined often by parents as their familial responsibilities. The effectiveness of these tactics was based on the fact that, in the context of family farming, parents, usually fathers, monopolized both the ideological and material means for the domination of children who, in turn, relied upon them for their material sustenance. The withdrawal of the material means for the sustenance of dependent children, whether actually carried out or threatened, reinforced the power fathers can exercise to reign in recalcitrant daughters and sons of the household.

Daughters, like sons, then, were often subjected to forms of domination as well as rewards and punishments. However, the experience of domination for daughters is different from that of sons. Sons eventually came to be established as the head of the household, and the power differences between fathers and sons were really in fact a phase in the life cycle of a male farmer. The power differential came to an end once the son inherited property. The situation of women in this context was rather different. The period of women's position as subordinates to male heads of households and farms is more sustained both as daughters then as wives. The majority of agricultural holdings tended to be registered in the names of men. One of the reasons for this was that the state reinforces the de facto if not the de jure male ownership of agricultural enterprises. Registering property in the names of males facilitated access to state subsidies, loans, and the dissemination of technical information. Since men were considered the rightful operators of any farm, credit facilities and subsidy programs were directed at men. The terms of loans, interests, and mortgage rates were more favorable to men, considered the primary income earners and property owners, irrespective of how much women may bring in through their wage work in other sectors of the economy.

So the juro-political apparatus of the state in these respects promoted the economic dependence of women on men. The state then participated in the cyclical process of establishing males as household heads, reinforcing male power and authority by providing an economic basis for patriarchal authority. The male head's control over labor and family members was mediated through a variety of ideological devices, especially those associated with the sanctity of the family. Marie Pons's father impressed upon Marie that life itself is associated with farming using the symbolism of blood and earth. But that control over labor in fact gained real force materially through the head's control over property. Moreover, men also tended to control the products of that labor. The income generated from the production of vines is paid to the head of the household—the owner of that property—who ultimately controls its distribution. Therefore, it is as dependents of the owner that members establish entitlement to the products of labor. In this sense, wives and husbands exchange their labor on the basis of what has been called the conjugal contract (Whitehead 1981). However, because women tended to surrender control and de facto as well as de jure ownership of their agricultural property to their husbands, husbands and wives entered into the conjugal contract on very different terms. Men entered as the owners of the means of production and their own labor power. Women entered as the owners of labor power only. In this light, it can be argued that not only are power differentials characteristic of family, but class-like relations are in evidence at the level of the family unit and class and gender converge. The authority of the male head is sanctioned by ownership of the means of production and control of the economic resources upon which the livelihood of the domestic unit depends. The dependent status of the other members of the domestic unit underlines the authority of the male head, who may withdraw, apportion, and appropriate goods, services, and labor. Moreover, the presence of class-like divisions and dynamics reveals the way women and women's labor is exploited by men as heads of households, particularly where a system of rewards and punishment is in place within a regime of familial authoritarianism based on patriarchal power.

CONCLUSION

I have discussed and examined the ways in which Languedoc women and men confront the problem of the reproduction of the family farm. I have used the conceptual schema of the regimes of regulation to apprehend the processes by which certain forms of action and choices become embodied in the men and women who commit their labor to run family winegrowing farms. I have illustrated how practices of regimes of familistic hegemony and familial authoritarianism are complementary and entwined in small holding Languedoc farms. Familial authoritarianism becomes salient when a regime based on familial hegemony falters. Familial hegemony becomes weakened as the alternatives to relying on winegrowing as a means for the reproduction of labor become multiplied under industrial and market capitalism. I have also discussed the specifically gendered aspects of the system of management on Languedoc family enterprises and demonstrated the ways women are inserted into and affected by the systems of labor control.

I have also proposed in this chapter some possibilities for appreciating the complexities of gender and generational issues in the reproduction of Languedoc farming by drawing on Bourdieu's idea of habitus and Gramsci's concept of hegemony. The concept of hegemony has been particularly apposite for my purposes here for it allows us to view a social world as made up of fields and institutions of power. Hegemony applies to political fields and is often used to discuss relations between the rulers and the ruled, the dominators and the dominated, and state and civil society. It permits an understanding of how groups in the social world establish their domination over others and the ways in which this is done, not through coercion or force but through achieving consent and defining the boundaries of a commonsense reality (Lears 1985, 572). Hegemony is a process through which the legitimacy of the power wielded by certain groups in society is established and the primacy of their political visions and project is accepted. Hegemonic processes are located in institutions of power in civil society, such as schools, churches, and the family, where those in positions of power aim to shape and form the worldview and collective wills.

I have adopted a perspective that views the institution of the family as characterized by a particular configuration of power, where certain subject categories rule and others are ruled. References to dominant groups in Gramsci's work largely apply to political elites and dominant classes. However, I have extended his notion of dominant groups to include the social category of men. Through the processes of capitalist transformation, men have established a position of dominance in the world of Languedoc production that allows them to define the legitimacy of their vision and projects. In a context in which women have come to rely increasingly on men for their own reproduction as a result of the rationalization and mechanization of family farming and the masculinization of viticulture, men have become produced as heads of the enterprise who manage, direct, and control the labor process. As a consequence of this, I argue, familial hegemony means, in fact, a consensus to assimilate to the imperative and interests of men. As Williams, among others, has pointed out, hegemony is never total (1977, 107). It captures some people but not others and can, in turn, fail. According to Foucault, the exercise of force and coercion in this respect represents frustrated and failed forms of discipline in the different institutions that make up the social world (1977). So the practices in regimes of familial authoritarianism are invoked. In many respects, as I have tried to show here, regimes of familial authoritarianism translate into regimes of regulation based on patriarchy. It is through the operation of these two different but complementary regimes that Languedoc farmers manage to keep their sons and daughters *down,* in the multiple senses of the word, on the farm.

NOTES

1. France's bacon needed to be saved because in the international wine market, sales of French wine dropped dramatically in the first years of the twenty-first century. For example, in Canada, since 1996, there has been a drop of nineteen percent in sales of wines from France. While this overall decline has occurred, there has actually been an increase in wine sold from the Languedoc region. In Quebec, for example, it has increased by 250 percent to fifty-three thousand hectoliters. The consumption of Languedoc wine has increased to such an extent that Languedoc has surpassed Bordeaux as France's leading exporter of wine to Canada (*Wine Access Magazine,* March 2002).
2. Most small-scale farmers tend to grow grapes and reply on cooperatives to manufacture and market wines. For a discussion of vinification and marketing cooperatives in France, see Ulin (1996).
3. It is generally held that one person and one tractor can run an operation of roughly eight hectares. Beyond that extra labor is needed. Increments in size demand increasing amounts of labor and the mobilization of that labor on a more sustained basis.
4. Fieldwork upon which this chapter is based was undertaken in several periods from 1990 to 2002 in three villages located near Béziers. The specific information that appears in this chapter is excerpted from life histories recorded for a total of twenty-one women and eighteen men who were members of households that operated family farms.
5. These terms are adaptations of a framework used by Ching Kwan Lee to contrast the systems of management in two factories in Asia (see Lee 1998). Lee, in turn, has borrowed and adapted Buroway's framework of

analysis, which uses the idea of "regimes of factory production" to describe management systems in industrial production systems (see Burawoy 1985).

6. *Habitus* is generally understood as a structure of dispositions that reflect a "field of objective possibilities open to agents at a particular historical moment" (Lane 2000, 25) or a system of internalized dispositions that mediate between social structures and practical activity (Brubaker 1985, 758). See also Maton (2008). Habitus is also discussed in Bourdieu (1977, 1984, and 1994).

7. Pseudonyms are used throughout this chapter.

8. Ontological narratives are the stories people tell to define themselves, to make sense of their lives and actions undertaken. For a discussion of this concept, see Somers (1994).

9. See Touraine et al., 1980.

10. Smith offers a well-developed discussion of hegemony (1999). Also see Kurtz (1996), Roseberry (1994), and Sider (1986).

11. The very sameness of the work done by women and men, however, did not constitute the basis for determining wage levels. Women were, in fact, customarily paid half men's wages. It has been argued that grievances over this specific form of inequity provoked women to join in the riots and protests in the early 1900s and that the issue of the exploitation of women was a rallying point for women in that period of particularly heightened political sensibilities (see Frader 1991).

12. Frader outlines some of the changes in women's work in the pre–World War II period as capitalist rationalization proceeded apace (1991).

13. The specific measures are detailed in Pech (1971).

14. They included legislation, subsidy programs, and plans for agricultural reform. To foster the growth of the capitalist sector, these laws made provisions and introduced a series of subsidies for the creation of S.A.F.E.R. (Société d'Aménagement Foncier et d'Etablissement Rural), a network of rural agencies—land banks, essentially—authorized to buy up land that became available on the market. The purpose of the land banks was first to consolidate "unviable" microfundia into what government legislation defined as "viable" farms. S.A.F.E.R. lands would then be upgraded and sold to those who conformed to what the legislation determined as "qualified" family farmers. This in fact meant the relatively prosperous and progressive sector of the farming population, which had assimilated the modernizing imperatives of the state, especially young farmers trained in degree and diploma programs sponsored by the state. Structural reform through

S.A.F.E.R. then favored the development of large-scale farming, as only relatively wealthy farmers, those with already large and profitable farms, could afford to buy and maintain upgraded land according to the strict guidelines imposed by the state (Keeler 1979 and 1981; Wright 1964).

15. After 1945, farm mechanization and the various plans for modernizing French agriculture resulted in a drop in the agricultural population from thirty-five percent in 1939 to six percent in 1990 (see Ardagh 1982; Hoggart, Buller, and Black 1995). The rural exodus in France has been discussed by Mendras (1984); Wright (1964); Duby and Wallon (1976); and Gervais, Jollivet, and Tavernier (1977).

16. For example, at the national level, Jean Monnet, who became commissioner general in the postwar administration of France, launched his First Plan for French recovery under the slogan "modernization or downfall." The Marshall Plan provided funds for the economic transformation and industrialization of France in 1947 (see Ardagh 1982).

17. A fuller discussion of this case appears in Lem 1999.

Technology and Nature

RACHEL E. BLACK AND ROBERT C. ULIN

Wine is a product of nature as much as it is a product of human craft and ingenuity. Although there are important microclimatic and geographic considerations, winegrowing involves human intervention in nearly every step of the process—from the pruning and training of vines to managing the process of fermentation in the cellar. Wine is a manifestation of human relationship to nature. At the same time, this is not always a harmonious relationship: the production of wine reveals tensions between humans and their natural environment.

The vineyard is usually envisioned and represented as a lush green space absent of humans. However, if we consider the viticultural landscape for just a moment, we become aware of the human presence in all aspects of the scenery. We are looking at a monoculture that human hands have carefully arranged and that human culture has shaped over centuries. Humans are not absent from the vineyard: skilled local and migrant laborers begin to shape the wine we drink as they work among the vines. Many a winemaker will tell you that all good wine is made in the vineyard. However, the commodification of wine and its sale on globalized markets obscures and naturalizes human labor, knowledge, and technology.

Elizabeth Saleh notes in her chapter that this naturalizing process plays an important part in the construction of wines' authenticity. Focusing on wine production in Lebanon, Saleh uncovers the complex technological and cultural relations that exist in the vineyard. In particular, Saleh focuses on the role of French oenologists and the production of quality wine. Interestingly, Lebanon offers no technical training for locals interested in learning how to make wine; the Lebanese attend French oenology schools and most of the large producers employ French oenologists. Saleh uncovers this French cultural hegemony and considers how it plays out in both the vineyard and the cellar. Technology is deeply cultural, and in this case it has played a key role in shaping social and economic relations that mirror the not-so-distant colonial past.

Consumers have become increasingly concerned with how their wine is produced. In part, this is an offshoot of the organic food movement and a growing interest in knowing the people who grow food and understanding the production methods. Organic, biodynamic, and natural wines are becoming more commonplace on wine shop shelves. Like with food, there is a great deal of consumer confusion and many misconceptions about what these labels and categories mean. Most consumers assume that a bottle of wine contains fermented grape juice, and they sometimes note that the label says that the wine may contain sulfites. There is an inherent assumption that wine is a simple, healthy, "pure" product. However, it is rarely the case that wine contains only grape. Commercial (and occasionally genetically modified) yeast, acidifiers, and fining agents made from animal products are just a few examples of the many substances potentially found in the average bottle of wine. Perhaps wine labels should include a list of ingredients.

This is one of the thoughts behind what has come to be known as the natural wine movement. In this section, Rachel Black explores the ways wine producers, importers, and consumers negotiate and shape the concept of nature through wine. Numerous contradictions exist between the philosophy behind natural wine and the practices involved in winegrowing. These tensions between human intervention and the production of a "natural" beverage are in many ways an attempt to break down the barriers and alienation commodification has created. Natural wine drinkers are interested in knowing the farmers who made their wine. Through narratives of production and the forging of producer-consumer relations (even by proxy), wine drinkers feel that wine brings them closer to nature. In the case of the natural wine movement, authenticity often means the eschewing of technology.

As Paul Cohen remarks in his chapter, if we look at the history of natural wine, technology is truly at the center of this movement's evolution. Cohen revisits the writings of Jules Chauvet, a French *négociant* and chemist often referred to as the father of natural wine. Interesting, Chauvet was heavily invested in developing technology that could be used in producing wines that were a clear expression of the places in which they were produced. Chauvet's writings spoke out against the use of commercial yeasts and the overworking of the vineyard. At the same time, Chauvet helped develop the technologically heavy process of carbonic maceration, which has come to be one of the hallmarks of his home region, the Beaujolais.

This section reveals a series of complex human relations and human-environment relations illuminated through the study of wine production and consumption. Wine cannot exist without human intervention and the ongoing development of technology used in the vineyard and the cellar. The naturalization of these processes brings to light our unease about the overmanipulation of nature and the negative side effects it might have on our bodies and the environment. In Western cultures, people have held wine above other food products because of its symbolic prestige and historical importance, and for this reason, wine has largely escaped the same scrutiny placed on other food products and agricultural activities. This section invites further critical analysis of wine production and Western conceptions of nature.

CHAPTER THIRTEEN

Pursuits of Quality in the Vineyards: French Oenologists at Work in Lebanon

ELIZABETH SALEH

The sun shone relentlessly down upon the vineyards in the Kefraya region of West Bekaa in Lebanon. It was the peak of summer and within weeks, or perhaps even just days, the grape harvest would begin in the country's largest winegrowing region. Starting in the winter months and continuing into spring, the vines had been pruned and their canes trained. During late spring and early summer, excess leaves were removed and the branches cut. By the early summer months, treatment was applied and the vines more or less left to their own devices until the start of the harvest. Given that the vineyards were a hub of activity until this point, it seemed that the respite in the shade from the sweltering heat would be welcomed by all. One late afternoon, I made a visit to the home of the head of agricultural affairs of one of the largest wineries in Lebanon, Château Kefraya. I asked Mr. Nabhane when the harvest would begin. We sat on his family's veranda in the Kefraya village, and Nabhane reclined back into his summer chair as he looked out beyond the villagers' *kouroum* (vineyards), mainly of the Cinsault variety, and finally rested his gaze upon the vineyards of the noble varieties such as Cabernet Sauvignon and Chardonnay on the winery estates surrounding the Château Kefraya.

Nabhane picked at some grapes from the fruit bowl placed by his wife on the table next to him, and proceeded to tell me that the harvest would begin soon. However, he could not confirm when exactly. That was up to Fabrice Guiberteau, the *muhandis al khamara* (wine engineer), who originates from the Cognac region of France and is employed by the Château Kefraya winery. Guiberteau would decide on the exact time of the harvest, and many of the vineyard owners in Kefraya depended upon his decision. I asked Nabhane how Guiberteau would decide when he wanted the harvest to begin. Nabhane smiled and informed me that the time of the harvest was subject to how Guiberteau wanted the wines to taste. Having already spent some time with Guiberteau learning about the vini/viticulture techniques he uses, I knew his main aim was to begin the process of augmenting both the quality and quantity of the wines produced by the Château Kefraya, and that this would begin in the vineyards. Yet, as this was Guiberteau's second harvest in Lebanon, I wondered what knowledge he would draw upon to decide when the grapes were ready to be reaped. Surely, as he had not experienced all the different possible weather conditions in the Bekaa Valley, he would face challenges and perhaps might even require advice and support from locals such as Nabhane. Nabhane told me Guiberteau would look to the sugar content in the grapes; this is all the knowledge needed to make the styles of wines desired.

Guiberteau's mission to increase and improve the overall quantity and quality of the wine was also part of a wider joint enterprising project envisioned by the Lebanese business association of wineries, the Union Vinicole du Liban (UVL). Château Ksara, Château Musar, and Château Kefraya established the UVL in 1997 as part of their pursuit to create and monopolize a niche in the international market for high-quality wines. These alliances were essential for overall symmetry in the production and reputation of good-quality wines in Lebanon, particularly as new wineries opened following the end of the civil war. That the shareholders—especially those in the Château Kefraya and Château Ksara wineries—belong to wider mercantile networks with links extending across different political and trade organizations in Lebanon and beyond is suggestive of their well-connected positions. The objectives to regulate and standardize production so as to follow international guidelines of production materialized through the UVL's successful campaigning and lobbying for the passing of a wine law in 2000. It was the first of its kind since wine legislation was passed in 1938, during the French mandate thrown out in 1983. Articles in the new wine law such as those stipulating the required sugar content of the different kinds of wines or that Lebanese wine can only be produced from *vitis vinifera* varieties, requires specialized oenologists who understand the overall process of wine production from the vineyard to the winery. The hiring of French oenologists was therefore also a critical part of the agenda for the other largest wine producer in Lebanon, Château Ksara, further north in the Bekaa Valley. There, Mr. James Palgé from the Champagne region of France has been employed since 1994 and holds an equally influential role to Guiberteau. Significant here is that oenology qualifications cannot be obtained at Lebanese universities and students interested in specializing in winemaking must travel abroad for further training. Thus, while there is an apparent labor market for Lebanese oenologists, decisions to hire and pay substantially high salaries to French oenologists were conterminous to strategies (both current and preemptive) deployed by these wineries to maintain and assert their social and economic power.

The positions of power held by Guiberteau and Palgé resonate with what Collier and Ong have noted as a culture of expertise where "technopreneurs" attempt to create symmetry across space while also ensuring that the singularity of the good produced is retained (2005). Harvey draws similar conclusions, where cultural commodities such as wine have a tendency to evoke notions of authenticity and history—especially in terms of its aesthetic values—important to those seeking monopoly privileges (2006). The globalization of specialized labor required in the production of these cultural commodities aimed at niche markets is essential in the postmodernity of capitalism, thereby guaranteeing the "special qualities" attributed to a good during production are not to the degree where it can no longer follow the requirements of tradability. Yet the strategies deployed to restrict production of wine and to control and fashion the concept of taste speak of a particular type of a "commodity spirit" (Appadurai 1986, 25). Here, a quality-quantity nexus emerges as a marker for singularity, exclusivity, and authenticity through an emphasis upon the natural ties associated with the region where the grapes are grown. Ulin observes that the seasonal process within viticulture speaks of a discourse of wine as something natural, held together with the seemingly unquestionable "customs or habits" practiced within winegrowing that eclipse the "cultural mediation of time" and, more important, the "social construction of the natural" (1996, 55). Strategies of power are therefore naturalized through the symbolic association with the "invention" of the château and through legislation that establishes a stable referential system of what good quality wine should be (Ulin 1996, 55). Linked to this is the Bordeaux 1855 wine classification for *grand cru* wines that constructed a hierarchy of regions and was a precursor for the

globalization of a dominant form in the spatial categorization of wine production where superior-quality wines are linked to limitations in their quantity—
and this began in the vineyard (Simpson 2011; Ulin 1996). Thus, despite the
significant roles of nonhuman and/or natural factors required in the production of quality wines such as the right location, the right weather conditions,
and the right kinds of grapes, it is apparent that wine enterprises seek to maintain a focus on organizing and controlling production, as is suggested in the
relationship between Guiberteau and the vineyard owners of Kefraya.

Such a discourse of nature is also articulated through a politics of the aesthetics acting to conceal a hierarchy in winegrowing, where elite growers in
France have historically come to monopolize production and the market in
diverse ways, at both the local and global levels. One aspect, as geographer
Lagendjik suggests, is that of "flying winemakers" who gained expertise in
wine-renowned regions such as Bordeaux and have become "quality and marketing symbols," instrumental in universalizing French methods of production
(2004, 13). Somewhat paradoxically, and more often than not, wines produced
in these countries were judged less upon the reputation of the *terroir* of their
region than from the status of the "international winemaker." The following sections examine this apparent replication, where these French oenologists
strive to transform grapes into high-end retail wines with skills, expertise, and
values that emerge from their extensive experiences working in wine production outside of Lebanon. In doing so, the chapter explores nuances in how the
quality-quantity nexus is perceived by Guiberteau and Palgé in their viticulture
practices and how attempts are made to naturalize this discourse of quality in
the contracts forged with vineyard owners in Kefraya and beyond, willing to
comply with expectations to maintain certain types of grape varieties.

The focus of this chapter arises out of my fieldwork doctoral research on
Lebanese wine producers and their ongoing pursuit to create and sustain a niche
in the international market for high-quality wines. By focusing upon the enterprising strategies deployed from within the Lebanese wine industry and the
types of business relations formed, I explore how knowledge required for the
construction of a market must also entail a capacity to (re)produce it as a social reality, with particular attention paid to the Kefraya region. Part of my
analytical narrative considers the history of the modernization of Lebanese
wine production as part of a wider and longer project of French cultural hegemony in the region that can be traced back to before the French mandate
during the early twentieth century and to the sericulture industry of the eighteenth century (Makdisi, 2000; Traboulsi 2007). Entangled within the French
agenda of hegemony are the political and economic interests of local actors with

extensive trade networks extending well beyond the peripheries of the rural plains of the Bekaa, the urban port of Beirut, and into the very heart of Europe (Makdisi, 2000; Traboulsi 2007). In this way, the current pursuit of the production of high-quality wines by elite entrepreneurs involved in such enterprises speaks of a history of social class and also of a particular perception of place that can be situated within a wider perspective of the Lebanese laissez-faire political economy and also of the globalization of wine production—both of which belong to a history of trade and market-driven economies (Gates 1998; Unwin 1991). The stance I take on the market draws broadly upon Mitchell's analysis of market coordination, where a series of overlapping arrangements and agreements are historically constituted and socially defined within a framework that excludes what cannot be exchanged within that market (2007). The discourse of nature that shapes the production of quality wines fits within such an understanding of the market, where practices of winegrowing not adhering to standards that serve as markers for singularity and authenticity result in lower rankings or even at times rankings not classified as wine at all. Given that such a winegrowing hierarchy perpetuates a cultural process of status and difference demonstrates the inherently political endeavors of such a discourse. The work of the oenologist in this regard is culturally situated and "proceeds, like science in general" in an attempt to control and reproduce nature (Ulin 2002, 700).

THE PREDICAMENT OF CINSAULT

Cinsault vines are grown across the Bekaa Valley, and research into the Jesuit archives at the Taanayel Monastery in the central Bekaa indicates that the first plantations began in the mid-nineteenth century. Their ambition to make wine in the French style required changes in the methods of wine production starting with the introduction of new grape varieties such as the Cinsault planted in the *gobelet* style. Archival research suggests that the proliferation of Cinsault across the valley is linked with the spread of phylloxera, which appears to have arrived at least by the end of the nineteenth century, resulting not only in a gradual destruction of many indigenous varieties, but also a loss of local techniques used in the plantations of these vines. It is apparent that the grafting of phylloxera-resistant root stock required the expertise used by the Jesuits in their vineyards and also the capital to invest in these vines. The transformation of the Bekaa viticulture landscape due to phylloxera is thus also a narrative of social and economic change, and it is perhaps no coincidence that the prevalence of Cinsault in Kefraya, where much of my fieldwork took place between late 2006 and early 2008, is entwined within this history.

Plantations of Cinsault across Kefraya began in the late 1940s with Michel de Bustros, who comes from a Beiruti mercantile family that can be traced back to the gentile classes of the eighteenth century. Following the modification of family lands in Kefraya, de Bustros turned to village residents, offering to pay up front for their expenses to plant Cinsault vines. Repayment started once the grapes reached optimum levels and sold off to wineries such as Château Ksara and Château Musar. Since then, the region has become a major winegrowing hub where approximately 121 hectares of vineyards belong to the Château Kefraya estate established by Michel de Bustros in 1979. Another 631 hectares or so belong to those residing in the Kefraya village who predominately sell Cinsault by the kilogram to wineries across Lebanon. However, following the end of the civil war (1975–1990) and the increasing attention paid to quality, there has been growing pressure over the years by Palgé, followed by Guiberteau, for vineyard owners to grow grapes other than Cinsault.

Both oenologists described their dislike for Cinsault in terms of its displeasing aesthetic qualities and incompatible quantities for making high-quality wines. One of the main problems for Guiberteau was that the Cinsault berries are bigger in size than other grapes, resulting in a higher volume of wine, but with weaker color and aroma. For Palgé, the sugar content of these grapes is very high, resulting in large volumes of wine unsuitable for aging. These perspectives evoke what Mansfield observes as the way in which quality techniques can be perceived as subjective and judged through the senses, while also objective and made "real" through measuring quantities (2003). The somewhat intangible properties such as the Cinsault wine's "weak" aroma and apparent inability to age are validated through tangible aspects such as its size and volume. The Cinsault grapes are thus also perceived to counter the required breaking down of production into what Callon and colleagues have suggested as an economy of qualities where the "mobilization of scarce resources" within the production of a market good entails a series of "rites of passage" in a quest for singularity (2002). A politics of aesthetics was also in this respect extended to the way the vines must look and the way they are to be maintained, elucidating further the properties of singularity associated with the wine. Guiberteau explains:

> The vines must be looked after properly. You must make sure that the grapes are planted in the right manner. So either trained along a wire or planted in a *gobelet* style. These must be planted at a certain distance apart and pruned in the correct way. The grapes yielded must be a certain amount too. Here, the relationship between quantity and quality is crucial. Limited amounts of grapes will make a good wine. You see all of this is important. Even if you stand at any point in the vineyard, all the

vines should line up equally. This is a good indicator—a basic one—but a start. And it looks beautiful!

The usages of aesthetic properties to describe the positive attributes of the vineyards also illustrate the articulation of quality discourses that occurs within enterprising strategies within agro-food production where the usages of visual imagery engage with a materiality of nature to classify the distinctive features and characteristics of a good, and, in doing so, create intimate links to the origin of the produce (see Goodman 2003; Murdoch, Marsden, and Banks 2000). Yet perhaps what distinguishes wines from the agro-food industries is that the aesthetic traits of the grapes have to be retained following transformation into another product (wine) so as to maintain intimacy with the origin of the grape. Yet the naturalization of the links between the region and the product (wine), Ulin argues, is inherently political, as it also entails the forging of ties of people to the process who are then, through time, spatially bound to a specific set of hierarchical labor relations (1996). That this universalistic discourse of quality arises historically from French dominating (locally and globally) viti-viniculture relationships brings forth once more the legacy of French cultural hegemony within the region. Given that the praxis of both oenologists is grounded within such practices of power can be illustrated by the way in which they seek to bring harmony between the viticulture and viniculture production spheres.

In my discussions with Guiberteau, the term *balance égale,* which can be roughly translated as *symmetry* or *harmony,* was frequently used when describing the aesthetic properties of the way the vineyards should be planted and pruned and what the right color of their leaves should be. These were important factors in the maintenance of the vines, the subsequent quality of the grapes, and finally the wines. Significantly, *balance égale* was also used in the process of judging if a *viticulteur* in Kefraya may share a similar philosophy with Guiberteau:

What do I see when I look out to the vineyards in the village of Kefraya? Of course I am looking at quality. How do I do this? Well, I must see if there is an attempt to look after the grapes—even if it is Cinsault that they are growing, then I must therefore also know the farmer (*viticulteurs*) and see if he is like me, also willing to look to the future. If not, then I must assume that the quality of his grapes will never be good and there is no harmony.

The interchanging qualities associated with the vineyard owner and the vineyard speaks of a particular reciprocal construction of value where it is the "transformative potential" of these qualities that is valorized by Guiberteau (Graeber 2007, 47; Munn 1986). Yet the usage of symmetry within commodified agricultural chains of production, as Busch and Tanaka observe, requires the symmetrical treatment of facts and values that become interdependent upon one another (1996). Within practices of ranking and standardization, nature and people are thus subjected to the same rites of passage that have equal intensity and force. Symmetry thus occurs following the successful completion of the stages of liminality whereby nonhuman bodies are transformed and the human actors involved are simultaneously valorized and attributed with corresponding positive qualities. A hierarchy of qualities emerges whereby a "good" vineyard owner is judged based upon, for example, a "good grape variety." Significantly, another important aspect of what makes a "good" vineyard owner for Guiberteau and Palgé is compliance and willingness to plant and grow what was deemed a "good grape." For both oenologists, the "good" qualities of the vineyard owner emerge when there is compliance to the changes imposed. Dependability and consistency were therefore of the essence and a "good" vineyard owner allowed the oenologists to have direct control over the maintenance of these vines.

While Palgé and Guiberteau share a similar objective, to terminate the use of the Cinsault variety and to promote the importance of harmony in the vineyards, their strategies differ because of nuances in the articulation of locality by the wineries they work for. Château Kefraya only sources grapes from the Kefraya region, and within Guiberteau's discourse of quality there appears to be an emphasis upon the natural properties of the land of the Kefraya region, where he believes the right conditions are readily available for making good-quality wines. The "natural environment" such as dry and rocky soils and the extreme cold and hot weather conditions allows the vines to "suffer" so that the grapes will not be full of juice and sugar. In this way, the flavors of the grapes would be just right to produce the styles of wines he desires. It is therefore the grape variety that is the problem and not the land in Kefraya:

> There are several factors that are expected in the production of good-quality wines. First of all, you must have good land and a good grape. Here in Kefraya, the land can produce good vines that will yield a good quality. But it is important that the right kinds of grapes are grown to make good wines. You cannot make a good wine from grapes such as Cinsault. You need noble varieties such as Cabernet Sauvignon or for a white wine, my favorite grape, which is Viognier.

Château Ksara's viticulture contracts on the other hand, currently extend across the Bekaa Valley. However, until 1997, Château Ksara sourced approximately

700 tons of the Cinsault variety from the Kefraya village. Starting in 1991, the winery began to set up contracts with landowners outside of Kefraya, planting vines of noble varieties such as Cabernet Sauvignon. Once the vines reached optimum levels for yielding grapes, Château Ksara ceased to buy the Cinsault from Kefraya. Palgé explains the process:

> Before I arrived, it was up to ninety percent Cinsault and I wanted to remove the grape completely from production. But even then we had to continue to buy Cinsault for another seven to eight years from Kefraya, since we still had to make wine. But we also started planting other varieties outside. In 1991, they began to plant Cabernet Sauvignon for red wines outside of Kefraya. But there was only Cabernet Sauvignon. So in 1994 when I arrived, I said that we must stop planting Cabernet Sauvignon. I suggested that we plant Syrah and Merlot as the two top priorities. By diversifying the grapes, we went from two red wines in Château Ksara to six reds. So we have a range that is much larger, and in each range there are specific varieties. The high ranges of wines are more tannic and more colorful. While the lighter wines, instead of using Cinsault, I replaced with new varieties such as Marselan. This is like Cinsault but lighter, more colorful and aromatic.

Such a diversification of the types of grape varieties now used by Château Ksara highlights how attention paid to the process of singularity within production functions to amplify the uniqueness of the wine produced. While Guiberteau may also be interested in diversifying the types of grapes used in Château Kefraya's wines, limitations in the ability to manipulate certain aspects of the production process are set apart through what Guiberteau described rather explicitly as "natural," and this differed to Palgé, who was less inclined to defining and demarcating particular regions in Lebanon to have a better potential for producing high-quality wines. In the pursuit for quality, conceptualizations of what was deemed "natural" thus had to do with what could not be controlled and organized. In this way, the quest for singularity in the vineyards entailed a further breaking down and reassembling of available resources that could potentially result in a more refined hierarchy of qualities. Significantly, the constraints faced by Guiberteau to extend viticulture relations beyond the Kefraya region are situated within discourses of wine that naturalize a distinctive locality brought about through the construction of a specialized relationship between a *château* and the vineyards that surround it (Ulin 1996). In this respect, the nuances in the perspectives of both oenologists in the way in which quality was or was not spatially attached to the Kefraya region speaks also

of how the application of their expertise and the conceptualization of quality
are discursive and contingent to a specific set of socioeconomic circumstances.
These conditions influenced the way practices of singularity could be materialized through contract agreements set up with vineyard owners across the
Bekaa Valley.

MAKING GRAPES TASTE LIKE TEACAKES

During the peak of harvest in Kefraya, the vineyards had once more become a
hub of activity. Migrant workers who traveled across from Syria a few weeks
earlier were moving up and down vineyards. Mostly young women were bent,
endlessly over the vines, sometimes with their children, cutting the berries
with kitchen knives or garden clippers and placing them into crates. A young
adolescent boy would then usually carry the crates back to the truck. There an
older man would grab the crate and throw the grapes into the truck. Meanwhile, local vineyard owners from Kefraya would visit regularly to check up
on the number of crates thrown into the trucks. Villagers were paid per kilogram
and I am informed that each crate of Cinsault is approximately twenty-five
kilograms. Counting the number of crates was a way for vineyard owners to
figure out a rough estimate of the amount of money they would receive for
their grapes.

Each year, before harvest, Château Kefraya would assess the surplus
amount of grapes needed and organize an agreement with some of the vineyard owners. Every so often, Nabhane would pass by in his jeep to see if the
whole process was running smoothly in these vineyards. At times, he would
come across vineyard owners who wanted to find out when their grapes
would be harvested, and it was important that this was done soon. After
all, once the grapes began to shrivel and reduce in weight, the vineyard
owners would lose money. Nabhane would assure them that this would
not happen. One day, while I joined Nabhane on his travels across the
vineyards of the Kefraya village, one vineyard owner stopped him and expressed these concerns. When Nabhane tried to assure him, the vineyard
owner pointed in the direction of the vines dotted on the slopes of the Château Kefraya estates:

> Ya Nabhane! How can you be sure? Look at what the *muhandis* is doing
> out there? I went walking up around the winery's vines and there are
> some grapes shriveling under the hot sun. What is he doing? Does he not
> want his grapes? Does he know what he is doing?

Nabhane reassured the vineyard owner that *Muhandis* Guiberteau did know what he was doing and that he would not do the same to the grapes belonging to vineyard owners in Kefraya. With that, Nabhane bid the worried man farewell and moved on to the next vineyard. I asked Nabhane about this, and he informed me that Guiberteau wanted to make a "special" and "important" wine with the grapes left shriveling on the vines. The next day, I paid a visit to Guiberteau in his office adjacent to the winery's laboratory and queried him about these grapes. Rather than explaining straight away, Guiberteau invited me to join him in the vineyards along with his agricultural engineer interns from Lebanese universities. I accepted, and a few minutes later we arrived at the sloping vines pointed out by the disconcerted vineyard owner only the day before. As we all jumped down from the jeep, Guiberteau handed us plastic bags to collect some of the grapes for sugar testing. He shouted out to us that we should also taste some of the grapes. This, he explained later, was important to assess the sugar and possible styles of the wines that could be produced. The grape variety was ugni blanc, a variety incidentally grown in Cognac, where Guiberteau grew up. The ugni blanc berries were no longer full and robust, and to me, they looked shriveled and brown. Nevertheless, I tasted some of its berries with the interns who also appeared somewhat suspicious. We were all surprised. One of the interns suggested that the berries tasted like cake. I, perhaps because of my somewhat Anglicized taste buds, had tea cakes come to mind.

The next day, those grapes were ready to be harvested to make Château Kefraya's Mistelle called Nectar Chateau Kefraya. As Guiberteau informed me, there had been a lot of problems with the quality of this. It would take another two years before the wine was ready to be bottled and consumed, and so hopefully in the coming years, the quality would be augmented. He told me of the importance of decreasing quantity to increase quality and how this extends to the type of grape and when to harvest it. There were similar ramifications when it came to making other styles of wines:

> At the moment our wine with the least quality is Les Bretèches, which is made up of Cinsault plus Carignan and Mourvèdre. Then there is the Château of Kefraya range and finally Comte de M, which is the highest quality and we blend Cabernet Sauvignon and Syrah for this wine. You see, to make the higher-quality wines we still have the potential to increase production by using grapes from our estates. This means that I can oversee directly what goes on in the vineyard. With wines such as Les Bretèches, it will be better for us to blend noble varieties and not Cinsault. However, it will not be necessary to control the quantity

(in terms of quality) of the grapes that will be used for these kinds of wines. So long as they are grapes which are known and recognized to be consistent, then the wines can be produced.

Since his arrival in 2006, Guiberteau has overseen plantations of different types of vines on lands belonging to the Château Kefraya estate further down in the flatter plains of the region. Significantly, a dimension related to this plan has to do with the issue of little control over the viticultural maintenance of the vineyards in the Kefraya village. At the same time, Guiberteau explained to me, he had to think of strategies to encourage the diversification of the grape varieties grown by vineyard owners in the Kefraya village. A main challenge Guiberteau faced was to find an incentive for vineyard owners in Kefraya to pull out their Cinsault vines. As the contractual agreements set up between vineyard owners in Kefraya and Château Kefraya are based solely upon quantity, quality is valued based upon the types of grape bought. Cinsault grapes are bought at thirty to thirty-four cents per kilogram, and the Chardonnay/Sauvignon/Cabernet Sauvignon/Syrah grapes are bought at fifty-four cents per kilogram. Guiberteau considers this a good system, but believes that further steps can be taken to decrease even more the price of Cinsault. In this way, the Cinsault will not be of interest for people and they will eventually change the variety. Yet, as I pointed out to Guiberteau, grapes are priced per kilogram and price varies dependent upon the type of grape rather than the quality. Guiberteau pointed once more to the importance of beginning the process by encouraging vineyard owners in Kefraya to pull out their Cinsault and plant the vines required by Château Kefraya. Given that vineyard owners in Kefraya could at any point sell their grapes to other wineries, Guiberteau was not keen to put too much effort into the maintenance of their vines. Finally, there was no intention to develop long-term contracts with Kefraya vineyard owners until the first steps had been take to plant the types of grape varieties Guiberteau required. As Guiberteau concluded:

> It is important that it is not us (Château Kefraya) who need the Kefraya village but rather that they need us...We might be able to develop long-term contracts but this will depend if they share the same philosophy as us and begin by pulling out all of their Cinsault. Then only if we need more vines to produce higher quality wines.

It remains to be seen what becomes of Guiberteau's plans in the coming years. However, upon my return for a visit in the harvest of 2008, it was clear that many in Kefraya had not heeded the advice of Guiberteau. During my visit to the Kefraya region in the early months of 2012, Nabhane informed me that this was still in fact the case. It was suggested that, given that the amount of capital required to pull out the Cinsault vines and plant new ones was rather substantial, vineyard owners would require support from the wineries to do this, perhaps in a similar manner to the agreements instigated by de Bustros during the initial stages of viticulture in Kefraya. Yet there was no indication that such an arrangement would be made. Also brought to the fore was that as a result of the shifting strategies deployed by first Château Ksara and currently Château Kefraya, the profits were no longer of strong financial significance for those who did not adhere to the pressure to change viticultural maintenance. This appears to have resulted in the emergence of enterprising individuals willing to accept the changes by the wineries. Most had accumulated wealth abroad and began to expand their vineyards by acquiring land from others in Kefraya unable (or unwilling) to plant the vines on demand in the market. While such changes across the Kefraya landscape are gradual, they are also indicative of changes in social relations among local residents in Kefraya. The construction of ornate villas surrounded by vineyards by these enterprising persons is a display of cultural capital and speaks of the perpetuation of a process of distinction that involves the necessity for claims to 'legitimate superiority" (Bourdieu 1984, 55). That this particular type of localism emulates spatial categorizations within discourses of quality wines is suggestive of the ways winegrowing hierarchy is naturalized and culturally reproduced. Significantly, while the history of viticulture in the region is quite long in comparison to other regions, it is apparent that such transformations have occurred partly in response to changes taking place across the Bekaa Valley as a consequence of the strategies to diversify grape plantations deployed by Palgé at the Château Ksara winery. Significantly, Palgé still has an interest to improve the quality of vines grown in Kefraya. The reasons for this, as Palgé explained, have to do with ensuring a shared and unified understanding of quality across the Bekaa Valley. Palgé spoke of his relationship with one of the most enterprising and largest vineyard owners in Kefraya:

Dr. Didi was the first to plant Sauvignon Blanc in 1988, and when I arrived in 1994, he grew both Sauvignon Blanc and Cinsault. And my advice was to give up on the Cinsault; to pull it out and replant other grape varieties. I said to him, "If you do this then, I am still with you." And he agreed. So we planted Chardonnay and Syrah. Thus, he restructured. He is someone who has twenty hectares of these vines as well as the Sauvignon Blanc, and all vines are now young. So you see here, the process of augmenting quality and quantity begins to slowly spread across the Bekaa Valley.

Palgé's plans to vary the types of grape varieties are extended to diversifying the regions across the Bekaa Valley where these grapes are planted—and branching out means greater control of quality is possible. On several occasions during my visits to Château Ksara in the harvest time, Palgé was present with his *chef d'atelier* to physically examine grapes about to be released from their crates down into the press to churn out the grape must. With six different ranges or grades of red wines all made from noble grape varieties, and in different vineyards recognized for their quality, Palgé made clear the importance of managing each vineyard plot separately:

> Everything is separated. Even during the harvest, I receive grapes by variety, per vineyard, and per *domaine* (parcel of land). So I can check the grapes, and after a few months taste each of the wines. We even have committees for tasting.

Palgé explains how this process enables flexibility to use the best quality grapes that came in for the higher categories of wines and so forth. In order to create symmetry between the vini-viticulture spheres, there are mainly two types of contract agreements set up with vineyard owners across the Bekaa Valley. Long-term contracts are characterized by vineyard owners who rented their lands outright to Château Ksara and so viticultural maintenance is the full responsibility of the winery. The grapes are bought by the kilogram and in this way the prices remain stable throughout each harvest. Palgé defines these contracts as reliable because there is less room for price negotiation. It is significant that the longer-term contracts are predominantly with large landowners who own properties in the West Bekaa; this includes the lands owned by elite Beiruti families such as the Itani family in Mansourah and the Rizk in Tal Ed Noub, but also the lands of the Ludwig Schneller School situated in Kherbet Kanafar. There appears to be little communication with these landowners and the Château Ksara winery appears to have direct control over their vineyards.

With the shorter-term agreements, vineyard owners maintain their vines on their own accord, but are expected to heed the advice of Château Ksara. Palgé informs me that prices for each harvest vary and depend upon the quality of these grapes. The differences in the long- and short-term contracts set up by Château Ksara with vineyard owners across the Bekaa Valley highlight the winery's methods of quality control. While the longer-term contracts may offer more stability in the sense that grapes are more or less guaranteed in each harvest, the shorter-term contracts allowed Palgé the room to maneuver during years when the harvest might not turn out as well as had hoped.

Significantly, these short-term agreements enabled vineyard owners to develop contracts with other wineries seeking to buy noble varieties. Such contracts can be simultaneous, so that Château Ksara may buy one type of grape variety and then another winery might buy other kinds. In spite of this, Palgé appears to have made it a point to maintain good relations with these vineyard owners and continues to offer them advice on issues related to viticultural mainte-nance; he makes clear the reasons for such motives:

> It is important to have contracts with only the vineyard owners who share the same view as Château Ksara. We want to make good wines, so they must grow the good grapes as we expect. This is good not just for us but for Lebanon.

Sometimes this even extended to viniculture when more than a couple of these smaller vineyard owners took the decision to start producing their own wines. In fact, more than two of the small-scale wineries that use grapes sourced exclusively from within their estates, which are now dotted across the Bekaa landscape, had started out by selling grapes to the Château Ksara winery. The encouragement by Palgé—and that some of these small-scale wineries were able to join the business association of Lebanese wineries (UVL) quite quickly—demonstrates the strategic efforts made by the larger wineries to ex-tend their discourses of quality across to the rest of the Lebanese wine industry. Indeed, as illustrated by Palgé, relations with vineyards owners are defined as good once there is compliance to the terms set out by Château Ksara not just for their production of wine but also for the rest of the wineries in Lebanon.

PROJECTIONS OF QUALITY

In both the perspectives of Guiberteau and Palgé, it is apparent that there is a clear sense as to how to classify regions, parcels of lands, grape varieties, and wines into a hierarchy of qualities. On one hand, their strategies materialized through the way their perspectives came to permeate winegrowing practices in Lebanon. Yet while symmetry or *balance égale* indicated a harmonious re-lationship with vineyard owners across the Bekaa, it served to exclude those unwilling to comply with standards of wine production that followed standard-ized and regulated procedure in line with international guidelines. Linked to this is that included in the 2000 wine law is a discussion concerning the start of a use of an appellation of origin system dependent upon the geographical area from where the grapes are sourced, and Article 12 concludes by stating that the "geographical area should be recognized for natural and human factors." While an AOC system has yet to be put in place in Lebanon, the strategies deployed by Guiberteau and Palgé invoke such ranking systems of quality.

The repercussions of such strategies have led to further socioeconomic changes where a winegrowing hierarchy is culturally regenerated across the Bekaa Valley. That most of the newer small-scale wineries that started out selling vineyards to Château Ksara are located in the central Bekaa is suggestive of the possibility of new emerging hierarchal classifications of space across the valley's viticulture landscape that once more replicate spatial categorizations within discourses of high-quality wine. In this respect, and much in the way that Kefraya emerged as the winegrowing hub of Lebanon, there is an apparent reproduction of an invented tradition, similar to Ulin's analysis of elite winegrowers of Bordeaux (1996). The usage of visual imagery such as an elaborately built villa surrounded by neatly aligned vineyards evokes a sense of cultural continuity while also naturalizing ties to the land specific to the production of high-quality wines. At the same time, the objectives to completely remove Cinsault vines present another layer to the discourse of quality where further refinement and categorization within wine production is yet another means in the quest of authenticity and singularity. Interestingly, Château Musar still continues the use of Cinsault in the production of its better known labels; making their wines quite distinctive (Karam 2005). Yet it appears that the amount of Cinsault planted and used in the production of wine will continue to decrease as long as Palgé and Guiberteau continue to work at Châteaux Kefraya and Ksara. For, as Guiberteau concluded during an interview, "in order to create something new, we have to destroy what was there before." Here, the term *create* speaks of power and the ability to control and monopolize the production and markets of Lebanese wines.

NOTE

For the data used in this chapter, I would like to thank Mr. Michel de Bustros, Mr. Nabhane Nabhane, Mr. Fabrice Guiberteau, and Mr. James Palgé for taking the time to answer and discuss my questions. Mr. Elia Ghorra and Brother Paul at the Taanayel Monastery were also extremely supportive in helping me gain access to the Jesuit archives. This chapter would not have materialized without the grant support from the following scholarships: Emslie Horniman Fieldwork Grant from the Royal Anthropological Institute, the Centre for British Research in the Levant, the Abdullah al-Mubarak Al-Sabah Foundation from the BRISMES Institute, and the Central Research Fund from the University of London. Post-fieldwork support has also been from the Anthropology Department of Goldsmiths, University of London.

CHAPTER FOURTEEN

The Artifice of Natural Wine: Jules Chauvet and the Reinvention of Vinification in Postwar France

PAUL COHEN

The emergence in France over the past two decades of what has come to be known as the natural wine movement represents a significant development in the history of wine. In both discourse and viticultural practice, natural wine-makers critique a mainstream of winemaking born after the Second World War and wedded to technological intervention in the vineyard and in the cellar. To take its stead, these winemakers call for a less interventionist approach, endorsing, in various combinations and to various degrees, organic (and in some cases biodynamic) agriculture in the vineyard, a refusal of synthetic yeasts in the fermentation process, and a rejection of a range of other practices including chaptalization (the adding of sugar before the start of fermentation to boost the final alcohol content), fining (the use of agents like egg whites or animal blood to precipitate out deposits), filtering (to remove deposits and microorganisms), the use of sulfites (to eliminate microorganisms), and the use of barrels made from new wood in barrel aging (to mark the wine's taste).

Though the share of "natural wine" in France's total wine production remains small, it is growing rapidly, has attracted a devoted following, and spawned a set of distinct commercial and consumption practices. A constellation of wine shops, restaurants and wine bars (primarily centered in Paris), annual tastings and natural wine festivals, specialized periodicals and blogs, inform, cater to, and attract a growing clientele interested in buying, drinking, and learning about natural wine.[1] Consumers, winemakers, restaurateurs, and importers have developed a host of new forms of sociability, consumption, and exchange around these sites. However modest its economic footprint, the movement has drawn sustained attention from French media and provoked angry polemics about natural wine's qualitative merits (Bettane 2007). As Rachel Black explores in her chapter on Italian natural wines, the movement has also begun to gain purchase outside of France.

Though it has yet to receive substantial scholarly attention, the natural wine movement offers a rich subject for historical, cultural, and social analysis. The emergence of what has quickly staked a dynamic place within France, home to the largest wine industry in the world by total production (International Organisation of Vine and Wine 2012, 23), is an important story in and of itself. But an examination of this phenomenon also makes it possible to track broader cultural and social currents in the history of food. Their proponents' claims that natural wines are "truer" situate their commodities within the cultural nexus of culinary authenticity. Their reimagining of what constitutes "good" and "authentic" wine in a nation that invented the very notion of premium wines, takes great pride in its viticultural traditions, and remains the leading per capita wine consumer in the world today raises important questions about contemporary French identity (Durand 1992; Guy 2003). A movement that has staked its very identity on a privileged link to nature and its suspicion of technical intervention has a place in the history of science and technology—particularly given the latter's prominence in state planning and the national imaginary in postwar France (Hecht 1998; Kuisel 1981; Muller 1984; Paul 1996). Natural winemakers' critiques of chemical additives and technical manipulation tie them to the environmental and organic food movements (Bess 2003; Guha 2000). To investigate the history of natural wine is to reconsider the place of wine in contemporary France and to trace the fault lines of the politics, culture, and economics of food and drink in the twenty-first century.

But what, precisely, does "natural" mean when referring to wine? Where does the boundary distinguishing "natural" from "nonnatural" wines lie? The proponents of this form of winemaking place great emphasis on the "natural"

character of their methods and their wines (Puzelat). The ideal of nonintervention and "letting grapes do what comes naturally" (Feiring 2011) can obscure
a simple fact known to all winemakers: it is simply not possible to make wine
from grapes without some form of human intervention. All natural winemakers must necessarily evaluate what constitutes acceptable and unacceptable
intervention, as Rachel Black's chapter demonstrates. How far can one go in
manipulating grapes, must (the grape juice derived just after pressing), fermentation, and fermented wine and still be considered a natural winemaker?

I propose in this chapter to interrogate the category of "natural" in both the
discourse and practices of the natural wine movement by revisiting the writings
of one of its most pivotal figures, Beaujolais biochemist, *négociant,* and winemaker Jules Chauvet (1909–1989). For the winemakers, critics, distributors,
and importers who have animated the movement, Chauvet represents a natural
wine pioneer, even a "spiritual father" (Binner). I examine Chauvet's published
scientific papers, which winemakers still study today, and published interviews
to retrace how he came to define natural wine.

Through a reading of Chauvet's work, I argue that to consider "nature"
analytically represents a necessary first step toward a critically informed appreciation of the natural wine movement and its history. Though this history has
already begun to be written, it has for the most part been the work of journalists, wine critics, and importers themselves sympathetic to natural wine and—
in many cases embedded within its commercial circuits. Wedded to a qualitative
appreciation of "good" and "bad" in describing wine, tracing clear boundaries
between those wines situated inside and beyond the natural pale, often offering
counsel to the consumer in the mode of wine guides, and frequently anecdotal
and autobiographical in character, their writings give voice to the perspectives
and values of natural winemakers themselves (Camuto 2008; Feiring 2008,
2011; Goode and Harrop 2011; Lapaque 2010; Lynch 1990; Rosenthal 2008).
A fuller, more rigorous appreciation of natural wine's place in the histories of
wine, food and foodways, and modern France will only be possible once we
recognize that the concept of "nature" around which the movement has come
to define itself is a historically specific, constantly renegotiated, and still evolving category. To adopt a critical perspective of the sort outlined here is by no
means to criticize natural wine, nor to dismiss its makers' values or practices.
By examining how Chauvet drew and redrew the frontier between "natural"
and "nonnatural" winemaking, we can discern the contours of what could be
characterized as the evolving ontology of the natural wine movement (how
people define what is natural and what is not). However obvious the distinction
between the natural and made environments might appear, societies and individuals differentiate between the two in a wide range of ways. The challenge of

defining "nature" is a familiar one to environmental historians (Cronon 1996; Glacken 1967; McNaughten and Urry 1998; Merchant 1980, 2003; Worster 1994). Following their lead, this chapter demonstrates that the "nature" in natural wine has a history and that identifying how various actors in the world of wine have defined it over time helps us to understand how they have chosen to cultivate their vineyards, vinify, consume and appreciate wine, and why.[2]

JULES CHAUVET

Jules Chauvet devoted his life to exploring the connections between science and wine. Born in 1909 into a wine *négociant* family in La Chapelle-de-Guinchay, a village in the Beaujolais, Chauvet pursued studies in chemistry and biology. Fascinated by how microbiology could shed light on winemaking, Chauvet began his career as a researcher in a biochemistry laboratory at the Université de Lyon. In 1934, he sank his savings into the construction of a personal laboratory in his family's home. After a stay in Berlin to work with German biochemist (and 1931 Nobel laureate) Otto Heinrich Warburg, he returned home in 1935 to work in his family's wine business, though he continued to pursue research one day a week at the Institut de Chimie Biologique in Lyon until the start of the war. With the death of his father and uncle (in 1942 and 1943, respectively), Chauvet took over the family business, making wine from the family's own vineyards and selling other winegrowers' product. Despite his professional commitments, he continued to conduct scientific experiments in his laboratory throughout his life. Though his commercial responsibilities kept him on the margins of institutional scientific life, conducting experiments in his home laboratory, Chauvet was by no means a marginal figure in the world of biochemical, microbial, and oenological research. His results won recognition from scientists in the French government's National Institute for Agronomic Research. Institut Pasteur de Paris scientist Paul Bréchot, with whom he collaborated for much of his life, made annual trips to La Chapelle-de-Guinchay to pursue experiments with Chauvet. He also received financial support from the Maison Loron, a sizeable family-run Mâcon and Beaujolais *négociant* concern, which purchased scientific equipment for Chauvet to assist him in his research (Chauvet 1998: 10–12; Chauvet 2007: 5–7).

SCIENCE IN THE SERVICE OF IMPROVING WINE

Chauvet did not see his scientific research and winemaking as distinct fields of endeavor. Instead, he conceived them as complementary, a unified field for experiment and intellectual investigation into the making of wine, all in the service of one goal: producing the best possible wine. Scientific experiments allowed Chauvet to identify and understand how particular phenomena influenced the taste of finished wine. Producing his own wine allowed him to test how particular vine management and vinification methods shaped the final product.

These considerations defined an ambitious research program. Which yeasts produced what flavors and aromas? How did different fermentation temperatures and speeds impact the final product? What effect did decantation have on musts? What roles did techniques like chaptalization, acidification, or deacidification play? (Chauvet 2007: 74–91). Chauvet spent a lifetime in his laboratory and vineyard exploring the internal microbiological, chemical, and biochemical mechanisms of a wide range of wine-related phenomena, testing new techniques, and assessing their impact on wine's taste. Scientific knowledge provided the framework for understanding how vines grew, how yeasts and bacteria participated in fermentation, and how particular processes influenced a wine's taste. Rigorous, controlled empirical experiment offered the means to test how particular variables influenced wine. His writings bear witness to a strong faith in the scientific method, a cult of rationality and empiricism, a scientist's cultivation of doubt and skepticism.

Chauvet's embrace of science as a tool for understanding and improving wine was by no means unique. A succession of figures who explored the science of wine, like Jean-Antoine Chaptal (1756–1832), the aristocrat chemist and minister under Napoleon who promoted adding sugar to grape must, and Louis Pasteur, who demonstrated microorganisms' role in fermentation, links Enlightenment science to the scientific rationales and technological infrastructure of modern agrobusiness (Paul 1996). Though Chauvet's research earned him a place in this scientific pantheon, he also used the conceptual apparatus, method, and language of science to critique the mainstream wine industry and invent natural wine.

DISCOVERING NONINTERVENTION

Though Chauvet came to preach nonintervention as a winemaking ideal—and is held up as a pioneer of such practices today—he did not always subscribe to these principles. Indeed, his own views on winemaking evolved substantially over the course of his career and research. In 1949, for example, he cosigned an article in a professional periodical offering winemakers advice on harvesting and vinifying in hot weather. "The sulfuring of harvests or musts, which is the normal rule, becomes an imperious necessity in a hot year," prescribed the article, though a footnote indicated Chauvet had already invented techniques that allowed for the diminution or elimination of SO_2 (Chauvet 2007, 64). The authors also specified that, in the event the temperature in the fermentation tank rose too high, thus halting fermentation, winemakers should inoculate with selected yeasts to restart fermentation (Chauvet 2007, 61–66). The article demonstrates two important features of Chauvet's approach in the immediate postwar period: first, he was opposed to neither sulfites nor selected yeasts; and second, he was already interested in exploring ways to diminish the doses of SO_2 needed to ferment wine safely.

A second article, published three years later, offers further insight into the evolution of Chauvet's thinking with regards to intervention in vinification. On the eve of the 1952 harvest, Chauvet signed another text offering much the same advice to Burgundian winemakers as he had in 1949. With intense heat again in the forecast, Chauvet warned makers of the dangers of precocious or overactive fermentations and counseled that "the use of sulfur dioxide in the 1952 harvest will therefore prove to be indispensable." In the event that high heat caused fermentation to halt before the must's sugars had completely transformed into alcohol, Chauvet suggested the use of selected yeasts in order to restart vinification (Chauvet 2007, 70–71). He proposed the use of tartaric acid to correct (i.e., increase) the wine's acidity in cases when it is deemed too low. Chauvet thus urged winemakers to borrow from a veritable arsenal of chemical and microbial weapons that scientific and food research placed at their disposal. But Chauvet offered alternatives. For makers faced with stalled fermentation, for example, he specified that "One should inoculate…either with the help of a commercial yeast starter, or with a starter prepared one or two days before from healthy grapes" (Chauvet 2007, 71) to restart the fermentation process—in short, leaving open the possibility of employing starters inoculated with indigenous yeasts (those naturally present on grape skins, also referred to as ambient yeasts). Going further, he also set sharp limits on what he considered acceptable forms of intervention. Chauvet emphatically condemned chaptalization as "useless," and went on to reject a range of additives: "Other than sulfur dioxide and tartaric acid, it will be perfectly useless and even harmful to use for vinifications in 1952 other oenological products like tannins, phosphates, ammonium salts and citric acid, etc., or any specialties derived from these same products" (Chauvet 2007, 73). Chauvet's winemaking blueprint in the late 1940s and early 1950s more closely resembled the vineyard practices that prevailed in postwar France than the natural wine movement's vision that would take shape decades later. It nonetheless betrays an intense concern with limiting the scope of chemical and other additives to only that which local conditions make necessary, and with tracing boundaries between salutary and harmful interventions. He repeatedly shifted these boundaries, placing ever-greater restrictions on interventions in the course of his career as his research, winemaking experiments, and thinking progressed.

INVENTING NATURAL WINE

Over time, Chauvet came to critique many of the practices he had previously endorsed. If the term *natural wine* does not figure in Chauvet's writing in this early period, he invoked the concept with increasing frequency as time progressed. In 1981, Chauvet explained to an interviewer that "the older I get, the more I want to see truly natural wines, well made wines" (Chauvet 1998, 38). He grounded his definition of natural wine in a sharp conceptual boundary separating the natural from the human-made world. As he told another interviewer shortly before his death:

> I will never cease repeating this: we must respect that which nature gives us, we must open our eyes wide. Life is beautiful; it's too bad that humankind is here…we walk by nature without even looking at it. Progress moves forward very rapidly, technology is more and more sophisticated, but we still have never succeeded in manufacturing our own tree leaf! (Léard-Viboux 2006, 30–31)

Chauvet here invokes a sharp dichotomy between nature and humanity that has a long history in Western thought (Cronon 1996; Merchant 1980, 2003). Pure, unspoiled, virgin nature is endowed with a host of positive values: deserving of respect, beautiful, and incomparably rich and complex. Indifferent to the grandeur of nature and imbued with an overinflated sense of its own intelligence and technical capacities, a flawed humankind suffers by comparison.

For Chauvet, to make natural wine meant to limit human intervention so as to leave as full rein to natural processes as possible. Wine made in this manner, being the product of natural mechanisms as admirable and inimitable as those that fashion leaves, embodies the qualities and virtues unique to nature. Given that natural processes were responsible for endowing wines with their intrinsic and characteristic aromatic identities, wine itself was therefore an *expression* of nature: "Wine contains in great intensity all that nature can synthesize in fermenting. Don't forget that wine is a reflection of the grape variety and above all of the *terroir*. The soil rules the plant. It is for this reason that one must respect nature" (Léard-Viboux 2006, 28). Winemakers thus should conceive of their work as a form of stewardship over the natural world of vine and wine:

> It is therefore necessary to preserve this precious capital which nature has bequeathed us, by taking several elementary precautions which will spare us subsequent treatments: don't let the harvest be crushed [before pressing], sort it when it isn't healthy, and let it ferment a long time, these are the most fundamental conditions in order to obtain as natural a wine as possible...It serves no purpose to add anything, because everything we add, amounts to a kind of medicine;...a wine isn't of higher quality when it is [more] alcoholic. It's a hoax, a sin of pride to want to make wines at 14 percent [through chaptalization]...And too bad for those who think that the alcohol content is too weak. To them, I answer: "Buy whisky and go to hell!" (Léard-Viboux 2006, 31–32)

Chauvet switches epistemological gears altogether in this passage, moving away from empiricism to critique chaptalization on philosophical grounds. To insist on making wines with more alcohol when, left to their natural course (i.e., in the absence of adding sugar to musts), they would contain less alcohol, is to make a wine *against* nature. If natural processes in a particular vat and a given vintage tended toward a lower-alcohol wine, Chauvet preached, then so be it—nature was right.

Chauvet's vision represented nothing less than a rejection of the dominant model of winemaking that had taken root in France after the Second World War. The wholesale embrace of mechanization, of chemical fertilizers, herbicides and pesticides, and of industrial modes of production and standardization exemplified by chaptalization had, in his view, badly compromised the quality of wines. The problem for Chauvet was not science or technology in and of themselves. It was that researchers and winemakers had developed these practices to increase yields, with no regard for wines' taste. He saw mechanization, the use of tractors in the place of horses, and chemical herbicides in the place of ploughing, as unhealthy for the soil. Plowing ensured the oxygenation of soil, necessary for the maintenance of a rich microbial ecosystem. Because vines that grow in soil poor in microbial life tend to be less resistant to disease, mechanized growers needed to treat their vineyards with ever more chemical pesticides and fungicides. The short-term consequence of this productivist model may have been higher yields, he warned, but its long-term consequences were poorer-tasting wines, the eradication of microbial life in the vineyard, polluted soils, and in the very long run, the risk of steadily declining yields.

"I consider this to be *very dangerous*. It disappoints me," is how Chauvet summed it up (Chauvet 1998, 30).

Chauvet saw other reasons to reject productivist agriculture. He preached the use of fewer or (better still) no chemicals not only for the sake of preserving the biological diversity present in the soil and the quality of wines, but also to avoid introducing poisons into the life cycle of an agricultural product destined for human consumption—"because wine, one drinks it after all!" (Chauvet 2007, 32). He thus explicitly linked his research and winemaking practices to a set of broader environmental and public health imperatives.

Chauvet extended his critique of mainstream viticultural practices from the vineyard to the winery. In the same way that he questioned the application of chemicals to vines and soil, Chauvet now rejected chemical interventions during vinification. He focused much of his criticism on the use of sulfites in the tank to control fermentation—a practice he had endorsed just after the war, as we have seen. In his view, sulfuring grape musts now occupied too important a place in vinification: "It is the easy way out. I think that we can do without SO_2, to a certain extent, if one practices good hygiene. What do people do? They treat with sulfur dioxide, and then they do whatever they want...SO_2, it's a poison" (Chauvet 2007, 32). Not only was sulfur dioxide a toxin that had no place in a foodstuff, effective alternatives existed. Scrupulously keeping vats clean to ensure that no potentially dangerous microorganisms make their way into the must and interrupt fermentation or produce flaws in the wine was one example (Chauvet in fact considered this the most important oenological discovery of his lifetime). And in many cases sulfuring was ineffective. Consider oxidasic casse, a fault that can develop in musts exposed to air, when certain enzymes attack pigments and tannins and produce an unpleasant taste (grapes harvested when they are overripe are especially vulnerable). At the doses high enough to stop oxidasic casse, SO_2 also arrests malolactic fermentation, a phase necessary to the evolution of all red and many white wines. Restarting malolactic fermentation requires reinoculating the must with selected yeasts. At lower doses, sulfur dioxide cannot prevent the casse. Rather than simplify the winemaker's life, Chauvet maintains, this particular intervention in fact complicates it and creates the need for subsequent, additional interventions (Chauvet 2007, 32–33).

Although Chauvet criticized a host of modern growing and vinification techniques, his vision corresponded more to an ethos than an all-or-nothing set of prescriptions and proscriptions. The goal was not to obtain a perfectly natural wine, but rather to make "as natural a wine as possible" (Léard-Viboux 2006, 31). Chauvet was not against chemical treatments in the vineyard, for example, as long as the molecules were biodegradable. Nor was he categorically opposed to SO_2. He allowed for its use when absolutely necessary to forestall faults and deviations during fermentation. Sulfites should only be added sparingly ("you treat *just what is necessary*, and not a [full] dose"), and in conjunction with other techniques aimed at reducing the quantities of the molecule needed (Chauvet 1998, 33). "But every time that a harvest is healthy, *healthy*, completely healthy," Chauvet insisted, "what point is there to give it sulfuric acid?" (Chauvet 1998, 33). His views on chaptalization were similar: "This does not mean that I am against chaptalization; but one must have recourse to it only in the event of a deficiency of alcohol" (Léard-Viboux 2006, 31). Chauvet thought winemakers should have the option of drawing from the panoply of technical solutions at their disposal, but only in an intelligent, cautious, and limited fashion. There were conditions under which practices normally ruled out of bounds could become acceptable. In years when harvests were not perfectly healthy, because of blight, hail, or too much rain, for example, intervention might be necessary to guide fermentation and save the vintage. "In other cases," Chauvet declared, "one must vinify naturally" (Léard-Viboux 2006, 31). Chauvet's line, in short, was a moveable one whose position was dictated by context.

Chauvet thus fashioned a program that married principle to pragmatism. This entailed navigating between two not always compatible imperatives: a celebration of nature and its fruits on the one hand, and a sober assessment of the difficulties and limits that real-world winemakers faced in the vineyard and winery on the other. Natural winemaking constituted an objective, an ideal, a goal towards which winemakers (with scientists' help) should work, rather than a recipe of clear-cut practices one could simply choose to adopt. Indeed, Chauvet never makes clear whether he believes the ideal of natural wine to be attainable—though he proudly affirmed that "I myself vinify my wines naturally, without sulfites, without chaptalization" (Léard-Viboux 2006, 30).

CECI N'EST PAS UNE INTERVENTION

Whether read as prescriptive commandment or as pragmatically inflected ethos, Chauvet's critique of mechanization, chemical treatments in the vineyard and wine vat, and selected yeasts appears straightforward because it is grounded on his own opposition between nature and humankind. Chauvet's lament that "Life is beautiful; it's too bad that humankind is here" suggests a longing for a pure, virgin planet not yet spoiled by humanity, regret for a lost prelapsarian Eden. Echoing this opposition between nature and humanity, and the close corollary opposing a golden age more in tune with nature against a modernity alienated from nature, Chauvet frequently spoke of the necessity of resurrecting more traditional ways of working: "we need to return to natural things" (Léard-Viboux 2006, 31). It was in precisely these terms that Chauvet sought to revive the older practice of tilling the vineyard: "I believe precisely that we must return to older things, that is, *to cultivate the vines* first and foremost, to stop putting chemical products all over the ground; we need to cultivate the vine" (Chauvet 1998, 27).

However straightforward Chauvet's rejection of (certain) modern agricultural techniques might appear, his own writings and work embody tensions between these principles that suggest a more complicated conception of nature. Consider three paradoxes present in Chauvet's texts. First, his scientific training and his active research program, as we have seen, testify to his wholehearted embrace of core components of modernity: scientific knowledge and empiricism. Chauvet was an active teacher to young oenologists, and he strongly encouraged winemakers to draw on oenologists' knowledge and services. Constantly searching for new approaches, Chauvet never hesitated to borrow techniques and technologies from other fields. In 1952, he tried heating unpressed grapes with a boiler to 70°C, then sulfuring, pressing, chaptalizing, and inoculating the now sterile musts in search of a method for salvaging wines made from harvests damaged by cold and humidity (Chauvet 2007, 92–96). Ten years later, he modified medical equipment to inject precise doses of oxygen into his fermenting must. Winemakers and oenologists recall that Chauvet "had...one of the most modern wineries" (Léard-Viboux 2006, 37). Science may have spawned the techniques that sent winemaking awry (namely mechanization and synthetic chemistry), but it also offered the path toward the "return to the natural" he so ardently desired. In a remark that crystallizes this tension between modernism and antimodernism within Chauvet's mind, winemaker Jacques Néauport remembers: "Jules Chauvet taught me everything; he taught me in particular to be wary of oenology, while at the same time proving to me that this new science was useful" (Léard-Viboux 2006, 47). On the one hand, Chauvet could convince a winemaker friend he should hire oenologists to help his firm make wine. On the other hand, he could joke with Néauport that it might be necessary to kidnap all the oenologists on the eve of the harvest and send them to Mauritius until the wine was done to ensure they could not interfere (Léard-Viboux 2006, 37, 47–48).

Second, though Chauvet's quest for less interventionist winemaking implies a faith in nature and its workings, it is a conditional, qualified faith. Nature itself dictates the circumstances under which winemakers can refrain from technical intervention and when they cannot. When nature "cooperates," by ensuring good weather and sparing vineyards disease from and pests, winemakers can happily dispense with proscribed interventions and vinify naturally. But it is precisely those moments when nature does not "cooperate" that winemakers must intervene. Nature, therefore, should not always be left entirely to its own devices.

And third, as Chauvet himself repeatedly emphasizes, the path of less intervention actually requires that the winemaker work *more,* not less. "Of course," Chauvet conceded, "this demands a great deal of attention and time" (Léard-Viboux 2006, 31). Chauvet's ideal for the vineyard, for example, entails substantial intervention of a particular sort. Regretting that mechanization and herbicides led winemakers to abandon working the soil, he imposes a labor-intensive regime: "I think that a real advance would have been to cultivate vines *even more*... [*sic*] And precisely to try through this cultivation, and perhaps through other means, to endow the vine, which is currently sensitive to all diseases, with natural resistance" (Chauvet 1998, 31). Though vines should be spared chemical showers, they should by no means be left to their own vegetal devices. By tilling the soil, growers can strengthen plants' resistance to diseases and pests. Nature then, can benefit from humankind's help and allow vines to produce grapes well-suited to making good wine.

These three examples cease to be paradoxes if we consider winemakers as embedded within nature (as opposed to situated outside, or opposed to, nature). This is precisely the move Chauvet makes in conceptualizing his natural winemaking methods. Science for Chauvet is not nature's enemy, but an effective instrument for better understanding nature. When properly used, technology too can serve rather than destroy nature.

The boundary that distinguishes "natural" from "nonnatural" wine is therefore not that separating the natural from the human world, but that differentiating between human activities deemed compatible with nature—like manually tilling the soil—and those which are not—like applying chemical herbicides. Although this distinction might appear the simple consequence of an antimodernist rejection of industrial agriculture and advanced technologies, Chauvet in fact embraced a certain number of modern technologies precisely because they allowed him to make wines in a way that he believed to be more natural. These concerns—and, indeed, the element of nature which was most important to Chauvet—were found at the microscopic scale.

Throughout his career, Chauvet privileged one specific aspect of wine in his scientific research, his winemaking, his thinking about what wine is, and his conclusions concerning how it should be made: yeast. Beginning with his very earliest scientific experiments, Chauvet pursued his conviction that yeasts played the most crucial role in wine. As he put it, "Biology is wine, wine is biology,... Because the job of making wine, to vinify wine, it's the job of a microbiologist, without any doubt" (Chauvet 2007, 11–12). Given yeast and bacteria's indispensable contribution to the production of wine—without fermentation, there is no alcohol—this remark on one level represents a simple statement of fact. But it also posits a hierarchy of values differentiating between the various elements, steps, and components that go into the making of a wine. By *equating* winemaking with microbiology, Chauvet assigns greater importance to the cellular processes of fermentation than, say, to farming in the vineyard, soil, geology, climate, or weather.

Chauvet's research into the mechanisms of fermentation count among his most influential contributions to the science of winemaking. By inoculating samples of the same grape must with different strains of yeast, he demonstrated that the resulting wines each possessed a different bouquet. The particular yeast strains responsible for fermentation in a given wine, therefore, represented a key variable in shaping that wine's aroma (Chauvet 2007, 15–24). In their study of the action of indigenous yeasts in fermentation, Chauvet and his Institut Pasteur collaborator Bréchot also demonstrated that a great range of different yeasts could become active during the fermentation process. Their interest in ambient yeasts also sent them out of the lab and into the field to inventory the yeasts native to grapes in the Beaujolais. They found each particular *terroir* to be home to a great diversity of locally specific microbial flora. Chauvet drew precise conclusions about winemaking from this work: individual yeast strains were responsible for endowing wines with particular aromas; wines vinified with indigenous yeasts were the product of many more yeast strains than those produced with selected yeasts; wines produced with indigenous yeasts therefore tended to be more aromatically complex than those with selected yeasts—and were certainly more clearly marked by the local microbial flora. As for selected yeasts, they had been bred to be particularly active—that is, to rapidly and doggedly pursue fermentation until all the must's sugars had been converted into alcohol—not to produce pleasurable aromas. In short—and all other things being equal, indigenous yeasts produced qualitatively better wines (Chauvet 1998, 25–26; Chauvet 2007, 25–33).

If wine was above all the fruit of microbiological processes, and indigenous yeasts produced the best wines qualitatively, then the winemaker-cum-microbiologist needed to focus attention on ensuring wild yeasts could

274 WINE AND CULTURE

play their full role. Though he cited a range of reasons to refrain from intro-ducing chemicals into the vineyard or winery, including their ineffectiveness and potential risks to the environment and human health, Chauvet's primary objection to synthetic compounds was that they attacked indigenous yeasts. He dramatized the loss of microbial diversity in untilled vineyard soils treated chemically: "there are no more microorganisms, they are all dead!" (Chauvet 1998, 31). Likewise in the fermentation tank. Sulfur dioxide at higher doses was certainly toxic for human beings, but the fact that it was a poison for microorganisms troubled Chauvet no less: "it poisons *not only the yeast*—the yeast can withstand it, but it gives better results when it hasn't been poisoned by sulfur dioxide—*but bacteria as well*" (Chauvet 1998, 32). The winemak-ers' mission was to protect wild yeasts so that they could transform the must's constituent elements into complex and pleasing aromas in the finished wine.

The imperative to rely on ambient yeasts for fermentation offered the con-ceptual basis upon which Chauvet ultimately grounded his definition of natu-ral wine. Wines produced from the action of the yeast and bacteria already present on grape skins at harvest were natural; those produced from selected, laboratory-bred yeasts were not. Within the rich natural world Chauvet so admired, when it came to producing good wine, the microbial scale mattered the most. To his mind, ambient yeasts were indispensable parts of winemak-ing for another reason as well: the particular "demographics" of the yeasts resident in a given region and even vineyard constitute one of the principal markers—the most important marker as far as Chauvet was concerned—of *terroir*. Because microorganisms unfailingly leave their stamp on a wine's taste, and each vineyard is home to a unique microbial population, yeasts define a *terroir*'s very identity, and by extension the identity imparted onto wines made there. Each wine's aroma is thus defined by a kind of organo-leptic identity card, a specific set of characteristics unique to each vineyard's microscopic ecosystem.

The sanctification of wild yeasts as the sole legitimate actors in fermen-tation dictated the criteria by which Chauvet differentiated between ac-ceptable and unacceptable interventions. Interventions that safeguarded the action of ambient yeasts and bacteria were acceptable; those that limited or eliminated their action were not. Chauvet's adherence to this impera-tive explains why banishing SO_2 from the fermentation tank took on such importance. As we have already seen, one of Chauvet's reasons for limiting the use of chemical herbicides, fungicides, and pesticides in the vineyard was to protect indigenous yeasts. As we have also seen, he maintained ex-tremely rigorous standards of hygiene during the harvest and in his winery to ensure that no stray yeasts or bacteria made their way into his musts and competed with the microorganisms resident on his grapes' skins. Chauvet preferred the use of metal tanks to traditional wood casks for vinification because "Metal, one can sterilize it; wood, one can't sterilize it" (Chauvet 1998, 35).

Chauvet also experimented extensively with the use of carbon dioxide gas during vinification and came to see in such methods a means to protect indigenous yeasts. He conducted extensive research into how yeasts and enzymes metabolize sugar in anaerobic environments, uncovering the mechanisms of fermentation in the absence of oxygen (Chauvet 1998, 25; Chauvet 2007, 34–57). His findings shed light on the traditional method for vinifying Beaujolais reds. Typically, grapes are harvested and placed intact in the fermentation vat. As the vat fills, the weight of the grapes on the top presses down on the lower grapes, crushing them. Fermentation begins in the resulting must collecting on the bottom of the vat, thus releasing carbon dioxide gas, which progressively drives oxygen from the tank. In the anaerobic environment within which the intact grapes above now find themselves, enzymes located inside the cells composing each intact grape initiate a distinct form of fermentation known as intracellular fermentation. After a prolonged period of maceration, the grapes are pressed, and the partially fermented juice allowed to complete its fermentation in an aerobic environment.

Excited by the distinctive aromatic possibilities of intracellular fermentation, Chauvet and Bréchot began to experiment with a process invented in 1934 by another oenologist, Michel Flanzy, called carbonic maceration. Traditional Beaujolais vinifications (known today as semicarbonic maceration) generate only partially anaerobic conditions: oxygen is present in the vat when grapes are introduced, the small quantities of must released when the lowest layers of grapes are crushed begin fermentation in an aerobic environment, and oxygen is only progressively expelled from the vat. In carbonic maceration, the empty vat is saturated with CO_2 gas (in liquid or dry ice form) *before* intact grapes are introduced, and the tank sealed when full, thus ensuring that *only* anaerobic fermentations begin and that the wine will be strongly marked by intracellular fermentations, before proceeding to the press and second fermentation phase (Tesnière and Flanzy 2011). Chauvet saw other advantages to working in an oxygen-free environment. Saturating the tank with carbon dioxide gas and sealing it when full protected the grapes and must from airborne microorganisms that might compete with ambient yeasts and bacteria. It offered a useful technique for controlling fermentations when harvests were marred by rot, to prevent faults and deviations (Chauvet 2007, 100–151). Chauvet, for example, argued that filling tanks with carbon dioxide was considerably more effective for preventing oxydasic casse than sulfuring: "so we said to ourselves: why treat with sulfur dioxide here? we are poisoning the yeasts, we are poisoning the bacteria...it's better to work under carbon dioxide all the way through: no air, no casse" (Chauvet 1998, 33).

Winemakers should, in Chauvet's view, indeed, they *had to,* intervene as little as possible. To allow nature to do its work, winemakers had to master relevant scientific disciplines and mobilize an array of elaborate, and in many cases novel, techniques and technologies. Good winemaking entailed liberating ambient microorganisms, but it also demanded that one "protect" musts and wines:

> [T]here are good things, for example to protect with nitrogen, to protect with argon, these are inert gases, yes this is progress...but obviously sulfur dioxide, avoid all those kinds of things. Filtration? Yes, if one absolutely must, but you filter because it's better than to fine...To fine, it's amazing how much one can take away from a wine when one fines! [Centrifuging] Ah yes, in that case, that's a torture...it's precisely there that one needs a great deal of knowledge in order to succeed in preserving the wine like that, naturally. (Chauvet 1998, 38)

Chauvet again traces a complex boundary separating acceptable from unacceptable interventions. Saturating tanks with CO_2 or noble gases and plunging dry ice into grape musts were acceptable manipulations that gave the winemaker better control over fermentation and reduced the need for sulfites; chemical treatments, above all SO_2, were beyond the pale. Displaying the same pragmatism we encountered earlier, Chauvet reluctantly preferred filtration to fining as a method for clarifying (removing deposits, including dead and living microorganisms) wines, but condemned centrifuging as "torture." The "return to natural things" depended upon the development of robust technologies that themselves protected, rather than eliminated, wild yeasts. Technology then was not the enemy—as long as it was not turned against yeasts and bacteria.

We discussed earlier Chauvet's conception of winemaking as a kind of "stewardship" over nature in the vineyard and tank. At a fundamental level, the scale of nature over which he believed winemakers held stewardship was the microscopic, and their mission was to protect indigenous microorganisms. In some sense, true winemakers were first and foremost shepherds of wild yeast (though the metaphor is an imperfect one, since Chauvet insisted on relying on wild rather than domesticated yeast).

CONCLUSION

What can we conclude concerning the history of natural wine from this examination of Chauvet's career as scientist and winemaker? First, Chauvet grounded his conception and practice of natural wine in scientific knowledge and research. Profoundly marked by his studies and research experiences in Lyon and Berlin, he always sought scientific explanations for phenomena and empirical confirmation for his ideas. Chauvet's invention of natural wine was born of his cult of scientific empiricism.

Second, Chauvet's own thinking on chemical and technical intervention evolved in the course of his career. This trajectory entailed changing attitudes toward the use of chemical additives, notably sulfites, and the best kinds of yeasts for fermentation.

Third, the "nature" with which Chauvet imagined and sought to anchor his research and his wines is, first and foremost, a microscopic one, imagined as the populations of microorganisms resident on grape skins. Winemakers needed to protect ambient yeasts so that they could mark the resulting wines with their characteristic, aromatically pleasing, organoleptic stamp. It is on the microscopic scale that he trained his research program, and it is here that he focused his winemaking energies.

Fourth, the "nonintervention" Chauvet held up as an ideal did not entail no intervention whatsoever. The nonintervention imperative concerned the microscopic scale—the need to preserve indigenous yeast—and solutions that served this goal were acceptable, however technologically complex and elaborate.

Fifth, "natural wine" for Chauvet was not a stable, clear-cut category. Instead, the quest to make natural wine was many things at once: a set of principles; a moving target; an unattainable but still admirable objective.

Chauvet's intellectual path represents an important chapter in the history of natural wine. He invented the principles and techniques behind its production as well as the conceptual framework with which it could be imagined. Active as a teacher, published scientist, and lecturer, Chauvet played a crucial role in training the first generation of winemakers who today count themselves part of this movement. Above all, his research on and commitment to vinifying with indigenous yeasts offered a specific vision of nature—one that privileged the microbiological scale—that the actors in the natural wine movement today have wholeheartedly embraced. However varied and moveable the boundaries natural winemakers draw to separate acceptable from unacceptable interventions, Chauvet's sanctification of wild yeasts stands at the very heart of their principles and practices.

NOTES

All translations are my own.

1. Natural wine shops in Paris include Les Caves Augé, Le Verré volé, and La Cave de l'Insolite (which closed in 2011). Like-minded wine bars and restaurants include Le Repaire de Cartouche, Le Baratin, L'Os à la moëlle, Le Chateaubriand, Racines, Que du bon, and Vivant. Annual wine tastings include the Dive Bouteille festival at the Château de Brézé. *Le Rouge et le blanc* is a quarterly natural wine magazine created in 1983. Natural wine blogs include: http://dumorgondanslesveines.20minutes-blogs.fr/; http://levindemesamis.blogspot.fr/; and http://ptijournalduvin.over-blog.fr/.

2. I am currently completing a book-length history of the natural wine movement. This chapter draws from this research.

CHAPTER FIFTEEN

Vino Naturale: Tensions between Nature and Technology in the Glass

RACHEL E. BLACK

Pruning vines and pressing grapes are examples of human intervention essential to the production of wine. In the end, wine is a cultural product. There is very little about winemaking that we can consider "natural," as in untouched by human hands. Nonetheless, more and more wines are sold as "natural wine." What is natural about natural wine? In this chapter, I discuss and critically evaluate how the international natural wine movement has constructed a discourse of nature in opposition to the technological and cultural processes involved in viticulture and oenology. In order to do this, I will look at the language used in wine tasting, production methods and the discourse of winegrowers, and the role of importers in the process of constructing natural wine. The naturalization of human labor and technology will be at the center of this discussion that uses ethnographic examples from natural wine production in Italy and its consumption in the United States. I carried out fieldwork in Italy in Piedmont in 2007 and 2008 and in the United States in San Francisco and Boston from 2009 to 2012. The Italian portion of the fieldwork consisted of interviewing wine producers in the Langhe area and attending wine trade shows. In the United States, I interviewed wine shop and wine bar owners and employees. I also attended tastings and talked to natural wine lovers and read blogs focused on natural wine to get a better sense of the ways American consumers understand the concept of natural wine.

THE NATURAL WINE MOVEMENT

The natural wine movement is an ill-defined and rag-tag movement. In each country, it takes on slightly different meanings. Most important, definitions of natural wine are amorphous, and producers, journalists, and consumers constantly debate them. Wine writers and journalists have noted that the natural wine movement defines itself just as much by what it stands against, as what it stands for (Goode and Harrop 2011, 141–142). Like many counterculture movements, the terms and rules of membership are not always clear. Natural wine can start with organic production, but on theoretical and esoteric levels these wines generally move far beyond the European Union regulations for organic agriculture.

Italy has long been one of the largest producers of organic agricultural products, which are mainly destined for export (European Commission Directorate-General for Agriculture and Rural Development 2010). However, thanks to groups like Slow Food, Italians are starting to take an interest in the impact of conventional and organic products on the land and on their health. What does it mean if a wine is labeled as organic? Organic wine is made by growing grapes using organic agricultural practices that include natural pest control and a very limited use of chemicals for fertilization or disease control. However, until recently, organic wine did not mean chemicals were not used in the winery during the production process. Organic used to stop at the winery door and this was generally a little-known fact. However, Europeans have recently ratified legislation that includes vinification in the parameters for organic wine (European Union 2012). Changes to European agricultural legislation demonstrate a larger shift in thinking about agriculture and food: European consumers are starting to desire greater transparency concerning the production methods of food products, including wine.

Besides organic agriculture, some producers have chosen to move away from conventional agricultural practices by going another route—biodynamic agriculture. The biodynamic philosophy is based on a series of 1924 lectures by Austrian philosopher Rudolf Steiner. Steiner believed that agriculture should respect nature's natural rhythms (Steiner 2004, 2005). According to American biodynamic winemaker Randall Grahm, "biodynamics seeks to invigorate the life force of the farm through a more intimate connection with energetic forces of the planetary and celestial spheres" (Grahm 2010, 311). Moon cycles are critical to this method and there is a complement of processes more ritually and spiritually based than scientifically proven. For instance, cow dung placed in a steer's horn is buried in the vineyard to ensure the fertility of the land. Despite a lack of scientific legitimacy, biodynamic farming has gained a growing following in Europe. During my fieldwork in Italy, I talked to numerous winemakers who told me, "I don't know how it works, but it does!" There was a certain suspension of disbelief among practitioners. Biodynamic agriculture even has a certifying body, Demeter. Most biodynamic producers have agreed upon a codified set of practices.[1]

While organic and biodynamic wines have certifications and agreed upon practices, the category of natural wine remains open to discussion and out of the reach of consensus. Many practitioners and believers feel that natural wine goes beyond the organic and biodynamic in its respect for natural grape growing practices and winemaking processes. Critics of natural wine argue otherwise: in *Drinks Business,* a trade publication, renowned French biodynamic producer Nicolas Joly snubbed natural wine as "nothing more than a drawer in which to pull all the winemakers who don't make enough effort to convert to organics and biodynamics" (Shaw 2012). It is apparent from the ongoing debate that this resistance to codification presents both strengths and weaknesses for this loosely knit movement.

Where did it all begin? Most wine writers and historians agree that the natural wine movement started in France. Jamie Goode and Sam Harrop declare that Jules Chauvet is the "father of the natural wine movement" (2011, 142). Paul Cohen's chapter in this volume looks more closely at the ways in which Chauvet's studies of winemaking methods contributed to the natural wine movement in the twentieth century. Wine writer and natural wine activist Alice Feiring points out that there were natural wine bars in Paris in the 1980s (2011). The natural wine movement in France has long been seen as part of a general movement to reject anonymous mass production of wine. The French still consider wine an important part of their culinary traditions and cultural identity. It took Italy a little longer to join the movement for a number of reasons. First, it was not until after the 1986 methanol scandal in Italy that Italians really began to focus on quality wine production (Barbera and Audifredi 2012; Negro et al. 2007). Quality meant first of all assuring the safety and genuine nature of wine. This led winemakers to focus on improving production methods, in particular cellar hygiene. In many cases, this was a recourse to modern technology and scientific methods, which also had its own set of challenges and tensions when it came to small-scale production (Negro et al. 2007). At the same time, the methanol scandal left Italians and foreign consumers wary of faceless, large-scale producers: consumers wanted to know who was making their wine and where it was from.[2] After 1987, the daily consumption of wine in Italy waned dramatically (Barbera and Audifredi 2012). In many ways, both the quality wine and natural wine movements were born of this reaction toward fraudulent and harmful industrial products (Brunori et al. 2012). Nonetheless, Italian *enoteche* (wine shops) and bars focused on natural wines are still the exception. In 2012, Italian anti-fraud authorities fined a wine shop in Rome for advertising natural wines, declaring that this labeling was misleading and fraudulent (Il Sole 24 Ore). This is one indication of the limited understanding of natural wine that exists in Italy and the murkiness of this category. In contrast to France, the natural wine movement in Italy has had a limited national audience, while natural Italian wines have a near cult-like following in the United States and Great Britain. One explanation for this lack of interest in natural wine could be that Italy was primarily an agricultural country until the 1960s and Italians still have a hard time feeling nostalgic about this agrarian past, which is largely associated with toil and hunger (Black 2012). Until recently, industrialization was considered progressive and positive. Only recently have Italians begun looking more closely at the impact of industrialization on their food system.

I have been inadvertently following natural wine since 2007, when I had a chance to attend Vinitaly in Verona and a number of wine trade shows and events in the Veneto. During a visit to Teobaldo Cappellano's cellar in Serralunga, Teobaldo presented me with invitations to an event called ViniVeri (Real Wines) held near Verona around the same time as Vinitaly.[3] The Cappellano family is a small-scale grower-producer in the Barolo DOCG area of Piedmont. Along with famed Barolo producer Bartolo Mascarello, Teobaldo Cappellano was a longtime activist against mass production and modernist winemaking techniques (Negro et al. 2007). Cappellano was one of the founders of ViniVeri, an off-Vinitaly event showcasing wines from smaller producers that follow a shared ethic for making what they referred to as "real wines." This was my first encounter with what I came to know as natural wine. In the following years, through the ViniVeri group of vintners and other Italian grower-producers, I learned more about the principles of nature that governed their practices in the vineyards and the winery, from the exclusion of chemical fertilizers and toxic pesticides in the vineyard to the very limited use of sulfur in the winery and an insistence on the use of only native yeasts. More important, I had an opportunity to understand how these producers articulated their perceptions of nature through their practices and in the way they communicate their wines.

I moved to San Francisco in 2009, and around this same time the natural wine movement started to make waves in the United States. The first Natural Wine Week was held in San Francisco that same year and a number of natural wine bars and shops opened in New York and San Francisco. Restaurants started boldly featuring natural wines on their lists as a distinguishing factor that denoted their culinary and moral identity—mainly that they stood in opposition to impersonal industrial food and wine. Having just arrived back from Italy, it was interesting to see how Italian winemakers were shaping the natural wine movement and how American consumers, who often call themselves *terroirists,* were interpreting it.

As wine blogger Jeremy Parzen puts it: "'Natural wine' is something of a misnomer. Wine is, after all, an act of humankind. Winemaking is also an inherently ideological act and while there are many winemakers—mostly French and Italian—who boast of their natural winemaking techniques (*natural techniques* is something of an oxymoron, isn't it?), there are also winemakers who produce 'natural wine' by virtue of the fact that their winemaking ideology naturally jives with those consciously engaged in natural winemaking" (2009). Interestingly, in this post, Parzen associates natural wines with the Old World. Although natural winemaking is starting to gain popularity in North America, it still remains a largely European phenomenon. One reason for this is perhaps scale: there are a larger number of small-scale family-owned grower-producers in Europe, while much of wine production in North America is large scale and highly mechanized.

In her blog dedicated to natural wine, Alice Feiring sets out some of the common parameters for natural wine after lamenting the growing presence of interlopers:

[I]n order to curb…dumbing down…, here are some simple guidelines for the criteria. Grapes, maybe a splish of SO2. Nothing gets added to the wine and nothing gets extracted. Short and Sweet. To The Point. Simple…1) Assume minimal chemical to no chemical farming. So if you're using the Monsanto poison Round Up? Sorry. 2) Wine with grapes and nothing else added. And that means yeast. Okay? Got that. If you add Yeast to spark fermentation OR Yeast Food to keep it going? Sorry. 3) No forceful machinery to alter the taste, texture or alcohol level of the wine. So, Reverse Osmosis or MOX? Sorry. 4) SO2? Softcore natural means a little SO2 at bottling. Hardcore natural, means non, no way, no how. (2009)

Alice Feiring and other wine writers and producers have identified these elements of grape growing and winemaking that must not be altered by the addition of chemicals such as sulfur dioxide or the use of heavy-handed processes like micro-oxygenation (MOX) that drastically alter the character of the final wine. Alice Feiring points out that there is a "hardcore" and "softcore" when it comes to natural winemakers: some eschew the use of temperature control during fermentation and others do not see a problem with adding some sulfur at the beginning and the end of the process (very wise since this antioxidant has been used since Roman times to facilitate the aging of wines and it is an antimicrobial agent that hinders the growth of fault-producing yeasts and bacteria). In this blog post, nature has degrees—making a clear definition of natural wine a challenge. In the world of American online wine writing, there is little consensus about what makes a wine "natural."

Interesting, Italian wine journalists have been a step behind their American counterparts when it comes to attempts at defining "natural" wine. Italian writers have tended to focus more on human skill and craft in the growing of grapes and production of wine. In contrast to the American focus on processes and technological interventions, Italian journalists tend to see wine as deeply connected to agricultural traditions and food culture. Recently, Italian wine writer Giovanni Bietti published a series of books entitled *Vini naturali d'Italia: Manuale del bere sano* (2010a, 2010b, 2011a, 2011b). In each book in this series of four, Bietti starts off by offering definitions of various aspects of natural wine. Unlike many of his American counterparts, Bietti argues that the definition of natural wine does not have to mean an extremist position; it should remain open to interpretation and discussion (2010a, 20). In the first volume, he offers a definition of natural wine broken down into four parts. First, natural wine should be an artisanal product. This precludes large-scale industrial production. For Bietti, it is important that a producer be able to follow the entire production cycle from start to finish. In this case, the coherence of knowledge and experience are critical to ensure a "natural" product (2010a, 20–21). Second, Bietti tells us that the vineyard must be healthy and that healthy grapes arrive in the cellar without any pesticides or chemicals. The author emphasizes the importance of seeing viticulture as part of a larger ecological system. He states that technology will not always save us here and that producers need to look to nature for pest control solutions and healthy vineyard arrangements (2010a, 21–22). Third, there must be a certain amount of respect shown for the grapes in the wine cellar. Invasive winemaking processes are to be avoided and wines should reflect the differences brought about by the vintage. Bietti notes that because of a lack of precise labeling, consumers need to be able to trust producers or the person selling them one. In this sense, purchasing wine is about human relations (2010a, 22–24). Fourth, Bietti tells us we need to know our wines. Most important, we need to approach natural wines with an open mind. Because of the variations that can occur from year to year, the evaluation of natural wines is particularly challenging (2010a, 24–26). This flies in the face of point systems and the standard approach to mainstream wine journalism. Last, the author tells us that we should consider the *digeribilità* (digestability) of wines and how well they go with food (2010a, 26–27). This salient point brings to light the importance Italians place on seeing wine as food and the role of food in health and nutrition.

DISCOURSES OF NATURAL WINE

Like with food products, the label "natural" has neither a legal definition nor a certification process. For wine, the term *natural* is negotiated between producers, importers/distributors, wine writers and bloggers, and consumers through manifestos, blogs, and informal conversations in wine bars, shops, and cellars. I have tried to analyze these vinous discourses to understand how the actors involved contest and construct this concept of nature. In particular, I have individuated three themes I would like to explore further here. The first mode articulates the romance of marketing, the second is expressed through sensory experience, and the third focuses on the question of honesty.

Conventional American wine marketing frequently plays on the romantic image of the vineyard and the romance of drinking wine. These powerful marketing images of rolling hills and couples swooning over glasses of Chardonnay all have something in common—they largely erase the process of winemaking. The farmers, crushing machine, stainless steel tanks, and hoses just do not fit the romantic image, but this machinery and the technology involved in winemaking is an integral part of modern wine production. This romantic view erases the human presence in production, turning wine into a neutral commodity shaped by marketing experts. In turn, the consumer is able to imagine his or her own fantasies about the origins of wine and his or her own connection to Old World traditions that can be tapped into by drinking wine.

While romance is free of workers and technology in these mainstream marketing campaigns for mass-produced wines, the natural wine movement cultivates another form of vinous romance. Natural wine places production in the spotlight and has scrutinized the utilization of technology. By focusing on the role of the grower-producer and the value in expressing the taste of place, natural wine producers and consumers create value in the uniqueness and limited reproducibility of their products. Anthropologist Marion Demossier has argued that the construction of the concept of *terroir* hinges on the specificity of place rather than production methods because place cannot be reproduced. This is also a strategy to protect economic interests tied to a unique geographic area (Demossier 2011). In contrast, most natural wine enthusiasts clearly espouse a desire to reconnect to production, which they view as tied to place. The presence of migrant workers is still obscured in natural wine narratives; instead, the romance of the small family farm and the dedicated artisan is put forward in the narratives that are an important part of the hand selling these wines often require.

Most of the wines considered natural come from small family farms, and the marketing and communication of these wines focuses on this small-scale, artisanal nature of production. Where Europeans sometimes see backwardness (Terrio 2000), Americans see romance in artisanal work that is part of natural wine production. In this case, natural wine transforms labor into a cultural product that has added value (Ulin 2002). From a practical perspective, natural wine producers need to add value to their products in order to charge more for their wines and to recover the costs of producing on such as small scale. Some journalists have called the natural wine movement "trendy" and "romantic" (De Blessi 2009; Richards 2012), and as the natural wine movement gains in popularity it ironically may be moving away from its counterculture roots.

The romance associated with agriculture is not the only discourse prevalent in the ways people talk and write about natural wine—sensory experience is also a common theme. This is something I have witnessed at numerous tastings. After taking a big whiff of the wine he had just poured, Sam pulled his nose out of his glass and declared: "Now this wine is funk-eeeee! It smells like cow dung. I feel like I am rolling around in a barn. Now, it is hard to get closer to nature than that. I love it!" As Sam's olfactory experience indicates, the sensory perception of natural wines can be quite intense. So, what does nature smell like? In the case of natural wine, it has some pretty distinctive odors and often a unique visual aesthetic.

Because of the limited or nonexistent quantities of sulfur dioxide used in the making and bottling of natural wine, these wines are often a breeding ground for yeasts that would otherwise be controlled or eliminated by the addition of SO_2. For instance, Brettanomyces, often referred to as Brett, is one of the prevailing yeasts that dominate the sensory experience of many natural red wines. Some wine geeks refer to this as B-Funk (a play on words with the P-Funk music genre), and this is certainly the cause of the barnyard aroma Sam experienced. Brett can lend some character and depth to a wine, but it can also take over and overshadow much of the complexity of a wine—Brettanomyces can continue to grow and reproduce in the presence of alcohol and in an anaerobic environment. This can translate into tasting notes that move out of the barn and into the pharmacy with hints of "Band-Aid" and "nail polish remover" on the nose. That said, natural wine enthusiasts see character and charm where oenology school graduates and wine professionals see faults. The natural wine fans will vehemently defend these funkier characteristics, declaring them indicators of greater biodiversity, individuality, craft, and expressions of nature in the glass. Unfortunately, the extremes of naturalness tend to taste disappointingly similar: often there is volatile acidity and the odors produced by Brettanomyces tend to predominate. There is little room in the bottle for the more subtle expressions often associated with the idea of *terroir* or a unique sense of place expressed through the sensory experience of wine.

Natural wines can also have a very different visual aesthetic from conventionally produced wines: natural white wines, in particular, are often cloudy. This is due to a lack of fining and filtering that leaves fine particles adrift that not only alter appearance, but potentially the mouth feel and taste of the wine. Again, the mainstream of the wine tasting would see this as a fault, but *terroirists* see this as another endearing indication that their wine has not been tampered with and is that much closer to nature.

Orange wines are another distinctive category of natural wines made from white grapes. Italian producer Josko Gravner's wines are an excellent example of this genre. Gravner's wines are made using long periods of skin contact. They are aged in amphorae that allow a certain amount of oxidation, which accounts for the striking visual presentation of these wines. Natural wine fans herald these ancient techniques as a more natural way of making wine. However, talking to producers about changes in production methods reveals that many winemakers in areas like the Veneto wanted to find a way to differentiate their products. Italy was not well known for white wines until the 1980s, when producers like Silvio Jermann showed that Italians could apply better cellar hygiene and the latest technology to produce excellent whites. The level of quality in white wines improved greatly in the Veneto and well-made, clean white wines came to epitomize this region. With the objective of differentiating their wines from this sea of perfectly passable white wine, houses like Gravner and Radikon looked beyond Italy and France to Georgia and Slovenia and the roots of wine production to find old ways to produce wine. This adaptation of old technology became a novelty. In addition to aging his wines in buried amphorae, Gravner uses lesser-known local grapes such as Ribolla Gialla.

The return to and valorization of indigenous grape varieties has become a hallmark of the natural wine movement, imbuing a greater sense of place through tradition. These wines go against the industrial grain and express the unique character of the winemaker and the place. Again, this return to tradition and nature falls into the discourse of romance.

For *terroirists,* quality can be something you see in the haze of your glass but it is also expressed in the way winemakers go about their business in the vineyard and in the cellar. Talking to Piemontese winemakers like Teobaldo Cappellano and Giuseppe Rinaldi, both small producers in the Barolo DOCG area, I often heard them say *"Io voglio produrre un vino onesto."* ("I want to produce honest wine.") The idea of honesty is deeply ingrained in the concept of natural wine—the wine reflects the growing season and the craft of the winemaker. Although technology and science are part of the process, they do not dominate. Tannin powders are not added to prop up flabby wine and overly ripe vintages are not acidified to balance out their richness and alcoholic nature. On the contrary, the producers I spoke to applauded a wine producer's ability to know when to pick his or her grapes, how to be patient through the fermentation process, and how to use naturally occurring variations in temperature as a means of clarifying their wine. Honest wine is about having skill in the craft of winemaking and not about mastery of chemistry. It is about listening to the natural processes (literally) and knowing how to intervene in the most appropriate way. The winemaker embodies the winemaking process through sensory experience using the apparatus of his or her body—listening to the sound of fermentation to understand how far along the process is and constantly smelling and tasting the wine to understand any microbial issues that might be transpiring in the wine are just a few simple examples of the techniques of the body used to make wine (Black 2012).

During a conversation about natural wine with Gian Luigi, an Italian wine producer who uses conventional production methods, he told me: "Natural wine used to be synonymous with faulty wines that just tasted bad. People would forgive all of these faults because they were told it was a natural product. I believe that you should taste a wine and if you like it, then you should ask how it is made—not the other way around." How much does the moral aspect of natural wine impact taste perception? What does nature taste like anyway? As my conversation with Gian Luigi unfolded, he told me, "fortunately, makers of *vini naturali* in Italy are starting to find a middle ground. They are no longer rejecting all technology and going back to the Stone Age. For example, rather than using a manual press, they are using a soft pneumatic press. Some forms of technology are less invasive than others." Gian Luigi told me about his experiments with using wild yeast rather than inoculating his wines. As we tasted through his experiments, he told me he was happy with the results, but that the move toward using all wild yeasts was gradual and had risks associated with a less predictable fermentation. Gian Luigi appreciated the diversity and character native yeasts brought to his wine; however, he was not ready to jump on the natural wine bandwagon. Gian Luigi told me he was interested in making good wines that were commercially viable. As natural wine begins to enter the mainstream, both conventional and natural winemakers are starting to meet in the middle, with beneficial results for everyone.

By looking at the winemaking practices of producers like Cappellano, Rinaldi, and Gravner, we can see how showing character, expressing a sense of place, and rallying around nonconformity comes up smack against concepts of modernization and homogeneity. The natural wine movement expresses both the producer's and the consumer's desire to not only get closer to agriculture and the land, but also to show and see the hand of the artisan in the production method. Modernization and technological advancement in the production of foodstuff has often been cited as the growing gap between the consumer and the producer (Raynolds 2000). So much so that the producer no longer has a name and is no longer an accountable individual tied to a specific place and product. Most wines deemed "natural" have great variation from vintage to vintage because they cannot be "spoofulated" (a popular term used by *terroirists* to indicate the overmanipulation, mechanical and chemical, of wine) to always taste the same. This taste of nature comes at a price: if a harvest fails because the grape grower did not spray his crop with copper sulfate or the wine turns to vinegar in the bottle for lack of sulfur dioxide, the small producer loses a year of work and income.

CRAFTSMANSHIP AND HUMAN INTERVENTION

In the case of the natural wine movement, the concept of nature is clearly not spontaneous. Wine does not spout out of the ground of its own accord. Wine is something cultural that requires a great deal of human intervention. The question is: when did that human intervention start becoming so problematic?

Honesty and transparency are at the core of the natural wine movement, but so is craft and artisanship. Interestingly these two concepts have rather conflicting etymologies. In his study of artisans and craft trades in Greece, Michael Herzfeld notes that in many languages to be crafty is to be cunning or to find a way to cheat: "In Italian, the highly formalized language of fine arts is parodied in popular phrase, *l'arte d'arrangiarsi,* that is similarly redolent of resistance to formal authority and means 'the art of fixing things for oneself'" (2004, 1). Herzfeld goes on to state that the ingenuity of the craftsman is not only about aesthetics but also about indirection and guile— the artisan is often accused of artifice. Artifice is a false reproduction of nature. Industrial production and the heavy use of technology challenges and threatens the craft aspects of wine production. This example of natural winemakers' and consumers' rejection of technology is also a reaction to changing social relation. As consumers become increasingly alienated from the production of goods and as the hands-on elements of production disappear, both consumers and producers are distanced from the social relations (vineyard and cellar labor in particular) inherent in wine. In the case of natural wine, it is industry that is framed as the producer of artifice and the craftsman who is the upholder of nature. Is this merely a crafty feat of reframing that turns the tables on the concepts of artifice and nature?

Within the natural wine movement, the concepts of craft and artisanship stand in opposition to mechanization and industrialization. The power of machines and technology to distance humans from one another has been a troubling train of thought in the Western world for some time. Social theorist Walter Benjamin, writing in the early twentieth century, was concerned with what kind of impact mass production would have on society and social relations. For Benjamin, the artisan imitated the processes of nature. With the introduction of mass production mediated by machines, reproduction becomes a "dead reiteration" distanced from unique, individual realities (Leslie 1998, 8). Machines distance humans from one another and from nature. This idea can also be applied to wine production. The mass production of wine, with a heavy application of mechanization and technology, leads to a product disconnected from its artisanal reality—the craftsman's attempt to reproduce nature. This reproduction of nature is more complicated than we first imagine because nature is never disconnected from human influence and construction.

Part of the heated discussion around natural wine focuses on interlopers. Because natural wine revolves around a set of changing and sometimes ill-defined practices, there is room for fakes and frauds. Interesting, the impostors are often of an industrial ilk and through false marketing these producers present their wines as natural despite a heavy industrial process that has little to do with respect for the environment or craftsmanship. Alessandro Stanziani explores fraud and counterfeiting of food and beverages in late nineteenth-century and early twentieth-century France, where the introduction of new technical and industrial processes in food production was seen as the source of fraudulence (2007). This question of the use of technology in food production in France continues today. European debates on the use of genetically modified organisms have brought the debate about naturalness into the public sphere (Heller 2007). Despite the necessity of mass production and technology in producing enough food to feed the world's growing population, consumers in Europe and North America are increasingly pushing back against the lack of transparency in food and, in this case, wine production.

Stanziani notes that lobbies and commercial interests have always been central to determining questions of quality and to judging counterfeits (2007, 377). Large commercial interests certainly dictate wine quality in Italy today. The creation of Appellation d'Origine Contrôlée (AOC) and Denominazione di Origine Controllata (DOC) regulations are certainly a reflection of this commercial reality (Bérard and Marchenay 2004). By moving outside of official legislative bodies and certification processes, the natural wine movement can be seen as a reaction against attempts to standardize and industrialize the production of wine. Stanziani states that "the idea of 'natural' was increasingly opposed to that of 'manufactured,' and also to 'adulterated' goods" in nineteenth-century France (2007, 380). According to Stanziani, the idea of natural in opposition to manufactured was a product of unfair competition. A very similar situation occurred in 1986 in Italy when, after the methanol scandal, Italians realized that cheap wine was not only not playing by the market rules, it was potentially dangerous. The real cost of the labor and input in making wine was much higher than the price of these adulterated forms of wine, which used methanol to increase their alcohol content. Natural wine is a reaction to unfair competition much in the same way as the nineteenth-century case presented by Alessandro Stanziani. The idea of nature becomes a foil for the manufactured—it is opposition to a false reproduction of nature.

What is meant by the term *natural* and how is nature perceived? As humans, we are part of the natural world and everything in this world is natural. As Tim Ingold warns, we need to overcome the Cartesian dualism that has constructed frames of knowledge that separate humans from the natural world and disengage human actions from the environment (2000). Following this line of argumentation, the "denaturing" of the world around us is certainly an act of human hands, as is the construction of artifice, which stands in opposition to nature. The construction of nature largely occurs in contrast to the creation of the category of artifice. By looking at winemaking practices and consumer perceptions of wine, we can see the tensions that exist among nature, technology, and artifice in wine production and consumption. In particular, the natural wine movement raises interesting questions about the ways nature is constructed through sensory experience and cultural perceptions of nature more generally.

Producers of natural wines face the challenge of treading a fine line between the use of technology and minimal intervention. As we have seen, winemaking is inherently a technology-heavy process: it requires human sensory evaluation and a large amount of equipment at every stage in order to produce a palatable alcoholic beverage. Discourses of natural wine from the production, distribution, and consumption sides express an unclear and difficult relationship with technology. For example, there is no doubt that a hydraulic press, a very modern and technologically involved piece of equipment, is the most gentle method for extracting grape must, better than human feet or the heavy-handed roto-fermentor. Although most winemakers who call their wine "natural" do not eschew technology altogether, there is a negotiation throughout the winemaking process. Often consumers conflate the use of technology with the process of industrialization and reject it completely as an attempt to homogenize the end product and erase the craftsmanship involved in making wine. The natural wine movement is still finding the middle ground in both the vineyard and the cellar, and the ways in which people talk about wine is shaping understandings of how wine is made.

COMMUNICATING NATURE

In the local and organic food movements, activist consumers operate on the logic that it is important to "know your farmer." If we know where our food comes from, we can ensure that it is produced in a sustainable manner. The same holds true for the case of natural wine. For natural wine consumers hearing the stories about how wine is made, the philosophy behind it, and learning about some of the challenges facing wine producers puts farmers back into the picture and connects wine drinkers with agriculture, the place where wine is made, and human processes behind production. Not all natural wine drinkers have a chance to meet winemakers: distance and language barriers often keep the two apart. Distributors and importers often mediate these dialogues. This poses its own series of ethical issues, and the commercial nature of wine is never far from the surface. Importers like Joe Dressner, who sadly passed away in 2011, have spent a lifetime searching out what they have deemed natural wines. Joe was a partner in Louis/Dressner Selections, one of the main importers of natural wines from Europe to the United States. Through his selection process, Dressner played a part in constructing what natural wine is in the United States. In addition, Joe traveled the country presenting his portfolio of wines, chaperoning wine producers on their stateside tours, and expounding the qualities of natural wine. In 2010, I attended a tasting of Louis/Dressner wines Joe was overseeing. Gregarious and outspoken, Joe corrected consumers about their ideas and perceptions; he even went so far as to declare that "wine is not an industry." This statement brought to light one of Joe Dressner's bigger projects: to bring wine back to the realm of human-to-human interactions, to make clear the human labor and relations behind the growing of grapes and making of wine—something industry clearly did not allow for in Joe's mind.

Wine importers and distributors are not the only people communicating natural wine: through social media and Internet technology, consumers can learn more about how their favorite wines are producers. Wine bloggers such as Alder Yarrow, Alice Feiring, and Jeremy Parzen have a strong following of natural wine drinkers who read these sites to find out more about the production of specific wines, native grape varieties, and traditions in wine-producing regions. These blogs are also a forum for discussing and debating the meanings of natural wine. Wine producers are less involved in these discussions; however, an increasing number of small producers now have their own sites where they can communicate the philosophy of their wine. Search engines like Able Grape make it easier for passionate wine drinkers to access information about wine. Sifting through all this information is often the challenge.

CONCLUSION

The natural wine movement is certainly full of contradictions. At the same time, it represents a larger desire on the part of both European and North American consumers to reconnect with agriculture and craftsmanship. These same actors, however, potentially reify nature and reproduce the same kind of artifice they set out to uncover and criticize. A rejection of technology and mass production methods can be seen as a broader rejection of modernity. The malaise of modernity represented by mass culture has led to a heightened sense of alienation of individuals in society, as well as individuals from nature (in this case as a symbol of cultural traditions) (Taylor 1991; Weber 1992).

At the same time, the natural wine movement in North America is largely about consumption. In Western cultures, defining the self through consumption is now perhaps the foremost form of identification. Giving meaning to consumption practices has a deeper ideological significance in consumer societies. Natural wine poses an interesting articulation between the worlds of American consumption and European production. American natural wine drinkers define themselves as alternative to mainstream wine drinking culture while still defining themselves through consumption. At the same time, the *terroirists* laud the work of natural wine grower-producers in Europe, helping to return the identity of these people back to their connection with craft and nature.

Wine, highly prized in so many Western cultures, has historically been the object of fraud and artifice. The present natural wine movement tells us a great deal about the ways in which we continue to fight battles against artifice, the copying of nature, while trying to maintain a connection to nature in an increasingly industrialized world. It has been argued that wine is one of the contributing factors in Western civilization (McGovern 2009), and it is certain that these complex human relations with vines have cemented links between culture and nature.

NOTES

1. For more information on the certification of biodynamic agriculture, please see the Demeter website: www.demeter.net/, accessed May 26, 2012.
2. In France, the many cases of fraud that came out of the industrialization of wine production in the late nineteenth century led to a similar consumer backlash and waves of government regulation in response to adulterated wine. See Stanziani 2007.
3. www.viniveri.net/en, accessed May 26, 2012. There other natural wine fairs, including Vin Natur (http://www.vinnatur.org/), which takes place at the same time as Vinitaly and ViniVeri.

CONTRIBUTORS

Rachel E. Black (editor) is an assistant professor and coordinator of the Gastronomy Program at Boston University. She is the author of *Porta Palazzo: The Anthropology of an Italian Market* (University of Pennsylvania Press, 2012) and editor of *Alcohol in Popular Culture: An Encyclopedia* (Greenwood, 2010). Black's current research focuses on the role of cooperative wine production in preserving living cultural heritage in northern Italy.

Robert C. Ulin (editor) received his PhD from the Graduate Faculty of the New School for Social Research. He is presently professor of anthropology at Rochester Institute of Technology, where he also served for two years as dean of the College of Liberal Arts. Prior to coming to RIT, Ulin served as the chair of anthropology at Western Michigan University. He is the author of *Vintages and Traditions* (Smithsonian Institution, 1996) and numerous articles on the anthropology of wine. He is also well known for his work on hermeneutics, critical theory, and historical anthropology.

Juraj Buzalka is a senior lecturer in social anthropology at the Institute of Social Anthropology, Comenius University, in Bratislava, Slovakia. His research interests include the anthropology of social movements, economic anthropology, nationalism, populism and religion, the politics of memory, and social transformations in Eastern Europe. He is the author of *Nation and Religion: The Politics Commemoration in South-East Poland* (Lit, 2007).

Christina M. Ceisel is a PhD candidate at the Institute of Communications Research at the University of Illinois at Urbana Champaign, and adjunct faculty at SUNY College at Oneonta. Her research considers the role of identity, hybridity, and authenticity in contemporary culture. She has presented and published on these themes as they relate to transnational children's media, popular Latin American celebrity, autoethnographic approaches to ethnic identity, and transnational foodways. Her dissertation work draws on cultural studies and qualitative methodologies to critically analyze the role of food in discourses of authenticity and hybrity within global commodity culture, as highlighted through a case study of Galicia, Spain.

Paul Cohen received a PhD in history from Princeton University. He is currently the director of the Centre for the Study of France and the Francophone World at the University of Toronto, where he is also an associate professor in French history. His research focuses on the early modern French history, the social history of language, the origins of national identity, the French Atlantic, and the social history of wine. He is the author of the forthcoming book *Kingdom of Babel: The Making of a National Language in France, 1400–1815* (Cornell University Press), as well as coauthor of *L'Introuvable unité du français. Contacts et variations linguistiques en Europe et en Amérique (XIIe–XVIIIe siècle)* (Presses de l'Université Laval, 2012).

Sarah Daynes is a cultural sociologist and an assistant professor of sociology at the University of North Carolina Greensboro and holds a PhD in sociology from the École des Hautes Études en Sciences Sociales in Paris, 2001. Her publications include *Desire for Race* (Cambridge University Press, 2008) and *Time and Memory in Reggae Music: The Politics of Hope* (Manchester University Press, 2010). She is currently conducting ethnographic fieldwork in France with winemakers and vineyard owners.

Marion Demossier is a professor in French and European studies at the University of Southampton, Modern Languages. She is the author of various works on wine producers, wine drinking cultures, and wine consumption. Her first monograph, "Hommes et Vins, une anthropologie du vignoble bourguignon" (1999) won the prix Lucien Perriaux, and her latest book, *Wine Drinking Culture in France,* was published by the University of Wales Press in 2011. Demossier holds a PhD in anthropology from EHESS and she is currently doing fieldwork in New Zealand and Burgundy.

Erica A. Farmer is a PhD candidate in anthropology at University College London. Her dissertation is a comparative project on legal geographical indication systems, focusing on the *appellation d'origine contrôlée* (AOC) system for wine in Bordeaux and on artisan food producers under the UK version of the EU Protected Food Names (PFN) system.

Yuson Jung holds a PhD in social anthropology from Harvard University and is an assistant professor in the department of anthropology at Wayne State University (Detroit, MI). She is working on a book project entitled the *Cultural Politics of Wine: The Transformation of the Bulgarian Wine Industry* based on her ethnographic research in the wineries in northwestern Bulgaria. The project explores the intersection of food, cultural politics, globalization, and transnational governance from the perspectives of marginal wine producers. Her research interests include the study of consumption, globalization, food and culture, and postsocialism as well as the anthropology of Europe.

Ewa Kopczyńska is an assistant professor in the Institute of Sociology at Jagiellonian University (Krakow, Poland). She teaches social anthropology and—for graduate students—anthropology of the body and anthropology of food. Her research and academic interests focus on the social meaning of obtaining, producing, and consuming food. She is currently conducting anthropological research on winemaking in Poland, homemade food processing, and alternative food networks.

Winnie Lem is a professor in the Departments of International Development Studies and Women's Studies at Trent University and holds a PhD from the University of Toronto. She has conducted research on farming in Languedoc, France, and is currently conducting research on migration between China and France. Lem is the author of *Cultivating Dissent: Work, Identity and Praxis in Rural Languedoc* (State University of New York Press, 1999).

Paul Manning received his PhD in linguistics from the University of Chicago and is currently an associate professor in the anthropology department of Trent University. His research focuses on linguistic and semiotic anthropology in Europe (Wales) and Eurasia (Georgia). He has done fieldwork on Welsh-speaking populations in Wales and Argentina and on Georgian-speaking populations in Georgia and Russia.

Elizabeth Saleh is a PhD candidate in social anthropology at Goldsmiths, University of London. The working title of her PhD thesis is *Trade-marking Tradition: An Ethnography of the Lebanese Wine Industry*. Her research interests include elites, agriculture, food studies, memory, and history.

Nicolas Sternsdorff Cisterna is a PhD Candidate in social anthropology at Harvard University. His research looks at food safety and food commodity chains. He is currently researching food safety after the meltdown at the Fukushima Dai-Ichi nuclear plant. He has done research on Chilean and New Zealand food exports to Japan and the phenomenology of wine tasting.

Robert Swinburn is a wine vineyard consultant and grape grower in Geelong, Australia. He is also a PhD candidate in anthropology at the School of Social and Political Sciences, The University of Melbourne, Australia.

Adam Walker is a PhD candidate in the department of anthropology of the City University of New York Graduate School and University Center. He is also a Graduate Teaching Fellow at Brooklyn College, where he teaches courses in anthropology and sexuality. His research interests include consumption, political economy, semiotics, and wine in Georgia.

BIBLIOGRAPHY

Abu-Lughod, L. 1991. "Writing against Culture." In *Recapturing Anthropology: Working in the Present,* ed. Richard G. Fox, 137–162. Santa Fe, NM: School of American Research Press.

Agulhon, M. 1982. *The Republic in the Village: The People of the Var from the French Revolution to the Second Republic,* trans. Janet Lloyd. Cambridge: Cambridge University Press.

Alcorso, C. 1994. *The Wind You Say: An Italian in Australia. A True Story of an Inspirational Life.* Sydney: Harper Collins Publishers.

Alexander, C. 2004. "Value, Relations, and Changing Bodies: Privatization and Property Rights in Kazakhstan." In *Property in Question: Value Transformation in the Global Economy,* eds. K. Verdery and C. Alexander. New York: Berg.

Anderson, K., ed. 2004. *The World's Wine Markets: Globalization at Work.* Northhampton: Edward Elgar Publishing.

Appadurai, A., ed. 1986. *The Social Life of Things: Commodities in Cultural Perspective.* Cambridge: Oxford University Press.

Appadurai, A. 1994. "Commodities and the Politics of Value." In *Interpreting Objects and Collections,* ed. S. M. Pearce. Oxon: Routledge.

Appadurai, A. 2002. "Disjuncture and Difference in the Global Economy." In *The Anthropology of Globalization: A Reader,* eds. J. X. Inda and R. Rosaldo, 47–65. Oxford: Blackwell.

Appadurai, A. 2008. *Modernity at Large: Cultural Dimensions of Globalization.* Minneapolis: University of Minnesota Press.

Arce, A. 1993. "New Tastes in Industrialized Countries and Transformations in the Latin-American Countryside: An Introduction to the Local Cases of Mexico and Chili." *International Journal of Sociology of Agriculture and Food* 3: 48–70.

Ardagh, J. 1995. *France in the 1980s.* London: Secker and Warburg.

Arendt, H. 1958. *The Human Condition.* Chicago: University of Chicago Press.

Asad, T., ed. 1973. *Anthropology and the Colonial Encounter*. New York: Humanities Press.

Assmann, J., and J. Czaplicka. 1995. "Collective Memory and Cultural Identity." *New German Critique* 65: 125–133.

Averyt, W. 1977. *Agropolitics in the European Community: Interest Groups and the Common Agricultural Policy*. New York: Praeger.

Banks, G., and J. Overton. 2010. "Old World, New World, Third World? Reconceptualizing the Worlds of Wine." *Journal of Wine Research* 21(1): 57–75.

Barbera, F., and S. Audifredi. 2012. "In Pursuit of Quality: The Institutional Change of Wine Production Market in Piedmont." *Sociologia Ruralis*. doi: 10:1111/j.1467–9523.2012.00567.x.

Barham, E. 2003. "Translating *Terroir:* The Global Challenge of French AOC Labeling." *Journal of Rural Studies* 19(1): 127–138.

Barnard, H., A. N. Dooley, G. Areshian, B. Gasparyan, and K. F. Faull. 2011. "Chemical Evidence for Wine Production around 4000 BCE in the Late Chalcolithic Near Eastern Highland." *Journal of Archaeological Science* 38(5): 977–984.

Barron, C. A. 1995. *Dreamers of the Valley of Plenty: A Portrait of the Napa Valley*. New York: Scribner.

Bateson, G., and M. C. Bateson. 1987. *Angels Fear: Towards an Epistemology of the Sacred*. New York: Macmillan.

Baudrillard, J. 1975. *The Mirror of Production*. St Louis: Telos Press.

Beeston, J. 2001. *Concise History of Australian Wine*. Sydney: Allen and Unwin.

Bell, D., and G. Valentine. 1997. *Consuming Geographies: We Are where We Eat*. London, New York: Routledge.

Benjamin, W. 1969. *Illuminations,* trans. Harry Zolin, ed. Hannah Arendt. New York: Schocken Books.

Benjamin, W. 2008. *The Work of Art in the Age of its Technical Reproducibility, and Other Writings on Media*. Cambridge: Belknap Press / Harvard University Press.

Beridze, G. I., and P. B. Azarashvili. 1965. *Wines and Cognacs of Georgia*. Tbilisi: Vsesojuznoje objedinenije Prodintorg.

Bess, M. 2003. *The Light-Green Society: Ecology and Technological Modernity in France, 1960–2000*. Chicago: University of Chicago Press.

Bessière, J. 1998. "Local Development and Heritage: Traditional Food and Cuisine as Tourist Attractions in Rural Areas." *European Journal of Rural Sociology* 38(1): 21–34.

Bestor, T. C. 2001. "Supply-Side Sushi: Commodity, Market, and the Global City." *American Anthropologist* 103: 76–95.

Bestor, T. C. 2003. "Markets and Places: Tokyo and Global Tuna Trade." In *The Anthropology of Space and Place: Locating Culture,* eds. S. Low and D. Lawrence-Zuniga. Malden: Blackwell.

Bettane, M. 2007. "Non aux bio-cons!" *Tast Pro* 40(July 30): 2.

Bietti, G. 2010–2011. *Vini Naturali d'Italia: Manuale del Bere Sano*. Vol. 1–4. Roma: Edizioni Estemporanee.

Binner, C. "L'AVN, qu'est-ce?" Accessed September 22, 2012. www.lesvinsnaturels.org/lassociation/l'avn-qu'est-ce/.

Black, R. 2010. *Alcohol in Popular Culture: An Encyclopedia.* Santa Barbara, CA: ABC Clio Press.

Black, R. 2012a. *Porta Palazzo: The Anthropology of an Italian Market.* Philadelphia: University of Pennsylvania Press.

Black, R. 2012b. "Wine Memory." *Sensate.* Accessed July 18, 2012. http://sensatejournal.com/2012/06/rachel-black-wine-memory/.

Boas, F. 1964. *The Central Eskimo.* Lincoln: University of Nebraska Press.

Bocock, R. 1986. *Hegemony.* London: Tavistock.

Bohmrich, R. 1996. "*Terroir:* Competing Perspectives on the Roles of Soil, Climate and People." *Journal of Wine Research* 7(1): 33–46.

Borislavov, Y. 2004. *Bulgarian Wine Book: History, Culture, Cellars, Wines.* Sofia: TRUD Publishers.

Borodziej, W., and A. Hajnicz. 1998. "Powojenne Przesiedlenia Ludności na Terenie Ziem Zachodnich w Świadomości Społecznej Polaków. Raport zbiorczy CBOS z badania jakościowego, Warszawa, lipiec 1996." In *Kompleks wypędzenia,* eds. W. Borodziej and A. Hajnicz. Kraków: Znak.

Botík, J., ed. 1988. *Hont. Tradície L'udovej kultúry (Hont. Traditions of Folk Culture).* Banská Bystrica: Krajské osvetové stredisko.

Bourdieu, P. 1977. *Outline of a Theory of Practice.* Cambridge: Cambridge University Press.

Bourdieu, P. 1979. *La Distinction: Critique Sociale du Jugement.* Paris: Les Editions de Minuit.

Bourdieu, P. 1984. *Distinction: A Social Critique of the Judgment of Taste.* Cambridge, MA: Harvard University Press.

Bourdieu, P. 1994. *In other Words: Essays towards a Reflexive Sociology.* Stanford, CA: Stanford University Press.

Bourdieu, P. 2007. *Distinction: A Social Critique of the Judgement of Taste.* New York: Routledge.

Bourgois, P. 1995. *In Search of Respect: Selling Crack in El Barrio.* Cambridge: Cambridge University Press.

Bowen, S., and A. Valenzuela Zapata. 2009. "Geographical Indications, *Terroir,* and Socioeconomic and Ecological Sustainability: The Case of Tequila." *Journal of Rural Studies* 25: 108–119.

Boyce, J. 2012. *1835: The Founding of Melbourne and the Conquest of Australia.* Melbourne: Black.

Braverman, H. 1974. *Labor and Monopoly Capital.* New York: Monthly Review Press.

Brillat-Savarin, J. A. (1825) 1994. *The Physiology of Taste.* London: Penguin Books.

Brubaker, R. 1985. "Rethinking Classical Theory: The Sociological Vision of Pierre Bourdieu." *Theory and Society* 14: 745–775.

Brunet, P. 1995. "Le *Terroir:* Fin ou Renouveau d'une Notion." *Cahiers Nantais* 43: 7–12.

Brunori, G., V. Malandrin, and A. Rossi. 2012. "Trade-Off and Convergences: The Role of Food Security in the Evolution of Food Discourses in Italy." *Journal of Rural Studies.* doi:10.1016/j.jrurstud.2012.01.013

Bunten, A. C. 2008. "Sharing Culture or Selling Out? Developing the Commodified Persona in the Heritage Industry." *American Ethnologist* 35(3): 380–395.

Burawoy, M. 1985. *The Politics of Production*. London: Verso.

Burkot, P. 2010. *Wino Gronowe z Polskich Winnic*. Biuro Produktów Roślinnych ARR. Accessed May 27, 2012. http://agroplony.pl/produkcja-rolna/produkcja-roslinna/267-wino-gronowe-z-polskich-winnic.html.

Busch, L., and K. Tanaka. 1996. "Rites of Passage: Constructing Quality in a Commodity Sector." *Science, Technology, & Human Value*, 21: 3–27.

Buzalka, J. 2007. *Nation and Religion: The Politics of Commemoration in South-East Poland*. Münster: Lit.

Buzalka, J. 2009. "Scale and Ethnicity in Southeast Poland: Tourism in the European Periphery." *Etnográfica* 13(2): 373–393.

Callon, M., C. Méadel, and V. Rabeharisoa. 2002. "The Economy of Qualities." *Economy and Society* 31: 194–217.

Campbell, G., and N. Guibert. 2007. *Wine, Society, and Globalization: Multidisciplinary Perspectives on the Wine Industry*. New York: Palgrave Macmillan.

Camuto, R. V. 2008. *Corkscrewed: Adventures in the New French Wine Country*. Lincoln: University of Nebraska Press.

Candea, M. 2007. "Arbitrary Locations: In Defence of the Bounded Field-Site." *Journal of the Royal Anthropological Institute* 13: 167–184.

Cavanaugh, J. R. 2007. "Making Salami, Producing Bergamo: The Transformation of Value." *Ethnos* 72(2): 149–172.

Centrum Badania Opinii Publicznej. 2010. *Postawy wobec alkoholi*, Komunikat z badań BS/116/2010, Warszawa. Accessed July 10, 2012. www.cbos.pl/SPISKOM.POL/2010/K_116_10.PDF.

Charters, S. 2008. *Wine and Society: The Social and Cultural Context of a Drink*. Oxford: Elsevier.

Chauvet, J. 1998. *Le Vin en question. Wine in Question*, ed. H. U. Kesselring. Paris: Jean-Paul Rocher.

Chauvet, J. 2007. *Études scientifiques et autres communications (1949–1988)*, eds. L. Chauvet and P. Pacalet. Paris: Jean-Paul Rocher.

Chauvin, P.-M. 2005. "Le critique et sa griffe. Ce que fait Robert Parker (aux vins de Bordeaux)." *Terrains & Travaux* 2(9): 90–108.

Chauvin, P.-M. 2009. "What Globalization Has Done to Wine." Review of *Le Marché de l'excellence. Les Grands crus à l'épreuve de la mondialisation* by Marie-France Garcia-Parpet, La vie des idées. July 27. Accessed May 31, 2012. www.laviedesidees.fr/What-Globalization-Has-Done-to.html.

Chauvin, P.-M. 2010. *Le marché des réputations. Une sociologie du monde des vins de Bordeaux*. Bordeaux: Féret.

Chevet, J.-M. 2009. "Cooperative Cellars and the Regrouping of the Supply in France in the Twentieth Century." In *Exploring the Food Chain: Food Production and Food Processing in Western Europe, 1850–1990*, eds. Y. Segers, J. Beileman, and E. Buyst, 253–277. Brepols: Turnhout.

Chiffoleau, Y., and C. Laporte. 2006. "Price Formation: The Case of the Burgundy Wine Market." *Revue Française de Sociologie* 5 (47) 157–182. Accessed June 6, 2012. www.cairn.info/load_pdf.php?ID_ARTICLE = RFS_475_0157.

Ching K. L. 1998. *Gender and the South China Miracle*. Berkeley: University of California Press.

Choy, T. et al. 2009. "Strong Collaboration as a Method for Multi-sited Ethnography: On Mycorrhizal Relations." In *Multi-sited Ethnography: Theory, Praxis and Locality in Contemporary Research*, ed. M. A. Falzon, 197–214. Farnham and Burlington: Ashgate.

Clifford, J. and G. E. Marcus, eds. 1986. *Writing Culture: The Poetics and Politics of Ethnography*. Berkeley: University of California Press.

Cole, S. 1991. *Women of Praia*. Princeton, NJ: Princeton University Press.

Collier, S, and A. Ong. 2005 *Global Assemblages: Technology, Politics, and Ethics as Anthropological Problems*. Oxford: Blackwell Publishing.

Colman, T. 2008. *Wine Politics: How Governments, Environmentalists, Mobsters, and Critics Influence the Wines We Drink*. Berkeley: University of California Press.

Comaroff, J., and J. Comaroff. 1992. *Ethnography and the Historical Imagination*. Boulder, CO: Westview Press.

Commission on the European Union. 2002. "Education and Culture at a Glance: Newsletter of the Education and Culture Directorate," Issue 7 (May), http://ec.europa.eu/dgs/education_culture/publ/news/07/newsletter_en2.htm.

Counihan, C. 2004. *Around the Tuscan Table: Food, Family, and Gender in Twentieth Century Florence*. New York: Routledge.

Cox, H. 1967. *The Wines of Australia*. London: Hodder and Stoughton.

Creed, G. 1998. *Domesticating Revolution: From Socialist Reform to Ambivalent Transition in a Bulgarian Village*. University Park: Penn State University Press.

Crenn, C. and I. Téchoueyres. 2007. "Local Heritage to Singularize a Wine *Terroir*: The Example of Pays Foyen (Gironde, France)." *Anthropology of Food* S2.

Cronon, W., ed. 1996. *Uncommon Ground: Rethinking the Human Place in Nature*. New York: W. W. Norton & Company.

Croser, B. 2010. *The Adelaide Advertiser*. February 9.

Czegledy, A. 2002 "Urban Peasants in a Post-socialist World: Small-Scale Agriculturalists in Hungary." In *Post-socialist Peasant? Rural and Urban Constructions of Identity in Eastern Europe, East Asia and the Former Soviet Union*, eds. P. Leonard and D. Kaneff, 200–220. Houndmills, Basingstoke: Palgrave.

Davidson, R. 2007. "*Terroir* and Catalonia." *Journal of Catalan Studies* 10: 58–72.

Daynes, S. 2010. *Time and Memory in Reggae Music*. Manchester: Manchester University Press.

Deflem, M., and F. C. Pampel. 1996. "The Myth of Postnational Identity: Popular Support for European Unification." *Social Forces* 75(1): 119–143.

del Pozo, J. 1995. "Vina Santa Rita and Wine Production in Chile since the Mid-19th Century." *Journal of Wine Research* 6(2): 133.

Demossier, M. 1999. *Hommes et Vins: Une Anthropologie du Vignoble Bourguignon*. Dijon: Editions Universitaires de Dijon.

Demossier, M. 2001. "The Quest for Identities: Consumption of Wine in France." *Anthropology of Food*. Special Issue 01.

Demossier, M. 2010. *Wine Drinking Culture in France: A National Myth or a Modern Passion?* Cardiff, UK: University of Wales Press.

Demossier, M. 2011. "Beyond *Terroir*: Territorial Construction, Hegemonic Discourses, and French Wine Culture." *Journal of the Royal Anthropological Society* 17: 685–705.

Denzin, N. K. 2003. *Performance Ethnography: Critical Pedagogy and the Politics of Culture.* Thousand Oaks, CA: Sage Publications.

Denzin, N. K. 2006. "Pedagogy, Performance, and Autoethnography." *Text and Performance Quarterly* 26(4), 333–338.

Denzin, N. K., and M. D. Giardina. 2011. "Introduction." In *Qualitative Inquiry and Global Crises,* eds. N. K. Denzin and M. D. Giardina, 9–27. Walnut Creek, CA: Left Coast Press.

de Roest, K., and A. Menghi. 2000. "Reconsidering 'Traditional' Food: The Case of Parmigiano Reggiano Cheese." *Sociologia Ruralis* 40(4): 439–451.

Di Bleasi, J. 2009. "Naturally Speaking." *Vinosseur.* July 19. Accessed June 2, 2012. http://vinosseur.com/naturally-speaking/.

Dion, R. 1990. *Le Paysage et la Vigne: Essais de Géographie Historique.* Paris: Editions Payot.

Dmitrów, E. 1998. "Przymusowe Wysiedlenie Niemców w Polskiej Opinii Publicznej 1945–1948." In *Kompleks Wypędzenia,* eds. W. Borodziej and A. Hajnicz. Kraków: Znak.

Douglas, M. 1996. *Natural Symbols: Explorations in Cosmology.* London: Routledge.

Douglas, M. 1997. "A Distinctive Anthropological Perspective." In *Constructive Drinking: Perspectives on Drink from Anthropology,* ed. M. Douglas, 3–15. Cambridge: Cambridge University Press.

Douglas, M. 2003. *Constructive Drinking: Perspectives on Drink from Anthropology.* London: Routledge.

Drábiková, E. 1988. "'Vinohradníctvo' Winegrowing." In *Hont. Tradície Ľudovej kultúry (Hont. Traditions of Folk Culture),* ed. J. Botík. Banská Bystrica: Krajské osvetové stredisko.

Drengson, A., and Y. Inoue, eds. 1995. *The Deep Ecology Movement: An Introductory Anthology.* Berkeley, CA: North Atlantic Books.

Duby, G., and A. Wallon. 1976. *Histoire de la France Rurale.* Paris: Seuil.

Dumas, A. 1962 [1853]. *Adventures in Caucasia,* trans. and ed. A.E. Murch. Westport, CT: Greenwood Press.

Dunn, E. 2008. "Postsocialist Spores: Disease, Bodies, and the State in the Republic of Georgia." *American Ethnologist* 35(2): 243–258.

Dunstan, D. 1994. *Better the Pommard: A History of Wine in Victoria.* Melbourne: Australian Scholarly Publishing.

Durand, G. 1992. "La Vigne et le vin." In *Les Lieux de mémoire,* III, *Les France,* 2, *Traditions,* ed. P. Nora. Paris: Gallimard.

Edelman, M. 1999. *Peasants against Globalization: Rural Social Movements in Costa Rica.* Stanford, CA: Stanford University Press.

Eliade, M. 1960. *Myths, Dreams and Mysteries: The Encounter between Contemporary Faiths and Archaic Realities.* London: Harvill Press.

Eliade, M. 1971. *Myth of the Eternal Return: Cosmos and History.* Princeton, NJ: Princeton University Press.

Encarnación, O. G. 2008. *Spanish Politics: Democracy after Dictatorship.* Malden, MA: Polity.

Engel, L. C. 2007. "'Rolling Back, Rolling Out:' Exceptionalism and Neoliberalism of the Spanish State." *Critical Studies in Education* 48(2): 213–227.

Enjalbert, H. 1953. "Comment naissent les grands crus: Bordeaux, Porto, Cognac." *Annales* 8: 315–328, 457–474.

Enjalbert, H., and B. Enjalbert. 1987. *L'Histoire de la vigne et du vin*. Paris: Bordas S.A.

Eriksen, T.-H. 2001. *Small Places, Large Issues*. London: Pluto Press.

Euromonitor International. 2012. *Wine in Poland*. March. Accessed May 27, 2012. www.marketresearch.com/Euromonitor-International-v746/Wine-Poland-6858135/.

European Commission Directorate-General for Agriculture and Rural Development. 2010. "An Analysis of the EU Organic Sector". Accessed May 26, 2012. http://ec.europa.eu/agriculture/organic/files/eu-policy/data-statistics/facts_en.pdf.

European Union. 2012. Regolamento di Esecuzione N. 203/2012 della Commissione dell'8 marzo 2012 che modifica il regolamento (CE) n. 889/2008 recante modalità di applicazione del regolamento (CE) n. 834/2007 del Consiglio in ordine alle modalità di applicazione relative al vino biologico. Accessed May 26, 2012. http://eur-lex.europa.eu/LexUriServ/LexUriServ.do?uri = OJ:L:2012:071:0042:01:IT:HTML.

Eyal, G., I. Szelenyi, and E. Townsley. 1998. *Making Capitalism without Capitalists: Class Formation and Elite Struggles in Post-Communist Central Europe*. London: Verso.

Fabian, J. 1983. *Time and the Other: How Anthropology Makes its Object*. New York: Columbia University Press.

Falzon, M. A., ed. 2009. *Multi-sited Ethnography: Theory, Praxis and Locality in Contemporary Research*. Farnham and Burlington: Ashgate.

Feenberg, A. 2010. *Between Reason and Experience: Essays in Technology and Modernity*. Cambridge, MA: The MIT Press.

Fehervary, K. 2009. "Goods and States: The Political Logic of State-Socialist Material Culture." *Comparative Studies in Society and History* 51(2): 426–459.

Feiring, A. 2008. *The Battle for Wine and Love: or How I Saved the World from Parkerization*. Orlando, FL: Houghton Mifflin Harcourt.

Feiring, A. 2009. "Natural Wine: The Definition." *The Feiring Line*. August 20. Accessed June 2, 2012. www.alicefeiring.com/blog/2009/08/natural-wines-the-definition.html.

Feiring, A. 2011a. "Natural Wine Movement, Just Noise?" *The Feiring Line*. December 27. Accessed June 2, 2012. www.alicefeiring.com/blog/2011/12/is-the-natural-wine-movement-just-noise.html.

Feiring, A. 2011b. *Naked Wine: Letting Grapes Do What Comes Naturally*. Cambridge, MA: Da Capo.

Fogarty, J. J. 2009. "A Review of Alcohol Consumption and Alcohol Control Policies." *Worldwide Hospitality and Tourism Themes* 1(2): 110–132.

Font, C. 2003. "Spain: Black Waters, Dirty Hands." *World Press Review* 50(2). http://worldpress.org/Europe/882.cfm.

Foster, W., and A. Valdes. 2004. "South America." In *The World's Wine Markets: Globalization at Work*, ed. K. Anderson, 210–227. Cheltenham, UK and Northampton, MA: Edward Elgar Publishing.

Foucault, M. 1979. *Discipline and Punish*. New York: Vintage.

Foucault, M. 1982. *The Archeology of Knowledge and the Discourse on Language*. New York: Vintage.

Frader, L. 1991. *Peasants and Protest: Agricultural Workers, Politics and Unions in the Aude, 1850–1914*. Berkeley: University of California Press.

Gade, D. W. 2004. "Tradition, Territory, and *Terroir* in French Viniculture: Cassis, France, and Appellation Contrôlée." *Annals of the Association of American Geographers* 94(4): 848–867.

Gade, D. W. 2009. "The Taste of Place: A Cultural Journey into *Terroir*." *Geographical Review* 99(2): 283–285.

Galasiska, A. and D. Galasiski. 2005. "Shopping for a New Identity." *Ethnicities* 5(4): 510–529.

Gangjee, D. 2012. *Relocating the Law of Geographical Indications*. Cambridge: Cambridge University Press.

Garcia-Parpet, M.-F. 2008. "Market, Prices and Symbolic Value: Grands Crus and the Challenges of Global Markets." *International Review of Sociology* 18(2): 237–252.

Gates, L. C. 1998. *The Merchant Republic of Lebanon: Rise of an Open Economy*. Oxford: The Centre for Lebanese Studies.

Geelong Wine. 2010. "Unleash your Senses, Media Kit." Geelong Winegrowers Association. Geelong, Australia.

Geertz, C. 1977. *The Interpretation of Cultures*. New York: Basic Books.

Gent, C. 2003. *Mixed Dozen: The Story of Australian Wine Since 1788*. Sydney: Duffy and Snellgrove.

Gervais, M., M. Jollivet, and Y. Tavernier. 1977. *La Fin de la France Paysanne: De 1914 à Nos Jours*. Paris: Seuil.

Giddens, A. 1991. *Modernity and Self-Identity: Self and Society in the Late Modern Age*. Cambridge: Polity Press.

Gilby, C. 2007. "Fast Forward into New Europe." *Harpers Supplement: Bulgaria* (March): 3–6.

Glacken, C. J. 1967. *Traces on the Rhodian Shore: Nature and Culture in Western Thought from Ancient Times to the End of the Eighteenth Century*. Berkeley: University of California Press.

Glick Schiller, N., A. Caglar, and T. C. Guldbrandsen. 2006. "Beyond the Ethnic Lens: Locality, Globality, and Born-Again Incorporation." *American Ethnologist* 33(4): 612–633.

Gmelch, G., and S. Bohn Gmelch. 2011. *Tasting the Good Life: Wine Tourism in the Napa Valley*. Bloomington: Indiana University Press.

Goode, J., and S. Harrop. 2011. *Authentic Wine: Toward Sustainable and Natural Winemaking*. Berkeley: University of California Press.

Goodman, D. 2003. "The Quality 'Turn' and Alternative Food Practices: Reflections and Agenda." *Journal of Rural Studies* 19: 1–7.

Goswami, M. 2004. *Producing India: From Colonial Economy to National Space*. Chicago: University Of Chicago Press.

Graeber, D. 2007. *Toward an Anthropological Theory of Value: The False Coin of our Dreams*. New York: Palgrave.

Grahm, R. 2010. *Been Doon So Long: A Randall Graham Vinthology*. Berkeley: University of California Press.

Gramsci, A. (1971) 1992. *Selections from the Prison Notebooks,* eds. and trans. Q. Hoare and G. N. Smith. New York: International Publishers.

Greer, G. 2003. "Whitefella Jump Up: The Shortest way to Nationhood." *Quarterly Essay* 11. Melbourne: Black Inc.

Gronow, J. 2003. *Caviar with Champagne: Common Luxury and the Ideals of the Good Life in Stalin's Russia.* Oxford: Berg.

Gudeman, S. 2008. *Economy's Tensions, the Dialectics of Community and Market.* New York and Oxford: Berghahn.

Guha, R. 2000. *Environmentalism: A Global History.* New York: Longman.

Guichard, F. 2000. "Le dit et le non-dit du vin: Le langage des étiquettes." *Annales de Géographie* 109 (614–615): 364–380.

Gupta, A., and J. Ferguson. 1992. "Beyond Culture: Space, Identity and the Politics of Difference." *Cultural Anthropology* 7(1): 6–23.

Gupta, A., and J. Ferguson. 1997. *Culture, Power, Place: Explorations in Critical Anthropology.* Durham, NC: Duke University Press.

Guthman, J. 2007. "The Polanyian Way? Voluntary Food Labels as Neoliberal Governance." *Antipode* 39(3): 456–478.

Guy, K. M. 2003/2007. *When Champagne Became French: Wine and the Making of a National Identity.* Baltimore: Johns Hopkins University Press.

Gwynne, R. N. 2008. "Value Chains and the Geographies of Wine Production and Consumption." *The Geographical Journal* 174(2) June: 95–96.

Habermas, J. 1971. *Knowledge and Human Interests.* Boston: Beacon Press.

Habermas, J. 1975. "Towards a Reconstruction of Historical Materialism." *Theory and Society* 2(Fall): 287–300.

Habermas, J. 1984. *The Theory of Communicative Action: Volume One.* Boston: Beacon Press.

Halbwachs, M. 1992. *On Collective Memory.* Chicago: University of Chicago Press.

Hall, S. 1996. "The Question of Cultural Identity." In *Modernity,* eds. S. Hall, D. Held, D. Hulbert, and K. Thompson. Oxford: Blackwell Publishing.

Handler, R., and J. Linnekin. 1984. "Tradition, Genuine or Spurious." *Journal of American Folklore* 97(385): 273–290.

Hann, C. 2006. *"Not the Horses We Wanted!" Postsocialism, Neoliberalism, and Eurasia.* Münster: Lit.

Hanson, F. A. 1989. "The Making of the Maori: Culture Invention and Its Logic." *American Anthropologist* 91: 890–902.

Hanson, F. A. 1993. *Testing Testing.* Berkeley: University of California Press.

Haraway, D. 1991. *Simians, Cyborgs and Women: The Reinvention of Nature.* New York: Routledge.

Harding, S. G. 1991. *Whose Science? Whose Knowledge: Thinking from Women's Lives.* Ithaca, NY: Cornell University Press.

Harper, D. 1987. *Working Knowledge. Skill and Community in a Small Shop.* Chicago: University of Chicago Press.

Harris, O. 1982. "Households and Their Boundaries." *History Workshop Journal* 13: 142–152.

Harvey, D. 2005. *A Brief History of Neoliberalism.* New York: Oxford University Press.

Harvey, D. 2006. *Spaces of Global Capitalism* London: Verso.

Heath, D., and A. Meneley. 2007. 'Techne, Technoscience, and the Circulation of Comestible Commodities: An Introduction." *American Anthropologist* 109(4): 593–602.

Hecht, G. 2009. *The Radiance of France: Nuclear Power and National Identity after World War II.* Cambridge, MA: MIT.

Hedetoft, U. 2002. *The Postnational Self: Belonging and Identity.* Minneapolis: University of Minnesota Press.

Heller, C. 2007. "Techne versus Technoscience: Divergent (and Ambiguous) Notions of Food 'Quality' in the French Debate over GM Crops." *American Anthropologist* 109(4): 603–615.

Hervieu-Léger, D. 2000. *Religion as a Chain of Memory.* New Brunswick, NJ: Rutgers University Press.

Herzfeld, M. 2004. *The Body Impolitic: Artisans and Artifice in the Global Hierarchy of Value.* Chicago: University of Chicago Press.

Hinnewinkel, J. C., C. Le Gars, and H. Vélasc-Graciet. 2008. *Philippe Roudié, Bordeaux, le vin et l'historien.* Bordeaux: Presses Universitaires de Bordeaux.

Hirsch, E. 2010. "Property and Persons: New Forms and Contests in the Era of Neoliberalism." *Annual Review of Anthropology* 39: 347–360.

Hobsbawm, E., and T. Ranger, eds. 1983. *The Invention of Tradition.* Cambridge: Cambridge University Press.

Hodder, I. 2010. "Cultural Heritage Rights: From Ownership and Descent to Justice and Well-Being." *Anthropological Quarterly* 83(4): 861–882.

Hoggart, K., H. Buller, and R. Black. 1995. *Rural Europe: Identity and Change.* London: Arnold.

Husserl, E. 1970. *The Crisis of European Sciences and Transcendental Phenomenology,* trans. David Carr. Evanston, IL: Northwestern University Press.

Il Sole 24 Ore. 2012. "Per niente naturale." July 8, 2012. Accessed September 7, 2012. www.ilsole24ore.com/art/cultura/2012–07–08/niente-naturale-081915. shtml?uuid = AbZwba4F.

Ingold, T. 2000. *The Perception of the Environment: Essays in Livelihood, Dwelling and Skill.* New York: Routledge.

International Organisation of Vine and Wine. 2012. *Statistical Report on World Viniculture.* Accessed September 22, 2012. www.oiv.int/oiv/files/0%20-%20Actualites/ EN/Report.pdf.

International Wine & Spirit Research and Wealth Solutions. 2011. *Rynek Wina w Polsce (The Wine Market in Poland).* Accessed May 27, 2012. www.wealth.pl/gfx/ wealth/files/raport_rynek_wina_w_polsce.pdf.

Ito, I. 2011. "Globalizing the Rural: The Use of Qualitative Research for New Rural Problems in the Age of Globalism." *International Review of Qualitative Research* 4(3): 279–290.

Jackson, M. 1998. *Minima Ethographica: Intersubjectivity and the Anthropological Project.* Chicago: University of Chicago Press.

Jefford, A. 2010. "Mateship with Place: A Fine-Wine Future for Australia." *The World of Fine Wine* 28: 96–105.

Johnson, H., and J. Halliday. 1992. *The Art and Science of Wine.* London: Mitchell Beazley.

Joseph, D. 2009. *"Harper's Wine and Spirit, Georgia: Georgian Wine at The Crossroads."* Supplement to *Harper's Wine and Spirit* April.

Judt, T. 1979. *Socialism in Provence.* Cambridge: Cambridge University Press.

Jung, Y. 2011. "Parting the Wine Lake: The Revival of the Bulgarian Wine Industry in the Age of CAP Reform." *Anthropological Journal of European Cultures* 20(1): 10–28.

Jung, Y. n.d. "Globalization, Wine Classification, and the Politics of Recognition: The Case of Bulgaria." Unpublished article currently under peer review.

Kaneff, D., and A. D. King. 2004. "Introduction: Owning Culture." *Focaal* 44(2): 3–19.

Karam, M. 2005. *Wines of Lebanon.* Beirut: Saqi Books.

Karp, I., C. Kratz, L. Szwaja, and T. Ybarra-Frausta, eds. 2006. *Museum Frictions: Public Cultures/ Global Transformation.* Durham, NC: Duke University Press.

Keeler, J. T. S. 1981. "Corporatism and Official Union Hegemony: The Case of French Agricultural Syndicalism." In *Organizing Interests in Western Europe,* ed. S. Berger. London: Cambridge University Press.

Kehrig, H. 1886. *Le Privilège des Vins à Bordeaux Jusqu'en 1789.* Bordeaux: Feret et fils.

Kelley, R. D. G. 1992. "Notes on Deconstructing 'The Folk.'" *The American Historical Review,* 97(5): 1400–1408.

Kirshenblatt-Gimblett, B. 1999. "Playing to the Senses: Food as a Performance Medium." *Performance Research* 4(1): 1–30.

Kirshenblatt-Gimblett, B. 1998. *Destination Culture: Tourism, Museums, and Heritage.* Berkeley: University of California Press.

Kotthoff, H. 1995. "The Social Semiotics of Georgian Toast Performances—Oral Genre as Cultural Activity." *Journal of Pragmatics* 24: 353–380.

Kramer, M. 2006. "The Destiny of Wine Nations." *Wine Spectator,* April 30.

Kramer, M. 2008. "The Notion of *Terroir.*" In *Wine and Philosophy: A Symposium on Thinking and Drinking,* ed. F. Allhoff, 225–334. Malden: Blackwell Publishing.

Kuisel, R. 1981. *Capitalism and the State in Modern France: Renovation and Economic Management in the 20th Century.* New York: Cambridge University Press.

Kuleba, M. 2005. *Ampelografia Zielonej Góry.* Zielona Góra: Pro Libris.

Kurtz, D. V. 1996. "Hegemony and Anthropology: Gramsci, Exegeses and Reinterpretations." *Critique of Anthropology* 16 (2): 103–135.

Ladurie, E. Le Roy. 1979. *Montaillou: The Promised Land of Error.* New York: Vintage Books.

La France. 1923. "Les appellations d'origine: Le 'Sauternes.'" December 31. Gironde Departmental Archives, Bordeaux. File 7M196.

Lagendijk, A. 2004. "'Global Lifeworlds' Versus 'Local Systemworlds': How Flying Winemakers Produce Global Wines in Interconnected Locals." *Tijdschrift voor Economische en Sociale Geografie* 95(5): 511–526.

Lagrave, R. 1987. *Celles de la Terre.* Paris: Editions de l'Ecole des Hautes Etudes en Sciences Sociales.

Lamoureux, F. et al. 2011. *Les entreprises viticoles professionnelles en Gironde: Dénombrement et description.* Rosace/Chambre d'Agriculture de la Gironde.

Lane, J. F. 2000. *Pierre Bourdieu: A Critical Introduction*. London: Pluto.

Lapaque, S. 2010. *Chez Marcel Lapierre*. Paris: La Table Ronde.

La Petite Gironde. 1932. "Le droit à l'appellation d'origine 'Sauternes.'" 20 Janvier. Gironde Departmental Archives, Bordeaux. File 7M196

Lash, S., and J. Urry. 1987. *The End of Organized Capitalism*. Madison: University of Wisconsin Press.

Lave, J. 2003. "Producing the Future: Getting to Be British." *Antipode* 35(3): 492–511.

Léard-Viboux, É., ed. 2006. *Jules Chauvet, naturellement... Témoignages, entretiens*. Paris: Jean-Paul Rocher.

Lears, T. Jackson. 1985. "The Concept of Cultural Hegemony: Problems and Possibilities." *American Historical Review* 90(3): 567–593.

Lecours, A. 2010. "Regionalism, Cultural Diversity and the State in Spain." *Journal of Multilingual and Multicultural Development* 22(3): 210–226.

Ledeneva, A. 1998. *Russia's Economy of Favours: Blat, Networking and Informal Exchange*. London: Cambridge.

Lee, C. K. 1998. *Gender and the South China Miracle*. Berkeley: University of California Press.

Leeuwen, C. van. 2006. "The Concept of *Terroir* in Viticulture." *Journal of Wine Research* 17(1): 1–10.

Lefebvre, H., and D. Nicholson-Smith. 1991. *The Production of Space*. City: Wiley-Blackwell.

Leiss, W. 1974. *The Domination of Nature*. Boston: Beacon Press.

Leitch, A. 2008. "Slow Food and the Politics of Pork Fat: Italian Food and European Identity." In *Food and Culture: A Reader*, eds. C. Counihan and P. Van Esterik. New York: Routledge.

Lem, W. 1999. *Cultivating Dissent: Work, Identity, and Praxis in Rural Languedoc*. Albany: State University of New York Press.

Leslie, E. 1998. "Walter Benjamin: Traces of Craft." *Journal of Design History* 11(1): 5–13.

Lindholm, C. 2008. *Culture and Authenticity*. Malden: Wiley-Blackwell.

Long, L. M. 2003. *Culinary Tourism*, illustrated edition. Lexington: University Press of Kentucky.

Loubere, L. A. 1990. *The Wine Revolution in France: The Twentieth Century*. Princeton: Princeton University Press.

Lynch, K. 1990. *Adventures on the Wine Route: A Wine Buyer's Tour of France*. New York: North Point Press.

Lyotard, J.-F. 1984. *The Postmodern Condition: A Report on Knowledge*. Minneapolis: University of Minnesota Press.

Magone, J. M. 2008. *Contemporary Spanish Politics*, second edition. New York: Routledge.

Makdisi, U. 2000. *The Culture of Sectarianism; Community, History, and Violence in Nineteenth-Century Ottoman Lebanon*. London: University California Press.

Manning, P. 2009. "The Epoch of Magna: Capitalist Brands and Postsocialist Revolutions in Georgia." *Slavic Review* 68(4): 924–945.

Manning, P. 2012. *The Semiotics of Drink and Drinking*. London: Continuum Books.

Manning, P., and A. Uplisashvili. 2007. "Our Beer: Ethnographic Brands in Postsocialist Georgia." *American Anthropologist* 109 (4): 626–641.

Mansfield, B. 2003. "Spatializing Globalization: A 'Geography of Quality' in the
Seafood Industry." *Economic Geography* 79(1): 1–16.

Marchenary, P., and L. Bérard. 2004. *Produits de terroir.* Paris: CNRS editions.

Markham, D. 1997. *1855: A History of the Bordeaux Classification.* New York: Wiley.

Mars, G., and Y. Altman. 1991. "Alternative Mechanisms of Distribution in a Soviet
Economy." In *Constructive Drinking,* ed. M. Douglas, 270–279. Cambridge:
Cambridge University Press.

Martin, E. 1987. *The Woman in the Body: A Cultural Analysis of Reproduction.*
Boston: Beacon Press.

Marx, K. 1967. *Capital,* vol.1. New York: International Publishers.

Massey, D. B. 2005. *For Space.* Thousand Oaks: Sage Publications.

Massey, D. B. 2007. *World City.* Malden: Polity.

Maton, K. 2008. "Habitus." In *Pierre Bourdieu: Key Concepts,* ed. M. Grenfell.
London: Acumen Press.

Mauss, M. 2004. *Seasonal Variations of the Eskimo.* London: Routledge.

Mayo, O. 1991. *The Wines of Australia.* London: Faber and Faber.

McCarthy, C., and L. Engel. 2007. "Introduction." In *Globalizing Cultural Studies:
Ethnographic Interventions in Theory, Method, and Policy,* eds. C. McCarthy,
A. S. Durham, L. C. Engel, A. A. Filmer, and M. D. Giardina. New York: Peter
Lang Publishing.

McGovern, P. E. 2003a. *Ancient Wine: The Search for the Origins of Viticulture.* Princeton: Princeton University Press.

McGovern, P. E. 2003b. "Georgia as Homeland of Winemaking and Viticulture." In
National Treasures of Georgia: Art and Civilization Through the Ages, ed. O. Z.
Soltes, 58–59. London: Philip Wilson Foundation for International Arts and
Education.

McGovern, P. E. 2009. *Uncorking the Past: The Quest for Wine, Beer and Other
Alcoholic Beverages.* Berkeley: University of California Press.

McNaughten, P., and J. Urry. 1998. *Contested Natures.* London: Sage.

Mendras, H. 1984. *La Fin des Paysans.* Paris: Actes-Sud.

Meneley, A. 2004. "Extra Virgin Olive Oil and Slow Food." *Anthropologica* 46:
165–176.

Meneley, A. 2007. "Like an Extra Virgin." *American Anthropologist* 109(4): 678–687.

Meneley, A. 2008. "Oleo-Signs and Quali-Signs: The Qualities of Olive Oil." *Ethnos*
73(3): 303–326.

Merchant, C. 1980. *The Death of Nature: Women, Ecology and the Scientific Revolution.* New York: Harper & Row.

Miller, T. 2007. *Cultural Citizenship: Cosmopolitanism, Consumerism, and Television
in a Neoliberal Age.* New York: New York University Press.

Milton, K. 2002. *Loving Nature: Towards an Ecology of Emotion.* London: Routledge.

Mintz, S. W. 1985. *Sweetness and Power.* New York: Penguin.

Miranda, V. 2010. "2020: La Reinvención De La Industria Vitivinícola." *Vitis*
November.

Mitchell, T. 2007. "The Properties of Markets." In *Do Economists Make Markets? On the Performativity of Economics,* eds. D. Mackenzie, F. Muniesa, and L. Siu. Princeton: Princeton University Press.

Molesworth, J. 2003. "Chile Strides Ahead: Investment in New Vineyards and Wineries Begins to Pay Off." *Wine Spectator* April 30.

Molesworth, J. 2007. "Chile." *Wine Spectator* May 15.

Mondovino, directed by Jonathan Nossiter. (2004; Belgium). Palace Films.

Moran, W. 1993. "The Wine Appellation as Territory in France and California." *Annals of the Association of American Geographers* 83(4): 694–717.

Morlat, R. 1998. "The Relationships Between *Terroir,* Vines and Wines." *Comptes Rendus de l'Academie d'Agriculture de France* 84(2): 19–32.

Moulton, K., A. Simova, and N. Young. 1994. "Wine and the Politics of Survival." In *Privatization of Agriculture in New Market Economies: Lessons from Bulgaria,* eds. A. Schmitz et al., 263–282. Norwell: Kluwer Academic Publishers.

Mühlfried, F. 2005. "Banquets, Grant-eaters and the Red Intelligentsia in Post-soviet Georgia." *Central Eurasian Studies Review* 4(1): 16–19.

Muller, P. 1984. *Le Technocrate et le paysan. Essai sur la politique française de modernisation de l'agriculture de 1945 à nos jours.* Paris: Économie et Humanisme.

Munn, N. 1986. *The Fame of the Gawa: A Symbolic Study of Value Transformation in a Massim (Papua New Guinea) Society.* Cambridge: Cambridge University Press.

Murdoch, J., T. Marsden, and J. Banks. 2000. "Quality, Nature and Embeddedness: Some Theoretical Considerations in the Context of the Food Sector." *Economic Geography* 76(2): 107–125.

Naess, A. 1992. *Ecology, Community and Lifestyle: Outline of an Ecosophy.* Translated and edited by D. Rothenberg. Cambridge: Cambridge University Press.

Negro, G., M. T. Hannan, and H. Rao. 2007. "No Barrique, No Berlusconi: Collective Identity, Contention, and Authenticity in the Making of Barolo and Barbaresco Wines." Research Paper 1972. Graduate School of Business, Stanford University, Stanford, CA.

Nguyen, V. 2002. "Introduction: A Crisis of Representation." *Race and Resistance: Literature and Politics in Asian America.* Oxford: Oxford University Press.

Noev, N. 2006. "The Bulgarian Wine Sector: Policy Issues and Implications After 15 Years of Transition." *Journal of Wine Research* 17(2): 73–93.

Nützenadel, A., and F. Trentmann, eds. 2008. *Food and Globalization: Consumption, Markets and Politics in the Modern World.* London: Berg Publishers.

Olejniczak, R. 2004. *Wino. Report of Instytut Badania Opinii i Rynku Pentor-Pozna&nacute.* Accessed May 27, 2012. www.poradnikhandlowca.com.pl/bezcms/archiwum/online04/12/raport4.html.

Olick, J. K. 1999. "Collective Memory: The Two Cultures." *Sociological Theory* 17(3): 333–348.

Paco and Lola. 2011. "Dossier de Prensa." www.pacolola.com/esp/prensa.html.

Pan, S., C. Chang, and J. Malaga. "Alcoholic Beverage Consumption in China: A Censored Demand System Approach." *Applied Economics Letters* 13–15: 975–979.

Parzen, J. 2009. "Nothing Natural about It." *Saignee.* June 20. Accessed March 1, 2011. http://saignee.wordpress.com/2009/06/20/day-2-nothing-natural-about-it/.

Pascual-de-Sans, A. 2004. "Sense of Place and Migration Histories—Idiotopy and Idiotope." *Area* 36: 348–357.

Patterson, C. T. 2007. "Diverging Pathways to the Periphery: The Case of Georgian and Moldovan Wines." Presented at the Annual SOYUZ Symposium. Princeton, New Jersey.

Paul, H. 1996. *Science, Wine and the Vine in Modern France*. Cambridge: Cambridge University Press.

Paxson, H. 2010. "Locating Value in Artisan Cheese: Reverse Engineering *Terroir* for New-World Landscapes." *American Anthropologist* 112(3): 444–457.

Peace, A. 2011. "Barossa Dreaming: Imagining Place and Constituting Cuisine in Contemporary Australia." *Anthropological Forum: A Journal of Social Anthropology and Comparative Sociology* 21(1): 23–42.

Pech, R. 1975. *Entreprise Viticole et Capitalisme en Languedoc Roussillon du Phylloxera Aux Crises de Mévente*. Toulouse: Publication de l'Université de Toulouse le Mirail.

Peterson, R. A. 1999. *Creating Country Music: Fabricating Authenticity*. Chicago: University of Chicago Press.

Peynaud, E. 1988. *Le Vin et les jours*. Paris: Bordas.

Phillips, L. 2006. "Food and Globalization." *Annual Review of Anthropology* 35: 37–57.

Pijassou, R. 1980. *Le Médoc: Un grand vignoble de qualité*. 2 vols. Paris: Tallandier.

Polanyi, K. 1944. *The Great Transformation: The Political and Economic Origins of Our Time*. City: Beacon Press, 2001.

Popelková, K. 2007. "Vinohradníci a vinohradníctvo v mestách pod Malými Karpatmi" (Winemakers and Winemaking in Towns under Small Carpathians). In *Mestá a dediny pod Malými Karpatmi. Etnologické S'túdie (Towns and Villages under Small Carpathians: Ethnological Studies)*, eds. O Danglová and Z. Juraj. Bratislava: Ústav Etnológie SAV.

Polski Instytut Wina i Winorośli. Accessed January 16, 2012. www.instytutwina.pl/4konwent.html.

Port, J. 2004. "…And in My Spare Time I Make Wine." *The Age, Epicure*. September 28.

Prange-Barczyński, T. 2009. "Slow and Steady in Poland." *Meininger's Wine Business International*. June 18. Accessed April 16, 2012. www.wine-business-international.com/156-bWVtb2lyX2lkPTM3NCZtZW51ZV9jYXRfaWQ9—en-magazine-magazine_detail.html.

Pratt, J. 2007. "Food Values. The Local and the Authentic." *Critique of Anthropology* 27(3): 285–300.

"Protection of Georgian Wine Appellations." 2008. Compilation of Project Documents. Food and Agriculture Organization of the United Nations, and the European Bank for Reconstruction and Development, April 2008. ftp://ftp.fao.org/docrep/fao/011/aj278e/aj278e01.pdf.

Puzelat, T. "L'Association AVN." Accessed 22 September 2012. www.lesvinsnaturels.org/lassociation/.

Rapp, R. 1999. *Testing Women: Testing the Fetus: The Social Impact of Amniocentesis in America*. New York: Routledge.

Rapp, R, E. Ross, and R. Bridenthal. 1979. "Examining Family History." *Feminist Studies* 5(1): 174–200.

Reddy, W. M. 1984. *The Rise of Market Culture: The Textile Trade & French Society, 1750–1900.* Cambridge: Cambridge University Press.

Remaud, H., and J.-P. Couderc. 2006. "Wine Business Practices: A New Versus Old Wine World Perspective." *Agribusiness* 22(3): 405–416.

Reynolds, L. 2000. "Re-Embedding Global Agriculture: The International Organic and Fair-Trade Movements." *Agriculture and Human Values* 17(3): 297–309.

Richards, P. 2012. "Natural Wine: Reviewed." *TV Masters of Wine: Susie and Peter.* Accessed June 2, 2012. http://susieandpeter.com/natural-wine-reviewed/.

Robinson, J. 2004. "Chilean Wine Comes of Age." *Financial Times* February 14.

Robinson, J. 2006. *The Oxford Companion to Wine.* Oxford: Oxford University Press.

Rogers, D., and K. Verdery. 2012. "Postsocialist Societies: Eastern Europe and the Former Soviet Union." In *Handbook of Social and Cultural Anthropology,* eds. J. Carrier and D. Gewertz. London: Berg.

Rogers, S. 1987. "Good to Think: The 'Peasant' in Contemporary France." *Anthropological Quarterly* 60: 56–63.

Roseberry, W. 1994. "Hegemony and the Language of Contention." In *Everyday Forms of State Formation: Revolution and the Negotiation of Rule in Modern Mexico,* eds. G. Joseph and D. Nugent, 355–366. Durham: Duke University Press.

Rosenthal, N. I. 2008. *Reflections of a Wine Merchant: On a Lifetime in the Vineyards and Cellars of France and Italy.* New York: Farrar, Strauss and Giroux.

Roudié, P. 1988. *Vignobles et vignerons du Bordelais (1850–1980).* Paris: CNRS.

Roudié, P. 2000. "Vous avez dit 'château'? Essai sur le succès sémantique d'un modèle viticole venu du Bordelais." *Annales de Géographie* 109(614–615): 415–425.

Roudié, P., and J.-C. Hinnewinkel. 2001. *Une Empreinte dans le Vignoble: XX Siècle: Naissance des Vins d'Aquitaine d'Origine Coopérative.* LPDA Editions.

Rousseau, J.-J. 1755. *Un discours sur l'origine et les fondements de l'inégalité parmi les hommes.*

Sahlins, M. 1976. *Culture and Practical Reason.* Chicago: University of Chicago Press.

Sakson, A. 2004."Stosunek mieszkańców zachodniego pogranicza Polski do wykupu ziemi przez Niemców." In *Transgraniczność w perspektywie socjologicznej. Teorie, studia interpretacje,* Volume II, ed. M. Zielińska. Zielona Góra: Lubuskie Towarzystwo Naukowe.

Sassoon, A. 1982. *Approaches to Gramsci.* London: Writers and Readers Publishing.

Schiefenhövel, W., and H. Macbeth. 2011. *Liquid Bread: Beer and Brewing in Cross-Cultural Perspective.* New York: Berghahn.

Scott, J. C. 1998. *Seeing Like a State: How Certain Schemes to Improve the Human Condition Have Failed.* New Haven: Yale University Press.

Scruton, R. 2007. "The Philosophy of Wine." In *Questions of Taste: The Philosophy of Wine,* ed. B. C. Smith, 1–19. Oxford: Signal Books.

Scruton, R. 2009. *I Drink Therefore I am: A Philosopher's Guide to Wine.* London: Continuum.

Sedlák, J. 2011. "Preslávil Slovensko rizlingom" (He made Slovakia famous for its Riesling). *Víno: Mimoriadna príloha Denníka Pravda 18. 11. 2011 (Wine: Special Dossier of Pravda Daily,* November 18, 2011), 22–26.

Sewell, W. H. Jr. 1980. *Work and Revolution in France: The Language of Labor from the Old Regime to 1848*. Cambridge: Cambridge University Press.

Shaw, L. 2012. "Joly: Natural Wine Means Nothing." *Drinks Business*, May 22. Accessed June 1, 2012. www.thedrinksbusiness.com/2012/05/joly-natural-wine-means-nothing/.

Shils, E. 1961. "Centre and Periphery." In *The Logic of Personal Knowledge: Essays Presented to Michael Polanyi*, ed. E. Shils, 117–130. London: Routledge & Kegan Paul.

Sider, G. 1986. *Culture and Class in Anthropology and History: A Newfoundland Illustration*. Cambridge: Cambridge University Press.

Silverstein, M. 2006a. "Talking about Wine as a Cultural Object and Denotational Domain." *Annual Review of Anthropology* 25: 179–213.

Silverstein, M. 2006b. "Old Wine, New Ethnographic Lexicography." *Annual Review of Anthropology* 35: 481–496.

Simpson, J. 2011. *The Emergence of a World Industry, 1840 -1914: Creating Wine*. Princeton: Princeton University Press.

Slater, D. 1999. *Consumer Culture and Modernity*. Malden: Polity.

Smith, G. 1999. *Confronting the Present: Towards a Politically Engaged Anthropology*. Oxford: Berg.

Somers, M. 1994. "The Narrative Construction of Identity: A Relational and Network Approach." *Theory and Society* 23: 605–649.

Souto, C. 2000. "El nacionalismo gallego (1916–1936). Una madurez inconclusa." *Espacio, Tiempo y Forma*, Serie V, H.a Contemporánea (13): 415–440.

Stanziani, A. 2007. "Negotiating Innovation in a Market Economy: Foodstuffs and Beverage Adulteration in Nineteenth-Century France. "*Enterprise and Society* 8(2): 375–412.

Steiner, R. 2004. *Agriculture Course: The Birth of the Biodynamic Method*. Herndon: Rudolf Steiner Press.

Street, R. S. 2005. *Beasts of the Field: A Narrative History of California Farmworkers 1769–1913*. Palo Alto: Stanford University Press.

Stronza, A. 2001. "Anthropology of Tourism: Forging New Ground for Ecotourism and Other Alternatives." *Annual Review of Anthropology* 30: 261–283.

Sutton, D.-E. 2010. "Food and the Senses." *Annual Review of Anthropology* 39: 109–223.

Taleng, F. 2008. *Les chefs d'exploitation du secteur vinicole français en 2005*. Direction des Etudes, des Répertoires et des Statistiques, Mutualité Sociale Agricole (MSA).

Taussig, M. 1980. *The Devil and Commodity Fetishism in South America*. Chapel Hill: University of North Carolina Press.

Taussig, M. 1987. "History as Commodity in some Recent American (Anthropological) Literature." *Food and Foodways* 2, 151–169.

Taylor, C. 1991. *The Malaise of Modernity*. Toronto: House of Anansi Press.

Taylor, C. 1994. *Multiculturalism: Examining the Politics of Recognition*. Princeton: Princeton University Press.

Tedlock, B. 2005. "The Observation of Participation and the Emergence of Public Ethnography." In *The Handbook of Qualitative Research*, third edition, eds. N. K. Denzin and Y. S. Lincoln. Thousand Oaks: Sage.

Teil, G. 2004. *De la Coupe aux Lèvres: Pratiques de la Perception et Mise en Marché de Vins de Qualité.* Toulouse: Octarès.

Teil, G. 2010. "The French Wine Appellation d'Origine Contrôlée and the Virtues of Suspicion." *The Journal of World Intellectual Property* 13(2): 253–274.

Teil, G., and S. Barrey. 2009. "La Viticulture Biologique: De la Recherche d'un Monde Nouveau au Renouvellement du Goût de *terroir.*" *Innovations Agronomiques* 4: 427–440.

Terrio, S. J. 2000. *Crafting the Culture and History of French Chocolate.* Berkeley: University of California Press.

Tesnière, C., and C. Flanzy. 2011. "Carbonic Maceration Wines: Characteristics and Winemaking Process." *Advances in Food and Nutrition Research* 63: 1–15.

Torrès, O. 2006. *The Wine Wars: The Mondavi Affair, Globalization and "Terroir."* New York: Palgrave Macmillan.

Touraine, A. et al. 1980. *Le Pays Contre l'Etat: Luttes Occitanes.* Paris: Edition du Seuil.

Traboulsi, F. 2007. *A History of Modern Lebanon.* London: Pluto Press.

Transparency International Georgia. 2009. "Food Safety in Georgia." Accessed December 12, 2009. www.amcham.ge/res/Bullets_on_1stPage/TI_Food_Safety.pdf.

Treadgold, T. 2011. *The Western Australian Business News.* Perth. June 8.

Trilling, L. 1972. *Sincerity and Authenticity.* Cambridge: Harvard University Press.

Trubek, A. B. 2004. "Incorporating *Terroir:* L'Affaire Mondavi Reconsidered." *Gastronomica* 4(3): 90–99.

Trubek, A. B. 2008. *The Taste of Place: A Cultural Journey into Terroir.* Berkeley: University of California Press.

Tuite, K. 2008. "The Autocrat of the Banquet Table: The Political and Social Significance of the Georgian *supra.*" Unpublished manuscript. http://mapageweb.umontreal.ca/tuitekj/publications/Tuite-supra.pdf.

Ulin, R. C. 1984. *Understanding Cultures: Perspectives in Anthropology and Social Theory.* Austin: University of Texas Press.

Ulin, R. C. 1991. "Critical Anthropology Twenty Years Later: Modernism and Postmodernism in Anthropology." *Critique of Anthropology* 11(1): 63–89.

Ulin, R. C. 1995. "Invention and Representation as Cultural Capital: Southwest French Winegrowing History." *American Anthropologist* 97(3): 519–527.

Ulin, R. C. 1996. *Vintages and Traditions: An Ethnohistory of Southwest French Wine Cooperatives.* Washington, DC: Smithsonian Institution Press.

Ulin, R. C. 2001. *Understanding Cultures: Perspectives in Anthropology and Social Theory,* second edition. London: Blackwell Publishers.

Ulin, R. C. 2002. "Work as Cultural Production: Labor and Self-identity Among Southwest French Wine-Growers." *Journal of the Royal Anthropological Institute* 8(4): 691–712.

Ulin, R. C. 2004. "Globalization and Alternative Localities." *Anthropologica* 46(2): 153–164.

Ulin, R. C. 2008. "Writing about Wine: The Uses of Nature and History in the Wine Growing of Southwest France and America." In *Wine, Society and Globalization: Multidisciplinary Perspectives on the Wine Industry,* eds. G. Campbell and N. Guibert, 43–62. New York: Palgrave MacMillan.

Unwin, T. 1991/1996. *Wine and the Vine: An Historical Geography of Viticulture and the Wine Trade*. London, New York: Routledge.

Vauban, S. Le Prestre de. (1707) 1933. *Projet d'une dixme royale, suivi de deux écrits financiers*. Paris: Alcan.

Verdery, K. 1996. *What Was Socialism and What Comes Next?* Princeton: Princeton University Press.

Verdery, K. 2003. *The Vanishing Hectare: Property and Value in Postsocialist Transylvania*. Ithaca: Cornell University Press.

Veseth, M. 2011. *Wine Wars. The Curse of the Blue Nun, The Miracle of Two Buck Chuck, and the Revenge of the Terroirists*. Lanham, MD: Rowman & Littlefield Publishers.

Visse-Causse, S. 2007. *L'appellation d'origine: valorisation du terroir*. Paris: ADEF.

Volkov, V. 2000. "The Concept of *Kul'turnost:'* Notes on the Stalinist Civilizing Process." In *Stalinism: New Directions*, ed. S. Fitzpatrick, 210–230. London: Routledge.

Warner, C. K. 1960. *The Winegrowers of France and the Government Since 1875*. New York: Columbia University Press.

Watson, J. L. 2006. *Golden Arches East: McDonald's in East Asia*, second edition. Stanford: Stanford University Press.

Watson, J. L., and M. L. Caldwell. 2005. *The Cultural Politics of Food and Eating: A Reader*. Malden: Wiley-Blackwell.

Weber, E. 1976. *Peasants into Frenchmen: The Modernization of Rural France 1870–1914*. Stanford: Stanford University Press.

Weber, M. 1906 (1992). *The Protestant Ethic and Spirit of Capitalism*. Trans. T. Parsons. London: Routledge.

Weber, M. 1978. *Economy and Society*. Berkeley: University of California Press.

Weber, M. 2004. *The Vocation Lectures*. New York: Hackett.

Werbner, R., ed. 1998. *Memory and the Postcolony: African Anthropology and the Critique of Power*. London: Zed books.

West, H. et al. 2012. "Naming Cheese." *Food, Culture, and Society* 15(1): 7–41.

White, P. 2010. *The Independent Weekly*. Melbourne. May.

Whitehead, A. 1981. "I'm Hungry, Mum: The Politics of Domestic Budgeting." In *Of Marriage and the Market: Women's Subordination in International Perspective*, eds. K. Young, C. Walkowitz, and R. McCullogh. London: CSE Books.

Wilk, R., ed. 2006. *Fast Food/ Slow Food: The Cultural Economy of the Global Food System*. Lanham, MD: Alta Mira Press.

Williams, R. 1977. *Marxism and Literature*. Oxford: Oxford University Press.

Williams, R. 1988. *Keywords: A Vocabulary of Culture and Society* (revised edition). London. Fontana.

Wilson, J. E. 1998. *"Terroir:" The Role of Geology, Climate, and Culture in the Making of French Wines*. London: Mitchell Beazley, Reed Consumer Books.

Wilson, T. M. 2006. *Food, Drink and Identity in Europe*. New York: Rodopi.

Winebiz. 2011. "Wine Industry Statistics." Accessed May 16. winebiz.com.au/statistics/wineries.asp.

"Wines of Chile." 2010. *Strategic Plan 2020: International Market*.

Wolf, E. 1982. *Europe and the People without History.* Berkeley: University of California Press.

Worster, D. 1994. Worster, *Nature's Economy: A History of Ecological Ideas.* Cambridge: Cambridge University Press.

Wright, G. 1964. *Rural Revolution in France: The Peasantry in the Twentieth Century.* Stanford: Stanford University Press.

Yoon, S. Y. S. 1975. "Provençal Wine Co-operatives." In *Beyond the Community: Social Process in Europe,* eds. J. Boissevain and J. Friedl, 140–165. The Hague: Department of Education and Science of the Netherlands.

Young, E. 2002. "Massive Oil Slick Reaches Spain." *New Scientist,* December 2. www.newscientist.com/article/dn3132-massive-oil-slick-reaches-spain.html.

Zeldin, T. 1983. *The French.* London: Fontana.

Zhao, W. 2005. "Understanding Classifications: Empirical Evidence from the American and French Wine Industries." *Poetics* 33: 179–200.

INDEX